FOURTH EDITION

KOVELS'
DEPRESSION GLASS & AMERICAN DINNERWARE PRICE LIST

**BOOKS BY
RALPH AND TERRY KOVEL**

American Country Furniture 1780–1875
Dictionary of Marks — Pottery & Porcelain
Kovels' Advertising Collectibles Price List
Kovels' American Silver Marks
Kovels' Antiques & Collectibles Price List
Kovels' Antiques & Collectible Fix-It Source Book
Kovels' Book of Antique Labels
Kovels' Bottles Price List
Kovels' Collector's Guide to American Art Pottery
Kovels' Collector's Source Book
Kovels' Depression Glass & American Dinnerware Price List
Kovels' Guide to Selling Your Antiques & Collectibles
Kovels' Illustrated Price Guide to Royal Doulton
Kovels' Know Your Antiques
Kovels' Know Your Collectibles
Kovels' New Dictionary of Marks — Pottery & Porcelain
Kovels' Organizer for Collectors
*Kovels' Price Guide for Collector Plates, Figurines, Paperweights,
    and Other Limited Editions*

FOURTH EDITION

KOVELS'
DEPRESSION GLASS
& AMERICAN
DINNERWARE
PRICE LIST

Ralph and Terry Kovel

CROWN PUBLISHERS, INC.
NEW YORK

Published by Crown Publishers, Inc., 201 East 50th Street,
New York, New York 10022.
Member of the Crown Publishing Group.
Manufactured in the United States of America

Library of Congress Cataloging-in-Publication Data
Kovel, Ralph M.
[Depression glass & American dinnerware price list]
Kovels' depression glass & American dinnerware price list/Ralph and Terry Kovel.—4th ed.
p.   cm.
1. Depression glass—Catalogs. 2. Ceramic tableware—United States—History—20th century
—Catalogs.   I. Kovel, Terry H.   II. Title.   III. Title: Depression glass & American dinnerware
price list.   IV. Title: Depression glass and American dinnerware price list.   V. Title: Kovels'
depression glass and American dinnerware price list.
NK5439.D44K67   1991   90-28595
738'.0973'075—dc20   CIP
ISBN 0-517-58444-1

10 9 8 7 6 5 4

CONTENTS

ACKNOWLEDGMENTS

We want to thank the following companies and collectors who knowingly or unknowingly helped us to find pictures and prices for this book:

Al-Lin's Antiques; Doug Albacete; Ann's Treasures; Atticana; Back Trak Depression & Antiques; Bad Habit; Kathy Baker; Barnes Antiques; David Becker; Big Timber Collectables; Roselyn A. Blum; Mrs. W. M. Bostwick; Paul Bourdeau; Elizabeth Boyce; M. Brookshire; L. Brown; Samantha Burdick; C & L Collectibles; Cats Paw Collectibles; The China Hutch; China Traders; C. & L. Chryanowski; Collectors Corner; Collectors Junction; Larry Cook; T. J. Cousins; Crow's Nest Antiques; D & G Collectibles; Dancing Girl; The Daze; Martha Deleo; Denelen's Glass; Depression Delights; DiSanto & Smondrowski; Pat Dole; Dorthe Durant; Eddie's Collectibles; Elegant Garage; Evelyn Felker; Fenner's Antiques; Fiesta Etc.; Fiesta Feast; Fiesta Plus; James Fletcher; Marv Fogleman; Bill Foos; Fore & Aft; David C. Gaydos; Anne & Bob Geary; Glass Connection; Glass Rainbow, Ltd.; Glass Slipper Antiques; Grandpa's Trading Company; A. Griggs; D. Hadley; A. Hoffmann; Hogues Antiques & Curios; J & J Antiques; Fran Jay; Kathy; Shirley King; Shirley D. King; Janet King-Farison; Diane Kosmal; Landsberg Orchids; Judy Lang; Ralph F. Leslie; R. Levine; S. Levine; L. A. Maness; Manic Depression; M. McGinnis; Memory Lanes; Dorothy Meyer; Milkweed Antiques, Ltd.; Phyllis J. Moorefield; Morris Antiques; Museum Shop; My Glass Duchess; The New Glaze; Betty Newbound; Christine Olson; Elsa Philcrantz; Robert Pierce; Popkorn; Rainbow Collectibles; Red Horse Inn; Kimberly Reinink; D. & P. Renner; Lavonne Rhodebeck; The Rose Antiques; Roselle Scheifman; Shir-Craft; Shuck's Antiques & Collectibles; R. Singer; Some Antiques; Clarence R. Souza; Jean E. Stack; Chris Stansell; Tom & Mary Stevenson; Carol Stone; Djanet Stumreiter; Sugar Hill Antiques; Sunshine & Friends Co.; T & J's Yesteryear Collectibles; M. E. Theobald; L. & K. Thompson; N. Tims; David & Kay Tucker; Bryant Turner; S. Visakay; Walnut Avenue Antiques; Dana & Penny Welch; Larry D. Wells; M. Welzel; Steve Williams; Winstead Antiques & Gifts; A. Yerger; Yesterday's Today; Ted Young; Delmer H. Youngen

Special thanks go to: *The Daze* for providing information on reproduction glass that regularly appears in that newspaper; Keith Robinson of the Manhattan Beach Historical Society; Ann Kerr, the Russel Wright expert; Homer Laughlin China Company; and the many authors whose works helped us with our research. The books, both current and out of print, are listed in the bibliographies. Another thanks to Crown Publishers, especially to our editor, Ann Cahn; to Deborah Kerner, who designed the layout; and to Jeffrey Clark, for the line drawings of patterns. It is fun to do the first work on a book like this—to do the research, locate objects and pictures, and struggle through problems. But then come the boring details—proofreading, matching up pictures, assembling the charts and tables, and meeting deadlines. An extra thank-you to those on the Kovels' staff who worked on this book.

DEPRESSION GLASS

DEPRESSION GLASS

Introduction

Clear and pastel-colored glassware in matching sets became popular about 1925. The Fostoria Glass Company of Fostoria, Ohio, made the first of these glass sets, which included dinner plates, coffee cups, and other pieces to be used at a dinner table. The glassware was expensive and its popularity led to similar pieces being made by other companies that were able to produce a less expensive glass.

Inexpensive glass was made by a method called tank molding: Silica sand, soda ash, and limestone were heated, and the molten glass mixture was passed through pipes to the automated pressing mold. Patterns were acid-etched or tooled into the mold so the finished glassware had a design. Because the pressing process made a glass that often had flaws or bubbles, patterns used as decoration were often lacy in appearance to help hide the flaws.

During the late 1960s, interest in the inexpensive pastel glass led to several books, and the term "Depression glass" came into general use, even though the glassware was made before, during, and after the Depression. The name has gradually come to include other glassware made from 1925 through the 1970s. This price list includes the lacy types, the pseudo-Sandwich glass patterns, the hobnail variations, the solid-colored wares of ruby, cobalt, or green, and the many opaque glass patterns. In the past few years another term, "elegant glassware of the Depression," has come to be used. This refers to the better-quality glass made at the same time. There is much overlap between these types of glass and even the exact name to use for a pattern may be in doubt. We have included those patterns most often offered for sale as Depression glass last year. Depression and some "elegant" patterns are included. The pattern names used are from original catalogs, Depression glass books, lists, or shows.

Depression-glass designs can be divided into groups. The etched designs, like Adam or Cherry Blossom, were made first, from about 1925 to 1935. Pastel colors were used.

Raised designs, often with fruit and flower patterns, such as Open Rose and Sharon, were made in the mid-1930s. Strong colors like cobalt blue or Royal Ruby, opaque glass, pastels, and clear glass were popular.

Geometric wares, such as Hobnail and Ribbon, were made during the late 1920s, and again in the late 1930s and early 1940s. Simple outlines and bold colors predominated. Art Deco-influenced geometric designs include Imperial Octagon and U.S. Octagon.

Enameled or silk-screened patterns were developed during the 1940s. White enameled designs were added to the glass. Cobalt blue, Royal Ruby, and clear glass were the most popular colors that were decorated this way. Shirley Temple glasswares and White Sail are two such enameled patterns.

A few patterns, Floral & Diamond Band for example, were made to resemble the cut glass of the nineteenth century, particularly the Lacy Sandwich patterns made by the Sandwich, Massachusetts, glassworks. About ten such pseudo-Sandwich patterns were made, and most of them were referred to as Sandwich in the manufacturers' catalogs.

Depression glass utility wares were also made. The dishes were meant to be used in the kitchen and not on the table, and included ice-box dishes, lemon reamers, or canister sets.

Opaque glass was popular in the 1930s. Each of the colors was given a special name by the company that produced it. Monax or Ivrene were opaque white glasswares.

Opaque green glass was known by a variety of names. Jade green is a generic name used by many companies. Jade-ite was the green color used by Anchor Hocking; Jadite was a color of glass and a pattern of green kitchenware made by Jeannette Glass Company. To avoid unnecessary confusion, we have chosen to always spell the word "jadite" in this book. Delphite, an opaque blue glass, is sometimes spelled "delfite" in the ads, but we have chosen to always use the delphite spelling.

This book is not an in-depth study of Depression glass. The beginner who needs more information about patterns, manufacturers, color groups, or how and where to buy should see the Bibliography and club lists we have included.

Hundreds of patterns, many not listed in other price books, are included here. But if you wish to specialize in one pattern of Depression glass, there may be a book available that includes many colored photographs of your pattern. There may also be a book available with special information about the factory making your pattern. The best way to learn about Depression glass is to attend the regional and national shows devoted to glass. Your local newspaper or the collectors' publications listed in this book will print the dates and locations.

There are lists of reproductions and known glass patterns and manufacturers following the last glass price entries.

This book is a price report. Prices are actual offerings in the market-place. They are not an average. The high and low prices represent different sales. Prices reported are not those from garage or house sales or flea markets. They are only from dealers who understand the Depression glass market and who sell at shops, at shows, or through national advertising.

Information about American ceramic dinnerwares and the prices for these pieces can be found in the second half of this book.

Particular patterns can be found by using either the Depression Glass or American Dinnerware main listings, both of which are arranged alphabetically. Depression Glass begins on page 11 and American Dinnerware on page 132. There is no index of pattern names in this book because it would only duplicate the main listings. However, we have compiled lists of known Depression glass and American Dinnerware patterns along with information on manufacturers, dates, alternate names, and descriptions. These can be found at the end of each section.

Patterns listed in the main sections of the book are those most popular with collectors. This book is a report of prices for pieces offered for sale during the past year. Most of the patterns included in earlier books are still to be found here because the collectors still buy these patterns. Many newly popular patterns are also included. We have made no effort to give an *exact* definition of the term "Depression glass." If a pattern of American glassware was made between 1925 and 1970 and if it is known to some collectors or dealers as Depression glass, we have included it here.

DEPRESSION GLASS
Bibliography

Archer, Margaret and Douglas. *Imperial Glass.* Paducah, Kentucky: Collector Books, 1978.

Birkenheuser, Fred. *Tiffin Glassmasters.* Privately printed, 1979 (P.O. Box 524, Grove City, OH 43123).

Cambridge Glass Co. (catalog reprint). Privately printed, 1976 (P.O. Box 416, Cambridge, OH 43725).

Fine Handmade Table Glassware (catalog reprint). Privately printed, 1978 (P.O. Box 416, Cambridge, OH 43725).

Florence, Gene. *Collector's Encyclopedia of Depression Glass,* 9th edition. Paducah, Kentucky: Collector Books, 1991.

Florence, Gene. *Elegant Glassware of the Depression Era,* 4th edition. Paducah, Kentucky: Collector Books, 1991.

Florence, Gene. *Kitchen Glassware of the Depression Years,* 3rd edition. Paducah, Kentucky: Collector Books, 1987.

Florence, Gene. *Pocket Guide to Depression Glass,* 7th edition. Paducah, Kentucky: Collector Books, 1990.

Florence, Gene. *Very Rare Glassware of the Depression Years.* Paducah, Kentucky: Collector Books, 1988.

Fountain, Mel. *Swankyswigs, with Price Guide.* Privately printed, 1979 (201 Alvena, Wichita, KS 67203).

Heacock, William. *Fenton Glass — The First Twenty-five Years.* Privately printed, 1978 (P.O. Box 663, Marietta, OH 45750).

Klamkin, Marian. *Collector's Guide to Depression Glass.* New York: Hawthorn Books, 1973.

Kovel, Ralph and Terry. *Kovels' Antiques & Collectibles Price List,* 23rd edition. New York: Crown Publishers, 1990.

Kovel, Ralph and Terry. *Kovels' Guide to Selling Your Antiques & Collectibles,* Updated Edition. New York: Crown Publishers, 1990.

Kovel, Ralph and Terry. *Kovels' Know Your Collectibles.* New York: Crown Publishers, 1981.

Luckey, Carl F. *Identification & Value Guide to Depression Era Glassware,* 2nd edition. Florence, Alabama: Books Americana, 1986.

McGrain, Pat. *1981 Price Survey.* Privately printed, 1980 (Box 219, Frederick, MD 21701).

McGrain, Patrick, ed. *Fostoria — The Popular Years.* Privately printed, 1982 (Box 219, Frederick, MD 21701).

Schliesmann, Mark. *Price Survey,* 3rd edition. Privately printed, 1986 (Box 838-PS, Racine, WI 53403).

Stout, Sandra McPhee. *Depression Glass in Color.* Radnor, Pennsylvainia: Wallace-Homestead Book Co., 1970.

Stout, Sandra McPhee. *Depression Glass Number Two.* Radnor, Pensylvainia: Wallace-Homestead Book Co., 1971.

Stout, Sandra McPhee. *Depression Glass III.* Radnor, Pensylvainia: Wallace-Homestead Book Co., 1976.

Stout, Sandra McPhee. *Depression Glass Price Guide.* Radnor, Pensylvainia: Wallace-Homestead Book Co., 1975.

Warner, Ian. *Swankyswigs, A Pattern Guide and Check List.* Privately printed, 1982 (Box 57, Otisville, MI 48463).

Weatherman, Hazel Marie. *Colored Glassware of the Depression Era.* Privately printed, 1970 (P.O. Box 4444, Springfield, MO 65804).

Weatherman, Hazel Marie. *Colored Glassware of the Depression Era 2.* Privately printed, 1974 (P.O. Box 4444, Springfield, MO 65804).

Weatherman, Hazel Marie. *Decorated Tumbler.* Privately printed, 1978 (P.O. Box 4444, Springfield, MO 65804).

Weatherman, Hazel Marie. *Fostoria — Its First Fifty Years.* Privately printed, 1972 (P.O. Box 4444, Springfield, MO 65804).

Weatherman, Hazel Marie. *Price Guide to the Decorated Tumbler.* Privately printed, 1979 (P.O. Box 4444, Springfield, MO 65804).

Weiss, Jeffrey. *Cornerstone Collector's Guide to Glass.* New York: Simon & Schuster, 1981.

Whitmyer, Margaret & Kenn. *Bedroom & Bathroom Glassware of the Depression Years.* Paducah, Kentucky: Collector Books, 1990.

DEPRESSION GLASS
Clubs and Publications

CLUBS

Fenton Art Glass Collectors of America, Inc., *Butterfly Net* (newsletter), P.O. Box 384, Williamstown, WV 26187.

Fostoria Glass Society of America, Inc., *Facets of Fostoria* (newsletter), P.O. Box 826, Moundsville, WV 26021.

Heisey Collectors of America, *Heisey News* (newsletter), 169 West Church Street, Newark, OH 43055.

Michiana Association of Candlewick Collectors, *MACC Spyglass* (newsletter), 17370 Battles Road, South Bend, IN 46614.

Morgantown Collectors of America, *Morgantown Newscaster* (newsletter), 420 First Avenue N.W., Plainview, MN 55964.

National Cambridge Collectors, Inc., *Cambridge Crystal Ball* (newsletter), P.O. Box 416, Cambridge, OH 43725.

National Candlewick Collectors Club, *Candlewick Collector* (newsletter), 275 Milledge Terrace, Athens, GA 30606.

National Depression Glass Association, *News & Views* (newsletter), P.O. Box 69843, Odessa, TX 79769.

National Duncan Glass Society, *National Duncan Glass Journal* (newsletter), P.O. Box 965, Washington, PA 15301-0965.

National Imperial Glass Collectors Society, *Glasszette* (newsletter), P.O. Box 534, Bellaire, OH 43906.

National Milk Glass Collectors Society, *Opaque News* (newsletter), 1113 Birchwood Drive, Garland, TX 75043.

National Reamer Collectors Association, *NRCA Quarterly Review* (newsletter), Rt. 3, Box 67, 405 Benson Road, Frederic, WI 54837.

Old Morgantown Glass Collectors' Guild, *Old Morgantown Topics* (newsletter), P.O. Box 894, Morgantown, WV 26507-0894.

Tiffin Glass Collectors Club, *Tiffin Glassmasters* (newsletter), P.O. Box 554, Tiffin, OH 44883.

Local clubs and their meeting dates are often listed in *The Daze*.

PUBLICATIONS

Antique Trader Weekly (newspaper), Box 57, Otisville, MI 48463.

The Daze (newspaper), Box 57, Otisville, MI 48463.

Glass Collector's Digest (magazine), P.O. Box 553, Marietta, OH 45750-9979.

Kovels on Antiques and Collectibles (newsletter), P.O. Box 22200, Beachwood, OH 44122.

Matching Services: China, Silver, Crystal (leaflet), Ralph and Terry Kovel (P.O. Box 22900, Beachwood, OH 44122).

Tea Room/Pyramid Newsletter (newsletter), 921 West Lynwood, Phoenix, AZ 85007.

Westmoreland Glass Collector's Newsletter (newsletter), P.O. Box 143, North Liberty, IA 52317.

DEPRESSION GLASS
Color Names

This is a list of some of the most confusing color names:

AMBER	Topaz, Golden Glow
BLUE GREEN	Ultramarine
CLEAR	Crystal
DEEP BLUE	Ritz blue, cobalt, dark blue, deep blue
GREEN	Springtime Green, emerald, Imperial Green, Forest Green, Nu-green
MEDIUM BLUE	Madonna
OPAQUE BLACK	Black
OPAQUE BLUE	Delphite
OPAQUE GREEN	Jadite
OPAQUE OFF-WHITE	Chinex, Clambroth, Cremax, Ivrene
OPAQUE WHITE	Milk white, Monax
PINK	Rose Marie, Rose, Rose Pink, Rose Tint, Rose Glow, Nu-rose, Wild Rose, Flamingo, Cheri-glo
PURPLE	Burgundy, amethyst
RED	Royal Ruby, Ruby Red, Carmen

A

ACCORDIAN PLEATS,
see Round Robin

Adam

Adam, sometimes called Chain Daisy or Fan & Feather, is a glass pattern made from 1932 to 1934 by the Jeannette Glass Company, Jeannette, Pennsylvania. Sets can be found in crystal, delphite, green, and pink. A few pieces are known in yellow, but this does not seem to have been a standard production color. Reproductions have been made in green and pink.

CRYSTAL

Ashtray 12.00
Plate, Square, 9 In. 16.00

GREEN

Ashtray, 4 1/4 In. 8.00
Bowl, 4 3/4 In. ...6.00 To 10.00
Bowl, 5 3/4 In. 30.00
Coaster, 3 1/4 In. 12.00
Cup & Saucer..............20.00
Grill Plate 12.00
Plate, Square, 7 3/4 In. 8.00
Platter, Oval, 11 3/4 In. ...15.00
Sugar, Cover..... 30.00 To 45.00
Tumbler, Footed,
  4 1/2 In..................15.00

PINK

Ashtray, 4 1/4 In. 24.00
Bowl, 7 3/4 In. 24.00
Bowl, Cover, 9 In...........48.00
Cake Plate 15.00
Candleholder, 4 In., Pair ...65.00
Creamer.....................13.00
Pitcher, 32 Oz., 8 In........27.00
Plate, Square, 7 3/4 In. 10.00
Plate, Square, 9 In..........22.50
Sherbet 17.00
Tumbler, Footed,
  4 1/2 In..................16.00
Tumbler, Footed,
  5 1/2 In..................45.00
Vase, 7 1/2 In............ 165.00

Akro Agate

Picture a marble cake with the irregular mixture of colors running through the batter. This is what Akro Agate is usually like—a marbelized mixture of colored glass. The Akro Agate Company, Clarksburg, West Virginia, originally made children's marbles. The marbelized dinnerware and other glass children's sets were made in many colors from 1932 to 1951.

AMBER

Ashtray 98.00
Child's Set, Stippled Band,
  17 Piece................ 180.00
Saucer, Transparent,
  Large Stippled Band........ 4.00

Tea Set, Child's, Stippled Band,
  16 Piece................. 285.00
Tea Set, Child's, Stippled Band,
  Box, 17 Piece 240.00

BLACK

Flowerpot, Ribbed Top,
  4 In........................15.00
Flowerpot, Stacked Disc,
  5 1/2 In...................25.00
Jar, Apothecary 65.00
Shaving Mug,
  Ring Handle 65.00

BLUE

Ashtray 15.00
Bowl, Cereal, Child's,
  Concentric Ring...........15.00
Bowl, Child's, Octagonal,
  Closed Handles............10.00
Bowl, Scalloped, 3-Footed,
  5 1/4 In...................50.00
Bowl, Stacked Disc 35.00
Bowl, Transparent,
  Large Concentric Ring.....50.00
Candleholder, Pair........ 165.00
Coaster, Westite 90.00
Creamer, Child's,
  Interior Panel 21.00
Creamer, Child's, Opaque,
  Raised Daisy,
  1 3/16 In..................18.00
Creamer, Stacked Disc,
  Interior Panel 8.00
Cup, Transparent,
  Ribbed Plain Jane 6.00
Flowerpot,
  1 White & 2 Red Rings,
  5 1/2 In...................75.00
Flowerpot, Hand Fluted,
  5 1/4 In...................10.00
Flowerpot,
  Hand Painted Siesta Scene,
  4 In........................85.00
Flowerpot, Stacked Disc, White,
  5 1/2 In...................27.00
Pitcher, Water, Opaque.....15.00
Planter, Scalloped, Oval,
  6 In........................ 2.50
Plate, Child's, Concentric Rib,
  3 1/4 In.................... 4.00
Powder Jar, Apothecary.....95.00

Powder Jar,
Colonial Lady..............22.00
Powder Jar, Concentric Ring,
White......................20.00
Powder Jar, Mexicali With Hat,
White......................25.00
Powder Jar,
Mortar & Pestle 16.00
Powder Jar, Scotty Dog.....95.00
Saucer, Marbelized, Stacked Disc,
Interior Panel 25.00
Sugar, Child's,
Interior Panel 21.00
Sugar, Child's, Stacked Disc,
1 7/8 In....................7.00
Tea Set, Marbelized,
Large Interior Panel,
15 Piece................. 850.00
Teapot, Child's, Cover,
2 1/2 In...................35.00
Vase, Scalloped, 3-Footed,
6 In.......................90.00

GREEN

Ashtray, Match Holder,
Hotel Lincoln..............45.00
Ashtray, Square, 3 In. 4.00
Cornucopia...................4.00
Creamer, Child's, Stacked Disc,
1 7/8 In....................6.00
Cup & Saucer, Child's,
Yellow Saucer.............22.00
Cup, Child's 6.00
Cup, Child's,
Concentric Rib 2.50
Cup, Child's, Transparent...15.00
Cup, Interior Panel,
Transparent.................9.00
Flowerpot, Banded Darts,
4 In.......................35.00
Jardiniere, Graduated Darts,
Smooth Top, 5 In...........5.00
Lamp, Wall, With Shade,
Marbelized.................35.00
Match Holder, White........8.00
Pitcher, Child's, Concentric Rib,
4 Pink Tumblers 30.00
Pitcher, Water, Child's......20.00
Planter, Dark, White, Footed,
2 In.......................12.00
Plate, Child's, Chiquita.......4.00
Plate, Child's,
Concentric Rib 3.00

Plate, Stippled Band &
Interior Panel,
Transparent.......9.00 To 15.00
Powder Jar,
Colonial Lady..............50.00
Powder Jar, Concentric Ring, 3-
Footed, Cover,
3 1/2 In...................40.00
Powder Jar, Cover, Round,
5 In.......................60.00
Powder Jar, Scotty Dog.....60.00
Saucer, Child's,
Chiquita ....2.00 To 3.00
Saucer, Marbelized...........7.00
Sugar, Child's, Chiquita......5.00
Tea Set, Child's, Chiquita,
22 Piece................. 155.00
Tea Set, Child's, Large,
10 Piece................. 275.00
Tea Set, Child's, Stacked Disc,
8 Piece 60.00
Tea Set, Marbelized,
Small Interior Panel,
15 Piece................. 300.00
Teapot, Child's, Chiquita,
Cover......................9.00
Teapot, Child's, Stacked Disc,
1 3/8 In....................7.00
Tumbler, Child's,
Stacked Disc & Interior Panel
..........................15.00
Vase, Flared, Ivory, 6 In....25.00
Vase, Ribs & Flutes,
8 In..................... 125.00
Vase, Tab Handle,
6 1/4 In...................40.00
Water Set, Stacked Disc,
7 Piece 45.00

IVORY

Planter, Ribbed,
4 X 8 In...................10.00

PINK

Creamer, Child's,
Stacked Disc................7.00
Cup, Child's ....6.00 To 11.00
Plate, Child's.................5.00
Powder Jar, Lady, White....75.00
Saucer, Child's,
Stacked Disc...............4.50
Tea Set, Child's,
16 Piece................. 325.00

PUMPKIN

Ashtray, Square, 3 In. 7.00
Bowl, Scalloped, 3-Footed,
5 1/4 In...................45.00
Candlestick, Pair 145.00
Cornucopia...................4.00
Cup, Child's,
Concentric Ring 15.00
Cup, Large Stacked Disc,
Interior Panel 18.00
Flowerpot, 5 1/2 In.........90.00
Flowerpot, 6 1/2 In.........20.00
Flowerpot, Banded Darts,
2 1/2 In...................35.00
Flowerpot, Hand-
Painted Floral Scene,
4 In.......................95.00
Saucer, Child's 2.50
Urn, Square-Footed,
White......................3.00
Vase, Ribs & Flutes,
8 In..................... 125.00
Vase, Tab Handle,
6 1/4 In...................45.00

RED

Ashtray, Rectangular,
4 In...................... 150.00
Cup, Flashed On, Chiquita...5.00

TAN

Saucer, Child's, Concentric Rib,
2 3/4 In....................4.00

WHITE

Bowl, Dart, 3-Footed,
5 1/4 In...................35.00
Box, Cigarette,
3 1/2 X 4 In..............12.50
Saucer, Child's, Concentric Rib,
2 3/4 In....................3.00
Tumbler, Child's, Stacked Disc,
2 In.......................8.00

YELLOW & RED

Cup, Child's,
Interior Panel 23.00
Teapot, Child's... 18.00 To 45.00

YELLOW

Cup & Saucer, Child's,
Pump Open 15.00

Cup, Child's,
Raised Daisy...............13.00

Flowerpot, Banded Dart,
4 In......................40.00

Jardiniere, Bell Shape,
Rectangular Top,
4 3/4 In...................8.00

Planter, Oval, Large 35.00

Plate, Child's,
Concentric Rib 7.00

Sugar & Creamer, Child's...12.00

Tumbler, Child's, Raised Daisy,
2 In......................15.00

Alice

An 8 1/2-inch plate, cup, and
saucer were apparently the
only pieces made in the Alice
pattern. This 1940s pattern
was made by the Anchor
Hocking Glass Company, Lancaster, Ohio, in opaque white
with a pink or blue border
and in jadite. Other related
sections in this book are Fire-
King, Jadite, Jane-Ray, Square,
Swirl Fire-King, and Tur-
quoise Blue.

BLUE ──────────────

Cup & Saucer...............6.00
Plate, 9 In..................9.00

JADITE ─────────────

Cup & Saucer.......2.50 To 4.00
Plate,
8 1/2 In........ 10.00 To 12.00
Saucer......................1.00

PINK ──────────────

Cup & Saucer.......1.50 To 4.00
Plate, 8 1/2 In.............15.00

Alpine Caprice

Caprice and Alpine Caprice
were made from the same
molds. Alpine Caprice has a
satin finish, Caprice is transparent. Alpine Caprice, made
by the Cambridge Glass Company, Cambridge, Ohio, about

1936, was made in blue, crystal, and pink satin-finished
glass.

**ALPINE CAPRICE, see
also Caprice**

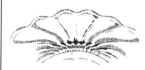

BLUE ──────────────

Bowl, 4-Footed,
12 1/2 In....... 65.00 To 70.00
Candleholder, 7 In., Pair ...75.00
Dish, Mayonnaise, Spoon ...65.00

CRYSTAL ─────────────

Bowl, 4-Footed, Oval,
11 In. 50.00
Candleholder, Pair..........50.00
Relish, 3 Sections, 8 In. 35.00

American

American is a pattern made to
resemble the pressed glass of
an earlier time. It was introduced by Fostoria Glass,
Moundsville, West Virginia,
in 1915 and remained in production until the factory
closed in 1986. Most pieces
were made of clear, colorless
glass known as crystal. A few
pieces are known in amber,
blue, green, yellow, and milk
glass. It is similar to Cube pattern, but after looking carefully, you will soon learn to
tell the two patterns apart.
Many pieces of American pattern were reproduced after
1987.

CRYSTAL ─────────────

Appetizer, Insert............27.50
Ashtray 8.50
Bottle, Bitters..............45.00
Bottle, Condiment,
Stopper 105.00
Bottle, Ketchup, Stopper....30.00
Bowl, 5 In. 15.00
Bowl, Deep, Oval,
11 1/2 In..................55.00
Bowl, Flower Frog, Cupped,
7 In.......................50.00
Bowl, Low, 13 In...........65.00
Bowl, Oval, 9 In............35.00
Bowl, Tricorner, 11 In......35.00
Butter, 1/4 Lb..............45.00
Butter, Cover,
Round.........42.50 To 100.00
Cake Stand, Square 75.00
Candleholder, 6 In., Pair ...60.00
Candy Dish, Cover,
3 Sections 65.00
Candy Dish, Cover,
Footed.....................38.00
Celery......................20.00
Cocktail, Footed,
2 7/8 In....................7.50
Compote, Cover, 9 In.......30.00
Creamer.....................15.00
Cruet, Stopper, 5 Oz........35.00
Cruet, Stopper, 7 Oz........46.00
Cup & Saucer...............10.00
Decanter, Whiskey..........80.00
Dish, Lemon, Cover 30.00
Dish, Mayonnaise, Footed,
Ladle 43.00
Dish, Sundae, 3 1/8 In. 9.50

Lamp, Hurricane, Base,
Pair...................... 175.00
Napkin Ring.................12.00
Pitcher, Ice Lip, 1/2 Gal.,
8 1/4 In...................85.00
Pitcher, Milk, 1 Pt. 30.00
Plate, 7 1/2 In.............. 7.00
Plate, 8 1/2 In..............12.00
Plate, 9 1/2 In..............22.00
Plate, Torte, 14 In. 35.00
Platter, Oval,
12 In. .... 43.00 To 65.00
Relish, 3 Sections, Oval,
9 1/2 In..................33.00
Salt & Pepper, Tray,
Small 35.00
Sauce, Liner, 8 In. 41.00
Soup, Cream 45.00
Sugar & Creamer, Tray,
Small 30.00
Sugar, Cover, Handle.......23.00
Syrup, Bakelite
Handle ....85.00 To 125.00
Toothpick 23.00
Tray, Round, 12 In. 165.00
Tumbler, 3 3/8 In...........12.00
Tumbler, 4 In......9.00 To 14.00
Vase, Bud, Cupped Top,
6 In.......................16.00
Vase, Flared, 5 1/4 In. 30.00
Vase, Flared, 9 1/4 In. 78.00
Vase, Sweet Pea 125.00
Whiskey.......... 12.00 To 15.00
Wine............. 12.50 To 15.00

PINK

Candy Jar, Cover, Round,
6 In...................... 225.00

AMERICAN BEAUTY,
see English Hobnail

American Pioneer

Panels of hobnail-like pro-
trusions and plain panels were
used in the design of American Pioneer. It was made by
Liberty Works, Egg Harbor,
New Jersey, from 1931 to
1934. Crystal, green, and pink
dishes are easily found.
Amber is rare.

CRYSTAL

Bowl, 5 In. 12.00
Bowl, Handle, 9 In. 13.00
Candlestick, 6 1/2 In.,
Pair.......................65.00
Cup & Saucer.......5.00 To 7.50
Goblet, 3 Oz.,
4 In............. 30.00 To 40.00
Goblet, 8 Oz., 6 In. 35.00
Plate, 8 In...........4.00 To 6.00
Saucer...................... 2.00
Sherbet, 3 1/2 In. 14.00

GREEN

Creamer, 3 1/2 In. 22.00
Cup 10.00
Cup & Saucer...............12.00
Mayonnaise 65.00
Saucer...................... 4.00
Sugar, 3 1/2 In. 22.00

PINK

Cheese & Cracker,
2 Piece 25.00
Coaster, 3 1/2 In. 20.00
Cup & Saucer................ 9.50
Ice Bucket, Handle 25.00
Plate, 8 In..........5.00 To 6.00
Sugar, 2 3/4 In..............13.00

American Sweetheart

In 1930 Macbeth-Evans Glass
Company introduced Ameri-
can Sweetheart. At first it was
made of pink glass, but soon
other colors were added. The
pattern continued in production until 1936. Blue, pink,
red, Cremax, and Monax
pieces were made. Sometimes
a gold, platinum, green, pink,
red, or smoky black trim was
used on Monax pieces. There
is a center design on most
plates, but some Monax plates
are found with plain centers.
One of the rarest items in this
pattern is the Monax sugar
bowl lid. The bowls are easy
to find but the lids seem to
have broken.

MONAX

Bowl, 6 In. ....8.00 To 10.00
Bowl, 9 In. ...... 30.00 To 45.00
Bread Plate ....2.00 To 3.00

Console, 18 In. 300.00
Creamer....................... 7.50
Cup .... 5.00 To 6.00
Cup & Saucer...... 8.50 To 10.00
Plate, 6 In........... 3.00 To 4.00
Plate, 8 In........... 4.50 To 6.00
Plate, 9 3/4 In.............. 16.00
Plate, 9 In.......... 6.00 To 13.00
Plate,
  10 1/4 In....... 15.00 To 18.00
Plate, 12 In. .... 9.00 To 12.00
Platter, Oval, 13 In. 35.00
Saltshaker, Footed......... 105.00
Saucer.............. 1.50 To 2.00
Sherbet, 4 1/4 In. 18.00
Sherbet, Footed,
  4 1/4 In................... 13.00
Sugar & Creamer... 13.00 To 15.00
Tidbit, 2 Tiers ... 45.00 To 75.00

PINK

Bowl, 6 In. .... 7.00 To 11.00
Bowl, 9 In. ...... 22.00 To 27.50
Bowl, Vegetable, Oval,
  11 In. 30.00
Creamer..................... 8.00
Cup & Saucer.... 10.00 To 15.00
Plate, 6 In.......... 2.00 To 4.00
Plate, 8 In.................... 9.00
Plate,
  9 3/4 In........ 16.00 To 20.00
Plate, Server,
  12 In. .... 8.00 To 13.00
Platter, Oval, 13 In. 20.00
Sherbet, 3 3/4 In............ 16.50
Sherbet, 4 1/4 In. 12.00
Soup, Cream, 4 1/2 In...... 35.00
Soup, Dish,
  9 1/2 In........ 28.00 To 35.00
Tumbler,
  4 1/4 In........ 42.00 To 52.50

RED

Plate, Server,
  15 1/2 In.............. 250.00
Sugar & Creamer,
  Cover................... 175.00

PINK

Salt & Pepper............. 250.00

Anniversary

Although pink Anniversary pattern was made from 1947 to 1949, it is still considered Depression glass by collectors. Crystal pieces are shown in a 1949 catalog. In the 1970s crystal and an iridescent carnival-glass-like amber color were used. The pattern was the product of the Jeannette Glass Company, Jeannette, Pennsylvania.

CRYSTAL

Bowl, 4 3/8 In. 2.00
Bowl, 9 In. 10.00
Butter, Cover 22.00
Cake Plate, Metal Cover..... 8.00
Cup & Saucer, Gold Trim ... 2.50
Plate, 6 1/4 In.............. 1.50
Plate, 9 In.................... 5.50
Sandwich Server,
  12 1/2 In.................. 5.00
Sugar & Creamer, Open 4.00
Tidbit, 2 Tiers, Chrome 20.00
Vase, 6 1/2 In..... 7.00 To 10.00

IRIDESCENT

Bowl, 7 3/8 In. .... 2.00 To 2.50
Cup & Saucer....... 3.00 To 4.00
Plate, 6 In.......... 1.00 To 2.00
Plate, 9 In.................... 4.00
Wall Pocket................ 20.00

PINK

Butter, Cover .... 40.00 To 47.00

Creamer..................... 8.00
Sugar & Creamer, Cover.... 25.00
Wine.............. 8.00 To 11.00

**APPLE BLOSSOM, see
Dogwood**

Aunt Polly

U.S. Glass Company, a firm with factories in Indiana, Ohio, Pennsylvania, and West Virginia, made Aunt Polly glass. The pattern can be found in blue, green, and iridescent. Pink Pieces have been reported. The pattern was made in the late 1920s.

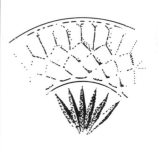

BLUE

Butter, Cover ... 70.00 To 125.00
Compote, 2 Handles........ 20.00
Plate, 6 In........... 7.50 To 9.00
Plate, 8 In.................. 13.50
Salt & Pepper............. 195.00
Sherbet .... 7.00 To 12.00
Sugar 32.50
Tumbler,
  3 5/8 In........ 18.00 To 30.00
Vase,
  6 1/2 In........ 23.00 To 45.00

GREEN

Bowl, Handles, 5 1/2 In.... 14.00
Butter, Cover 200.00
Creamer..................... 24.00
Sugar, Cover................ 95.00
Vase, 6 1/2 In.............. 20.00

IRIDESCENT

Compote, 2 Handles........18.00
Sherbet, 6-In. Underplate...11.50
Vase, 6 1/2 In..............15.00

Aurora

The Hazel Atlas Glass Company made Aurora pattern glass in the late 1930s. Crystal, cobalt blue, green, and pink pieces were made.

BLUE

Bowl, 5 3/8 In. 8.00
Cup..........................5.00
Plate, 6 1/2 In...............6.00
Tumbler, 4 3/4 In..........14.00

GREEN

Bowl, 5 3/8 In. 6.50

PINK

Bowl, 5 3/8 In. 6.00

Avocado

Although the center fruit looks more like a pear, the pattern has been named Avocado. It was made originally from 1923 to 1933 by the Indiana Glass Company, Dunkirk, Indiana, in crystal, green, and pink. In 1973, a reproduction line of pitchers and tumblers appeared in amethyst, blue, frosted pink, green, and pink. In 1982, amber-colored creamers and sugars, cups and saucers, plates, and serving dishes were made. Pieces have also been made in red and yellow. The pattern is sometimes called Sweet Pear or No. 601.

CRYSTAL

Bowl, Oval, 2 Handles,
8 In......................10.00
Soup, Dish...................7.00
Sugar & Creamer, Cover....25.00

GREEN

Bowl, 2 Handles,
5 1/4 In..................24.00
Bowl, 7 1/2 In. 32.50
Bowl, Handles, 7 In. 14.00
Bowl, Oval, 2 Handles,
8 In......................21.50
Cake Plate 33.00
Creamer.......... 24.00 To 38.00
Cup..........................22.00
Cup & Saucer...............55.00
Plate,
6 3/8 In........ 10.00 To 13.00
Plate,
8 1/4 In........ 14.00 To 18.50
Relish, Footed, 6 In.........18.00
Sherbet .... 30.00 To 60.00
Sugar .... 28.00 To 38.00

PINK

Bowl, 2 Handles,
5 1/4 In..................22.00
Cup..........................25.00
Cup & Saucer...............50.00
Pitcher.................... 525.00
Plate, 6 3/8 In..............11.00
Sherbet .... 30.00 To 40.00

B

B PATTERN, see Dogwood

BALLERINA, see Cameo

Bamboo Optic

Bamboo Optic pattern was made by Liberty Works of Egg Harbor, New Jersey, about 1929. Pink and green luncheon sets and other pieces were made. The pattern resembles Octagon.

GREEN

Cup..........................4.50
Cup & Saucer................6.50
Plate, 12 3/4 In. 10.00
Plate, Octagonal, 8 In........6.00
Sandwich Server,
Center Handle..............25.00
Sherbet 5.00
Sugar & Creamer 7.50

PINK

Cup ....4.00 To 5.00
Plate, 7 1/4 In............... 5.00
Plate, 8 In.................... 3.75
Saucer........................ 2.00
Sugar 10.00

BANDED CHERRY, see Cherry Blossom

BANDED FINE RIB, see Coronation

BANDED PETALWARE, see Petalware

BANDED RAINBOW, see Ring

BANDED RIBBON, see New Century

BANDED RINGS, see Ring

Baroque

Fostoria Glass Company of Moundsville, West Virginia, made Baroque, or No. 2496, from 1936 to 1966. The pattern was made in crystal, blue (azure), Gold Tint, yellow (topaz), and green. The same molds were used to make other glass patterns decorated with etched designs.

BLUE

Ashtray 10.00
Bonbon, 3-Footed...........95.00
Bowl, Handle, 10 1/2 In.... 9.00
Butter.................... 295.00
Candleholder, 3-Light,
  6 In......................27.50
Candleholder, 5 1/2 In.,
  Pair......................45.00
Cup.........................15.00
Cup & Saucer...............25.00
Goblet,
  6 3/4 In....... 22.00 To 30.00
Jelly, Cover, Footed,
  7 1/2 In..................85.00
Mustard, Cover & Ladle 75.00
Plate, 6 In.................. 7.00
Plate, 7 In..........9.00 To 14.00
Plate, 8 In.................18.00
Plate, 9 In.................37.00
Punch Bowl Set,
  12 Cups 1500.00
Punch Cup..................25.00
Saucer........................ 5.00

Sherbet 18.00
Sugar & Creamer 22.00
Tidbit, Footed, 8 1/4 In....35.00
Tray, Oval, 8 In.............85.00
Tumbler, 3 1/2 In..........39.00
Tumbler, 3 3/4 In..........85.00
Tumbler, 4 1/4 In..........24.00
Tumbler, 5 3/4 In..........39.00

CRYSTAL

Bonbon 15.00
Candelabrum, 2-Light, Bobeche,
  Prisms, 8 1/2 In...........70.00
Candleholder, 3-Light,
  6 In........................35.00
Candleholder, Lustres,
  7 3/4 In....................40.00
Cruet, Stopper 60.00
Cup & Saucer...............12.00
Dish, Pickle, 8 In. 14.00
Goblet,
  6 3/4 In........ 10.00 To 14.50
Ice Bucket 20.00
Mayonnaise, 3 Piece 38.00
Oyster Cocktail, 3 In........10.00
Plate, 7 In..........4.00 To 6.00
Plate, 9 In..................24.00
Punch Cup..................15.00
Sherbet ....6.00 To 9.50
Sugar & Creamer,
  Individual..................17.00
Sugar, Individual............. 5.00
Sweetmeat 17.50
Tumbler, 3 1/2 In..........30.00
Tumbler, 4 1/4 In..........22.50
Tumbler, 5 3/4 In..........27.50

YELLOW

Bowl, Flared,
  12 In. .... 25.00 To 27.00
Bowl, Handle, 5 In. 12.00
Bowl, Vegetable, Oval,
  9 1/2 In...................40.00
Candleholder, 5 1/2 In.,
  Pair......................28.00
Compote, 4 3/4 In..........22.50
Cruet, Stopper 295.00
Goblet,
  6 3/4 In........ 22.00 To 27.50
Ice Bucket 45.00

Jelly, Cover 30.00

Plate, 9 In...................42.50

Relish, 2 Sections,
6 1/2 In...................15.00

Relish, 3 Sections,
10 In. .... 20.00 To 27.50

Rose Bowl,
3 3/4 In........ 80.00 To 85.00

Salt & Pepper, Large........95.00

Sherbet 16.00

Sugar & Creamer 25.00

Tray, Oval, Handle,
6 1/2 In...................25.00

BASKET, see No. 615

Beaded Block

Imperial Glass Company, Bellaire, Ohio, made Beaded Block from 1927 to the 1930s. It was made in amber, crystal, green, ice blue, pink, red, vaseline, and white. Frosted or iridescent pieces were also made, leading some collectors to name the pattern Frosted Block. Some iridescent pink pieces made recently have been found marked with the IG trademark used from 1951 to 1977.

AMBER ——————

Creamer.....................12.00

Plate, Square,
7 3/4 In...........3.00 To 4.50

Soup, Cream 18.00

BLUE ——————

Bowl, Square, 5 1/2 In.....38.00

Creamer.....................17.50

Sugar & Creamer 65.00

Vase, 6 In...................17.00

CRYSTAL ——————

Bowl, Round, 4 1/2 In.....15.00

Pitcher, 1 Pt.,
5 1/4 In....... 47.00 To 52.00

Vase, 6 In...................12.00

GREEN ——————

Bowl,
6 1/4 In........ 10.00 To 12.00

Pickle, 2 Handles, Oval.....21.00

Pitcher.....................35.00

IRIDESCENT ——————

Bowl, 2 Handles,
4 1/2 In...................35.00

Bowl, 5 1/2 In. 10.00

Bowl, 6 1/2 In. 10.00

PINK ——————

Bowl, Plate, 7 1/2 In.......18.00

Vase, 6 In........ 10.00 To 14.00

VASELINE ——————

Bowl, Cupped, 5 1/4 In....37.00

Sugar 37.00

Sugar & Creamer 65.00

BERWICK, see Boopie

**BEVERAGE WITH
SAILBOATS, see White
Ship**

BIG RIB, see Manhattan

BLOCK, see Block Optic

Block Optic

Block Optic, sometimes called Block, was made from 1929 to 1933 by the Hocking Glass Company, Lancaster, Ohio. Slight variations in the design of some pieces, like creamers and sugars, show that the pattern was redesigned at times. Blue, crystal, green, and pink pieces are common. Yellow examples are harder to find. Some pieces were made with a black stem or a black flat foot.

CRYSTAL ——————

Sherbet, Pedestal.............3.00

Wine........................5.00

GREEN ——————

Bottle, 6 In. 13.00

Bowl, 5 1/4 In. ....2.00 To 9.00

Butter........................4.00

Cup & Saucer.... 10.00 To 13.00

Cup, Fluted 5.00

Cup, Round..................5.00

Goblet, 5 3/4 In............19.00

Ice Bucket 30.00

Pitcher, 54 Oz.,
8 1/2 In........ 28.00 To 30.00

Pitcher, Bulbous, 68 Oz.,
7 5/8 In..................60.00

Plate, 6 In...................1.50

Plate, 8 In..........3.00 To 4.50

Plate, 9 In........ 12.00 To 14.00

Salt & Pepper, Footed 25.00

Salt & Pepper, Squat........60.00

Sugar & Creamer, Footed...19.00

Sugar, Fluted.................9.00

Sugar, Round 9.00

Tumble-Up 55.00

Tumbler, 5 Oz..............14.00

Tumbler, 10 Oz.............12.00

PINK

Butter Tub.................68.00
Candleholder, Pair..........50.00
Cup..........................3.00
Sherbet, 4 3/4 In...........10.00
Sugar & Creamer 19.00
Sugar, Cone.................8.00
Whiskey, 1 Oz.,
  1 5/8 In........ 25.00 To 31.00

YELLOW

Candy Jar, Cover 35.00
Plate, 9 In..................25.00
Salt & Pepper, Short........50.00
Tumbler, Footed, 10 Oz.,
  6 In.......................13.00

Boopie

With a name like Boopie, it must have some other attraction. This Anchor Hocking pattern was made in the late 1940s and 1950s. Only glasses of various sizes are known, including the 3 1/2-ounce, 4-ounce, 6-ounce, and 9-ounce. The pattern came in crystal, forest green, and royal ruby.

CRYSTAL

Tumbler, Footed,
  3 1/2 In....................2.00
Tumbler, Footed,
  5 1/2 In....................4.00

GREEN

Tumbler, Crystal Base,
  5 1/2 In....................5.50

Tumbler, Footed,
  3 7/8 In....................4.00

ROYAL RUBY

Tumbler, Footed,
  3 3/4 In....................5.50

BOUQUET & LATTICE, see Normandie

Bowknot

The Bowknot pattern remains a mystery. The manufacturer is still unidentified. The swags and bows of the pattern were mold-etched. There does not seem to be a full dinner set of this pattern. Only the 7-inch plate, cup, sherbet, two sizes of bowls, and two types of 10-ounce tumblers have been found. Green pieces are found easily. The pattern was also made in crystal.

CRYSTAL

Plate, 7 In...................7.50

GREEN

Bowl, 4 1/4 In. 12.00
Bowl,
  5 1/4 In........ 13.00 To 16.00
Bowl, 7 In. 5.00
Cup..........................7.00
Plate, 7 In..........4.00 To 9.00
Tumbler, 5 In...............14.00
Tumbler, Footed, 5 In. 11.00

BRIDAL BOUQUET, see No. 615

Bubble

Names of Depression glass patterns can be depressingly confusing. Bubble is also known as Bullseye, the original name given by Anchor Hocking Glass Company, or as Provincial, the 1960s name. Bubble was made in many colors, originally in crystal, pale blue, and pink. Dark green was issued in 1954. Later, milk white and ruby red were made. Recently, yellow pieces have been seen, possibly made in the 1950s. Reproductions have appeared in the 1980s in green, jadite, pink, and royal ruby. They usually have an anchor mark on the bottom.

BLUE

Bowl, 4 In. 9.00
Bowl, 4 1/2 In. ....5.00 To 6.00
Bowl, 5 1/4 In. ....6.00 To 8.50
Bowl, 8 3/8 In. ...8.00 To 10.00
Bowl, 9 In. 13.00
Bowl, 10 In.................10.00
Butter.......................3.50
Creamer.....................26.00
Cup.................2.00 To 3.00
Cup & Saucer.......3.00 To 6.50
Grill Plate 6.00
Grill Plate, 9 3/8 In........12.00

Plate, 6 3/4 In......1.25 To 3.50
Plate, 9 3/8 In......4.00 To 6.50
Platter, Oval,
   12 In. ....9.00 To 12.00
Saucer......................... 1.00
Soup, Dish,
   7 3/4 In..........7.00 To 10.50
Sugar .... 10.00 To 13.00
Sugar & Creamer... 26.00 To 39.00

CRYSTAL ─────────

Bowl, 4 In. ....2.00 To 3.00
Bowl, 4 1/2 In. 2.00
Bowl, 5 1/4 In. ....4.00 To 6.00
Bowl, 8 3/8 In. ....3.00 To 7.00
Candleholder........4.75 To 6.00
Cup ....1.50 To 2.50
Plate, 9 3/8 In.............. 3.50
Saucer....................... 2.00
Sugar & Creamer.... 5.00 To 10.00
Tumbler, 9 Oz.............. 7.00
Tumbler, 12 Oz.............. 9.00

GREEN ─────────

Cup & Saucer.......7.50 To 9.50
Plate, 9 3/8 In.............. 5.00
Saucer....................... 2.50
Sherbet 4.50
Sugar 6.00
Sugar & Creamer... 15.00 To 17.50

PINK ─────────

Bowl, 8 3/8 In. 8.00

RED ─────────

Bowl, 4 1/2 In. 5.00
Cup & Saucer.......5.50 To 9.50
Pitcher,
   64 Oz.......... 32.00 To 45.00
Plate, 9 3/8 In.............. 5.50
Tumbler, 6 Oz.,
   3 In...............4.50 To 6.50
Tumbler, 9 Oz., 5 In. 7.50
Tumbler, 12 Oz.....7.50 To 9.00

WHITE ─────────

Bowl, 8 3/8 In. 6.00
Creamer...................... 2.00

BULLSEYE, see Bubble

Burple ─────────

Burple is not a mistype but a real name used by the factory. Anchor Hocking Glass Company, Lancaster, Ohio, made crystal, forest green, and ruby red dessert sets in this pattern in the 1940s. There are also two sizes of bowls.

CRYSTAL ─────────

Bowl, 8 1/2 In. 3.00
Bowl, Footed, 4 1/2 In...... 3.00

GREEN ─────────

Bowl, 4 1/2 In. ....2.00 To 6.50
Bowl, 8 1/2 In. ...4.50 To 15.00
Cocktail, Crystal Foot 7.50
Sherbet, Crystal Foot........ 3.75
Tumbler, Footed,
   3 5/8 In.................... 4.00

BUTTERFLIES & ROSES, see Flower Garden with Butterflies

BUTTONS & BOWS, see Holiday

By Cracky ─────────

A strange cracked-ice look to the glass must have inspired the name By Cracky for this pattern. It was made in the late 1920s by L. E. Smith Glass Company, Mt. Pleasant, Pennsylvania. Candleholders, flower frogs, 8-inch octagonal

plates, and luncheon sets with sherbets were made. The luncheon set dish had several compartments. Amber, canary yellow, crystal, and green pieces were made. The pieces have an overall crackled pattern.

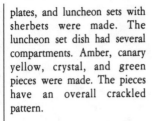

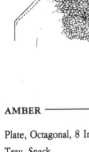

AMBER ─────────

Plate, Octagonal, 8 In........ 2.00
Tray, Snack 4.00

CRYSTAL ─────────

Pitcher......................15.00
Sherbet 1.50

GREEN ─────────

Plate, 6 In.................... 1.50
Sherbet 3.00
Sherbet, Crimped 3.50

C

CABBAGE ROSE, see Sharon

CABBAGE ROSE WITH SINGLE ARCH, see Rosemary

Cameo

Cameo is understandably called Ballerina or Dancing Girl because the most identifiable feature of the etched pattern is the silhouette of the dancer. This pattern must have sold well when made by Hocking Glass Company from 1930 to 1934 because many different pieces were made, from dinner sets and servers to cookie jars and lamps. The pattern was made in crystal with a platinum rim and in green, pink, and yellow. In 1981 reproductions were made of both pink and green Cameo salt and pepper shakers. Children's dishes have recently been made in green, pink, and yellow; but there were never any old Cameo childrens' dishes.

CRYSTAL

Tumbler, Platinum Rim, 9 Oz., 4 In. 8.00

GREEN

Bottle, Vinegar 20.00
Bowl, 8 1/2 In. 24.00
Bowl, Vegetable, 10 In. 24.00
Cup & Saucer.... 12.00 To 16.50
Dish,
  Mayonnaise..... 28.00 To 30.00
Goblet, 4 In................. 45.00
Goblet, 6 In................. 49.50
Grill Plate, 2 Tab Handles,
  10 1/2 In.................. 50.00
Ice Bowl .... 125.00 To 150.00
Pitcher, 5 3/4 In.......... 150.00
Pitcher, 6 In. .... 35.00 To 52.50
Plate, 6 In.................... 3.50
Plate, 8 In.................... 7.50
Plate, 9 1/2 In.............. 12.00
Plate, Square, 8 1/2 In. 22.00
Platter, Closed Handle,
  12 In. 15.00
Salt & Pepper............... 45.00
Sherbet, 3 1/8 In. 9.50
Sherbet,
  4 7/8 In........ 24.00 To 25.00
Soup, Dish................. 13.50
Sugar & Creamer 27.00
Sugar, 3 1/4 In. 10.50
Tumbler, 3 3/4 In.......... 22.00
Tumbler, Footed, 5 In. 24.50
Vase, 5 3/4 In. 130.00

PINK

Creamer.................... 65.00
Goblet, 6 In....125.00 To 150.00
Plate, 8 In................... 21.00
Plate, 10 In. 35.00

YELLOW

Bowl, 5 1/2 In. 25.00
Bowl, Oval, 10 In........... 30.00
Cup 6.50
Cup & Saucer.......8.00 To 8.50
Grill Plate,
  10 1/2 In..........6.00 To 7.50
Plate, 6 In...........2.00 To 2.25
Plate, 8 In.................... 3.25
Plate, 9 1/2 In......6.00 To 7.50
Tumbler, Footed, 5 In. 12.00

Candlewick

Candlewick was made by Imperial Glass Company, Bellaire, Ohio, from 1937 to 1982. Many similar patterns have been made by other companies. The beaded edge is the only design. Although the glass was first made in crystal, it has also been produced in black, nut brown, sunshine yellow, ultra blue, and verde (green). Some pieces of crystal are decorated with gold. Pieces have been found in red, pink, lavender, and amber, and with fired-on gold, red, blue, or green beading. Some sets were made with etchings and hand-painted designs.

• • • • • • • • • • • • • • •
If two tumblers get stuck when stacked, try putting cold water into the inside glass, then put both into hot water up to the lower rim.
• • • • • • • • • • • • • • •

Candlewick

BLACK ───────────

Plate, 2 Handles............60.00

BLUE ───────────

Bowl, 11 In.............. 100.00
Bowl, Handle, 7 In. 45.00

CRYSTAL ───────────

Ashtray, 3 Piece 15.00
Ashtray, Eagle 50.00
Basket, 6 1/2 In. 32.00
Bouillon, Liner.............50.00
Bowl, Float, 11 In. 30.00
Bowl, Heart, Handle,
   6 1/2 In..................18.00
Bowl, Vegetable, Cover,
   8 In...........90.00 To 140.00
Butter Tub, 2 Handles,
   7 In..................... 175.00
Butter, Cover,
   1/4 Lb......... 20.00 To 25.00
Cake Plate, Birthday........15.00
Cake Stand,
   Floral.......... 15.00 To 20.00
Candleholder, 3-Footed,
   Pair......................55.00
Celery, Open Handle.......45.00
Clock, Boudoir........... 250.00
Cologne, Stopper 32.00
Compote, Pedestal,
   5 1/2 In........ 15.00 To 18.00
Console Set, 3 Piece........70.00
Cruet, Handle 32.00
Cup & Saucer,
   After Dinner 14.00
Dish, Jelly, Cover...........20.00
Eggcup.....................39.00

Goblet, 9 Oz...............12.00
Gravy Boat, Underplate,
   2 Ball Handle 75.00
Ice Bucket, Handles,
   7 In..................... 200.00
Mayonnaise,
   3 Piece .... 22.00 To 35.00
Mayonnaise, Chrome Underplate,
   Ladle 50.00
Muffin, 2 Handles,
   8 1/2 In..................28.00
Nappy, Gold Beaded 30.00
Pitcher, 80 Oz. 205.00
Plate, 6 In...................6.50
Plate, 7 In...................7.00
Plate, Torte, 2 Handles,
   14 In. 25.00
Platter, 13 In...............60.00
Relish, 2 Sections, 8 In.....15.00
Relish, 4 Sections,
   8 In........... 16.00 To 18.00
Relish, 4 Sections, Handle,
   12 In. 75.00
Relish, 5 Sections,
   10 1/2 In..................15.00
Relish, 13 In. 35.00
Salt & Pepper..............22.00
Salt & Pepper, Beaded......45.00
Sugar, Ruby Flashed 65.00
Tray, Center Handle,
   6 In.......................18.00
Tray, Center Handle,
   8 1/2 In..................28.00
Tray,
   Deviled Egg.... 75.00 To 87.50
Vase, Bud, Footed,
   5 3/4 In..................40.00
Vase, Crimped, 2 Handles,
   Star Cut, 8 In.............35.00

GREEN ───────────

Bowl, 5 1/4 In. 124.00
Bowl, 6 In. 125.00

PINK ───────────

Ashtray, 6 In................7.00

YELLOW ───────────

Ashtray, 5 In...............6.00

Cape Cod

Cape Cod was a pattern made by the Imperial Glass Company, Bellaire, Ohio, from 1932. It is usually found in crystal, but was also made in amber, azalea, light blue, cobalt blue, green, milk glass, and ruby. In 1978 the dinner set was reproduced. The cruet was reproduced in 1986 without the rayed bottom.

AMBER ───────────

Cruet........................26.00

BLUE ───────────

Sherbet .... 20.00 To 26.00

CRYSTAL ───────────

Bowl, 4 1/2 In. 5.00
Bowl, 12 In.................30.00
Bowl, Handle, 7 1/2 In. ...30.00
Cake Stand, 11 In...........50.00
Candleholder, 5 In..........13.00
Compote, Cover, 6 In.......50.00
Cruet, Stopper 20.00
Cup & Saucer................ 8.00
Cup, Punch 10.00
Decanter, 26 Oz., Pair.... 120.00
Eggcup.....................26.00
Mug, Tom & Jerry..........33.00
Parfait...................... 7.00
Pitcher, 60 Oz. 70.00
Pitcher, Milk, 10 Oz. 25.00
Plate, 7 In................... 6.00
Plate, 8 In................... 9.00

Plate, 10 In. 33.00
Plate, 13 In. 18.00
Plate, Cupped, 14 In. 33.00
Plate, Serving, 2 Handles,
  11 1/2 In. 40.00
Plate, Torte, Flat, 14 In. 30.00
Punch Set, 15 Piece 175.00
Relish, 2 Sections,
  Handle 28.00
Relish, 3 Sections, Handle,
  9 1/2 In. .... 30.00 To 35.00
Relish, 5 Sections, 11 In. ...50.00
Saltshaker 10.00
Spoon Rest. 6.00
Tumbler, Footed, 10 Oz. 6.00
Tumbler, Footed, 12 Oz. 8.00

RED

Candleholder, 5 In. 7.50
Candleholder, 8 In., Pair 7.00
Decanter....................15.00
Tumbler, 10 Oz. 8.00

Caprice

Caprice was advertised in 1936 as the most popular crystal pattern in America. It was made until 1953. Over 200 pieces were made in the line. Frosted pieces were called Alpine Caprice, the name given by the maker, Cambridge Glass Company, Cambridge, Ohio. The sets were made in amber, amethyst, blue, cobalt blue, moonlight blue, crystal, emerald green, light green, pink, and milk glass. Reproductions are being made in cobalt and moonlight blue.

CAPRICE, see also Alpine Caprice

BLUE

Ashtray, 5 In. 17.00
Bowl, 4-Footed, Crimped,
  11 In. 60.00
Bowl, Oval, 13 In. 70.00
Cruet, Oil & Vinegar, Holder,
  3 Oz. 145.00
Cup & Saucer...............28.00
Dish, Mayonnaise,
  3 Piece 70.00
Ice Bucket, Handle,
  Tongs................... 150.00
Pitcher, Ball, 80 Oz. 260.00
Plate, 8 1/2 In. 19.00
Saucer...................... 5.00
Sugar & Creamer, Tray,
  Miniature.................45.00
Tumbler, Footed, 12 Oz. ...40.00

CRYSTAL

Bowl, 10 In. 14.00
Bowl, 4-Footed, Oval,
  13 In. 28.00
Bowl, Handles Down, Square,
  7 In......................10.00

Bowl, Handles Up, Square,
  5 In........................10.00
Bowl, Ruffled, Square,
  8 In.......................18.00
Bowl, Underplate, Divided,
  2 Handles 35.00
Candleholder, 3-Light.......22.00
Candy Dish, Cover, 3-
  Footed....................35.00
Candy Dish, Cover, Shell ...40.00
Champagne 12.50
Cigarette Box, Small 17.00
Compote, Footed 22.00
Cup & Saucer.... 16.50 To 32.00
Oyster Cocktail 50.00
Plate, 4-Footed,
  13 1/2 In..................30.00
Plate, 6 In...................12.00
Plate, 7 1/2 In.....7.50 To 11.00
Plate, 8 1/2 In..............12.00
Relish, 3 Sections 30.00
Saucer....................... 3.00
Sherbet .... 12.50 To 27.50
Sugar 6.00
Tumbler, Footed,
  5 1/4 In...................15.00
Wine.......................52.00

PINK

Cup & Saucer...............32.00
Dish, Lemon, 6 In. 22.50
Plate, 8 1/2 In..............24.00
Sherbet, Tall 30.00

Caribbean

The rippled design of Caribbean is slick and modern in appearance and has attracted many collectors. It was made by Duncan and Miller Glass Company, Pittsburgh, Pennsylvania, from 1936 to 1955. Sets were made of crystal, amber, blue, and red glass. The Duncan and Miller catalogs identify the line as No. 112.

BLUE

Candy Dish, Cover 60.00

Cheese & Cracker, Liner....30.00

Relish, 2 Sections...........18.00

Sherbet 13.00

Sugar & Creamer 60.00

Tumbler, Footed,
   5 1/2 In...................30.00

CRYSTAL

Ashtray, Footed.............15.00

Candleholder, Prisms,
   Pair........................45.00

Cup, Punch,
   Amber Handle 10.00

Cup, Punch,
   Blue Handle...............10.00

Cup, Punch,
   Red Handle ......6.00 To 10.00

Jar, Cigarette, Cover 30.00

Plate, 6 In....................4.00

Plate, 8 1/2 In...............8.00

Punch Bowl, 10 In..........75.00

Punch Set, Underplate, Ladle,
   12 Cups 225.00

Relish, 5 Sections, 10 In. ...45.00

Sugar 13.00

Sugar & Creamer 15.00

Syrup, 4 1/2 In..............40.00

Vase, 5 3/4 In..............18.00

Vase, Ball, 7 1/4 In. 17.00

Century

Century pattern was made by Fostoria Glass Company from 1926 until 1986. It is a plain pattern with a slightly rippled rim. Full dinner sets were made.

CRYSTAL

Bonbon, 3-Footed...........16.50

Bowl, 8 1/2 In. 35.00

Bowl, Triangular, 7 In. 13.00

Candleholder, 4 1/2 In.,
   Pair........................22.00

Candy Dish, Cover,
   Footed......... 37.00 To 43.00

Compote......... 15.00 To 18.00

Creamer, Individual.......... 3.00

Cruet, Oil..................40.00

Cup & Saucer...............10.00

Dish, Mayonnaise, Liner 30.00

Goblet,
   5 3/4 In........ 12.00 To 25.00

Mustard Pot, Cover.........45.00

Pitcher, 6 1/8 In............45.00

Plate, 7 1/2 In.....9.00 To 15.00

Plate, 8 1/2 In...............6.00

Plate, Triangular, 7 In. 17.50

Platter, 12 In..... 40.00 To 45.00

Relish, 2 Sections,
   7 3/8 In....................8.00

Relish, 3 Sections, Oval,
   11 In. 20.00

Sherbet 10.00

Sugar & Creamer, Tray,
   Individual..................23.00

Sugar, Large 4.00

Tidbit, 3 Tiers, 8 1/4 In....15.00

Tray, Center Handle........20.00

Tumbler, Footed,
   4 3/4 In...................13.00

Tumbler, Footed,
   5 3/8 In...................25.00

CHAIN DAISY, see Adam

Chantilly

As late as the 1960s the Jeannette Glass Company, Jeannette, Pennsylvania, made a pattern called Chantilly that is collected by Depression glass buffs. It was made in crystal and pink.

CRYSTAL

Bowl, Handle,
   11 1/2 In..................30.00

Cake Plate 70.00

Candleholder, 3-Light.......38.00

Cocktail, 3 Oz...............25.00

Dish, Mayonnaise, Ladle 25.00

Goblet, 5 3/4 In............16.00

Tumbler, Footed, 12 Oz.,
   5 7/8 In...................16.00

Vase, 10 In. 25.00

Vase, Footed, 8 In. 20.00

Wine........................35.00

Cherokee Rose

The Tiffin glass factory can be traced back to the 1840s, when Joseph Beatty made glass in Steubenville, Ohio.

The factory failed and was purchased by Alexander Beatty in 1851. He was joined by his sons and moved to Tiffin, Ohio, in 1888. The company became part of U.S. Glass Company in 1892 and was still operating in 1963 when U.S. Glass went bankrupt. Employees bought the plant and it went through several changes of ownership until it closed in 1980. Cherokee Rose was one of the popular glass patterns made by Tiffin in the 1940s and 1950s. The glass was made only in crystal.

CRYSTAL

Candlestick, 2-Light,
    Pair............ 60.00 To 65.00
Goblet, 9 Oz.............. 20.00
Plate, 8 In....... 10.00 To 12.00
Plate, 10 In. 8.00
Sherbet 15.00
Tidbit, 3 Tiers 20.00
Vase, Bud, 8 In. 32.00
Vase, Bud, 10 1/2 In...... 42.00

CHERRY, see Cherry Blossom

Cherry Blossom

Cherry Blossom is one of the most popular Depression glass patterns. It has been called Banded Cherry, Cherry, or Paneled Cherry Blossom by

some collectors. The pattern was made by the Jeannette Glass Company, Jeannette, Pennsylvania, from 1930 to 1939. Full dinner sets and serving pieces were made in a wide range of colors. Pieces were made in crystal, delphite (opaque blue), green, jadite (opaque green), and pink. Many reproductions of Cherry Blossom pieces have been made and sold in recent years.

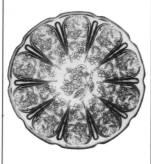

DELPHITE

Bowl, 4 3/4 In. 12.00
Creamer, Child's 34.00
Cup & Saucer 32.50
Cup, Child's 27.50
Dinner Set, Child's,
    14 Piece................ 170.00
Plate, 6 In................. 10.00
Plate, 9 In..........9.00 To 11.00
Plate, Child's........6.00 To 9.00
Saucer, Child's 4.00
Sugar & Creamer, Child's...70.00

GREEN

Bowl,
    5 1/2 In........ 25.00 To 30.00
Bowl, 8 In. 35.00
Bowl, Handle, 9 In. 20.00
Bowl, Vegetable,
    Oval .... 25.75 To 32.00
Cake Plate,
    Footed.......... 18.50 To 20.00
Coaster....................... 10.00
Creamer.......... 10.00 To 12.00
Cup .... 15.00 To 18.00
Cup & Saucer 19.00
Pitcher, 8 In. 38.00
Pitcher, Footed, 8 In........ 40.00
Plate, 6 In.................... 4.50
Plate, 7 In........ 15.00 To 17.50
Plate, 9 In........ 17.00 To 18.00
Platter, 11 In............... 30.00
Salt & Pepper,
    Scalloped 750.00
Sherbet 13.00
Soup, Dish.................. 26.00
Sugar, Cover..... 25.00 To 34.50
Tumbler,
    3 1/2 In........ 20.00 To 25.00
Tumbler,
    4 1/4 In........ 17.00 To 18.00
Tumbler, Footed,
    3 3/4 In........ 13.00 To 15.00
Tumbler, Footed,
    4 1/2 In........ 27.00 To 30.00

PINK

Bowl, 4 3/4 In. ...8.00 To 13.50
Bowl, 5 3/4 In. 24.00
Cake Plate, 3-Footed........ 22.00
Coaster..................... 15.00
Creamer..................... 16.50
Creamer, Child's 27.50
Cup & Saucer.... 13.00 To 20.00
Dinner Set, Child's,
    14 Piece................ 160.00
Grill Plate,
    9 In............. 15.00 To 17.00
Mug, 7 Oz. 150.00
Plate, 6 In..........4.50 To 5.00
Plate, 9 In........ 12.00 To 17.50
Platter, Oval, 9 In......... 700.00

Salt & Pepper,
Scalloped 1000.00
Sherbet .... 11.00 To 12.50
Sugar 10.00
Sugar & Creamer, Cover....36.00
Tumbler,
3 1/2 In........ 10.00 To 12.50
Tumbler, 4 1/4 In.......... 16.50
Tumbler, Footed,
3 3/4 In........ 11.00 To 14.50
Tumbler, Footed,
4 1/2 In........ 24.00 To 25.00
Tumbler, Footed, 5 In. 24.00

Cherry-Berry

Two similar patterns, Cherry-Berry and Strawberry, can be confusing. If the fruit pictured is a cherry, then the pattern is called Cherry-Berry. If the strawberry is used, then the pattern has that name. The dishes were made by the U.S. Glass Company in the early 1930s in crystal, green, iridescent amber, and pink.

CHERRY-BERRY, see also Strawberry

CRYSTAL

Bowl, 7 1/2 In. 16.00

GREEN

Bowl, 6 In. 32.00
Bowl, 7 1/2 In. 20.00
Dish, Olive,
Handle .... 32.00 To 35.00

Sherbet 6.00

Chinex Classic

Chinex Classic and Cremax are very similar patterns made by Macbeth-Evans Division of Corning Glass Works from about 1938 to 1942. Chinex and Cremax are both words with two meanings. Each is the name of a pattern and the name of a color used for other patterns. Chinex is ivory-colored, Cremax is a bit whiter. Chinex Classic, the dinnerware pattern, has a piecrust edge, and just inside the edge is an elongated feathered scroll. It may or may not have a decal-decorated center and colored edging. The Cremax pattern has just the piecrust edge. The decals used on Chinex Classic are either floral designs or brown-toned scenics.

CHINEX CLASSIC, see also Cremax

IVORY WITH DECAL

Bowl, 5 3/4 In. 6.00
Bowl, 8 3/4 In. 15.00
Creamer...................... 6.00
Cup 5.00
Plate, 6 In................... 4.00
Plate, 9 3/4 In.............. 6.00
Sherbet 1.50

IVORY

Bowl, 5 3/4 In. 4.00
Cup & Saucer.......4.00 To 6.00
Plate, 6 In..................... .85
Plate, 8 In................... 5.00
Plate, 9 3/4 In......3.00 To 3.50
Sherbet, Footed.............. 8.00
Sugar & Creamer 12.00

Chintz

Several companies made a glass named Chintz. To identify the pieces of Chintz pattern, remember the design is named for the etched pattern, not the shape, of the glass. Fostoria Glass Company made Baroque, a glass shape that included molded fleur-de-lis-shaped handles and ridges. This glass blank was then etched with design No. 338 and then sold as Chintz pattern. The etched design pictures branches of leaves and flowers. It was also used on some vases and other pieces that were not Baroque blanks. Only crystal pieces were made. Pieces were made from 1940 to 1972. To confuse this even more, the company made other etched designs (Navarre) on the Baroque blanks. Another Chintz pattern was made by A. H. Heisey Company from 1931 to 1938. It was an etched design of butterflies and encircled flowers. This Chintz pattern was made in crystal, green (Moongleam), orchid (Alexandrite, a glass that turned from blue to purple depending on the lighting source), pink (Flamingo), and yellow (Sahara). Pieces listed in this book are for Fostoria Chintz.

CRYSTAL

Bonbon, 3-Footed
.... 20.00 To 35.00
Candleholder, 2-Light,
Pair........................60.00
Candleholder, 3-Light,
Pair........................90.00
Candy Dish, Cover,
3 Sections ...... 85.00 To 95.00
Champagne, 5 1/2 In.......18.00
Cocktail, 5 In. ... 19.00 To 24.50
Cordial,
3 7/8 In........ 42.50 To 47.50
Goblet,
7 5/8 In........ 22.00 To 26.00
Jelly, Cover,
7 1/2 In........ 85.00 To 95.00
Mayonnaise Set,
3 Piece .... 40.00 To 60.00
Oyster Cocktail,
3 3/8 In...................25.00
Plate,
7 1/2 In........ 10.00 To 12.00
Plate, 9 1/2 In..............45.00
Plate, 13 1/2 In. 45.00

Relish, 3 Sections,
10 1/2 In.................39.50
Saucer.......................5.00
Sherbet, 4 3/8 In...........16.00
Sugar & Creamer,
Individual 39.50
Sugar & Creamer, Large....35.00
Sugar & Creamer, Tray,
Individual 75.00
Tumbler, 5 Oz..............19.50
Tumbler, 9 Oz..............15.00
Tumbler, Footed,
13 Oz.......... 18.00 To 24.00
Wine,
5 3/8 In....... 28.00 To 45.00

Christmas Candy

Christmas Candy, sometimes called Christmas Candy Ribbon, was made by the Indiana Glass Company, Dunkirk, Indiana, in 1937. The pattern, apparently only made in luncheon sets, was made in crystal, a light green called seafoam green, a bright blue called teal blue, and dark emerald green.

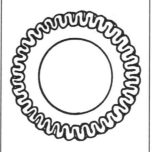

CRYSTAL

Creamer ....5.00 To 7.00
Cup..........................3.50
Cup & Saucer................5.00
Fruit Cup 5.00
Plate, 8 1/2 In......5.00 To 5.50
Sugar ....5.00 To 7.50
Sugar & Creamer.... 7.00 To 12.00

TEAL BLUE

Creamer 16.00
Plate, 6 In. 5.50
Plate, 8 In. ....4.00 To 9.00
Plate, 9 5/8 In..............25.00
Saucer.......................3.00
Soup, Dish, 7 3/8 In. 23.00

CHRISTMAS CANDY RIBBON, see Christmas Candy

Circle

Circles ring the Circle pattern made by Hocking Glass Company, Lancaster, Ohio, in the 1930s. It is often found in green, but is less available in crystal and pink.

CRYSTAL

Goblet, 8 Oz., 4 In. 8.50
Sherbet, Green Stem........12.00
Sugar 6.00

GREEN

Bowl, 5 1/8 In. 9.00
Bowl, Flared, 5 1/2 In. 12.00
Champagne ....9.00 To 9.50
Cup ....2.50 To 3.00
Cup & Saucer, Footed 4.75
Cup & Saucer, Side Cone....4.50
Goblet, 8 Oz.,
4 In............ 10.00 To 12.00
Pitcher, Water, 80 Oz. 30.00
Plate, 6 In. 2.00
Salt & Pepper..............25.00

Sherbet,
3 1/8 In...........2.25 To 5.50
Sherbet,
4 3/4 In...........4.50 To 9.00
Sugar, Footed...............6.00
Tumbler, 5 In...............12.00
Water Set, 6 Piece..........57.00
Wine,
4 1/2 In........11.50 To 12.00

PINK

Creamer.....................18.75
Cup.........................10.00
Plate, 6 In..................5.75
Plate, 8 1/4 In.............11.75
Sherbet, 3 1/8 In...........10.00
Sugar......................18.75

CIRCULAR RIBS, see Circle

CLASSIC, see Chinex Classic

Cleo

In 1930 the Cambridge Glass Company, Cambridge, Ohio, introduced an etched pattern called Cleo. Many pieces are marked with the Cambridge C in a triangle. Sets were made in amber, blue, crystal, green, pink, and yellow.

AMBER

Bowl, Decagon, 10 In. 20.00
Pitcher, 22 Oz. 110.00
Saucer......................3.50

BLUE

Basket, 11 In...............75.00
Bonbon, 5 1/2 In...........35.00
Bowl, 6 1/2 In. 15.00
Bowl, Console, 12 In. 40.00

GREEN

Candleholder, Pair..........45.00
Cup.........................18.00
Ice Bucket, Tongs 40.00
Relish, 2 Section...........20.00

PINK

Bowl, 11 1/2 In. 27.50
Cup & Saucer................18.00
Goblet, 9 Oz................25.00
Sugar, Footed..............15.00

Cloverleaf

Three-leaf clovers form part of the border of Cloverleaf pattern made by Hazel-Atlas Glass Company from 1930 to 1936. It was made in black, crystal, green, pink, and topaz.

BLACK

Ashtray, 5 1/2 In...........70.00
Creamer...........9.00 To 12.50
Cup & Saucer....10.00 To 13.00
Plate, 6 In..................27.50
Plate, 8 In...................8.00
Salt & Pepper..............60.00
Sherbet, Footed.............15.00
Sugar ....9.00 To 12.50
Sugar & Creamer...18.00 To 26.00

CRYSTAL

Cup & Saucer................5.00
Plate, 8 1/4 In..............4.00
Tumbler, 3 3/4 In..........25.00

GREEN

Bowl, 5 In. ...... 20.00 To 24.00
Bowl, 7 In. ...... 30.00 To 32.00
Bowl, 8 In. 40.00
Candy Dish 20.00
Creamer......................7.00
Cup ....5.00 To 8.00
Cup & Saucer................8.00
Grill Plate 15.00
Plate, 6 In...................3.50
Plate, 8 In...................5.00
Salt & Pepper..............18.00
Saucer......................2.50
Sherbet 4.00
Tumbler, 4 In..............32.00
Tumbler, Footed,
5 3/4 In........ 15.00 To 18.50

PINK

Bowl, 4 In. 15.00
Sherbet ....4.50 To 7.50

YELLOW

Candy Dish, Cover 80.00
Creamer.....................12.50
Sugar .... 10.00 To 12.50

Colonial

Sometimes this pattern is called Knife & Fork, although Colonial is the more common name. It was made by Hocking Glass Company, Lancaster, Ohio, from 1934 to 1938. Colors include crystal, green, opaque white, and pink.

• • • • • • • • • • • • • • • •
Don't use ammonia on glasses with gold or silver decorations.
• • • • • • • • • • • • • • • •

CRYSTAL ─────────

Cocktail, 4 In. 7.00
Goblet, 5 3/4 In. 12.00
Plate, 8 1/2 In. 3.00
Saltshaker 18.00
Spoon Holder...............50.00
Tumbler, 12 Oz.............18.00
Water Set, 6 Piece..........50.00

GREEN ─────────

Bowl, 8 In. 15.00
Butter, Cover .... 45.00 To 50.00
Claret, 5 1/4 In.............20.00
Cocktail, 4 In. ... 20.00 To 22.00
Cordial,
3 3/4 In........ 21.00 To 24.00
Cup & Saucer...............13.00
Goblet, 5 1/4 In............20.00
Goblet,
5 3/4 In........ 18.00 To 25.00
Plate, 6 In................... 2.00
Plate, 10 In. 45.00
Soup, Cream ..... 22.00 To 40.00
Spoon Holder............. 110.00
Tumbler, Footed, 4 In. 25.00
Whiskey..................... 9.00
Wine.......................22.00

PINK ─────────

Cup & Saucer......7.00 To 12.50
Grill Plate 22.00
Pitcher, 54 Oz. 30.00
Plate, 10 In. 38.00
Sherbet, 3 In..... 11.00 To 15.00
Sherbet, 4 3/8 In. 7.00
Soup, Cream 55.00

Soup, Dish..................13.50
Tumbler, Footed,
3 1/4 In........ 12.00 To 12.75
Tumbler, Footed, 4 In. 9.50
Tumbler, Footed,
5 1/4 In..................25.00
Whiskey....................15.00

Colonial Block

A small set of dishes, mostly serving pieces, was made in Colonial Block pattern by Hazel-Atlas Glass Company, a firm with factories in Ohio, Pennsylvania, and West Virginia. The dishes were made in the 1930s in green and pink and in the 1950s in white.

GREEN ─────────

Butter, Cover 35.00
Candy Jar,
Cover.......... 27.50 To 30.00
Goblet ....7.50 To 8.50
Sugar & Creamer, Cover....25.00
Sugar, Cover...............16.50

PINK ─────────

Butter, Cover 42.00

WHITE ─────────

Creamer..................... 5.50
Sugar & Creamer, Cover....14.00

Colonial Fluted

Federal Glass Company made Colonial Fluted pattern from 1928 to 1933. It was made in crystal and green.

CRYSTAL ─────────

Bowl, 7 1/2 In. 10.00

GREEN ─────────

Bowl, 6 In. 8.50
Bowl,
7 1/2 In........ 11.00 To 12.00
Creamer............4.75 To 5.00
Plate, 8 In................... 3.00
Saucer....................... 2.00
Sherbet ....4.00 To 5.50
Sugar, Cover...............13.00

Colony

Colony is a pattern that has also been called Elongated Honeycomb or Hexagon Triple Band because of the features in the molding. It was made by Hazel-Atlas Glass Company in the 1930s in crystal, green, and pink. Another pattern, also named Colony, was made by Fostoria Glass Company.

CRYSTAL —————————

Bowl, Handle, 8 1/2 In. ...22.00

Butter, Cover, 1/4 Lb. 43.00

Cake Plate, Handle,
   10 In. 20.00

Candleholder, 2-Light,
   Pair.......................35.00

Candy Dish, Cover,
   6 1/2 In.................30.00

Compote, Cover 35.00

Goblet, 3 7/8 In............10.00

Pitcher, Ice Lip 65.00

Pitcher, Ice Lip, 2 Qt. 95.00

Plate, 9 1/2 In..............30.00

Relish, 2 Sections, Handle,
   7 In.......................18.00

Salt & Pepper, Tray,
   Individual.................. 8.00

Sherbet, 6 In................ 7.00

Tumbler, Footed, 12 Oz.,
   5 3/4 In..................14.00

PINK —————————

Sherbet, 6 In...............20.00

Columbia

Columbia pattern can be
found in crystal but is rare in
pink. It was made by Federal
Glass Company, Columbus,
Ohio, from 1938 to 1942.

CRYSTAL —————————

Bowl, 5 In. ....8.00 To 11.00
Bowl,
   8 1/2 In....... 12.00 To 15.00
Bowl, Ruffled,
   10 1/2 In...... 12.50 To 16.00
Butter, Cover ......6.00 To 16.00
Cup..........................4.00
Cup & Saucer.......4.50 To 6.00
Plate, 6 In..........1.25 To 3.00
Plate, 8 In....................2.50
Plate, 9 1/2 In......3.75 To 6.00
Plate, 11 In. 6.00
Plate, 12 In. 1.75
Soup, Dish..................12.00

Coronation

Coronation was made by Anchor Hocking Glass Company,
Lancaster, Ohio, from 1936 to
1940. Most pieces are crystal
or pink, but there are also
dark green and ruby red sets.
The pattern is sometimes
called Banded Fine Rib or
Saxon. Some of the pieces are
confused with those in Lace
Edge pattern.

PINK —————————

Bowl, 4 1/4 In. 5.00
Bowl, Handle, 4 1/4 In. 3.00
Bowl, Handle, 6 1/2 In. ...12.00
Bowl, Handle,
   8 In...............4.50 To 13.50
Cup..........................3.00
Plate, 6 In...........1.00 To 2.50
Plate, 8 1/2 In...............4.00
Sherbet ....3.00 To 4.50
Tumbler 14.50

RED —————————

Bowl, 4 1/4 In. 4.50
Bowl, 6 1/2 In. 14.00
Bowl, 8 In. 10.00
Bowl, Handles, 4 1/4 In..... 5.00
Bowl, Handles,
   8 In............. 12.00 To 20.00
Candy Dish, Cover,
   Footed.....................35.00

Cosmos

Cosmos glass was made by the
Jeannette Glass Company of
Jeanette, Pennsylvania, from
the 1950s. It was made in
crystal or golden iridescent
glass.

IRIDESCENT

Pitcher, White Deco,
  9 5/8 In.................19.00

Saucer....................... 3.00

Soup, Dish...................6.00

Sugar & Creamer 12.00

Tumbler, White Deco 5.00

Cracked Ice

Cracked Ice is an Art Deco-
looking geometric pattern
made by Indiana Glass Company in the 1930s. It was
made in green and pink.

GREEN

Candleholder, 3 3/8 In.,
  Pair.......................12.00

PINK

Sherbet, 4 1/8 In............5.00

Tumbler, Footed.............7.50

Craquel

Craquel was made by the
United States Glass Company
in 1924. It has an overall stippled finish. Pieces were made
in crystal with green trim and
in blue and yellow.

GREEN

Cup, Child's 5.00

Plate, 8 In................... 2.00

Tumbler, 5 1/2 In........... 5.00

YELLOW

Cup, Child's 4.50

Plate, 8 In................... 1.50

Cremax

Cremax and Chinex Classic
are confusing patterns. There
is an added piece of molded
design next to the fluted rim
trim on Chinex Classic. Also
the names Cremax and Chinex
refer to colors as well as patterns. Cremax, made by
Macbeth-Evans Division of
Corning Glass Works, was
popular in the late 1930s to
the early 1940s. It is a cream-
colored opaque glass, some-

times decorated with floral or
brown-tinted decals or with a
colored rim.

**Cremax, see also Chinex
  Classic**

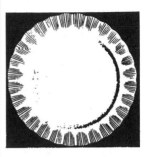

CREAM-COLORED WITH BLUE DECAL

Plate, 9 1/2 In...............5.50

Soup, Dish, 7 1/2 In. 25.00

CREAM-COLORED

Bowl, 5 3/4 In. 6.00

Cup & Saucer,
  Green Border 4.00

Cup & Saucer,
  Pink Border................3.00

Cup & Saucer, After Dinner,
  Pink Border...............12.00

Cup & Saucer.................4.00

Cup, Pink Border............3.50

Cup, Red Border 3.00

Plate, 9 1/4 In..............6.00

Plate, 12 In. 15.00

Plate, Brown Castle,
  9 1/2 In....................1.75

Plate, Green Border, 6 In....2.00

Plate, Green Border,
  9 1/2 In....................5.50

Plate, Pink Border, 6 In. ...2.00

Plate, Pink Border, 11 In....5.00

Plate, Yellow Border,
  12 In. 20.00

Saucer, After Dinner.........4.00

**CRISS CROSS, see X
  Design**

CUBE, see Cubist

Cubist

Cubist, or Cube, molded with the expected rectangular and diamond pattern, was made by Jeannette Glass Company from 1929 to 1933. It was made in amber, blue, canary yellow, crystal, green, pink, ultramarine, and white. It has been made recently in amber, opaque white, and avocado.

CRYSTAL ──────────

Bowl, 4 1/2 In. 3.50
Bowl, 6 1/2 In. 3.50
Candy Dish,
    Cover........... 20.00 To 22.50
Sugar & Creamer, 2 In....... 4.00
Sugar & Creamer, 3 In....... 5.00
Sugar & Creamer, Tray,
    3 Piece 7.50
Tray, Handle, Round,
    Gold Trim................. 3.00

GREEN ──────────

Bowl, 4 1/2 In. 5.00
Creamer, 3 In................ 7.00
Pitcher, 8 3/4 In......... 170.00
Plate, 8 In.................. 5.00
Powder Jar.................. 17.50
Salt & Pepper............... 22.00
Shaker 10.00
Sherbet 4.00
Sugar, 3 In.................. 6.00

PINK ──────────

Bowl, 4 1/2 In. 4.50
Bowl, 6 1/2 In. 4.00
Bowl, 7 1/2 In. 8.00
Candy Dish 22.50
Coaster...................... 6.00
Creamer, 3 1/4 In. 7.00
Plate, 8 In.................. 4.50
Powder Jar,
    Cover........... 10.00 To 15.00
Salt & Pepper............... 18.00
Saltshaker 10.00
Sherbet, 3 In................. 3.00
Sugar & Creamer, 2 In....... 6.00
Sugar, 2 In.........1.50 To 5.00
Sugar, 3 In.................. 4.00

ULTRAMARINE ──────────

Bowl, 6 1/2 In. 50.00

D

DAISY, see No. 620

DAISY PETALS, see Petalware

DANCING GIRL, see Cameo

Decagon

Decagon, named for its 10-sided outline, was made by the Cambridge Glass Company of Cambridge, Ohio. The pattern, dating from the 1930s, was made in amber, dark blue (cobalt), light blue (Moonlight), green, pink, and red.

AMBER ──────────

Cup & Saucer.......7.00 To 9.00
Goblet, 5 1/2 In............12.00
Ice Bucket .... 30.00 To 35.00
Liner, 6 1/2 In. 3.00
Plate, 6 1/4 In............... 5.00
Plate, 7 1/2 In............... 4.75
Plate, 8 1/2 In.......6.50 To 9.00
Saltshaker, 4 1/8 In.........15.00
Sandwich Server,
    Center Handle.............18.00
Sandwich Server, Center Handle,
    11 In. 19.00
Sugar 9.00
Sugar & Creamer 15.00
Tray, Pickle, 9 In. 15.00
Tumbler, Footed, 10 Oz. ...12.00

BLUE ──────────

Tumbler, Footed, 8 Oz......13.00

GREEN ―――――――

Sugar & Creamer, Tray 30.00

PINK ―――――――

Candy Dish, Cover 77.00
Plate, 6 1/4 In............... 5.00
Plate, 8 3/8 In............... 6.50
Platter, 2 Handles,
   10 1/2 In.................27.00
Sugar & Creamer, Footed,
   3 1/4 In.................24.00
Sugar, Scalloped 9.00

Della Robbia

Della Robbia is a heavy glass with raised pears and apples as part of the design. It was made by the Westmoreland Glass Company, Grapeville, Pennsylvania, from the 1920s to the 1940s. The pattern was made in crystal, Roselin, green, and amber. Crystal pieces often have fruit stained in natural colors.

CRYSTAL ―――――――

Bowl, 5 1/2 In. 4.00
Bowl, 6 In. 4.50
Bowl, 9 In. ...... 12.00 To 15.00
Butter, Cover 18.00
Compote, 3 3/4 In..........25.00
Creamer.....................13.00
Cup & Saucer......6.00 To 25.00
Dish, Cheese................18.00
Goblet 10.00
Pitcher.....................75.00

Plate, 7 1/4 In..............15.00
Plate, 8 In...................25.00
Plate, 10 1/2 In. 25.00
Plate, 14 In. 45.00
Punch Set, 14 Piece 800.00
Salt & Pepper...............15.00
Sugar & Creamer 12.00
Tumbler, Footed,
   4 3/4 In..................30.00
Tumbler, Footed,
   5 3/4 In..................35.00
Tumbler, Footed, 6 In. 35.00

Dewdrop

Although Dewdrop was made in 1954 and 1955, it is collected by some Depression glass buyers. It was made by Jeannette Glass Company, Jeannette, Pennsylvania, in crystal.

CRYSTAL ―――――――

Creamer...................... 4.00
Dish, Maple Leaf 6.00
Jug, 64 Oz. 16.00
Lazy Susan, Gold 14.00
Nappy, 8 1/2 In............. 8.00
Punch Set, 14 Piece 40.00
Snack Plate & Cup...........6.00
Sugar, Cover................. 4.00

DIAMOND, see Windsor

**DIAMOND PATTERN,
   see Miss America**

Diamond Quilted

Imperial Glass Company, Bellaire, Ohio, made Diamond Quilted, sometimes called Flat Diamond, in the 1920s and early 1930s. It was made in amber, black, blue, crystal, green, pink, and red. Dinner sets, luncheon sets, and serving pieces, including a large punch bowl, were made, but not all items were made in all colors.

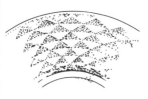

AMBER ―――――――

Cup........................... 6.00

BLACK ―――――――

Bowl, 7 In. 24.00
Candleholder, Pair..........40.00
Cup........................... 8.00

BLUE ―――――――

Bowl, 5 In. 10.00
Bowl, 7 In. 12.00

Creamer....................14.00
Sugar & Creamer 25.00

GREEN ————————————

Bowl, Flared, 7 In. 5.00
Candleholder, Curved........9.00
Plate, 6 In...................2.00
Plate, 8 In...................6.00
Sugar ....3.50 To 6.00

PINK ————————————

Candleholder.................9.00
Creamer......................6.00
Plate, 8 In...................6.00
Punch Set, 14 Piece 400.00
Sherbet ....4.00 To 6.00
Sugar ....5.00 To 6.00

Diana

Diana is one of the many Depression glass patterns with swirls in the glass, which often causes confusion. Federal Glass Company, Columbus, Ohio, made this pattern, sometimes called Swirled Sharp Rib, from 1937 to 1941. It was made in amber, crystal, green, and pink. A pink bowl was reproduced in 1987.

AMBER ————————————

Cup.........................5.00
Cup & Saucer.......5.50 To 9.00
Salt & Pepper...............65.00
Sugar ....4.00 To 5.00

Sugar & Creamer... 12.00 To 16.00
Tumbler, 4 1/8 In..........16.50

CRYSTAL ————————————

Bowl, 5 In. 3.50
Bowl, 9 In. ....5.00 To 6.00
Bowl, 12 In.................6.50
Creamer......................3.00
Cup.........................2.50
Cup & Saucer,
    After Dinner ......4.00 To 6.50
Saucer.......................1.00
Soup, Cream 6.50
Sugar 2.50
Sugar & Creamer 6.50

GREEN ————————————

Cup & Saucer................5.00
Plate, 6 In...................2.00

PINK ————————————

Cup & Saucer................6.50
Plate, 6 In...................1.75

Dogwood

Dogwood is decorated with a strange flower that has been given many names. Collectors have called this pattern Apple Blossom, B pattern, Magnolia, or Wildrose. It was made from 1929 to about 1934 by Macbeth-Evans Glass Company. It is found in Cremax, crystal, green, Monax, pink, and yellow. Some pieces were made with such thin walls the factory redesigned the molds to make the pieces thicker.

• • • • • • • • • • • • • • • •

Never allow water to evaporate in a glass vase. It will leave a white residue that may be impossible to remove.

• • • • • • • • • • • • • • • •

CREMAX ————————————

Bowl, 5 1/2 In. 2.00
Bowl, 6 1/2 In. 15.00
Cake Plate, 13 In. 150.00
Cup.........................30.00

CRYSTAL ————————————

Butter, Cover...............90.00
Plate, 8 In...................3.00
Vase, 5 1/2 In..............16.00

GREEN ————————————

Cake Plate, 13 In. 50.00
Creamer, Thin, 2 1/2 In....38.00
Cup & Saucer.... 23.00 To 25.00
Plate, 6 In...................4.00
Plate, 8 In...........4.00 To 6.00
Saucer.......................4.00
Sherbet 55.00
Sugar 35.00
Sugar & Creamer 75.00

MONAX ————————————

Plate, 12 In. ..... 15.00 To 18.00

PINK ————————————

Ashtray 8.00
Bowl, 8 1/2 In. 33.00
Creamer, Thin, 2 1/2 In....25.00
Cup.........................11.00
Cup & Saucer.... 12.00 To 16.00
Grill Plate,
    10 1/2 In....... 10.00 To 16.50
Plate, 6 In..........3.50 To 4.50
Plate, 8 In..........4.00 To 5.00
Plate, 9 1/4 In.............21.00

Saucer..............2.50 To 4.00
Sugar & Creamer,
  Thin........... 20.00 To 33.50
Sugar, Thick.......9.50 To 13.00
Sugar, Thin.................20.00
Tumbler, 4 In.... 25.00 To 30.00
Tumbler, 5 In..............45.00

YELLOW

Cup & Saucer..............27.00
Sugar & Creamer..........35.00

Doric

Doric was made by Jeannette Glass Company, Jeannette, Pennsylvania, from 1935 to 1938. The molded pattern has also inspired another name for the pattern—Snowflake. It was made in delphite, green, pink, and yellow. A few white pieces may have been made.

DELPHITE

Bowl, 4 1/2 In. 5.00
Candy Dish, 3 Sections 4.00
Creamer..................... 7.00
Saucer...................... 5.00
Sherbet 4.50

GREEN

Bowl, 8 1/4 In. 12.50
Cake Plate, 10 In. 15.00
Cup & Saucer..............11.00
Grill Plate, 9 In.............10.00
Plate, 6 In....................3.00
Plate, 9 In..................12.50

Salt & Pepper..............22.00
Sherbet 8.00

PINK

Bowl, 4 1/2 In. ....5.00 To 5.50
Candy Container,
  3 Sections 4.00
Cup.........................10.00
Grill Plate, 10 1/2 In.......10.00
Plate, 9 In................... 8.00
Salt & Pepper..............20.00
Sugar, Cover................. 9.00
Tray, Handles, 10 In......... 8.00

Doric & Pansy

The snowflake design of Doric alternates with squares holding pansies, so, of course, the pattern is named Doric & Pansy. It, too, was made by Jeannette Glass Company, but only in 1937 and 1938. It was made in crystal, pink, and ultramarine. The ultramarine varied in color from green to blue. A set of child's dishes called Pretty Polly Party Dishes was made in this pattern.

CRYSTAL

Cup & Saucer................ 9.00
Sandwich Server,
  2 Handles 70.00

PINK

Creamer, Child's............22.50
Cup & Saucer, Child's 25.00

Dinner Set, Child's,
  14 Piece................. 135.00
Plate, Child's................. 5.50
Plate, Sherbet,
  6 In...............5.00 To 6.00
Sugar, Child's...............22.50

ULTRAMARINE

Butter, Cover 375.00
Cup & Saucer.... 18.00 To 20.00
Plate, 6 In...........7.00 To 8.50
Sugar 170.00
Sugar & Creamer 250.00
Tray, Handles, 10 In........22.50

**DORIC WITH PANSY,
  see Doric & Pansy**

**DOUBLE SHIELD, see
  Mt. Pleasant**

**DOUBLE SWIRL, see
  Swirl**

**DRAPE & TASSEL, see
  Princess**

DUTCH, see Windmill

**DUTCH ROSE, see
  Rosemary**

E

**EARLY AMERICAN, see
  Princess Feather**

**EARLY AMERICAN
  HOBNAIL, see Hobnail**

**EARLY AMERICAN
  ROCK CRYSTAL, see
  Rock Crystal**

**ELONGATED
  HONEYCOMB, see
  Colony**

English Hobnail

Westmoreland Glass Company, Grapeville, Pennsylvania, made English Hobnail pattern from the 1920s through the 1970s. It was made in amber, blue, cobalt, crystal, green, pink, red, and turquoise. There is much variation in the shading. Red English Hobnail has been made in the 1980s, a darker amber in the 1960s. Red and pink reproductions have been made since 1980.

ENGLISH HOBNAIL, see also Miss America

AMBER ———————

Candy Dish, Cover, Cone...44.00
Tidbit, 2 Tiers 40.00

BLUE ———————

Sherbet 25.00

CRYSTAL ———————

Bowl, Footed, 6 1/2 In.....35.00
Butter.......................20.00
Candleholder, 3 1/2 In. 10.00
Candleholder, 4 In., Pair ...20.00
Candy Basket 15.00
Cocktail, Round Base 6.00
Compote, Round Foot,
  5 In........................15.00
Creamer, Footed 8.00
Cup 5.00
Goblet, 5 In.................10.00
Jar, Jam, Chrome Cover,
  Ladle 12.00
Lamp, Electric, 6 1/4 In. ...25.00
Lamp, Oil, 9 1/2 In. 55.00
Mustard, Cover, Spoon,
  3 1/2 In....................25.00
Salt & Pepper.... 20.00 To 37.50
Soup, Cream................. 5.50
Sugar 9.00
Sugar & Creamer,
  Footed.......... 18.00 To 20.00
Toothpick, Top Hat 6.00

Tumbler, Footed,
  3 3/4 In.................... 6.50
Tumbler, Footed,
  5 3/4 In.................... 8.50
Wine, Round Base........... 8.00

GREEN ———————

Bottle, Cologne 25.00
Bowl, 3-Footed, 6 In........12.00
Candy Dish, Cover 40.00
Cup, Black Handle..........15.00
Goblet, Black Foot,
  6 Oz.......................20.00
Lamp, Oil, 9 1/2 In. 75.00
Pitcher, 8 1/2 In............. 7.00
Plate, 6 In.................... 4.00
Plate, Square, Black Trim,
  8 In........................12.00
Salt & Pepper...............65.00
Salt Dip.......... 12.00 To 16.00
Saucer, Black Trim........... 5.00
Sherbet, Black Foot.........15.00

PINK ———————

Bottle, Cologne 20.00
Candy Dish, 15 In. 350.00
Creamer.....................20.00
Goblet, 6 1/4 In............18.00
Plate, 13 In. 20.00
Saltshaker 30.00
Sherbet 12.00
Sugar 18.00

RED ———————

Sugar & Creamer 30.00

TURQUOISE ———————

Plate, 8 In..................15.00
Salt Dip.....................24.00

• • • • • • • • • • • • • • • •

Never put hot glass in cold water, or cold glass in hot water. The temperature change can crack the glass.

• • • • • • • • • • • • • • • •

Fairfax

Fairfax was made by Fostoria Glass Company, Fostoria, Ohio, from 1927 to 1960. The name Fairfax refers to a glass blank and to an etching pattern. The same glass blanks were used for other etched designs including June, Trojan, and Versailles. The undecorated blank, also known as No. 2375, is popular with collectors. The same shapes were used to make other patterns with etched designs. The glass was made in amber, black, blue, green, orchid, pink, ruby, and topaz.

AMBER ———————

Celery, Oval 11.00
Ice Bucket, Handle 45.00
Plate, 6 In..........1.50 To 2.50
Plate, 9 1/2 In.............11.00
Saucer..............1.50 To 5.00
Tray, Center Handle,
  11 In. .... 22.00 To 30.00
Wine........................16.00

BLACK ———————

Salt & Pepper...............85.00

BLUE ———————

Ashtray 9.00

Bowl, Centerpiece,
15 In. 43.00
Candy Dish, Cover 45.00
Cocktail, Trojan Stem.......21.00
Cup, Footed ....7.00 To 8.00
Sherbet, Trojan Stem 15.00
Sugar, Miniature 6.00
Tray, Center Handle,
11 In. .... 15.00 To 30.00
Wine, Trojan Stem..........25.00

GREEN ―――――――――

Candleholder, Pair..........45.00
Candy Dish, Cover 20.00
Celery, Oval, 11 1/2 In. ...14.50
Compote, 7 In. 12.00
Cup & Saucer,
After Dinner 17.50
Cup & Saucer, Footed 7.00
Cup, Flat....................9.00
Mayonnaise Set, 2 Piece 35.00
Plate, 6 In....................2.00
Plate, 7 In....................5.00
Plate, 9 1/2 In...............9.00
Sugar & Creamer 35.00
Sugar, Footed, Open.........8.00

ORCHID ―――――――――

Bowl, 6 In. 14.00
Cup 5.00
Mayonnaise 10.00
Plate, 10 1/4 In. 18.00

PINK ―――――――――

Butter, Cover 70.00
Cup & Saucer................8.00
Cup, Footed 6.00
Pitcher, Footed 170.00
Relish, 3 Sections,
11 1/2 In..................20.00
Saucer........................2.50
Sugar & Creamer, Cover....25.00

TOPAZ ―――――――――

Plate, 8 In....................5.00
Relish, 11 1/2 In. 12.00

FAN & FEATHER, see
Adam

FINE RIB, see Homespun

Fire-King

Fire-King or Fire-King Oven
Glass, Fire-King Oven Ware,
and Fire-King Dinnerware
were all made by Anchor
Hocking Company, Lancaster,
Ohio, from 1942 through the
1960s. Fire-King oven glass is
a transparent, pale blue glassware with a lacy decoration. A
matching dinnerware set is
called Philbe. It was made in
crystal and pale blue. Philbe is
listed under its own name in
this book. Fire-King Oven
Ware is an opaque glass made
by Anchor Hocking in the
1950s. It was made in blue,
jadite, pink, and white, or
ivory with gold or colored
trim. Some mixing bowls and
kitchen sets were made with
tulips or red kitchen objects
pictured on the sides. Fire-
King Dinnerware sets were
made in patterns named Alice,
Jadite, Jane-Ray, Square, Swirl
Fire-King, and Turquoise
Blue. These are listed in this
book in their own sections.

BLUE ―――――――――

Baker, Square, 1 Pt. 5.00
Bowl, 4 3/8 In. ....2.50 To 8.50
Bowl, 5 3/8 In. ...9.00 To 15.00
Bowl, Measuring,
16 Oz.......... 17.50 To 27.50

Cake Pan, 8 3/4 In.........18.00
Casserole, Cover,
Individual....... 10.00 To 12.00
Coffee Mug.................18.00
Measuring Cup,
No Spout................ 123.00
Custard Cup,
5 Oz...............2.50 To 3.00
Custard Cup, 6 Oz. 3.50
Loaf Pan,
9 1/8 In........ 14.00 To 20.00
Measuring Cup, 1 Spout,
8 Oz.......................12.00
Measuring Cup, 3 Spouts,
8 Oz.......................20.00
Mixing Bowl, 6 7/8 In. 9.00
Mixing Bowl, 8 3/8 In. 12.00
Mixing Bowl, 10 1/8 In. ...12.00
Mug, Coffee 15.00
Nurser, 4 Oz................12.00
Percolator Top......3.00 To 5.00
Pie Plate,
8 3/8 In...........5.50 To 7.50
Pie Plate, 9 In. .....4.00 To 8.00
Pie Plate, Individual 9.00
Roaster, Cover,
10 3/8 In....... 55.00 To 60.00
Server,
Tab Handles.... 11.50 To 20.00

CRYSTAL ―――――――――

Server, Tab Handles 5.00

IVORY ―――――――――

Bowl, Red Design, 8 In......9.00
Cake Pan, 9 In...............7.00
Custard Cup, Large 1.00
Loaf Pan, 6 X 10 In.........7.00
Measuring Cup..............10.00
Mixing Bowl, 4 Piece.......16.00
Mixing Bowl, 7 In. 4.00
Mixing Bowl, 8 In. 4.00
Pie Plate....................3.00
Server, Tab Handles 5.00

JADITE ―――――――――

Butter.......................5.00
Butter, 1/4 Lb. 15.00
Refrigerator Jar, Cover,
4 X 4 In..........4.00 To 7.00

Mixing Bowl, 6 In. 5.00
Mixing Bowl, 7 In. 5.00
Mixing Bowl, 8 In. 6.00
Mixing Bowl, 9 In. 7.00

PINK

Mixing Bowl, 7 In. 5.00
Refrigerator Jar, Cover,
   4 X 4 In. 6.00

TURQUOISE

Mixing Bowl,
   8 1/2 In. . . . . 6.00 To 12.00

Flanders

Flanders dinnerware was made
by the U.S. Glass Company,
at the Tiffin, Ohio, plant from
1914 to 1935. It was made in
crystal and in pink or yellow
(Mandarin) with crystal trim.

CRYSTAL

Champagne 15.00
Cocktail 15.00
Cordial 55.00
Cup & Saucer 35.00
Dish, Mayonnaise 25.00
Parfait 22.00
Plate, 6 In. . . . . 10.00 To 12.00
Plate, 8 In. 12.00
Plate, 10 1/2 In. 35.00
Sherbet 15.00
Sugar & Creamer, Footed . . . 95.00
Tumbler, Footed, 9 Oz. 17.50
Tumbler, Footed, 12 Oz. . . . 17.50

PINK

Bowl, Console, 13 In. 95.00
Candleholder, Blown 75.00
Champagne 25.00
Cocktail 40.00
Cordial 75.00
Cup & Saucer 40.00
Nut Cup, Blown 75.00
Oyster Cocktail 40.00
Plate, 6 In. 12.50
Plate, 8 In. 17.50
Tumbler, Footed, 9 Oz. 35.00
Tumbler, Footed, 12 Oz. . . . 40.00
Vase 195.00
Whiskey, Footed 65.00

YELLOW

Champagne 18.00
Cup, Loop Handle 25.00
Plate, 10 1/2 In. 35.00
Tumbler, Footed, 12 Oz. . . . 24.00
Wine 30.00

FLAT DIAMOND, see
   Diamond Quilted

Floragold

The iridescent marigold color
of carnival glass was copied in
this 1950s pattern made by
Jeannette Glass Company,
Jeannette, Pennsylvania. The
pattern is called Floragold or
Louisa, the name of the original carnival glass pattern that
was copied. Pieces were made
in crystal, iridescent, ice blue,
shell pink, and reddish yellow.

• • • • • • • • • • • • • • •
**Shallow nicks and
rough edges on glass
can sometimes be
smoothed off with fine
emery paper.**
• • • • • • • • • • • • • • •

CRYSTAL

Bowl, 4 1/2 In. 5.00
Bowl,
   5 1/2 In. . . . . 22.00 To 25.00
Bowl, Deep, 9 1/2 In. 27.50
Bowl, Ruffled, 5 1/2 In. 7.00
Bowl, Square, 8 1/2 In. 12.00
Butter, Cover, Oblong,
   1/4 Lb. . . . . 16.00 To 23.00
Butter, Cover, Round 35.00
Butter, Round 15.00
Candy Dish, Footed,
   5 1/4 In. 5.00
Creamer. . . . . 4.50 To 6.50
Cup 4.00
Cup & Saucer 13.00
Pitcher,
   64 Oz. . . . . 22.00 To 26.00
Plate, 8 1/2 In. 22.00
Plate, 13 1/2 In. 14.00
Plate, Indent, 13 1/2 In. . . . 32.00
Salt & Pepper 34.00
Sugar 6.00
Sugar, Cover 13.00
Tumbler, Footed,
   10 Oz. . . . . 10.00 To 14.00

IRIDESCENT

Bowl, Deep, 9 1/2 In. 26.50
Bowl, Ruffled,
   9 1/2 In. . . . . 6.50 To 8.00
Bowl, Ruffled, 12 In. 12.00
Bowl, Square, 4 1/2 In. 4.50
Bowl, Square,
   8 1/2 In. . . . . 12.00 To 13.00
Butter, Cover, Oblong,
   1/4 Lb. 22.00

Butter, Cover, Round,
1 Lb. .... 29.00 To 40.00
Candleholder, 2-Light.......15.00
Candy Dish, Footed,
5 1/4 In.................... 5.50
Creamer............4.75 To 6.50
Cup 4.50
Cup & Saucer......7.50 To 10.50
Pitcher,
64 Oz........... 21.00 To 25.00
Plate,
8 1/2 In........ 17.50 To 23.50
Plate, Indent, 13 1/2 In. ...35.00
Salt & Pepper.... 28.00 To 40.00
Saucer........................ 8.50
Sherbet ....7.00 To 10.00
Sugar, Cover................14.00
Tumbler, Footed, 10 Oz. ...14.00
Tumbler, Footed, 11 Oz. ...14.00
Tumbler, Footed, 15 Oz. ...85.00

PINK

Bowl, 5 1/2 In. 17.50
Cup & Saucer................ 9.50
Tumbler, Footed, 11 Oz. ...15.00

Floral

Poinsettia blossoms are the decorations on Floral pattern made by Jeannette Glass Company from 1931 to 1935. The pattern was made in amber, crystal, delphite, green, jadite, pink, red, and yellow.

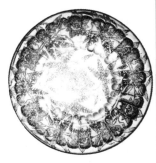

GREEN

Bowl, 4 In. ...... 12.00 To 16.00

Bowl,
7 1/2 In........ 12.00 To 18.00
Bowl, Vegetable, Cover,
8 In............. 30.00 To 35.00
Bowl, Vegetable, Oval,
9 In.........................17.00
Butter.......................19.00
Candleholder................40.00
Coaster,
3 1/4 In...........7.00 To 8.50
Creamer...........8.50 To 10.00
Cup.........................11.50
Cup & Saucer...............15.00
Pitcher, Footed, Cone,
8 In.........................27.50
Plate, 9 In..................13.00
Relish,
2 Sections ...... 10.00 To 12.00
Salt & Pepper...............30.00
Sherbet 13.50
Sugar, Cover................22.00
Tumbler, Footed,
4 3/4 In...................16.00
Tumbler, Footed,
5 1/4 In...................39.00
Vase, 8 Sides, 7 In........ 750.00

PINK

Bowl, 4 In. 15.00
Bowl, Vegetable, Cover,
8 In.........................45.75
Butter.......................10.00
Butter, Cover 50.00
Candy Jar,
Cover.......... 27.00 To 32.50
Coaster......................10.00
Creamer..................... 8.00
Cup & Saucer.... 14.00 To 17.50
Pitcher,
10 1/4 In.....175.00 To 180.00
Pitcher, Footed, Cone,
8 In........... 15.00 To 23.00
Plate, 6 In.................. 4.00
Plate, 8 In..........7.50 To 8.50
Plate, 9 In....... 11.00 To 13.00
Platter, Oval, 10 3/4 In. ...10.00
Salt & Pepper...............40.00
Saucer....................... 6.00
Sherbet .... 10.00 To 12.00
Sugar 7.00
Sugar & Creamer, Cover....26.00

Sugar, Cover...............16.00
Tumbler, Footed,
4 3/4 In........ 11.00 To 16.00

FLORAL RIM, see
Vitrock

Floral & Diamond Band

Floral & Diamond Band was made by the U.S. Glass Company in the 1920s. It features a large center flower and pressed diamond bands of edging. The pattern was made in black, crystal, green, pink, and yellow. Some pieces are iridescent marigold color and are considered carnival glass, called Mayflower by the collectors.

BLACK

Sherbet 10.00
Sugar & Creamer 30.00
Tumbler, 5 In...............14.00

GREEN

Bowl, 8 In. 16.00
Butter, Cover 93.00
Sherbet 5.00

PINK

Creamer.....................12.00
Plate, 8 In..................22.50
Sherbet 5.00
Tumbler, 5 In...............18.00

Florentine No. 1

Florentine No. 1, also called Poppy No. 1, is neither Florentine in appearance nor decorated with recognizable poppies. The plates are hexagonal, differentiating them from Florentine No. 2. The pattern was made by the Hazel-Atlas Glass Company from 1932 to 1935 in cobalt blue, crystal, green, pink, and yellow.

COBALT BLUE ───────

Bowl, 5 In.	15.00
Creamer	12.00
Creamer, Ruffled	45.00
Pitcher, Footed, 6 1/2 In.	650.00

CRYSTAL ───────

Cup & Saucer	8.00
Salt & Pepper	16.00 To 18.00
Saltshaker	13.00
Sugar	6.00

Sugar & Creamer, Ruffled	35.00
Sugar, Ruffled	19.00 To 22.50

GREEN ───────

Bowl, 5 In.	9.50
Coaster, 3 3/4 In.	9.50
Cup & Saucer	8.00 To 10.00
Pitcher, Footed, 6 1/2 In.	25.00
Platter, Oval, 11 1/2 In.	8.00
Saltshaker	15.00
Sherbet	7.00
Sugar & Creamer, Cover	26.00
Sugar, Cover	15.00

PINK ───────

Sherbet	5.00
Soup, Cream, Ruffled	9.00
Sugar & Creamer, Cover	28.50
Sugar & Creamer, Ruffled	50.00
Sugar, Ruffled	22.00

YELLOW ───────

Butter, Cover	85.00
Cup	8.00
Grill Plate, 10 1/4 In.	8.00
Pitcher, Footed, 6 1/2 In.	40.00
Plate, 6 In.	4.00
Plate, 8 1/2 In.	7.00
Salt & Pepper	36.00
Sherbet	8.50 To 10.00
Sugar	10.00
Tumbler, Footed, 4 7/8 In.	22.00

Florentine No. 2

Florentine No. 2, sometimes called Poppy No. 2 or Oriental Poppy, was also made by Hazel-Atlas Glass Company from 1932 to 1935. It has round plates instead of the hexagonal pieces of Florentine No. 1. It was made in amber, cobalt, crystal, green, ice blue, pink, and yellow.

AMBER ───────

Pitcher, 7 1/2	65.00
Tumbler	60.00

CRYSTAL ───────

Ashtray	10.00
Candy Dish, Cover	25.00
Cup	4.00
Plate, 10 In.	6.00 To 10.00
Platter, Oval, 11 In.	8.00
Salt & Pepper	30.00
Soup, Cream, 4 3/4 In.	8.50 To 10.00
Sugar, Cover	23.00
Tumbler, Footed, 4 In.	6.00

GREEN ───────

Bowl, 4 1/2 In.	9.00 To 10.00
Bowl, 8 In.	20.00
Bowl, Vegetable, Oval, 9 In.	20.00
Candleholder, Pair	47.50
Cup	5.00 To 7.50
Grill Plate	6.00

Plate, 6 In................... 4.00
Plate, 8 1/2 In......6.00 To 7.50
Plate, 10 In. ....7.00 To 11.00
Relish, 10 In................12.00
Relish, 3 Sections,
10 In. .... 17.50 To 25.00
Salt & Pepper.... 28.00 To 35.00
Sherbet ....6.50 To 8.00
Soup, Cream.......8.50 To 10.50
Sugar 5.00
Tumbler, 3 3/8 In..........12.00
Tumbler, Footed,
3 1/4 In...................10.00
Tumbler, Footed,
4 In............. 12.00 To 12.50
Tumbler, Footed, 5 In. 18.50
Vase, 6 In...................30.00

PINK

Soup, Cream.......7.00 To 10.00
Sugar & Creamer 20.00
Sugar, Ruffled 25.00

YELLOW

Ashtray, 3 3/4 In...........18.00
Ashtray, 5 1/2 In...........35.00
Bowl, 6 In. 30.00
Bowl, 8 In. 25.00
Butter,
Cover.........100.00 To 130.00
Candleholder, Pair..........40.00
Coaster, 3 1/4 In. 16.50
Cup..........................6.50
Cup & Saucer................9.00
Custard Cup 60.00
Gravy Boat ...... 36.00 To 38.00
Gravy Boat, Underplate 65.00
Grill Plate 8.00
Pitcher, 48 Oz.,
7 1/2 In...................85.00
Pitcher, Footed,
7 1/2 In........ 15.00 To 25.00
Plate, 6 In...........3.00 To 4.00
Plate, 8 1/2 In......7.00 To 8.50
Plate, 10 In. ....9.00 To 12.50
Platter, 11 1/2 In...........58.00
Platter, Oval, 11 In. 12.50
Salt & Pepper.... 32.00 To 45.00
Saltshaker .... 14.50 To 17.00
Sherbet ....7.50 To 9.00

Sugar & Creamer 16.50
Sugar, Cover................20.00
Tumbler, 3 3/8 In..........12.00
Tumbler, 4 In.... 10.50 To 14.50
Tumbler, Footed,
3 1/4 In...................11.00
Vase, 6 In........ 35.00 To 50.00

**FLOWER, see Princess
Feather**

**FLOWER & LEAF
BAND, see Indiana
Custard**

**FLOWER BASKET, see
No. 615**

Flower Garden With Butterflies

There really is a butterfly hiding in the flower on this U.S. Glass Company pattern called Flower Garden with Butterflies, Butterflies and Roses, Flower Garden, or Wildrose with Apple Blossom. It was made in the late 1920s in a variety of colors, including amber, black, blue, canary yellow, crystal, green, and pink.

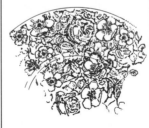

AMBER

Ashtray 175.00
Candy Dish, Cover 125.00
Plate, 7 In..................15.00

BLACK

Bowl, 9 In. 215.00
Plate, 9 In................ 100.00

BLUE

Candy Dish, Cover,
Cone ....125.00 To 190.00
Compote,
4 3/4 X 10 1/4 In...... 125.00
Compote, Footed,
2 7/8 In...................75.00
Powder Jar, Footed,
7 1/2 In................. 125.00
Tray, 11 X 7 In........... 100.00

CANARY YELLOW

Ashtray, Match Holder ... 180.00
Plate, Gold Trim, 8 In......45.00

CRYSTAL

Candy Jar, Cover, Cone.....75.00
Plate, 8 In...................14.00
Vase, 6 1/4 In..............68.00

GREEN

Perfume Bottle,
Stopper................... 200.00
Candy Jar, Cover,
Cone ....130.00 To 190.00
Compote,
4 3/4 X 10 1/4 In...... 125.00
Compote,
5 7/8 X 11 In.............65.00
Compote,
7 1/4 X 8 1/4 In.........85.00
Cup & Saucer............. 125.00
Dish, Mayonnaise, Footed,
Spoon 90.00
Powder Jar,
6 1/4 In......80.00 To 130.00
Plate, 8 In..................22.00
Sandwich Server,
Center Handle.............75.00
Saucer.....................13.00

PINK

Candy Jar, Cover, Cone... 120.00
Plate, 10 1/4 In. 70.00
Tray, Oval .... 60.00 To 65.00

FLOWER RIM, see Vitrock

Forest Green

There is no need to picture Forest Green in a black-and-white drawing because it is the color that identifies the pattern. Anchor Hocking Glass Company, Lancaster, Ohio, made this very plain pattern from 1950 to 1957. Other patterns were also made in this same deep green color, but these are known by the pattern name.

Bowl, 4 3/4 In. ....3.50 To 4.00
Bowl, 7 3/8 In. 8.00
Bowl, Deep, 5 1/4 In. 3.00
Creamer, Square 4.50
Cup & Saucer................ 3.50
Juice Set, 7 Piece 30.00
Mixing Bowl, 6 In. 6.00
Pitcher, 22 Oz. 15.00
Pitcher, 3 Qt................20.00
Plate, 6 3/4 In............... 4.50
Plate, 8 3/8 In......4.00 To 6.00
Platter .... 20.00 To 23.50
Punch Bowl.................22.00
Punch Cup..........1.50 To 2.50
Punch Set, 18 Piece 70.00
Saucer....................... 1.50
Soup, Dish, Square,
  6 In................4.00 To 8.00
Sugar & Creamer 8.00
Tumbler, 3 1/2 In........... 2.00
Tumbler, 4 1/2 In........... 2.00
Vase, 6 1/2 In.....3.00 To 4.00
Vase, 9 In.................... 8.00

Fortune

Anchor Hocking made Fortune pattern in 1937 and 1938. The simple design was made in crystal or pink.

CRYSTAL ────────

Bowl, 4 1/2 In. 2.00
Tumbler, 4 In............... 5.00

PINK ────────

Bowl, 4 In. 3.00
Bowl, 4 1/2 In. 2.25
Bowl, Handle,
  4 1/2 In...........2.25 To 4.00
Candy Dish,
  Cover............6.00 To 15.00
Cup........................... 3.50
Plate, 6 In.................... 3.00
Saucer....................... 2.00
Tumbler, 3 1/2 In........... 5.00
Tumbler, 4 In............... 7.00

FOSTORIA, see American

FROSTED BLOCK, see Beaded Block

Fruits

Pears, grapes, apples, and other fruits are displayed in small bunches on the pieces of Fruits pattern. Hazel-Atlas and several other companies made this pattern about 1931 to 1933. Pieces are known in crystal, green, pink, and iridized finish.

GREEN ────────

Cup & Saucer.......5.75 To 9.00
Plate, 8 In.................... 3.50
Sherbet ....9.00 To 10.00

PINK ────────

Bowl, 8 In. 30.00
Plate, 8 In.................... 4.00
Saucer....................... 2.50

G

Georgian

Georgian, also known as Lovebirds, was made by the Federal Glass Company, Columbus, Ohio, from 1931 to 1935. The pattern shows alternating sections with birds in one, a basket of flowers in the next. It was made in crystal and green. Notice that it is mold-etched and in no way resembles the Fenton glass pattern called Georgian, listed in this book as Georgian Fenton.

• • • • • • • • • • • • • • • • •

For a pollution-free glass cleaner use a mixture of white vinegar and water.

• • • • • • • • • • • • • • • • •

CRYSTAL

Bowl, 4 1/2 In. 6.00
Bowl, Deep, 6 In. 35.00
Creamer, 3 In. 9.00
Plate, 6 In. 3.00
Saucer. 2.00
Sherbet 9.00
Sugar, Cover, 3 In. 32.00
Wine. 17.00

GREEN

Bowl, 4 1/2 In. 5.50
Bowl,
  6 1/2 In. .... 60.00 To 98.50
Bowl, 7 1/2 In. 52.00
Butter, Cover .... 15.00 To 30.00
Creamer, Footed, 3 In. 8.50
Cup. 7.50
Cup & Saucer............... 9.00
Plate, 8 In. ....5.50 To 6.50
Sherbet 10.00
Sugar & Creamer,
  3 In. .... 20.00 To 33.00
Sugar & Creamer, 4 In......30.00
Tumbler, 5 1/4 In..........90.00

Georgian Fenton

Fenton Glass Company made this Georgian pattern tableware from about 1930. It came in many colors, some pale but many in the popular dark shades. Look for amber, black, cobalt blue, crystal, green, pink, ruby, and topaz. It is very different from the

Georgian or Lovebirds pattern made by the Federal Glass Company.

AMBER

Cup & Saucer................ 7.50
Goblet, 5 1/2 In............. 4.00
Tumbler, 4 In................ 3.50

COBALT BLUE

Bowl, 4 1/2 In. 5.00
Goblet, 5 1/2 In............. 5.00

Tumbler, 4 In............... 4.00

CRYSTAL

Cup & Saucer................ 8.00
Goblet, 5 1/2 In............13.00
Tumbler, 4 In............... 3.00

RUBY

Cup & Saucer...............17.00
Sherbet 4.25
Wine, 4 1/2 Oz............18.00

GLADIOLA, see Royal Lace

Gloria

Gloria is an etched glass pattern made by Cambridge Glass Company about 1930. It is similar to the Tiffin pattern called Flanders. Gloria was made in amber, crystal, emerald green, green, Heatherbloom (pink-purple), pink, and yellow. Full dinner sets were made as well as serving pieces, vases, and candlesticks.

CRYSTAL

Candleholder, Pair..........75.00
Compote, Tall, 7 In........37.50
Plate, 8 1/2 In..............10.00
Salt & Pepper..............25.00

GREEN

Basket, 2 Handles, 6 In.....20.00
Bowl, Oval, 12 In..........55.00

Cocktail, Footed, 3 In.......20.00
Dish, Mayonnaise, Liner,
    Ladle 50.00
Pitcher, Ball, 80 Oz....... 150.00
Plate, 14 In. 50.00

PINK

Bowl, 10 In.................55.00
Plate, 7 1/2 In..............12.00
Soup,
    Cream Square Saucer......32.00

YELLOW

Bowl, 6 In. 15.00
Bowl, Square, 5 In..........15.00
Candlestick, 6 In., Pair 60.00
Cordial......................65.00
Goblet, 9 Oz................25.00
Plate, Tab Handle,
    10 In. 30.00
Sandwich Server,
    Center Handle.............28.00

HAIRPIN, see Newport

**HANGING BASKET, see
    No. 615**

Harp

The pattern name Harp describes the small lyre-shaped instruments that are included on the borders of these pieces of glass. This Jeannette Glass Company pattern was made from 1954 to 1957. Pieces are found in crystal, crystal with gold trim, light blue, and pink.

CRYSTAL

Ashtray ....3.00 To 3.50
Cake Plate, Footed, Gold Trim,
    9 In............. 14.00 To 22.50
Coaster Set, 4 Piece 12.50
Coaster, Gold Trim 3.50
Plate, 7 In...........4.50 To 8.00

Tray, Handle, Gold Trim,
    12 3/4 In....... 22.00 To 32.50

LIGHT BLUE

Cake Plate 23.00

PINK

Cake Plate 22.00

Heritage

Federal Glass Company, Columbus, Ohio, made Heritage in the 1930s through the 1960s. Evidently the serving pieces were made in blue, light green, and pink, but the plates and dinnerware pieces were made only in crystal. Amber and crystal reproduction bowls were made in 1987.

CRYSTAL

Bowl, 5 In. ....3.00 To 4.50
Bowl, 8 1/2 In. 20.00
Bowl,
    10 1/2 In.........6.00 To 12.00
Cup & Saucer.......4.00 To 8.00
Plate, 8 In.................. 4.00
Plate, 9 1/4 In.............. 7.00
Sandwich Server, 12 In. 9.00
Saucer..............1.75 To 2.00
Sherbet 3.00
Sugar 5.00
Sugar & Creamer... 18.00 To 25.00
Tumbler, Footed,
    6 In............. 10.00 To 12.00
Wine.........................3.00

**HEX OPTIC, see
    Hexagon Optic**

Hexagon Optic

Hexagon Optic, also called Honeycomb or Hex Optic, really does have an accurate, descriptive name. Pink or green sets of kitchenware were made in this pattern by Jeannette Glass Company, Jeannette, Pennsylvania, from 1928 to 1932. In the years near 1960 some iridized sets and some blue-green pieces were made.

GREEN

Ice Bucket 12.50
Pitcher, 5 In. 10.00
Pitcher, Footed, 9 In........45.00
Salt & Pepper.... 12.00 To 22.00
Tumbler,
    3 3/4 In...........3.00 To 4.00
Whiskey, 2 In.....5.00 To 12.00

IRIDESCENT

Creamer.............3.00 To 3.50
Tumbler, Footed,
    5 3/4 In.................... 5.00

PINK

Plate, 6 In................... 1.50
Plate, 8 In................... 4.00
Saucer....................... 2.75
Tumbler, Footed,
    5 3/4 In...........4.50 To 7.50

HEXAGON TRIPLE BAND, see Colony

HINGE, see Patrician

Hobnail

Hobnail is the name of this pattern, although many similar patterns have been made with the hobbed decorations. Hocking Glass Company, Lancaster, Ohio, made this pattern from 1934 to 1936. It was made in crystal or pink. Some pieces were made with red rims or black feet.

HOBNAIL, see also Moonstone

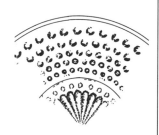

CRYSTAL ─────

Coaster	4.00
Cup & Saucer	12.50
Decanter, Stopper, 32 Oz.	35.00
Goblet, 13 Oz.	14.50
Plate, 8 In.	2.00
Tumbler, 15 Oz.	5.00
Whiskey	4.00

PINK ─────

Cup	2.00
Cup & Saucer	5.00
Pitcher, 18 Oz.	35.00
Plate, 6 In.	1.00
Plate, 8 In.	1.50
Whiskey	6.00

Holiday

Holiday is one of the later Depression glass patterns. It was made from 1947 through 1949 by Jeannette Glass Company. The pattern is found in dinnerware sets of crystal, iridescent, and pink. A few pieces of opaque shell pink were made. The pattern is sometimes also called Buttons & Bows or Russian.

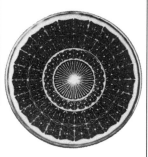

CRYSTAL ─────

Bowl, 5 1/8 In.	3.00 To 5.00
Bowl, Vegetable, Oval, 9 1/2 In.	10.00
Butter, Cover	25.00 To 30.00
Creamer	5.00 To 6.00
Cup & Saucer	7.00 To 9.50
Pitcher, 6 3/4 In.	22.00
Plate, 6 In.	2.50
Plate, 9 In.	7.50 To 9.00
Platter, 11 3/8 In.	7.00
Sherbet	4.00 To 7.00
Sugar & Creamer, Cover	18.00
Sugar, Cover	13.00
Tray, Sandwich, 10 1/2 In.	7.00
Tumbler, 4 In.	14.00
Tumbler, Footed, 4 In.	25.00

PINK ─────

Bowl, 5 1/8 In.	6.50 To 8.00
Bowl, 7 3/4 In.	37.50
Bowl, 8 1/2 In.	18.00
Bowl, 10 3/4 In.	75.00
Bowl, Vegetable, Oval, 9 1/2 In.	15.00
Butter, Cover	30.00 To 35.00
Console, 10 3/4 In.	100.00
Creamer	6.00 To 6.50
Cup	4.50 To 5.00
Cup & Saucer	7.00 To 18.00
Pitcher, 16 Oz.	40.00 To 45.00
Pitcher, 6 3/4 In.	24.00 To 35.00
Plate, 6 In.	3.00
Plate, 9 In.	9.50 To 12.50
Plate, Sherbet	2.75 To 3.00
Platter, 11 3/8 In.	13.00
Sherbet	4.75 To 8.50
Soup, Dish, 7 3/4 In.	25.00 To 35.00
Sugar & Creamer, Cover	21.00
Sugar, Cover	14.00 To 15.00
Tray, Sandwich, 10 1/2 In.	9.00 To 12.00
Tumbler, 4 In.	14.00 To 20.00

Homespun

Homespun, often called Fine Rib, is a cause of confusion. Several writers have presented different views about whether this is really one pattern or two. We prefer to call all of these pieces Homespun because that is the way most collectors use the name. Jeannette Glass Company made crystal and pink pieces in this pattern in 1939 and 1940. Hazel-Atlas made other pieces in crystal and cobalt blue.

CRYSTAL ───────────────

Cup 4.50
Plate, 9 1/4 In. 10.00
Plate, Child's. 6.00
Saucer. 2.00

PINK ───────────────

Cup . . . . 5.00 To 6.50
Plate, 6 In. 3.00
Plate, 9 1/4 In. 9.50
Platter, 13 In. 13.00
Sherbet 9.00
Sugar 6.00
Tea Set, Child's,
  12 Piece 140.00
Tumbler, 4 In. . . . . 4.00 To 6.00
Tumbler,
  5 1/4 In. . . . . 20.00 To 22.50

YELLOW ───────────────

Tumbler, 4 In. 5.00

HONEYCOMB, see
  Hexagon Optic

HORIZONTAL FINE
  RIB, see Manhattan

HORIZONTAL RIBBED,
  see Manhattan

HORIZONTAL
  ROUNDED BIG RIB,
  see Manhattan

HORIZONTAL SHARP
  BIG RIB, see
  Manhattan

HORSESHOE, see No.
  612

Indiana Custard

The design makes the old name Flower & Leaf Band clear, but collectors prefer to call this pattern Indiana Custard. It is an opaque glassware of custard color and ivory made by the Indiana Glass Company. The sets were made from the 1930s to the 1950s. Some pieces have bands that are decorated with pastel colors or decal designs. The same pattern was made of milk glass in 1957. It was called Orange Blossom.

IVORY ───────────────

Bowl, 4 7/8 In. . . . . 4.00 To 6.00
Bowl, 5 3/4 In. . . . 6.50 To 15.00
Bowl, 8 3/4 In. 22.00
Bowl, Vegetable, Oval,
  9 1/2 In. . . . . 20.00 To 22.00
Butter, Cover . . . . 43.00 To 50.00
Creamer. . . . . 9.00 To 10.00
Cup 31.00
Cup & Saucer 38.00
Platter, 11 1/2 In. 18.00

Sherbet 75.00
Sugar 6.00
Sugar & Creamer, Cover 32.00
Sugar, Cover . . . . . 11.00 To 22.00

Iris

The design of Iris is unusually bold for Depression glass. Molded representations of stalks of iris fill the center of a ribbed plate. Other pieces in the pattern show fewer irises, but the flower is predominant. Edges of pieces may be ruffled or beaded. It was made by Jeannette Glass Company, Jeannette, Pennsylvania, from 1928 to 1932 and then again in the 1950s and 1970s. Early pieces were made in crystal, iridescent, and pink; later pieces were made in blue-green, reddish yellow, or white. The pattern is also called Iris & Herringbone. Reproduction candy vases have been made in a variety of colors since 1977.

IRIS & HERRINGBONE,
  see Iris

CRYSTAL ───────────────

Bowl, 4 1/2 In. 28.00
Bowl, 5 In. . . . . . . 33.00 To 45.00
Bowl, Beaded, 8 In. 52.00
Bowl, Ruffled, 5 1/2 In. . . . 6.50
Bowl, Ruffled, 9 1/2 In. . . . 8.00

Bowl, Ruffled,
11 1/2 In.................20.00
Bowl, Straight, 11 In........32.00
Butter, Cover .... 20.00 To 27.00
Candleholder................10.00
Candleholder, Pair..........30.00
Candy Dish, Cover 75.00
Coaster Set, 8 Piece 40.00
Creamer.............6.00 To 7.50
Cup.........................9.00
Cup & Saucer.... 13.50 To 20.00
Cup,
After Dinner ... 20.00 To 22.50
Goblet,
4 1/4 In........ 11.00 To 16.00
Goblet,
5 3/4 In........ 15.00 To 18.00
Lamp Shade.................30.00
Pitcher, Footed,
9 1/2 In........ 18.50 To 25.00
Plate, 8 In........ 35.00 To 38.00
Plate, 9 In........ 25.00 To 40.00
Plate, 11 3/4 In. 20.00
Saucer...............5.00 To 6.00
Sherbet, Footed,
2 1/2 In...................16.00
Sherbet, Footed,
4 In............. 12.00 To 14.00
Sugar, Cover..... 10.00 To 15.00
Tumbler, 4 In.... 50.00 To 70.00
Tumbler, Footed,
6 1/2 In........ 15.00 To 19.00
Tumbler, Footed,
6 In............ 10.00 To 13.00
Wine,
4 1/2 In........ 12.00 To 16.00

IRIDESCENT ─────────

Bowl, Beaded,
4 1/2 In...........7.00 To 8.00
Bowl, Beaded,
8 In............. 20.00 To 25.50
Bowl, Ruffled, 11 In........15.00
Butter, Cover .... 27.50 To 32.50
Candleholder,
Pair............. 22.00 To 25.00
Creamer..............8.00 To 8.50
Cup ....8.00 To 9.00
Cup & Saucer.... 13.50 To 18.00
Goblet, 4 In...... 16.00 To 22.50
Plate, 5 1/2 In...............9.00

Plate, 9 In........ 25.00 To 32.50
Plate, 11 3/4 In. 17.00
Sherbet .... 10.00 To 15.00
Tumbler, Footed,
6 In............. 12.00 To 14.00
Vase, Footed, 9 In. 7.00

**IVEX, see Chinex Classic;
Cremax**

J

Jadite

Jadite is a color as well as a pattern. Kitchenware was made in jadite from 1936 to 1938 by Jeannette Glass Company. A matching set of dinnerware in the same green glass was called Jane-Ray. These pieces are listed in their own section. All of the pieces of kitchenware made of jadite were also made of a blue glass called delphite, but it is incorrect to call any but the green dishes by the name Jadite. For more information about related patterns and colors, see Alice, Fire-King, Jane-Ray, Philbe, Square, Swirl Fire-King, and Turquoise Blue in this book.

GREEN ─────────

Ashtray 6.00
Baker, Oval, 5 X 7 In. 12.00

Bowl, 4 1/4 In. 2.50
Bowl, 4 1/2 In. ....3.00 To 4.00
Bowl, 5 In. ....4.00 To 8.00
Bowl, 9 In. 12.00
Bowl, Batter 20.00
Crock, 40 Oz................55.00
Cup, Measuring,
1/4 Cup...................8.00
Cup, Measuring,
1/2 Cup...................12.00
Refrigerator, Dish Cover,
4 X 4 In...................10.00
Eggcup.......................4.50
Mixing Bowl, 6 1/2 In. 14.00
Mixing Bowl, 9 In. 6.00
Refrigerator, Dish Cover,
4 X 4 In....................8.00
Salt Box, Wooden Lid 17.50
Shaker, Spice................28.00
Sugar & Creamer, Square.... 5.00

Jane-Ray

A plain dinnerware set with ribbed edge was made of jadite from 1945 to 1963 by Anchor Hocking Glass Company, Lancaster, Ohio. It is called Jane-Ray. The matching kitchenware sets of the same green glass are called Jadite. Other related sections in this book are Alice, Fire-King, Philbe, Square, Swirl Fire-King, and Turquoise Blue.

JADITE ─────────

Bowl, 5 In. ....2.50 To 4.50
Bowl, 6 In. ....4.00 To 6.00

Bowl, 8 1/4 In. ....8.00 To 8.50
Creamer.............1.75 To 2.00
Cup & Saucer.......2.00 To 3.50
Mug 4.00
Plate, 7 In...........2.50 To 3.50
Plate, 9 In.................... 2.50
Plate, 10 In. 3.50
Platter ....6.00 To 9.00
Saucer.................50 To 1.00
Soup, Dish..........5.00 To 6.50
Sugar & Creamer,
  Cover.............6.50 To 10.00
Sugar, Cover........3.50 To 6.50

Jubilee

In the early 1930s the Lancaster Glass Company, Lancaster, Ohio, made this dinnerware decorated with etched flowers. It was made in a yellow shade, called topaz, and in pink. Collectors will find many similar patterns. The original Lancaster Jubilee had twelve petals on the flower.

PINK ─────────────

Sandwich Server,
  Center Handle.... 70.00 To 85.00

TOPAZ ─────────────

Cake Plate, Handle,
  11 In. .... 24.00 To 47.00
Creamer......... 17.00 To 20.00
Cup & Saucer...............18.00
Goblet, 6 In................40.00
Plate, 7 In....................6.50

Plate, 7 In..................12.00
Plate, 8 3/4 In.....8.00 To 14.00
Saucer...................... 4.00
Sugar .... 15.00 To 16.50
Sugar & Creamer 35.00

June

June is one of very few patterns that can be dated with some accuracy from the color. Fostoria Glass Company, Fostoria, Ohio, made full dinnerware sets but changed the color. From 1928 to 1944 the glass was azure, green, or rose. Crystal was made from 1928 to 1952. If your set is topaz, it dates from 1929 to 1938. Gold-tinted glass was made from 1938 to 1944. Pieces made of color with crystal stems or bases were made only from 1931 to 1944. Reproductions have been made in blue, crystal, pink, and yellow.

AZURE ─────────────

Baker, Oval, 9 1/2 In. 55.00
Bowl, 5 In. 35.00
Bowl, 6 In. 28.00
Bowl, Bouillon, Footed 50.00
Bowl, Handle, 9 In. 145.00
Bowl, Vegetable, Oval,
  9 In...................... 145.00
Bowl, Whipped Cream......42.50
Cake Plate, Handle,
  10 In. 95.00

Candleholder, Scroll,
  5 In........................47.50
Celery, 11 In...............32.00
Champagne,
  6 In............. 35.00 To 39.50
Chop Plate, 13 In......... 125.00
Creamer....................35.00
Cup 38.00
Cup & Saucer.... 37.50 To 47.50
Finger Bowl 33.00
Goblet,
  8 1/4 In........ 32.00 To 45.00
Goblet, Cocktail,
  5 1/4 In........ 45.00 To 60.00
Ice Bucket 130.00
Oyster Cocktail,
  5 1/2 Oz..................60.00
Pitcher.........450.00 To 550.00
Plate, 6 In..................12.50
Plate, 7 1/2 In.....9.00 To 15.00
Plate, 9 1/2 In..............45.00
Platter, Oval, 12 In. 145.00
Platter, Oval,
  15 1/2 In................ 295.00
Relish, Divided,
  8 1/2 In........ 25.00 To 60.00
Salt & Pepper............. 200.00
Sauce Boat, Underplate.....85.00
Sherbet, 4 1/4 In...........37.50
Sugar, Footed...............35.00
Sweetmeat, Handle 42.50
Tray, Center Handle,
  11 In. 95.00
Tumbler, Footed,
  5 1/4 In........ 35.00 To 39.50

CRYSTAL ─────────────

Bowl, 9 In. 55.00
Cordial, 4 In. 55.00
Cup & Saucer.... 17.00 To 22.00
Cup & Saucer,
  After Dinner 35.00
Finger Bowl 25.00
Goblet,
  8 1/4 In........ 19.00 To 29.50
Goblet, Cocktail,
  5 1/4 In........ 10.00 To 22.00
Oyster Cocktail,
  5 1/2 Oz..................22.00
Pitcher.........195.00 To 285.00
Plate, 7 1/2 In..............14.00

Relish, 8 1/2 In. 60.00
Sherbet, 4 1/2 In. 20.00
Sugar, Cover, Flat Top......90.00
Tumbler, 6 In.... 24.00 To 27.50
Tumbler, Footed,
4 1/2 In........ 10.00 To 27.50
Whiskey.....................35.00

PINK ——————

Bowl, Bouillon... 50.00 To 80.00
Cake Plate, Handle,
10 In. 85.00
Cup & Saucer...............42.50
Cup, After Dinner 75.00
Goblet, Cocktail,
5 1/4 In....................55.00
Grapefruit......125.00 To 175.00
Ice Bucket 165.00
Oyster Cocktail,
5 1/2 Oz. 45.00
Plate, 6 In...................12.00
Relish, Divided,
8 1/2 In...................60.00
Sugar 27.50
Sweetmeat, Handle 42.50
Tumbler, 6 In...............55.00
Tumbler, Footed,
4 1/2 In....................45.00

YELLOW ——————

Bonbon 35.00
Candleholder, 2 In., Pair ...50.00
Candleholder, Scroll,
5 In.......................37.50
Candy Dish, Cover 95.00
Console, Scroll..............75.00
Creamer.....................27.50
Cup 22.00
Cup & Saucer...............27.00
Cup & Saucer,
After Dinner 75.00
Goblet, 5 1/2 In...........45.00
Goblet,
8 1/4 In........ 26.00 To 27.50
Goblet, Cocktail,
5 1/4 In........ 21.00 To 35.00
Mayonnaise Set,
3 Piece 125.00
Parfait, 5 1/4 In. 40.00
Pitcher.........325.00 To 495.00
Plate, 6 In................... 6.00

Plate, 7 1/2 In............... 8.50
Plate, 9 1/2 In..............27.50
Salt & Pepper............. 150.00
Sherbet,
4 1/4 In........ 17.50 To 25.00
Soup, Soup..................27.00
Sugar .... 27.50 To 47.50
Tumbler, 6 In...............35.00
Tumbler, 8 1/4 In..........22.00
Tumbler, Footed,
5 1/4 In...................22.00
Whiskey.....................50.00

KNIFE & FORK, see Colonial

Lace Edge

To add to the confusion in the marketplace, this pattern, which is most often called Lace Edge, has been called Loop, Open Lace, or Open Scallop. The pieces themselves are often confused with other similar patterns, and cups or tumblers may be mixed up with Queen Mary or Coronation. Most of the pieces of Lace Edge were made of pink, although crystal is also found. It was made by Hocking Glass Company, Lancaster, Ohio, from 1935 to 1938.

LACE EDGE, see also Coronation

• • • • • • • • • • • • • • • •
Decorated glasses given as promotions often fade in sunlight.
• • • • • • • • • • • • • • • •

CRYSTAL ——————

Bowl, 3-Footed,
10 1/2 In................ 152.00
Bowl,
6 3/8 In........ 10.00 To 16.50
Bowl, Ribbed, 9 1/2 In.....13.00
Butter, Cover 46.00
Candy Jar, Cover, Ribbed...45.00
Compote, Cover 45.00
Cookie Jar, Cover...........48.00
Creamer.....................15.00
Plate, 10 1/2 In. 20.00
Tumbler, 4 1/2 In..........12.00

PINK ——————

Bowl,
6 3/8 In........ 10.00 To 14.00
Bowl, 9 1/2 In. 15.00
Bowl, Ribbed, 7 3/4 In.....45.00
Butter, Cover .... 40.00 To 46.00
Candleholder, Pair........ 145.00
Compote,
7 In............. 15.00 To 18.00
Creamer.....................15.00
Cup .... 15.00 To 19.00
Cup & Saucer.... 20.00 To 27.00
Flower Bowl,
Crystal Frog .... 16.00 To 19.50
Grill Plate ....6.00 To 15.00
Plate,
8 1/4 In........ 12.00 To 15.00
Plate,
8 3/4 In........ 10.00 To 12.50
Plate,
10 1/2 In....... 18.00 To 22.00
Plate, 4 Sections, 13 In. 28.00
Platter, 5 Sections...........22.00

Relish,
3 Sections ...... 40.00 To 55.00
Saucer........................6.00
Sugar 14.00
Tumbler, 4 1/2 In..........12.50
Tumbler, Footed,
5 In............. 40.00 To 58.00

LACY DAISY, see No.
618

Lake Como

Lake Como looks more like a piece of ceramic than a piece of glass at first glance. It is opaque white with blue decal decorations picturing a lake and part of an ancient ruin. It was made by Hocking Glass Company from 1934 to 1937.

Bowl, 6 In. 15.00
Bowl, 9 3/4 In. 35.00
Plate,
9 1/4 In........ 15.00 To 22.00
Platter 30.00
Salt & Pepper.... 30.00 To 32.00
Soup, Dish............... 100.00

Laurel

Opaque glass was used by McKee Glass Company, Jeannette, Pennsylvania, to make Laurel dinnerware. The pattern, with a raised band of flowers and leaves as the only decoration, was sometimes called Raspberry Band. A few pieces have decals of a dog in the center, and that group is called Scottie Dog. The dinnerware was made of French Ivory, jade green, powder blue, or white opal. A child's set was made with a colored rim.

BLUE

Bowl, 5 In. 10.00
Bowl, 11 In. 35.00
Bowl, Oval, 9 3/4 In. 30.00
Plate,
9 1/8 In........ 11.00 To 20.00
Sugar & Creamer 70.00

GREEN

Bowl, 5 In. ....6.00 To 6.50
Bowl, 11 In. ..... 21.00 To 24.00
Bowl, Oval,
9 3/4 In........ 15.00 To 18.00
Cheese Dish, Cover.........45.00
Creamer,
Child's.......... 33.00 To 50.00
Creamer, Tall 6.50
Cup & Saucer.... 12.50 To 15.00
Grill Plate 8.50
Plate, 9 1/8 In...............9.00
Plate, Child's................13.00
Platter 18.00
Saucer........................2.50
Sherbet ....4.00 To 8.50
Sugar & Creamer, Tall......18.00

IVORY

Bowl, 5 In. 6.50
Bowl, 6 In. 5.00
Bowl, 9 In. ...... 14.00 To 20.00
Bowl, 11 In. ..... 25.00 To 37.50
Bowl, Oval,
9 3/4 In........ 12.00 To 18.00
Candleholder,
Pair............. 20.00 To 26.50

Cheese Dish,
Cover.......... 35.00 To 50.00
Creamer, Child's............35.00
Creamer, Tall......9.00 To 10.00
Cup...........................6.00
Cup & Saucer...............8.50
Cup & Saucer, Child's,
Red Rim 27.50
Cup, Child's, Red Rim......20.00
Grill Plate ....6.50 To 7.00
Plate, 6 In...........3.00 To 3.50
Plate, 7 1/2 In.....7.00 To 15.00
Plate, 9 1/8 In......5.00 To 9.00
Plate, Child's, Red Rim.....12.50
Platter .... 15.00 To 20.00
Saucer........................2.00
Sherbet ....6.00 To 9.00
Sugar & Creamer, Child's,
Red Rim 65.00
Sugar & Creamer, Tall......19.50
Sugar, Tall.........8.00 To 10.00
Tea Set, Child's, Red Trim, Box,
14 Piece................. 240.00
Tumbler, 4 1/2 In..........24.00
Tumbler, 5 In..............45.00

WHITE

Sherbet 6.00

Lido

Lido pattern was made by the Federal Glass Company of Columbus, Ohio, in the mid-1930s. The glass was offered in crystal, Golden Glow, green, or Rose Glow.

BLUE ────────

Cocktail 25.00
Cruet, Oil, Stopper 450.00

CRYSTAL ────────

Compote, 4 3/4 In 22.50
Compote, 5 1/2 In 20.00
Creamer 12.50
Cup & Saucer .... 15.00 To 18.00
Goblet, Water 17.50
Plate, 6 In 4.00
Plate, 7 1/2 In 5.50
Sauce, 6 1/2 In 25.00
Sugar 12.50
Sugar & Creamer, Large 30.00
Tumbler, Footed, 9 Oz 9.00

**LILY MEDALLION, see
American Sweetheart**

**LINCOLN DRAPE, see
Princess**

Lincoln Inn

Lincoln Inn was made by the Fenton Glass Company, Williamstown, West Virginia, in 1928. The ridged dinnerware sets were made of amber, amethyst, black, light blue, cobalt, crystal, green, jadite (opaque green), pink, and red. A recent copy of the Lincoln Inn pitcher was made by Fenton Glass Company in iridized carnival glass.

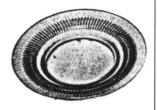

COBALT ────────

Compote 42.00
Creamer 20.00
Cup & Saucer .... 16.00 To 20.00
Goblet,
  5 7/8 In .... 25.00 To 28.00
Plate, 8 In 12.00
Plate, 12 In. 25.00
Sugar & Creamer 70.00

CRYSTAL ────────

Goblet, 5 7/8 In 14.00

GREEN ────────

Tumbler, 9 Oz. 35.00

RED ────────

Cup & Saucer 15.00
Goblet,
  5 7/8 In .... 17.00 To 20.00
Plate, 8 In 12.50

**LINE 300, see Peacock &
Wild Rose**

**LINE 994, see Popeye &
Olive**

**LITTLE HOSTESS, see
Moderntone Little
Hostess Party Set**

LOOP, see Lace Edge

LORAIN, see No. 615

LOUISA, see Floragold

**LOVEBIRDS, see
Georgian**

**LYDIA RAY, see New
Century**

• • • • • • • • • • • • • • •

To clean wax from glass candlesticks, scrape with a wooden stick, then wash off the remaining wax with rubbing alcohol.

• • • • • • • • • • • • • • •

MacHOB

MacHOB is the name devised for the Macbeth-Evans pattern made with a hobnail design. This pattern was made from 1928 of crystal, Monax, or pink.

CRYSTAL ────────

Iced Tea Set, 7 Piece 45.00
Pitcher, Pear Shape,
  10 1/2 In 25.00
Tumbler, 3 3/4 In. 4.50

Madrid

Madrid has probably had more publicity than any other Depression glass pattern. It was originally made by the Federal Glass Company, Columbus, Ohio, from 1932 to 1939. It was made of amber, blue, crystal, green, and pink. In 1976 Federal Glass reworked the molds and made full sets of amber glass called Recollection. These can be identified by a small 76 worked into the pattern. In 1982 crystal pieces of Recollection were made. In more recent years blue, pink, and crystal pieces have been reproduced by the Indiana Glass Company.

AMBER

Bowl, 5 In. 5.00
Bowl, 9 1/2 In. 20.00
Bowl, Vegetable, Oval,
  10 In. 10.00
Butter, Cover 52.50
Cake Plate, 11 3/4 In.......14.00
Creamer............5.50 To 6.00
Cup.................4.00 To 5.00
Grill Plate 8.00
Jar, Jam, 7 In...............18.50
Jello Mold,
  2 1/8 In...........7.00 To 9.00
Pitcher, 5 1/2 In............35.00
Plate, 6 In...........2.50 To 3.50
Plate, 7 1/2 In.............. 8.00
Plate, 8 7/8 In......4.00 To 6.50
Platter, Oval,
  11 1/2 In........8.00 To 10.50
Relish, 10 1/4 In. 14.50
Saucer....................... 2.00
Sherbet, 6 In................. 6.50
Soup, Cream,
  4 3/4 In..........9.00 To 13.00
Soup, Dish, 7 In. 8.50
Sugar 6.00
Sugar & Creamer 10.00
Tumbler, 4 1/2 In..........10.00
Tumbler,
  5 1/2 In........ 15.00 To 20.00

BLUE

Bowl, Vegetable, Oval,
  10 In. 25.00
Cup..........................12.00
Grill Plate 50.00

Pitcher, Square,
  8 In..........115.00 To 125.00
Plate, 6 In.................... 6.50
Plate, 7 1/2 In..............15.00
Tumbler, 5 1/2 In..........30.00

CRYSTAL

Butter.......................12.00
Pitcher, 5 1/2 In.......... 150.00
Plate, 9 In................... 4.50
Sherbet 4.00
Sugar 5.00

GREEN

Butter, Cover 70.00
Creamer.....................11.00
Grill Plate 12.00
Platter, Oval, 11 1/2 In. 6.00
Salt & Pepper...............55.00
Sauce 6.00
Sherbet, 6 In................. 9.75
Sugar, Cover................40.00
Tumbler, Footed,
  5 1/2 In....................37.50

PINK

Bowl, 9 3/8 In. 16.00
Cup.......................... 6.50
Cup & Saucer................ 9.00

**MAGNOLIA, see
  Dogwood**

Manhattan

Manhattan is another modern-looking pattern with a design made of molded circles. It was made by Anchor Hocking Glass Company from 1938 to 1941 in crystal and pink. A few green and red pieces are also known. The pattern has been called many names, such as Horizontal Fine Rib, Horizontal Ribbed, Horizontal Rounded Big Rib, Horizontal Sharp Big Rib, and Ribbed.

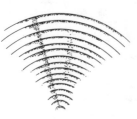

CRYSTAL

Ashtray, Round,
  4 In..............7.00 To 10.00
Ashtray, Square,
  4 1/2 In........ 12.00 To 17.00
Bowl, 4 1/2 In. 6.00
Bowl, 8 In. 13.00
Bowl, 9 In. 12.00
Bowl, Handle,
  5 3/8 In........ 11.00 To 16.50
Candleholder, Square,
  Pair............. 10.00 To 13.00
Candy Dish,
  Cover.......... 25.00 To 30.00
Coaster, 3 1/2 In. 7.00
Compote 18.00
Cup.........................11.00
Cup & Saucer...............20.00
Pitcher,
  24 Oz.......... 19.00 To 20.00
Plate, 6 In...........3.50 To 7.00
Plate, 8 1/2 In..............10.00
Plate,
  10 1/4 In....... 12.00 To 16.50
Punch Set, Red Handles,
  18 Piece................. 350.00
Relish, 4 Sections,
  14 In. .... 14.00 To 15.00
Salt & Pepper, Square,
  2 In.......................16.00
Sherbet ....4.00 To 7.00
Tumbler 12.00
Wine, 3 1/2 In. ....3.50 To 4.00

PINK

Bowl, Handle, 5 3/8 In. ...13.00
Candy Dish, 3-Footed........ 7.00

Compote......... 19.50 To 22.00
Sugar 9.00
Tumbler 10.00

MANY WINDOWS, see Roulette

Martha Washington

The Cambridge Glass Company of Cambridge, Ohio, started manufacturing Martha Washington pattern in 1932. The glass was made in amber, crystal, forest green, Gold Krystol, Heatherbloom, royal blue, and ruby.

AMBER

Mug, 12 Oz................. 35.00

BLUE

Cocktail, 3 Oz.............. 12.00

CRYSTAL

Candy Dish, Cover,
  Footed.................... 32.50
Cup & Saucer.............. 15.00
Plate, 6 In.................... 9.00
Plate, 8 In.................. 12.00
Plate, 10 1/2 In. 56.00

FOREST GREEN

Sugar & Creamer,
  Individual................. 18.00

GOLD

Stein, 8 Oz.................. 12.00
Tumbler, 1932............. 25.00

GREEN

Mug, 10 Oz................. 35.00

RUBY

Mug, 12 Oz................. 40.00

MAYFAIR, see Rosemary

Mayfair Federal

The Mayfair patterns can easily be recognized; but if you are buying by mail, the names are sometimes confusing. Mayfair Federal is the pattern sometimes called Rosemary Arches. It was made in amber, crystal, or green by Federal Glass Company from 1934. The other pattern is called Mayfair Open Rose.

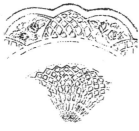

AMBER

Bowl, Sauce, 5 In. 6.00
Bowl, Vegetable, Oval,
  10 In. .... 20.00 To 25.00
Creamer............ 6.00 To 10.00
Cup .... 7.00 To 10.00
Cup & Saucer...... 8.00 To 12.00
Grill Plate 7.00
Plate, 6 3/4 In.............. 7.00
Plate, 9 1/2 In..... 8.00 To 12.00
Platter, Oval,
  12 In. .... 20.00 To 25.00
Saucer........................ 2.00
Soup, Cream,
  5 In............. 8.00 To 15.00
Sugar .... 8.50 To 10.00
Sugar & Creamer... 13.00 To 20.00

Tumbler,
  4 1/2 In........ 15.00 To 16.00

CRYSTAL

Bowl, 6 In. 14.00
Creamer..................... 8.00
Cup .... 2.75 To 3.50
Cup & Saucer....... 4.50 To 5.50
Grill Plate .... 6.50 To 11.00
Plate, 9 1/2 In..... 7.50 To 10.00
Sugar & Creamer... 11.00 To 20.00
Sugar, Footed....... 8.00 To 8.50

GREEN

Bowl, 5 In. 8.00
Cup 12.00
Sugar, Footed............... 9.00

Mayfair Open Rose

Mayfair Open Rose was made by Hocking Glass Company from 1931 to 1937. It was made in light blue, crystal, green, pink, and yellow. The cookie jar and the whiskey glass have been reproduced.

BLUE

Bowl, 5 1/2 In. 50.00
Bowl, Deep, 12 In.......... 65.00
Bowl, Vegetable, 10 In. 40.00
Bowl, Vegetable, Oval,
  9 1/2 In.................. 35.00
Butter,
  Cover......... 235.00 To 250.00
Cookie Jar, Cover......... 155.00
Cup .... 34.00 To 40.00

Cup & Saucer.... 50.00 To 52.50
Goblet, 4 1/2 In............70.00
Goblet, 7 1/4 In.......... 150.00
Pitcher,
   8 1/2 In......125.00 To 195.00
Plate, 5 3/4 In.............17.50
Plate, 8 1/2 In.............27.50
Plate, 9 1/2 In.............65.00
Salt & Pepper....112.50 To 225.00
Sandwich Server,
   Center Handle.............55.00
Sherbet, 2 1/4 In...........95.00
Sherbet, 4 3/4 In...........75.00
Sugar & Creamer 125.00
Sugar, Footed...............65.00
Tumbler, 3 1/4 In..........95.00
Tumbler, 4 1/4 In..........95.00
Tumbler, 4 3/4 In....... 125.00
Tumbler, Footed,
   5 1/4 In....................65.00

CRYSTAL

Sugar, Footed...............13.00

GREEN

Sandwich Server,
   Center Handle.... 20.00 To 25.00
Sugar 180.00

PINK

Bowl,
   5 1/2 In........ 15.00 To 18.00
Bowl, Vegetable,
   7 In............ 15.00 To 22.00
Bowl, Vegetable,
   10 In. .... 14.00 To 17.00
Cake Plate, Footed,
   10 In. 17.50
Cocktail, 4 In. ... 70.00 To 85.00
Creamer,
   Footed.......... 14.00 To 16.50
Cup.............. 10.00 To 13.00
Cup & Saucer.... 20.00 To 25.50
Goblet,
   5 3/4 In........ 44.00 To 48.50
Goblet, Wine, 4 1/2 In.....70.00
Grill Plate 23.00
Pitcher, 6 In. .... 31.00 To 36.00
Pitcher, 8 In. .... 35.00 To 38.00
Plate, 6 1/2 In............. 8.00
Plate, 8 1/2 In.............22.00

Plate, 9 1/2 In..............45.00
Sandwich Server,
   Center Handle.............33.00
Saucer, Cup Ring...........24.50
Sherbet, Footed, 3 In. 10.00
Sherbet, Footed,
   4 3/4 In....................75.00
Soup, Cream,
   5 In............. 32.75 To 35.00
Soup, Dish,
   11 3/4 In....... 37.50 To 42.00
Sugar .... 16.00 To 17.00
Tumbler, 3 1/2 In..........40.00
Tumbler,
   5 1/4 In........ 35.00 To 37.50
Tumbler, Footed,
   5 1/4 In....................26.00
Tumbler, Footed,
   6 1/2 In........ 26.00 To 32.00

YELLOW

Bowl, 5 1/2 In. 12.00
Creamer......................9.00
Cup...........................6.00
Cup & Saucer................8.00
Plate, 9 1/2 In...............9.00
Sugar 9.00

**MEADOW FLOWER, see
   No. 618**

**MEANDERING VINE,
   see Madrid**

Miss America

Miss America, or Diamond
Pattern, was made by Hocking Glass Company from 1933
to 1936. It was made in many
colors, including crystal,
green, ice blue, pink, red, and
Ritz blue. In 1977 some reproduction butter dishes were
made of amberina, crystal,
green, ice blue, pink, or red.
Saltshakers, pitchers, and tumblers are also being
reproduced.

**MISS AMERICA, see also
   English Hobnail**

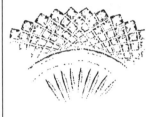

CRYSTAL

Bottle, Condiment 80.00
Bowl, 6 1/4 In. ....5.00 To 7.50
Butter, Cover............. 185.00
Cake Plate,
   Footed.......... 15.00 To 17.00
Candy Dish, Cover 55.00
Celery, 10 1/2 In............8.00
Coaster, 5 3/4 In. 11.00
Compote,
   5 In............. 10.00 To 11.00
Creamer......................6.00
Cup...........................7.00
Cup & Saucer................9.50
Goblet,
   3 3/4 In........ 15.00 To 18.00
Goblet, 4 3/4 In............18.00
Goblet,
   5 1/2 In........ 15.00 To 16.00
Grill Plate ....7.00 To 9.50
Plate, 10 1/2 In. 12.00
Platter, Oval, 12 In. 12.00
Relish, 4 Sections,
   8 3/4 In...........7.00 To 8.50

Relish, Divided,
11 3/4 In.... 15.00 To 17.00
Salt & Pepper.... 18.00 To 30.00
Sherbet ....5.50 To 8.00
Sugar ....6.00 To 7.00
Sugar & Creamer 14.50
Syrup, Glass Cover..........80.00

GREEN

Cup.......................... 8.00
Salt & Pepper............ 160.00
Tumbler,
4 1/2 In........ 12.00 To 15.00

ICE BLUE

Plate, 10 1/2 In. 75.00
Tumbler, 4 In...............75.00

PINK

Bowl, 6 1/4 In. ...9.50 To 16.00
Bowl, Curved, 8 In. 85.00
Bowl, Straight, 8 3/4 In. ...80.00
Bowl, Vegetable, Oval,
10 In. 24.00
Cake Plate, Footed,
12 In. .... 18.00 To 38.00
Candy Dish,
11 1/2 In............... 110.00
Celery,
10 1/2 In....... 15.00 To 17.00
Coaster, 5 3/4 In. 20.00
Cup & Saucer...............20.00
Goblet, 3 3/4 In............60.00
Goblet, 4 3/4 In............45.00
Goblet,
5 1/2 In........ 32.00 To 38.00
Grill Plate 16.00
Plate, 5 3/4 In......5.00 To 7.50
Plate,
8 1/2 In........ 14.00 To 16.00
Plate, 10 1/2 In. 24.00
Platter, Oval, 12 In. 12.00
Relish, 4 Sections,
8 3/4 In...................15.00
Saucer..............3.50 To 8.00
Sherbet ....9.00 To 12.50
Sugar .... 12.00 To 13.00
Tumbler, 4 In...............45.00
Tumbler, 5 3/4 In..........57.50

Water Set, 8 1/2-In.Pitcher,
7 Piece 190.00

MODERNE ART, see Tea
Room

Moderntone

Moderntone, or Wedding
Band, was made by Hazel-
Atlas Glass Company from
1935 to 1942. The cobalt
blue and the simple pattern
are popular today with Art
Deco enthusiasts. The pattern
was made of amethyst, cobalt
blue, crystal, and pink glass. It
was also made of a glass
called Platonite, which was
covered with a variety of
bright fired-on colors, including black, light or dark blue,
light or dark green, red, orange, yellow, and white
trimmed with a small colored
rim.

AMETHYST

Cup & Saucer.......6.00 To 9.00
Plate, 5 7/8 In......3.00 To 4.00
Plate, 8 7/8 In......6.00 To 9.00
Plate,
10 1/2 In....... 15.00 To 23.00
Platter, Oval, 12 In. 23.00
Saucer....................... 2.50
Soup, Cream ....9.50 To 12.00
Sugar 7.00
Sugar & Creamer 10.00

COBALT

Ashtray 240.00
Bowl, 5 In. ...... 17.00 To 19.50
Creamer.............7.00 To 8.00
Cup..........................8.00
Cup & Saucer.... 10.00 To 11.00
Custard Cup 10.00
Plate, 5 3/4 In......3.00 To 4.00
Plate, 6 3/4 In......5.00 To 8.00
Plate, 7 3/4 In......5.00 To 7.50
Plate, 9 In...................10.00
Plate, 10 1/2 In. 33.00
Platter, 11 In...............35.00
Salt & Pepper.... 27.50 To 32.50
Sherbet ....7.00 To 10.00
Soup, Cream................13.50
Sugar ....4.00 To 9.00
Sugar & Creamer... 16.50 To 17.50

CRYSTAL

Whiskey, 1 1/2 Oz. 9.00

GREEN

Creamer......................4.00
Cup..........................3.00
Saucer.......................1.00
Sherbet 3.50
Whiskey.....................12.00

LIGHT GREEN

Sugar 4.00

PINK

Berry Bowl, Large...........6.50
Berry Bowl, Small 4.50
Sherbet 3.50

WHITE

Sugar, Platonite..............4.00

YELLOW

Creamer......................4.00
Creamer, Platonite...........4.00
Saltshaker 6.00

Moderntone Little Hostess Party Set

The Moderntone Little Hostess Party Set was also made by Hazel-Atlas in the 1940s. This was a child's set of dishes made in Platonite with fired-on colors. We have seen blue, gray, green, maroon, orange, pink, turquoise, and yellow, but other colors were probably made.

BLUE

Sugar & Creamer 20.00

GOLD

Cup 3.50

GRAY

Cup & Saucer 12.50
Plate 9.00

GREEN

Sugar 2.25

MAROON

Creamer, Platonite 4.00
Plate 12.50
Teapot, Cover 45.00

ORANGE

Cup 3.50
Plate 4.00
Salt & Pepper 12.00

PASTELS

Service For 4, 14 Piece 50.00

PINK

Cup & Saucer 10.00
Saucer 4.00
Sugar, 2 Bands 6.00

PUMPKIN

Plate 9.00
Sugar 9.00

TURQUOISE

Cup 3.50
Cup & Saucer, Large 10.00

YELLOW

Cup .... 6.50 To 7.00
Saucer 4.00

Moondrops

The New Martinsville Glass Company, New Martinsville, West Virginia, made Moondrops from 1932 to the late 1940s. Collectors like the pieces with the fan-shaped knobs or stoppers. The pattern was made in amber, amethyst, black, cobalt, crystal, Evergreen, ice blue, jade, light green, medium blue, pink, Ritz Blue, rose, ruby, and smoke.

AMBER

Ashtray 14.00
Butter, Cover, Round 90.00
Cocktail Shaker ..... 15.00 To 20.00
Creamer, 2 3/4 In. 7.50
Cup & Saucer ...... 9.00 To 13.00
Plate, 8 In. 3.50
Plate, 14 In. 14.00
Sugar, 2 3/4 In. 7.00
Whiskey, Handle,
    2 3/4 In. 5.00

AMETHYST

Decanter, 10 1/2 In. 50.00
Tumbler, 3 5/8 In. 5.50

COBALT

Casserole, Cover 125.00
Tumbler, 3 5/8 In. 10.00
Wine, 4 In. 16.00

ICE BLUE

Butter, Metal Cover 75.00
Creamer, 3 3/4 In. 14.00
Sugar, 4 In. 14.00
Wine, 5 1/2 In. 20.00

PINK

Whiskey, 2 3/4 In. 12.00

RUBY

Ashtray 24.50
Cocktail Shaker, Handle 45.00
Compote, 4 In. 20.00
Creamer, Individual 12.00
Cup .... 5.00 To 9.00

Cup & Saucer 9.50

Goblet, Metal Stem,
5 1/8 In. 8.00

Sherbet, 2 5/8 In. 9.50

Sugar & Creamer,
2 3/4 In. .... 18.00 To 25.00

Sugar, 2 3/4 In. 12.00

Whiskey,
2 3/4 In. .... 7.00 To 10.50

Whiskey, Handle,
2 3/4 In. .... 11.00 To 12.00

Wine, 4 In. 15.00

Wine, Metal Stem,
5 1/2 In. .... 8.00 To 12.00

Moonstone

The opalescent hobnails on this pattern gave it the name Moonstone. It was made by Anchor Hocking Glass Company, Lancaster, Ohio, from 1941 to 1946. A few pieces are seen in green.

CRYSTAL

Bonbon, Heart Shape,
Handle 8.50

Bowl, 5 1/2 In. 12.00

Bowl, 7 1/2 In. 11.00

Bowl,
Cloverleaf Shape ... 6.00 To 11.00

Bowl, Crimped,
5 1/2 In. .... 5.50 To 7.00

Bowl, Crimped, Handle,
6 1/2 In. 12.00

Bowl, Divided, 7 1/2 In. 7.50

Bowl, Handle, 6 1/2 In. 6.00

Candleholder, Ebony Base,
8 In. 15.00

Candleholder,
Pair .... 14.00 To 17.50

Candy Dish,
Cover .... 10.00 To 24.50

Cigarette Box,
Cover .... 16.50 To 18.00

Creamer .... 6.00 To 8.00

Cup .... 6.00 To 6.50

Cup & Saucer 9.00

Goblet, 10 Oz. 16.00

Plate, 6 In. 2.50

Plate, 8 1/2 In. 8.50

Plate, Fluted, 10 In. 18.00

Powder Jar, Cover 14.50

Relish, Divided,
7 3/4 In. .... 6.50 To 12.00

Sherbet .... 4.00 To 8.50

Sugar .... 5.00 To 6.00

Sugar & Creamer.... 8.00 To 12.50

Vase, 3 1/2 In. 15.00

Vase, Bud, 5 3/4 In. 8.50

GREEN

Candlestick, Pair 16.00

Gravy Boat 9.00

Mt. Pleasant

Mt. Pleasant, sometimes called Double Shield, was made by L. E. Smith Company, Mt. Pleasant, Pennsylvania, from the mid-1920s to 1934. The pattern was made in black amethyst, a very deep purple that appears black unless held in front of a strong light, cobalt blue, crystal, green, and pink. Some pieces have gold trim.

• • • • • • • • • • • • • • • •

Watch burning candles in glass candlesticks. If the candle burns too low, the hot wax and flame may break the glass.

• • • • • • • • • • • • • • • •

BLACK

Bowl, Square, 2 Handles,
8 In. 22.00

Candleholder, Pair 34.00

Cup & Saucer 8.00

Dish, Mayonnaise, 3-Footed,
5 1/2 In. 20.00

Tray, Center Handle,
9 1/2 In. 15.00

BLUE

Bowl, Footed, Square,
4 In. 18.00

Candleholder, 2-Light,
Pair 30.00

Creamer 12.00

Cup 9.00

Dish, Mayonnaise, 3-Footed,
5 1/2 In. 24.00

Plate, 6 1/4 In. 5.00

Sherbet .... 11.00 To 12.00

Mt. Vernon

Mt. Vernon was made in the late 1920s through the 1940s by the Cambridge Glass Company, Cambridge, Ohio. It was made in amber, blue, crystal, emerald green, heatherbloom, red, and violet.

Navarre

Fostoria Glass Company, Fostoria, Ohio, made Navarre pattern glass from 1937 to 1980. It is an etched pattern. Some of the pieces were made on the Baroque glass blank, others on more modern shapes. It was originally made only in crystal. A few later pieces were made in color.

AMBER

Cup & Saucer	3.00
Mug, 14 Oz.	35.00
Sherbet, 4 1/2 Oz.	6.00

CRYSTAL

Butter, 5 In.	20.00
Butter, Cover, Round	65.00
Cup & Saucer	14.00
Goblet, 10 Oz.	3.00 To 8.00
Pitcher, 8 1/4 In.	55.00
Relish, 5 Sections, 12 In.	32.00
Salt & Pepper, Metal Covers	10.00
Sherbet, 4 1/2 Oz.	6.00
Sherbet, 6 1/2 Oz.	9.00
Sugar & Creamer	18.00
Tumbler, Footed, 3 Oz.	4.00

RED

Goblet, 7 Oz.	15.00
Plate, Square, 8 In.	12.00
Sherbet, 6 1/2 Oz.	12.50

BLUE

Bell, 6 1/2 In.	55.00
Champagne, 5 5/8 In.	24.00
Claret, 6 1/2 In.	24.00
Sherbet, 4 3/8 In.	22.00
Tumbler, 5 3/8 In.	25.00
Tumbler, 5 7/8 In.	27.50

CRYSTAL

Bowl, Flared, 12 In.	37.00 To 45.00
Cake Plate, 2 Handles, 10 In.	30.00
Candleholder, 4 In.	17.00
Candleholder, Double, Pair	45.00 To 65.00
Champagne, 5 5/8 In.	16.00 To 18.00
Claret, 6 1/2 In.	24.00 To 35.00
Compote, 5 In.	32.00
Cordial	40.00
Cup & Saucer	17.00 To 24.00
Dish, Cheese Center	35.00
Plate, 7 1/2 In.	12.00
Plate, 8 1/2 In.	17.50
Plate, Torte, 14 In.	55.00
Relish, 2 Sections, 6 In.	29.50
Relish, 3 Sections, 10 1/2 In.	45.00
Salt & Pepper	40.00
Salt & Pepper, Footed	50.00
Sherbet, 4 3/8 In.	17.00
Sugar & Creamer	35.00
Sugar & Creamer, Individual	17.00
Sugar, Individual	12.50
Tidbit, 3-Footed	27.50
Tumbler, Footed, 4 5/8 In.	16.00
Tumbler, Footed, 5 3/8 In.	18.00
Vase, 5 In.	47.50 To 75.00
Vase, 10 In.	55.00
Wine, 5 1/2 In.	22.00 To 24.00

New Century

There is vast confusion about the patterns called New Century, Lydia Ray, Ovide, and related pieces. After studying all the available books about Depression glass, the old advertisements, and checking with dealers who sell the glass, we have made these decisions. Most dealers and most people who advertise Depression glass call the pattern pictured here New Century. It has a series of ribs in the glass design. New Century was made by the Hazel-Atlas Glass Company, a firm with factories in Ohio, Pennsylvania, and West Virginia, from 1930 to 1935. It is found in amethyst, cobalt, crystal, green, and pink. In 1970 a book listed the pattern with ribs by Hazel-Atlas as Lydia Ray. In this same book,

New Century was a very plain ware with no impressed or raised pattern. Sometimes it was made in black or white with fired-on colors and was called Ovide. Research shows that the ribbed pattern was advertised in the 1930s as New Century by Hazel-Atlas. The plain glassware was also called New Century. With added enamel designs, it was sometimes called Ovide, Floral Sterling, or Cloverleaf. In this book, we list no Lydia Ray or Floral Sterling. The plain glass we call Ovide.

NEW CENTURY, see also Ovide

AMETHYST ──────────

Cup	15.00
Pitcher, 8 In.	32.00
Tumbler, 3 1/2 In.	9.00

COBALT ──────────

Tumbler, 3 1/2 In.	9.00

CRYSTAL ──────────

Cocktail, 4 1/4 In.	12.00
Cup	5.00
Pitcher, 60 Oz.	8.00
Plate, 8 1/2 In.	7.00
Salt & Pepper	20.00
Saucer	2.00
Soup, Cream	10.00
Tumbler, 4 In.	5.00

Tumbler, Red Trim, 3 1/2 In.	3.00

GREEN ──────────

Creamer	6.00 To 8.50
Salt & Pepper	20.00 To 28.00
Sherbet, 3 In.	7.00
Sugar, Cover	15.00
Tumbler, 3 1/2 In.	9.00
Whiskey	19.00

PINK ──────────

Cup	15.00
Tumbler, 4 1/4 In.	10.00
Tumbler, 5 1/4 In.	12.00

Newport

Newport, or Hairpin, was made by Hazel-Atlas Glass Company from 1936 to 1940. It is known in amethyst, cobalt blue, pink, Platonite (white), and a variety of fired-on colors.

AMETHYST ──────────

Bowl, 4 3/4 In.	10.00
Bowl, 5 1/2 In.	18.50
Creamer	7.00
Cup	6.00
Cup & Saucer	10.00 To 11.00
Plate, 6 In.	3.50
Plate, 8 1/2 In.	7.00 To 8.00
Plate, 9 1/4 In.	18.00
Plate, 11 1/2 In.	20.00
Platter, Oval, 11 3/4 In.	27.00
Saucer	2.00

Sherbet	8.00
Soup, Cream	11.00 To 15.00
Sugar	7.00 To 11.50
Sugar & Creamer	16.00 To 23.00
Tumbler, 4 1/2 In.	21.00 To 28.00

COBALT ──────────

Bowl, 4 1/4 In.	10.00
Bowl, 5 1/4 In.	22.00
Creamer	9.50 To 14.00
Cup & Saucer	10.00 To 12.00
Plate, 6 In.	3.50
Plate, 8 1/2 In.	3.25 To 7.50
Plate, 11 1/2 In.	22.50
Saltshaker	15.00 To 30.00
Sherbet	12.50
Soup, Cream	9.00 To 12.00
Sugar	8.00 To 9.00
Sugar & Creamer	16.00 To 18.00
Tumbler, 4 1/2 In.	22.50 To 27.50

WHITE ──────────

Creamer	3.50 To 5.00
Cup & Saucer	5.00
Plate, 8 1/2 In.	3.50 To 3.75
Saltshaker	8.00
Sherbet	5.00
Sugar	4.00 To 5.00
Sugar & Creamer	7.00
Sugar, Gold Trim	3.50

Normandie

A few Depression glass patterns were made in iridescent marigold color, which has been collected as carnival glass. Iridescent Normandie appears in the carnival glass listings as Bouquet and Lattice; when the pattern is in the other known colors, it is called Normandie. Look for it in amber, crystal, iridescent, and pink. One author also lists green. It was made from 1933 to 1940.

AMBER ────────────

Bowl, 5 In. ....5.00 To 9.00
Bowl, Vegetable, Oval,
  10 In. 12.50
Cup 4.50
Cup & Saucer.................7.00
Plate, 11 In. .....15.00 To 20.00
Salt & Pepper....28.00 To 35.00
Sherbet ....2.25 To 5.50
Sugar, Cover................60.00

CRYSTAL ────────────

Bowl, 5 In. 4.00
Creamer......................6.50
Plate, 6 In....................2.50
Plate, 9 1/4 In...............9.50

IRIDESCENT ────────────

Bowl, 5 In. ....2.50 To 4.00
Bowl, 6 1/2 In. ....4.50 To 6.00
Bowl, 8 1/2 In. 8.00
Creamer......................4.50
Cup 3.50

Cup & Saucer.......2.00 To 5.50
Grill Plate ....5.00 To 7.00
Plate, 6 In...........1.75 To 2.00
Plate, 7 1/4 ....50.00
Platter,
  11 3/4 In.........7.00 To 12.00
Saucer........................1.00
Sherbet ....4.00 To 5.50
Sugar ....3.50 To 5.00
Sugar & Creamer 10.00

PINK ────────────

Cup 6.00
Cup & Saucer.................9.50
Plate, 11 In. 75.00
Plate, 9 1/4 In..............10.00
Salt & Pepper...............40.00

NO. 601, see Avocado

No. 610

Many patterns are listed both by the original pattern number and by a name. No. 610 is often called Pyramid or Rex. It was made from 1926 to 1932 by the Indiana Glass Company. The pattern was made of crystal, green, pink, white, and yellow. In 1974 and 1975 reproductions were made in black and blue.

CRYSTAL ────────────

Sugar, Cover................22.00

GREEN ────────────

Pickle 37.00

YELLOW ────────────

Ice Bucket .....150.00 To 215.00
Relish,
  9 1/2 X 5 3/4 In.........45.00
Sugar & Creamer, Tray ... 100.00

No. 612

Indiana Glass Company, Dunkirk, Indiana, called this pattern No. 612, but collectors call it Horseshoe. It was made from 1930 to 1933 in green, pink, and yellow. Sugar and creamer sets were made in crystal. Plates came in two styles, one with the center pattern, one plain.

Sugar & Creamer... 28.00 To 33.00
Tumbler, 4 3/4 In..........20.00

No. 616

No. 616 is called Vernon by some collectors. It was made by Indiana Glass Company from 1930 to 1932. The pattern was made in crystal, green, and yellow. Some crystal pieces have a platinum trim.

GREEN

Creamer.....................10.00
Cup..........................7.00
Cup & Saucer......9.00 To 13.00
Grill Plate .... 25.00 To 50.00
Relish, 3 Sections...........16.50
Sandwich Plate,
  11 1/2 In.........9.00 To 13.00
Saucer...............2.50 To 4.00
Sherbet .... 11.00 To 12.50
Sugar 10.00

YELLOW

Relish, 3 Sections,
  Footed....................29.00
Sherbet 11.00
Sugar 10.50

No. 615

No. 615 is often called Lorain or sometimes Basket, Bridal Bouquet, Flower Basket, or Hanging Basket. It was made by the Indiana Glass Company from 1929 to 1932 of crystal, green, and yellow. Sometimes crystal pieces have blue, green, red, or yellow borders. Reproduction pieces were made of milk glass or olive green.

CRYSTAL

Bonbon, 3-Footed...........27.50
Compote....................20.00
Cup & Saucer...............11.50
Relish, 4 Sections...........15.00

GREEN

Bowl,
  7 1/4 In........ 32.50 To 45.00
Bowl, Deep, 8 In. 70.00
Bowl, Vegetable, Oval,
  9 3/4 In...................40.00
Butter........................4.00
Cup & Saucer...............13.00
Plate, 5 1/2 In..............5.50
Plate, 7 3/4 In..............8.00
Plate, 8 3/8 In.....9.00 To 13.50
Plate, 10 In. 37.00
Platter, 11 1/2 In...........17.00
Sherbet .... 15.00 To 17.50
Tumbler, 4 3/4 In..........17.00

YELLOW

Bowl,
  6 1/2 In........ 35.00 To 47.50
Bowl, Vegetable, Oval,
  9 3/4 In........ 45.00 To 48.75
Cup..........................18.50
Cup & Saucer.... 16.00 To 20.00
Plate, 6 In...................7.50
Plate,
  7 3/4 In........ 10.00 To 12.50
Plate,
  8 3/8 In........ 15.00 To 22.50
Relish, 4 Sections,
  8 In............. 25.00 To 30.00
Sherbet .... 20.00 To 30.00

CRYSTAL

Cup & Saucer,
  Platinum Rim...............6.00
Plate, Platinum Rim, 8 In....3.00
Sugar & Cream,
  Platinum Rim.............18.00
Sugar & Creamer, Footed,
  Platinum Rim.............18.00

GREEN

Bowl, Vegetable, Oval,
  9 In......................60.00
Creamer, Footed............25.00
Cup..........................8.00
Cup & Saucer...............22.00
Plate, 11 In. 18.00
Saltshaker 60.00
Saucer.......................4.50
Sugar 23.00

YELLOW

Cup & Saucer.... 10.00 To 12.00
Plate, 8 In...................5.50
Sugar & Creamer... 35.00 To 40.00

No. 618

Another Indiana Glass Company pattern made from 1932 to 1937 was No. 618, or Pineapple & Floral. It is also called Meadow Flower, Lacy Daisy, or Wildflower. The pattern was made of amber, crystal, and fired-on green and red. Reproductions were made in olive green in the late 1960s.

AMBER

Creamer 10.00
Cup 7.00
Cup & Saucer 10.00
Plate, 6 In. 4.00
Plate, 9 3/8 In. 12.50
Soup, Cream ..... 16.50 To 20.00
Sugar 8.50
Sugar & Creamer 18.00
Vase, 9 In. 95.00

CRYSTAL

Ashtray .... 12.50 To 16.50
Bowl, 6 In. ...... 10.00 To 20.00
Bowl, 7 In. 5.00
Cake Plate, Handle,
    10 In. .... 38.00 To 45.00
Candy Dish, 3 Sections, 3-
    Handled Cover 55.00
Celery, 11 In. 45.00
Compote,
    4 3/4 In. .... 29.00 To 35.00
Creamer 6.00

Cup 7.50
Cup & Saucer 8.50
Nappy, Handle, 5 In. 18.00
Pickle, Oval, 7 In. 20.00
Plate, 6 In. 8.00
Plate,
    7 1/2 In. .... 11.00 To 14.00
Plate, 8 3/8 In. ..... 4.00 To 6.00
Plate, 9 3/8 In. 9.00
Plate, Indentation,
    11 1/2 In. ...... 17.50 To 23.00
Plate, Sandwich,
    11 1/2 In. 12.00
Platter, Closed Handles,
    11 In. 8.00
Relish, 2 Sections,
    11 1/2 In. .... 9.00 To 15.00
Saucer 2.00
Sherbet,
    Footed .... 12.00 To 18.50
Sugar .... 6.00 To 7.00
Sugar & Creamer 12.00
Tumbler,
    4 1/4 In. .... 15.00 To 30.00
Tumbler, 5 In. ... 28.00 To 37.50
Vase, Cone, 12 In. 28.00

No. 620

No. 620, also known as Daisy, was made by Indiana Glass Company. In 1933 the pattern was made in crystal, and in 1940 in amber; in the 1960s and 1970s reproductions were made in dark green and milk glass.

AMBER

Bowl, 4 1/2 In. .... 5.00 To 7.00
Bowl, 9 3/8 In. 22.00
Bowl, Vegetable, Oval,
    10 In. 12.00
Creamer 5.50
Cup 4.00
Cup & Saucer .... 5.00 To 5.50
Grill Plate 8.00
Plate, 6 In. .... 1.75 To 2.00
Plate, 8 3/8 In. 5.00
Plate, 9 3/8 In. 5.50
Sherbet .... 6.00 To 8.00
Soup, Cream .... 5.00 To 6.00
Sugar 5.00
Sugar & Creamer 13.00
Tumbler, Footed,
    9 Oz. .... 7.00 To 12.00

CRYSTAL

Bowl, 6 In. 10.00
Creamer 6.50
Cup 2.50
Grill Plate 10.00
Plate, Sandwich 6.00

NO. 622, see Pretzel

NO. 624, see Christmas Candy

OATMEAL LACE, see Princess Feather

Old Cafe

Old Cafe is one of the few patterns with only one name. It was made by the Anchor Hocking Glass Company, Lancaster, Ohio, from 1936 to 1938. Pieces are found in crystal, pink, and red.

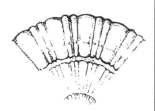

CRYSTAL

Bowl, Handle, 3 3/4 In. 5.00
Candy Dish, Low, 8 In......14.00
Nappy, With Frog,
5 1/2 In....................15.00
Pitcher, 6 In. 42.50
Vase, 7 1/4 In...............7.50

PINK

Bowl, 3 3/4 In. 3.00
Bowl, 9 In. 9.00
Bowl, Handle,
5 1/2 In...........4.00 To 7.50
Candy Dish, Low, 8 In.......4.00
Cup..........................4.50
Dish, Olive, Oblong,
6 In................3.00 To 5.50
Tumbler, 3 In...............11.00

RED

Candy Dish, Low,
8 In...............9.50 To 12.00
Cup.................6.00 To 8.00

Old English

Old English, or Threading, was made by the Indiana Glass Company, Dunkirk, Indiana, in the late 1920s and early 1930s. It was first made in amber, crystal, emerald green, and light green. Pink was a later color.

CRYSTAL

Eggcup.......................5.00
GREEN

Candleholder, 4 In.,
Pair............. 20.00 To 22.00
Tumbler, Footed,
4 1/2 In....................15.00
Tumbler, Footed,
5 1/2 In....................25.00

OLD FLORENTINE, see Florentine No. 1

OPALESCENT HOBNAIL, see Moonstone

OPEN LACE, see Lace Edge

OPEN ROSE, see Mayfair Open Rose

OPEN SCALLOP, see Lace Edge

OPTIC DESIGN, see Raindrops

Orange Blossom

Indiana Glass Company made Orange Blossom in 1957. The pattern is the same as Indiana Custard but the milk glass items are called Orange Blossom.

WHITE

Bowl, 5 1/2 In. 2.75
Creamer.............2.00 To 5.00
Cup..........................3.75
Plate, 9 3/4 In..............3.50

Orchid

Orchid was made by the Paden City Glass Manufacturing Company, Paden City, West Virginia, in the early 1930s. Colors used were cobalt blue, crystal, green, pink, red, or yellow.

CRYSTAL

Bowl, Deep, 10 1/2 In. 85.00
Candleholder................22.00
Candy Dish, Cover,
6 In...................... 145.00
Compote, Footed,
6 1/2 In...................42.00
Dish, Mayonnaise,
5 1/2 In...................40.00

Salt & Pepper, Footed 65.00
Tumbler, 12 Oz.............45.00
Vase, Fan, 6 1/2 In.........35.00

ORIENTAL POPPY, see
Florentine No. 2

Ovide

Hazel-Atlas made Ovide pattern from 1929 to 1935. It was made in green at first. By 1931-1932 it was black and by 1933-1935 Platonite or opaque white glass was used with fired-on colors. A bright fired-on pattern of black, green, orange, yellow, and black circles and lines was one of the popular designs. Some other patterns were white with colored rims. There is great confusion between Ovide and New Century. Read the explanation under New Century.

OVIDE, see also New
Century

BLACK ───────────────

Cup..........................2.50
Cup & Saucer...............13.00
Salt & Pepper...............20.00
Saucer........................1.50
Sugar ....4.00 To 5.00
Sugar & Creamer 8.00

GREEN ───────────────

Bowl, 5 In. ....2.50 To 4.00
Cocktail, Footed 2.00
Creamer.............2.50 To 3.50
Cup..........................2.00
Cup & Saucer.................3.00
Plate, 8 In....................1.00
Sherbet 2.00
Sugar 2.50

WHITE ───────────────

Bowl, Fired On, 5 In. 2.50
Mug, Fired On 3.00
Platter, Fired On.............6.00
Salt & Pepper,
   Black Flower 2.25
Salt & Pepper, Large.........7.00
Sherbet, Black Flower 4.00

OXFORD, see Chinex
Classic

Oyster & Pearl

Anchor Hocking Glass Company, Lancaster, Ohio, made Oyster & Pearl pattern from 1938 to 1940. It was made in crystal, pink, red, and white with fired-on colors. The outside of these fired-on pieces is white, the inside is either pink or green.

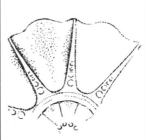

CRYSTAL ───────────────

Bowl, 10 1/2 In. 18.00
Bowl, Heart Shape,
   5 1/4 In....................6.00

Candleholder,
   3 1/2 In...........4.00 To 7.50
Plate, Sandwich,
   13 1/2 In........8.00 To 15.00
Relish, 10 1/4 In. 6.00

FIRED-ON GREEN ───────────

Bowl, Heart Shape,
   5 1/4 In....................5.00
Candleholder, 3 1/2 In.,
   Pair........................15.00

PINK ───────────────

Bowl, Heart Shape,
   5 1/4 In...................12.00
Candleholder, 3 1/2 In.,
   Pair........................30.00
Plate, Sandwich,
   13 1/2 In..................16.00
Relish, Oval, 10 1/4 In.....10.00

RED ───────────────

Bowl, Deep,
   6 1/2 In........ 14.00 To 16.00
Bowl, Handle,
   5 1/4 In........ 10.00 To 15.00
Candleholder, 3 1/2 In.,
   Pair............. 20.00 To 38.00

P

PANELED ASTER, see
Madrid

PANELED CHERRY
BLOSSOM, see Cherry
Blossom

PANSY & DORIC, see
Doric & Pansy

PARROT, see Sylvan

Patrician

Federal Glass Company, Columbus, Ohio, made Patrician, sometimes called Hinge or Spoke, from 1933 to 1937. Full dinner sets were made. It was made in amber, crystal, green, pink, and yellow.

AMBER

Bowl, 5 In. ....7.00 To 8.50
Bowl, 6 In. ...... 16.00 To 18.00
Bowl,
    8 1/2 In........ 30.00 To 33.00
Bowl, Vegetable, Oval,
    10 In. .... 18.00 To 30.00
Butter, Cover .... 70.00 To 75.00
Creamer...................... 8.00
Cup 4.00
Cup & Saucer.... 11.00 To 14.00
Grill Plate ....8.50 To 9.00
Pitcher, Molded Handle,
    8 In............. 85.00 To 90.00
Plate, 7 1/2 In.....4.00 To 10.00
Plate, 9 In...........5.50 To 7.50
Plate, 10 1/2 In. ...5.50 To 8.00
Platter, Oval,
    11 1/2 In....... 15.00 To 20.00
Salt & Pepper.... 42.50 To 43.00
Saucer...............5.00 To 8.50
Sherbet ....6.50 To 9.00
Soup, Cream ....8.00 To 13.50
Sugar 8.50
Sugar & Creamer, Cover....60.00
Tumbler, 5 1/2 In..........22.00
Tumbler, Footed,
    5 1/4 In...................35.00

CRYSTAL

Bowl, 5 In. ....6.50 To 9.00
Bowl, Vegetable, Oval,
    10 In. .... 14.00 To 20.50
Cup 6.00
Cup & Saucer...............11.00
Plate, 9 In.................. 8.00

Plate, 10 1/2 In. 8.00
Platter, Oval, 11 1/2 In. ...17.50

GREEN

Bowl, 8 1/2 In. 25.00
Creamer..................... 7.00
Cup 7.00
Cup & Saucer...............12.00
Dish, Jam 23.00
Plate, 7 1/2 In.....8.00 To 10.00
Platter, Oval, 11 1/2 In. ...19.00
Saucer....................... 5.00
Sherbet, Footed ....8.00 To 10.00
Sugar ....6.00 To 9.00
Sugar & Creamer 15.00
Tumbler, Footed,
    5 1/4 In...................36.00

PINK

Bowl, 5 In. 9.00
Butter, Cover 200.00
Cup 7.00
Grill Plate 10.00
Plate, 6 In................... 5.00
Plate, 10 1/2 In. 18.00
Sugar & Creamer, Cover....56.00
Tumbler, 4 1/2 In..........18.00

Patrick

Patrick pattern was made by the Lancaster Glass Company of Lancaster, Ohio, about 1930. The pattern was etched in rose or topaz glass.

TOPAZ

Goblet, 6 In.................26.00
Plate, 7 In..................10.00
Plate, 8 In.................. 8.00
Saucer....................... 4.00
Sugar & Creamer 25.00

**PEACOCK & ROSE, see
    Peacock & Wild Rose**

Peacock & Wild Rose

Line 300 was the name used by Paden City Glass Company, Paden City, West Virginia, for the pattern now called Peacock & Wild Rose. It was made in the 1930s of black, cobalt blue, green, pink, and red. A few of the lists call this pattern Peacock & Rose.

PINK

Ice Tub, 4 3/4 In...........70.00
Plate, 2 Handles,
    10 3/8 In..................32.00

Pear Optic

Pear Optic, sometimes called Thumbprint, was made in 1929 and 1930 by the Federal Glass Company. It was made only in green.

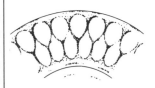

GREEN

Bowl, 6 In. 5.00
Goblet, Water 4.00
Plate, 8 In. 4.00

PEBBLE OPTIC, see Raindrops

PETAL SWIRL, see Swirl

Petalware

Macbeth-Evans made Petalware from 1930 to 1940. It was first made in crystal and pink. In 1932 the dinnerware was made in Monax, in 1933 in Cremax. The pattern remained popular and in 1936 cobalt blue and several other variations were made. Some pieces were handpainted with pastel bands of ivory, green, and pink. Some pieces were decorated with a gold or red rim. Flower or fruit designs in bright colors were used on some. Bright bands of fired-on blue, green, red, and yellow were used to decorate some wares. All of these patterns have their own names. These include Banded Petalware, Daisy Petals, Diamond Point, Petal, Shell, and Vivid Bands.

COBALT

Bowl, 4 1/2 In. 20.00
Bowl, 5 3/4 In. 8.00
Creamer.....................12.00

Cup & Saucer................9.75
Plate, 8 In. 8.50
Sugar 4.00
Tumbler, 4 1/2 In..........15.00
Plate, 11 In. 12.00
Tumbler, 4 1/2 In..........10.00

CREMAX

Cup & Saucer................9.00
Cup & Saucer, Floral Trim...6.00
Cup & Saucer,
   Gold Trim.........5.00 To 6.00
Cup & Saucer,
   Red Flowers...............14.00
Cup, Gold Trim 4.00
Plate, 6 In..........1.75 To 5.00
Plate, 8 In....................2.75
Plate, 9 In.........3.50 To 5.00
Plate, 11 In. ....6.50 To 12.00
Plate, Floral Trim, 8 In. 4.00
Plate, Gold Trim,
   8 In................2.75 To 4.00
Salver, 11 In. ......6.00 To 10.00
Salver, Bands, 11 In. 12.00
Salver, Bands, 12 In. 15.00
Saucer................1.50 To 2.00
Soup, Cream ....5.00 To 8.00
Sugar & Creamer.... 8.00 To 10.00
Sugar & Creamer,
   Floral Trim.................6.00
Sugar & Creamer,
   Gold Trim...................6.00
Sugar, Bands, Pink Trim.....7.50

CRYSTAL

Bowl, 5 3/4 In. 9.00
Bowl, 9 In. 7.00
Cup & Saucer................16.50
Cup & Saucer, Floral Trim...8.50
Goblet 15.00
Plate, Floral Trim, 8 In. 6.00
Salver, Floral Trim,
   11 In. 12.00
Saucer.......................1.00
Sherbet, 4 In................15.00

MONAX

Bowl, 9 In. 12.00
Cup & Saucer................6.50
Cup & Saucer, Gold Trim ... 5.50

Luncheon Set, Gold Trim,
   15 Piece...................65.00
Plate, 6 In....................2.00
Plate, 8 In. 2.75
Plate, 9 In..........4.50 To 8.00
Salver, Bands, 11 In. 15.00
Salver, Gold Trim, 11 In....12.00
Sherbet, 4 1/2 In. 5.50
Soup, Cream 5.00
Soup, Cream, Gold Trim 9.50
Sugar & Creamer 8.50
Sugar & Creamer,
   Gold Trim..................8.50

PINK

Bowl, 5 3/4 In. 7.50
Bowl, Footed, 9 In..........15.00
Cake Plate, Footed..........24.00
Candleholder, 2-Light,
   Pair.......................35.00
Candy Dish, Cover,
   Square....................35.00
Compote, 6 In. 18.00
Cookie Jar 125.00
Cup ....3.00 To 7.00
Cup & Saucer................8.50
Goblet, 8 Oz..... 10.00 To 15.00
Juice Set, 5 Piece 65.00
Plate, 9 In..........3.50 To 8.50
Snack Set, 8 Piece 40.00
Sugar & Creamer, Cover....30.00
Tray, 16 1/2 In.............28.00

Philbe

Philbe is a Fire-King dinnerware made by the Anchor Hocking Glass Company from 1937 to the 1940s. It was made in blue, crystal, green, and pink. The blue sometimes has platinum trim. Philbe is the dinnerware pattern; the matching kitchenware is called Fire-King Oven Glass.

PHILBE, see also Fire-King

BLUE ───────────

Cup........................25.00

Grill Plate 30.00

PINK ───────────

Ashtray 2.00

Cup.................2.00 To 2.50

Cup & Saucer................ 3.00

Plate, 7 3/4 In.............. 2.00

Plate, 9 In. 3.00

Sugar & Creamer 6.50

PIE CRUST, see Cremax

Pillar Flute

Pillar Flute was made by Imperial Glass Company, Bellaire, Ohio, in amber, blue, crystal, green, and a pink called Rose Marie. It was made about 1930.

BLUE ───────────

Bowl, 5 In. 25.00

Bowl, 6 In. 25.00

Compote, Shallow,
6 3/4 In...................25.00

Plate, 8 In. 10.00

Tray, Celery 22.50

Tumbler 15.00

PINK ───────────

Pitcher, 80 Oz. 21.00

**PINEAPPLE & FLORAL,
see No. 618**

PINWHEEL, see Sierra

Pioneer

Pioneer by Federal Glass Company, Columbus, Ohio, was first made in pink in the 1930s. In the 1940s the dishes were made in crystal and the pattern continued to be made into the 1970s.

CRYSTAL ───────────

Bowl, 11 In........9.00 To 10.00

Candleholder, 3 In., Pair ...12.00

Nappy, 5 3/8 In............. 8.00

Plate, 11 In. 9.00

POINSETTIA, see Floral

Popeye & Olive

Line 994 was the original name for this Paden City Glass Company pattern. The popular name today is Popeye & Olive. It was made in cobalt blue, crystal, green, and red. The pattern was made in the 1930s and a 1932 ad shows the red as a new color.

RED ───────────

Bowl, 8 In. 35.00

Bowl, Berry.................. 3.50

Candleholder, Pair..........25.00

Plate, 8 In. 9.00

Sugar & Creamer 15.00

Tumbler, 9 Oz. 20.00

**POPPY NO. 1, see
Florentine No. 1**

**POPPY NO. 2, see
Florentine No. 2**

**PRETTY POLLY PARTY
DISHES, see Doric &
Pansy**

Pretzel

Pretzel, also called No. 622 or Ribbon Candy, was made by Indiana Glass Company, Dunkirk, Indiana, in the 1930s. Crystal and teal pieces were made. Some reproductions appeared in the 1970s.

CRYSTAL

Bowl, 4 1/2 In. 6.00
Bowl, 9 3/8 In. 9.00
Creamer......................4.50
Cup...........................3.50
Cup & Saucer................4.50
Plate, 11 1/2 In. ...5.00 To 7.00
Plate, 3 Sections, Square,
  7 1/4 In....................5.50
Plate, 6 In..........1.25 To 2.50
Plate, 9 3/8 In......5.00 To 6.00
Plate, Indentation, Square,
  7 1/4 In...........3.00 To 4.00
Relish, 3 Sections, Square,
  7 1/4 In....................4.00
Sherbet 10.00
Soup, Dish..........6.00 To 7.00
Sugar 3.50
Sugar & Creamer 8.00
Sugar & Creamer, Square Tray,
  3 Piece 12.00

Primo

Green and mandarin yellow are the two colors of Primo advertised in the 1932 catalog for U.S. Glass Company.

GREEN

Cake Plate, Footed,
  10 In. 13.00
Creamer......................15.00
Cup & Saucer................8.00
Grill Plate ....7.50 To 14.00
Plate, 7 1/2 In......4.00 To 5.00
Saucer.......................2.00

YELLOW

Creamer......................7.00
Saucer.......................2.00
Sugar 7.00
Tumbler,
  5 3/4 In.........9.00 To 13.00

PRIMUS, see Madrid

Princess

Hocking Glass Company, Lancaster, Ohio, made the popular Princess pattern from 1931 to 1935. The first sets were made in green, then in topaz. The amber sometimes came out a rather yellow shade, so if you are assembling a set, be careful of the color variations. Pink was added last. There are blue pieces found in the West, but there is a debate about the age or origin of

these pieces. Some pieces had a frosted finish, some are decorated with hand-painted flowers. Green is sometimes trimmed with gold, other colors are trimmed with platinum.

AMBER

Bowl, Hat Shape,
  9 1/4 In..................21.00
Cup...........................6.25
Cup & Saucer...............10.50
Grill Plate 9.00
Saucer.......................5.00

BLUE

Cup 100.00

GREEN

Bowl, 5 In. ......20.00 To 23.00
Bowl, 9 In. 25.00
Bowl, Hat Shape,
  9 1/4 In..................30.00
Bowl, Vegetable, Oval,
  10 In. ....16.50 To 20.00
Cake Stand, 10 In...........14.00
Coaster.....................20.00
Cup ....6.75 To 8.00
Cup & Saucer....10.00 To 15.00
Grill Plate ....10.00 To 20.00
Pitcher, 6 In. ....31.00 To 35.00
Pitcher, 8 In. ....35.00 To 40.00
Plate, 5 1/2 In..............4.50
Plate, 8 In.........9.00 To 12.00
Plate, 9 In........17.00 To 25.00
Relish, Divided,
  7 1/2 In..................18.00

Salt & Pepper 35.00
Saltshaker 12.00
Saucer 5.00
Shaker, Spice 25.00
Sherbet .... 12.00 To 15.00
Sugar, Cover 20.00
Tumbler, 3 In 20.00
Tumbler, 4 In 17.00

PINK ─────────────

Bowl, 5 In. 15.00
Bowl, Octagon, 9 In. 40.00
Butter, Cover 70.00
Cup 5.25
Cup & Saucer 8.25
Pitcher, 8 In. 29.00
Plate, 9 In .... 12.00 To 14.00
Salt & Pepper 50.00
Saucer 3.00
Sugar, Open 8.00
Tumbler, 3 In 15.00
Tumbler, Footed,
  5 1/4 In 20.00

YELLOW ─────────────

Bowl, 5 In. ...... 20.00 To 22.00
Bowl, Vegetable, Oval,
  10 In. 48.00
Butter, Cover 115.00
Creamer 10.00
Cup & Saucer ...... 8.00 To 10.00
Grill Plate, 9 In. 6.00
Grill Plate, Handle,
  10 1/2 In 5.00
Plate, 8 In. 8.00
Plate, 9 In. .... 9.00 To 11.00
Salt & Pepper 70.00
Sherbet .... 24.00 To 27.00
Sugar, Cover 23.00
Tumbler, 4 In 16.00
Tumbler,
  5 1/4 In .... 18.00 To 20.00
Tumbler, Footed,
  5 1/4 In 16.00

Princess Feather

Westmoreland Glass Company
made Princess Feather pattern
from 1939 through 1948. It
was originally made in aqua,
crystal, green, and pink. In
the 1960s a reproduction appeared in an amber shade
called Golden Sunset. The
pattern is sometimes called
Early American, Flower, Oatmeal Lace, Scroll & Star, or
Westmoreland Sandwich.

CRYSTAL ─────────────

Bowl, Heart Shape, Handle,
  5 In 12.00
Cup & Saucer 8.00
Saltshaker 20.00
Sherbet 4.50

PINK ─────────────

Goblet,
  4 3/8 In .... 12.00 To 20.00

**PRISMATIC LINE, see
  Queen Mary**

**PROVINCIAL, see
  Bubble**

PYRAMID, see No. 610

Queen Mary

Queen Mary, sometimes called
Prismatic Line or Vertical
Ribbed, was made by Anchor
Hocking Glass Company from
1936 to 1940. It was made in
crystal, pink, and red.

CRYSTAL ─────────────

Bowl, 4 In. 2.50
Bowl, 8 3/4 In. 6.00
Butter, Cover .... 12.50 To 18.00
Candy Dish, Cover 20.00
Celery, 5 X 10 In 9.50
Coaster-Ashtray, 4 1/4 In ... 3.50
Creamer .... 3.50 To 4.00
Cup 5.00
Cup & Saucer 6.00
Plate, 6 5/8 In 2.00
Plate, 8 1/2 In 4.00
Plate, 12 In. .... 5.00 To 8.00
Relish, 3 Sections, 12 In. ... 10.00
Salt & Pepper 15.00
Saltshaker 5.00
Sherbet .... 2.50 To 3.00
Sugar 4.00
Sugar & Creamer ... 7.25 To 8.00
Tumbler, 5 In 16.00

PINK ─────────────

Bowl, 4 In. .... 2.70 To 4.25
Bowl, 6 In. ...... 15.00 To 16.00
Bowl, 7 In. 22.00

Bowl, Handle,
4 In.................3.00 To 6.00
Bowl, Open Handle,
5 1/2 In.....................7.50
Butter, Cover...............90.00
Creamer ....3.00 To 5.00
Cup.................4.00 To 4.75
Cup & Saucer................6.50
Plate, 12 In. 18.50
Plate, 6 5/8 In......2.00 To 5.00
Plate,
9 3/4 In........ 19.00 To 30.00
Saucer.......................2.75
Sherbet, Footed.....3.00 To 6.00
Sugar 4.50
Sugar & Creamer 9.00
Tumbler,
3 1/2 In...........5.25 To 9.00
Tumbler, 4 In.....5.00 To 10.00
Tumbler, 5 In..............25.00

RED
Coaster-Ashtray, 4 1/4 In.... 6.00

R

Radiance

New Martinsville Glass Company, New Martinsville, West Virginia, made Radiance pattern from 1936 to 1939. It was made of amber, cobalt, crystal, emerald green, ice blue, and red.

AMBER

Celery.......................6.00
Cup.........................9.00
Sugar 9.00
Tumbler, 9 Oz...............8.00

BLUE

Candleholder, Double,
Pair.......................150.00
Compote, 6 In. 48.00
Cup & Saucer...............18.00
Dish, Mayonnaise, Liner....45.00
Ladle, Punch...............33.00
Sugar 16.00

CRYSTAL

Bowl, 5 1/4 In. 3.00
Bowl, Footed, 10 In. 15.00
Butter, Cover...72.00 To 115.00
Condiment Set, Tray,
4 Piece 85.00
Creamer 12.00
Plate, 10 In. 10.00
Platter, Oval, 11 1/2 In. ...11.00
Soup, Dish, 8 1/2 In. 8.00
Sugar .... 12.00 To 18.00
Tumbler, Frosted,
5 1/2 In..................14.00

RED

Ladle, Punch...............165.00
Punch Cup...................9.00
Sugar & Creamer... 37.50 To 45.00
Tumbler,
9 Oz............ 18.00 To 25.00
Vase, Crimped, 12 In.......60.00

Raindrops

Watch out for confusion with Raindrops and another pattern called Thumbprint or Pear Optic. The pattern for Raindrops is on the inside of the pieces, the other pattern is on the outside. Federal Glass

Company made crystal and green Raindrops dinnerware from 1929 to 1933.

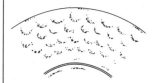

CRYSTAL

Cup.........................4.00
Whiskey, 1 7/8 In...........4.00

GREEN

Bowl, 6 In. 4.00
Cup................4.00 To 4.50
Cup & Saucer.......5.00 To 6.50
Plate, 8 In. ....3.00 To 3.50
Plate, Sherbet................1.50
Saucer.......................1.00
Tumbler, 5 In..............12.00
Whiskey,
1 7/8 In...........4.50 To 6.00

RASPBERRY BAND, see Laurel

REX, see No. 610

RIBBED, see Manhattan

Ribbon

Black, crystal, and green pieces were made in Ribbon pattern in the 1930s. It was made by the Hazel-Atlas Glass Company.

RIBBON CANDY, see Pretzel

CRYSTAL ————————

Bowl, 4 In. 5.50
Bowl, 8 In. 10.00
Candy Dish, Cover 22.50
Cup & Saucer 5.00
Plate, 6 1/4 In. 1.50
Plate, 8 In. 3.00
Saltshaker 5.00
Sherbet, Footed 4.50
Sugar & Creamer 12.00

GREEN ————————

Bowl, 4 In. 3.00
Bowl, 8 In. ...... 20.00 To 25.00
Candy Dish, Cover 26.00
Creamer............6.50 To 12.00
Cup ....3.00 To 4.50
Cup & Saucer 4.50
Plate, 6 1/4 In. ...... 1.50 To 3.00
Plate, 8 In. .... 2.50 To 3.00
Plate, Sherbet, Footed,
    6 In. 2.00
Salt & Pepper............... 18.00
Saltshaker 11.00
Saucer....................... 1.50
Sherbet, Footed 4.50
Sugar 7.00
Sugar & Creamer,
    Footed.......... 15.00 To 17.50
Tumbler, 6 In. .... 16.00 To 23.50

Ring

Hocking Glass Company made Ring from 1927 to 1932. The pattern is sometimes clear-colored glass and sometimes has colored rings added. The clear glass is crystal, green, or pink, which may or may not be decorated with rings of black, blue, orange, pink, platinum, red, or yellow.

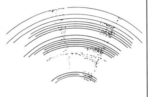

CRYSTAL ————————

Cocktail Shaker,
    Multicolored Rings 19.50
Cocktail Shaker,
    Platinum Rim.............. 20.00
Cocktail Shaker 7.75
Creamer...................... 2.50
Cup 2.50
Cup, Platinum Rings 3.25
Decanter Set, Blue Trim,
    6 Tumblers,
    7 Piece .... 38.00 To 50.00
Decanter, Black Rim........ 16.00
Decanter,
    Multicolored Rings 20.00
Goblet, 8 In........ 5.50 To 8.50
Ice Tub .... 12.00 To 20.00
Pitcher, 8 In. .... 15.00 To 20.00
Pitcher, 8 1/2 In............ 25.00
Pitcher, Platinum Rim,
    8 1/2 In........ 15.00 To 22.50
Plate, 6 1/4 In............... 2.25
Plate, Multicolored Rings,
    8 In........................ 5.00
Plate, Multicolored Rings,
    11 1/4 In.................. 12.00

Plate, Platinum Rim,
    6 1/4 In.................... 1.40
Plate, Platinum Rim, 8 In.... 3.00
Sherbet,
    4 3/4 In...........3.50 To 7.50
Soup, Dish, Platinum Rim ... 5.50
Sugar 4.50
Sugar & Creamer,
    Platinum Rim......5.50 To 9.50
Sugar, Footed................ 4.50
Sugar, Platinum Rim......... 3.50
Tumbler, 3 1/2 In........... 4.00
Tumbler, Footed,
    3 1/2 In.................... 5.00
Tumbler, Footed,
    6 1/2 In...........4.50 To 5.00
Tumbler, Footed, Platinum Rim,
    3 1/2 In.................... 6.00
Tumbler, Footed, Platinum Rim,
    6 1/2 In.................... 7.75
Tumbler, Multicolored Rings,
    3 1/2 In.................... 5.00
Tumbler, Multicolored Rings,
    5 1/2 In.................... 7.50
Tumbler, Pink Rim,
    5 1/8 In.................... 4.50
Tumbler, Platinum Rim,
    3 1/2 In.................... 5.50
Vase, Multicolored Rings,
    8 In....................... 17.00
Whiskey, Multicolored Rings,
    2 In........................ 5.00

GREEN ————————

Bowl, 5 In. 3.75
Pitcher,
    8 1/2 In........ 22.50 To 29.00
Plate, 6 1/4 In.............. 1.75
Plate, Off-Center Ring,
    6 1/2 In...........4.00 To 4.50
Sandwich Server,
    Center Handle............. 18.00
Tumbler, 4 1/4 In........... 7.00
Tumbler, Footed,
    5 1/2 In.................... 6.00

Ring-Ding

Ring-ding was made in 1932 by Hocking Glass Company of Lancaster, Ohio. Painted bands of green, orange, red, and yellow decorated the clear glass and gave the pattern its name.

CRYSTAL

Bowl, 5 In. 3.00
Sherbet, Low................10.00
Tumbler, Juice 6.00
Whiskey.............4.00 To 4.50
Wine........................10.00

Rock Crystal

Rock Crystal, sometimes called Early American Rock Crystal, was made in many solid colors by McKee Glass Company. Crystal was made in the 1920s. Amber, blue-green, cobalt blue, crystal, green, pink, red, and yellow pieces were made in the 1930s.

AMBER

Creamer,
  Footed......... 35.00 To 50.00

Goblet, Flared, 7 1/2 In....10.00
Goblet, Footed, 11 Oz......31.00
Parfait......................13.00
Plate, 7 1/2 In............... 5.00
Plate, 8 1/2 In............... 8.00
Sugar 30.00

CRYSTAL

Bonbon, 7 1/2 In...........15.00
Bowl, 4 1/2 In. ....5.00 To 9.50
Bowl, 10 1/2 In. 20.00
Bowl, Footed, 12 1/2 In....20.00
Butter, Cover 50.00
Candleholder, 2-Light,
  Pair........................35.00
Candy Dish,
  Cover.......... 25.00 To 40.00
Celery, 12 In...............21.00
Champagne,
  6 Oz.............6.00 To 11.00
Cocktail, Footed,
  3 1/2 Oz. ....9.00 To 14.00
Compote, 7 In. 27.50
Cordial, Footed,
  1 Oz.............9.00 To 14.00
Cruet, Stopper 48.00
Eggcup, Footed ....6.00 To 12.00
Finger Bowl, 5 In...........10.00
Goblet, 8 Oz..... 10.00 To 13.50
Goblet, 11 Oz...............12.00
Parfait......................28.00
Pitcher, 6 1/2 In...........90.00
Pitcher, 7 1/2 In......... 130.00
Plate, 7 1/2 In............... 4.00
Plate,
  10 1/2 In....... 35.00 To 40.00
Plate,
  11 1/2 In....... 20.00 To 30.00
Plate, Deviled Egg,
  11 1/2 In....... 75.00 To 98.00
Relish, 6 Sections, 14 In. ...25.00
Salt & Pepper...............50.00
Salt & Pepper, Bulbous.....95.00
Sherbet 9.00
Sugar & Creamer, Cover,
  Footed....................60.00
Sugar, Cover.................20.00
Tankard.................. 140.00
Tray, 13 In..................30.00
Tumbler, 5 Oz......6.00 To 9.00

Whiskey, 6 Piece 50.00
Wine, 3 Oz. ..... 10.00 To 15.00

GREEN

Cake Stand, Footed,
  11 In. .... 30.00 To 40.00
Goblet, Footed, 8 Oz. 18.00
Sandwich Server,
  Center Handle.............55.00
Sugar & Creamer, Footed...75.00
Sundae, Low, 6 In. 18.50

RED

Finger Bowl, Liner..........60.00
Tumbler, 12 Oz.............38.00
Tumbler, Straight, 9 Oz.....40.00
Wine, 3 Oz. 14.00

ROPE, see Colonial Fluted

Rose Cameo

Rose Cameo was made by the Belmont Tumbler Company, Bellaire, Ohio, in 1933. It has been found only in green.

GREEN

Plate, 7 In..........4.00 To 6.00
Sherbet ....5.00 To 8.00
Tumbler, Footed,
  5 In............. 11.00 To 12.00

ROSE LACE, see Royal Lace

Rosemary

Rosemary, also called Cabbage Rose with Single Arch or Dutch Rose, was made by Federal Glass Company from 1935 to 1937. It was made in amber, green, and pink. Pieces with bases, like creamers or cups, are sometimes confused with Mayfair Federal. The lower half of the Rosemary pieces are plain, the lower half of Mayfair Federal has a band of arches.

ROSEMARY, see also Mayfair Federal

AMBER

Bowl, 5 In. ....4.00 To 4.50
Bowl, 6 In. 20.00
Bowl, Vegetable, Oval,
  10 In. ....6.50 To 10.25
Creamer....................... 8.00
Cup......................... 4.00
Cup & Saucer......5.00 To 12.00
Grill Plate 6.50
Plate, 6 3/4 In......3.00 To 5.00
Plate, 9 1/2 In......5.00 To 7.00
Platter, Oval, 12 In. 10.00
Saucer...............1.25 To 2.00
Soup, Cream......8.00 To 12.00
Sugar ....6.50 To 8.00
Sugar & Creamer,
  Footed.......... 14.00 To 17.00
Tumbler,
  4 1/4 In........ 17.50 To 22.00

GREEN

Bowl, 6 In. ...... 14.00 To 25.00
Cup & Saucer...............15.00
Plate, 6 3/4 In.............. 9.00

PINK

Bowl, Vegetable, Oval,
  10 In. 25.00
Plate, 6 3/4 In.............. 9.00
Plate, 9 1/2 In..............14.00
Sugar 9.00

Roulette

Anchor Hocking Glass Company made Roulette pattern from 1935 to 1939. It can be found in crystal, green, and pink. Collectors originally called the pattern Many Windows.

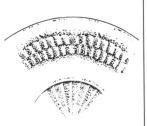

CRYSTAL

Sherbet 4.00

GREEN

Bowl, 9 In. 11.00
Cup.................2.75 To 5.00
Cup & Saucer.......4.75 To 6.50
Pitcher, 8 In. 24.00
Plate, 6 In..........1.75 To 2.50
Plate, 8 1/2 In......3.50 To 4.75
Plate, 12 In. 10.00
Saucer...............1.00 To 4.00
Sherbet ....3.00 To 4.75
Tumbler,
  5 1/8 In........ 17.50 To 19.50

Tumbler, Footed,
  5 1/2 In........ 12.00 To 18.50

PINK

Cup & Saucer...............18.00
Pitcher, 8 In. 20.00
Plate, 6 In.................... 8.00
Whiskey, 2 1/2 In........... 6.50

Round Robin

Sometimes a pattern was advertised by the wholesaler, but the manufacturer is unknown today. One of these is Round Robin, sometimes called Accordion Pleats. It was pictured in the catalogs of the late 1920s and 1930s and offered in green, crystal, and iridescent marigold.

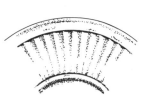

GREEN

Bowl, 4 In. 6.00
Creamer...................... 5.00
Cup........................... 4.50
Cup & Saucer............... 6.00
Plate, 6 In.................... 1.50
Sherbet ....4.50 To 5.00
Sugar 4.50

IRIDESCENT

Creamer....................... 5.00
Plate, 6 In.................... 1.50
Sherbet 4.00

Roxana

Hazel-Atlas Glass Company made Roxana pattern in 1932. It was made in crystal, yellow, and white. Although there seems to be a full luncheon set, collectors cannot find a cup for the saucer.

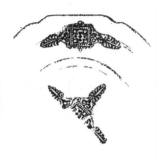

CRYSTAL ――――――――

Sherbet 5.00
Tumbler,
4 1/4 In.......... 7.00 To 8.50

YELLOW ――――――――

Plate, 6 In.................... 1.75
Sherbet, Footed 5.00
Tumbler, 4 1/4 In......... 10.00

Royal Lace

Royal Lace was made from 1934 to 1941. The popular pattern by Hazel-Atlas Glass Company was made in amethyst, cobalt blue, crystal, green, and pink. It is sometimes called Gladiola or Rose Lace.

• • • • • • • • • • • • • • • •
When the weather is bad, the auction will probably be good. Brave storms and cold and attend the auctions in bad weather when the crowd is small and the prices are low.
• • • • • • • • • • • • • • • •

AMETHYST ――――――――

Cider Set................. 110.00
Sherbet, Metal Holder 35.00

BLUE ――――――――

Bowl, 3 Legs, Straight Edge,
10 In. 45.00
Bowl, Round,
10 In. .... 35.00 To 45.00
Bowl, Vegetable, Oval,
11 In. 38.00
Candleholder, Straight Edge,
Pair........................ 75.00
Cookie Jar, Cover......... 230.00
Creamer.................... 30.00
Cup 27.50
Cup & Saucer .... 33.00 To 35.00
Pitcher,
48 Oz......... 85.00 To 125.00
Pitcher, 96 Oz. 250.00
Plate, 6 In.........6.00 To 12.50
Plate,
9 7/8 In........ 13.00 To 24.00
Platter, Oval, 13 In. 34.00

Saltshaker 95.00
Sherbet, Footed 35.00
Soup, Cream 28.00
Sugar .... 21.50 To 25.00
Sugar & Creamer,
Cover................... 160.00
Tumbler,
3 1/2 In........ 32.50 To 35.00
Tumbler, 4 1/8 In.......... 22.00

CRYSTAL ――――――――

Butter, Cover .... 60.00 To 65.00
Candleholder, Rolled Edge,
Pair............. 32.00 To 37.00
Cookie Jar,
Cover... 35.00 To 38.00
Creamer...................... 9.50
Cup 6.00
Plate, 9 7/8 In.............. 7.00
Salt & Pepper............... 28.00
Saucer....................... 2.50
Sugar 7.00
Sugar & Creamer 13.50
Sugar, Cover................ 18.00
Tumbler, 3 1/2 In.......... 12.50
Tumbler,
4 1/8 In.......... 8.50 To 9.50

GREEN ――――――――

Butter, Cover 235.00
Cookie Jar,
Cover........... 53.00 To 65.00
Creamer.......... 14.50 To 17.00
Cup 12.00
Cup & Saucer............... 18.00
Pitcher, 48 Oz. 80.00
Plate, 6 In..........4.00 To 5.00
Plate, 8 In.................. 10.00
Plate, 9 7/8 In.............. 17.00
Platter, Oval, 13 In. 22.50
Salt & Pepper... 83.00 To 100.00
Saltshaker 45.00
Sherbet 25.00
Soup, Cream ..... 22.00 To 23.00
Soup, Dish.................. 20.00
Sugar, Cover................ 48.00
Tumbler, 3 1/2 In.......... 22.00
Tumbler,
4 1/8 In........ 15.00 To 19.00
Tumbler, 5 3/8 In.......... 45.00

PINK

Bowl, 3-Footed, Rolled,
  10 In. 50.00
Bowl, 3-Footed, Ruffled,
  10 In. 45.00
Butter.......................6.00
Candleholder, Ruffled,
  Pair.......................55.00
Cookie Jar, Cover...........45.00
Cup................9.00 To 12.00
Cup & Saucer...............16.50
Pitcher, 48 Oz. 50.00
Salt & Pepper.... 44.00 To 55.00
Soup, Cream................16.50
Sugar ....9.00 To 11.00
Sugar & Creamer 25.00
Tumbler, 4 1/8 In..........14.00

Royal Ruby

There is no reason to picture
this pattern because it is the
plain shape and bright red
color that identifies it. Anchor
Hocking Glass Company made
it from 1939 to the 1960s
and again in 1977. The same
shapes were made in green
and called by the pattern
name Forest Green. Repro-
duction tumblers were made
in 1977-1978.

Ashtray, Square, 4 1/2 In.... 3.00
Berry Set, 9 Piece 50.00
Bowl, 4 1/4 In. ....4.00 To 5.00
Bowl, 8 1/2 In. 14.00
Bowl, 11 1/2 In. 22.00
Bowl, Vegetable, Oval,
  8 In.......................30.00

Cardholder.................45.00
Creamer............4.00 To 6.00
Creamer, Footed 6.00
Cup..........................3.50
Cup & Saucer...............5.50
Cup & Saucer,
  Square............4.00 To 6.00
Goblet,
  Ball Stem.........9.50 To 11.00
Pitcher Set, 9 Piece.........60.00
Pitcher, Tilt, 22 Oz. 20.00
Pitcher, Upright,
  3 Qt. .... 30.00 To 38.00
Plate, 6 1/2 In......2.00 To 3.00
Plate, 7 3/4 In...............6.50
Plate, Square, 9 In. 7.00
Punch Set,
  14 Piece........ 60.00 To 79.00
Saucer.......................1.50
Sherbet, Footed .....6.00 To 7.50
Soup, Dish....... 10.00 To 12.00
Sugar ....4.00 To 6.00
Sugar & Creamer, Cover....20.00
Sugar & Creamer, Footed...15.00
Tumbler, 5 Oz. .....3.00 To 7.00
Tumbler, 9 Oz. 5.00
Tumbler, 10 Oz.....3.00 To 5.00
Tumbler, 13 Oz....8.00 To 10.00
Tumbler, Footed, 6 In. 10.00
Vase, Flared, Large 15.00
Vase, Large 12.00
Vase, Medium 7.00
Vase, Small 4.00
Wine, 2 1/2 Oz.....7.00 To 8.50

RUSSIAN, see Holiday

• • • • • • • • • • • • • • •
When moving,
remember there is no
insurance coverage for
breakage if the items
are not packed by the
shipper.
• • • • • • • • • • • • • • •

S

S Pattern

Macbeth-Evans Glass Company
made S Pattern, or Stippled
Rose Band, from 1930 to
1935. It was made before
1932 in crystal, pink, topaz,
and crystal with gold, blue, or
platinum trim. The 1934-1935
listing mentions red, green,
and Monax. Other pieces
were made in amber, ruby,
Ritz Blue, and crystal with
many colors of trim including
amber, green, rose, platinum,
red, silver, or white.

AMBER

Bowl, 5 1/2 In. 3.50
Creamer............5.00 To 6.00
Cup.................3.00 To 3.50
Cup & Saucer...............5.50
Cup & Saucer,
  Platinum Rim...............4.00
Cup, Platinum Rim 3.00
Grill Plate 6.00
Plate, 6 In....................2.00
Plate, 8 1/4 In......2.50 To 3.00
Saucer.......................1.50
Sherbet 6.00
Sugar & Creamer 5.00

CRYSTAL

Creamer............3.75 To 4.00
Creamer, Yellow Band.......5.50

Cup .... 2.00 To 2.50
Cup & Saucer 3.50
Plate, 8 1/4 In. 2.00
Plate, 9 1/4 In. 4.00
Plate, Green Band,
  8 1/4 In. 2.00
Sugar .... 3.50 To 4.00
Sugar & Creamer.... 7.00 To 12.00
Sugar, Platinum Rim......... 3.50
Tumbler, 4 3/4 In. 3.00
Tumbler, 5 In. 6.00

SAIL BOAT, see White Ship

SAILING SHIP, see White Ship

Sandwich Anchor Hocking

Many patterns were called Sandwich. Each company seemed to have one design with that name. The Anchor Hocking Glass Company Sandwich pattern was made from 1939 to 1964. Pink and royal ruby were used in 1939-1940; crystal, forest green, and opaque white were used in the 1950s and 1960s; amber was used in the 1960s. A reproduction line was introduced in 1977 by another company in amber, blue, crystal, and red.

AMBER

Bowl, 6 1/2 In. 10.00
Bowl, Deep, 9 In. 22.50
Bowl, Smooth, 4 7/8 In. 3.00
Cookie Jar, Cover,
  9 1/4 In. .... 15.00 To 25.00
Cup 3.00
Cup & Saucer....... 5.00 To 6.00
Plate, 9 In. .... 4.00 To 7.00

CRYSTAL

Bowl, 4 7/8 In. .... 3.00 To 4.00
Bowl, 6 1/2 In. 24.00
Bowl, 7 In. 6.00
Bowl, 8 In. .... 5.00 To 8.50
Bowl, 9 In. 15.00
Bowl, Ruffled, 4 7/8 In. 8.00
Bowl, Scalloped,
  5 1/4 In. 6.00
Bowl, Scalloped,
  6 1/2 In. 5.50
Bowl, Vegetable, Oval,
  8 1/4 In. .... 4.75 To 5.00
Butter, Cover .... 26.00 To 32.50
Cup 1.50
Cup & Saucer....... 2.00 To 4.00
Custard Cup .... 2.50 To 3.50
Plate, 7 In. .... 6.00 To 8.00
Plate, 8 In. .... 3.00 To 5.50
Plate, 9 In. ....7.50 To 11.00
Plate, Indentation,
  9 In. .... 3.00 To 4.50
Punch Set, 14 Piece 45.00
Sherbet, Footed ..... 4.50 To 6.00
Sugar 4.00
Sugar & Creamer, Cover ... 22.00
Tumbler,
  3 9/16 In. .... 4.00 To 5.00
Tumbler, 9 Oz. 8.00

FOREST GREEN

Bowl, 4 5/16 In. .... 2.00 To 3.00
Cookie Jar, Cover........... 16.00
Cup .... 15.00 To 20.00
Cup & Saucer.... 27.50 To 30.00
Custard Cup .... 1.50 To 2.50

Custard Cup Liner.....1.50 To 3.00
Pitcher, 6 In. 125.00
Plate, 9 In. 63.00
Punch Set, 14 Piece 45.00
Saucer........................ 6.00
Sugar 20.00
Sugar & Creamer 35.00
Tumbler,
  3 9/16 In.......... 3.00 To 5.00
Tumbler, 9 Oz. 3.00

PINK

Bowl, 4 7/8 In. 6.50
Bowl, Scalloped, 8 In. 9.50

RUBY RED

Bowl, 6 1/2 In. 10.00
Bowl, Scalloped,
  5 1/4 In. 13.50

WHITE

Punch Cup.................... 1.25
Punch Set, 14 Piece 40.00

Sandwich Indiana

Another Sandwich pattern was made by the Indiana Glass Company, Dunkirk, Indiana, from the 1920s through the 1980s. Only the colors changed through the years. Amber was made from the late 1920s to the 1970s, crystal in the late 1920s to the 1980s, light green in the 1930s, pink in the late 1920s through the 1930s, red from 1933 to the 1970s, and teal blue in the 1950s. The scroll design varies with the size of the plate. In 1969 reproduction dinner sets were made in amber, blue, crystal, green, and red. Other items have been reproduced in amber and light green since 1982.

AMBER

Bowl, 4 1/4 In.	4.00
Goblet	10.00
Tumbler, Footed, 12 Oz.	12.00

CRYSTAL

Ashtray, Club Shape	3.00
Bowl, 6 Sides, 6 In.	4.00
Butter	85.00
Cup & Saucer	4.00
Plate, Indentation, Oval, 8 In.	3.00
Sherbet	4.00
Sugar & Creamer, Tray	10.00 To 12.00
Tray	3.00
Wine, 3 In.	17.00

SAWTOOTH, see English Hobnail

SAXON, see Coronation

SCROLL & STAR, see Princess Feather

SHAMROCK, see Cloverleaf

Sharon

Sharon, or Cabbage Rose, was made by the Federal Glass Company from 1935 to 1939. The pattern was made in amber, crystal, green, and pink. A cheese dish was reproduced in 1976 in amber, blue, dark green, light green, and pink. Other items have been reproduced in various colors.

AMBER

Bowl, 5 In.	6.50
Bowl, 10 1/2 In.	14.00
Bowl, Vegetable, Oval, 9 1/2 In.	13.00
Butter, Cover	29.00 To 42.50
Cup & Saucer	8.00
Platter, Oval, 12 1/2 In.	9.00 To 13.50
Salt & Pepper	25.00
Sherbet, Footed	6.75
Sugar	6.00
Sugar & Creamer	16.00 To 20.00

GREEN

Bowl, 5 In.	11.50
Bowl, 8 1/2 In.	23.00
Bowl, Vegetable, Oval, 9 1/2 In.	20.00
Butter, Cover	70.00
Candy Jar, Cover	135.00
Cup & Saucer	20.00
Plate, 6 In.	4.00 To 4.50
Plate, 7 1/2 In.	12.75 To 17.00
Plate, 9 1/2 In.	13.00
Salt & Pepper	45.00 To 55.00
Soup, Cream	27.00
Sugar, Cover	40.00
Tumbler, Thick, 5 1/4 In.	75.00
Tumbler, Thin, 4 1/8 In.	50.00
Tumbler, Thin, 5 1/4 In.	80.00

PINK

Bowl, 5 In.	6.00 To 8.00
Bowl, 6 In.	16.00
Bowl, 10 1/2 In.	33.00 To 40.00
Bowl, Vegetable, Oval, 9 1/2 In.	16.00
Butter, Cover	31.00 To 37.00
Cake Plate, Footed, 11 1/2 In.	26.00 To 30.00
Creamer	12.50
Cup	10.00 To 12.50
Cup & Saucer	15.00
Plate, 6 In.	3.50 To 4.50
Plate, 7 1/2 In.	21.00
Plate, 9 1/2 In.	9.00 To 13.00
Platter, Oval, 12 1/2 In.	12.00 To 14.00
Salt & Pepper	35.00 To 40.00
Saltshaker	18.00
Saucer	6.00
Sherbet, Footed	10.00 To 11.00
Soup, Cream	24.00 To 30.00
Soup, Dish, 7 1/2 In.	25.50 To 35.00
Sugar	7.50 To 12.00
Sugar & Creamer	12.00
Tumbler, Footed, 6 1/2 In.	30.00
Tumbler, Thick, 4 1/8 In.	30.00
Tumbler, Thin, 4 1/8 In.	24.00 To 28.00
Tumbler, Thin, 5 1/4 In.	32.00

SHEFFIELD, see Chinex Classic

SHELL, see Petalware

Shirley Temple

Shirley Temple is not really a pattern, but the dishes with the white enamel decoration picturing Shirley have become popular with collectors. The most famous were made as giveaways with cereal from 1934 to 1942. Several companies, including Hazel-Atlas

Glass Company and U.S. Glass, made the glassware. Sugars and creamers, bowls, plates, and mugs were made. The milk pitcher and mug have been reproduced since 1982 and the bowl has been reproduced since 1986. Other items with the Shirley Temple decal include Fostoria Mayfair green sugar bowl and tea cup, a white mug, and an 8 7/8-inch Moderntone cobalt plate. In 1972 Libbey glass made six different sized tumblers.

BLUE

Bowl, Cereal.....	45.00 To 50.00
Creamer..............	45.00
Mug	42.00
Plate	275.00
Sugar	45.00

Sierra

Sierra, or Pinwheel, was made by Jeannette Glass Company from 1931 to 1933. It is found in green and pink.

• • • • • • • • • • • • • • • •

The best time to buy an antique is when you see it.

• • • • • • • • • • • • • • • •

GREEN

Bowl, 5 1/2 In.	8.00
Bowl, 8 1/2 In.	8.00
Butter, Cover	28.00 To 50.00
Cup	9.00
Plate, 9 In..................	14.00
Salt & Pepper....	22.00 To 48.00
Saucer.......................	4.00
Sugar	17.50
Sugar & Creamer	34.00
Sugar, Cover.....	25.00 To 30.00

PINK

Bowl, 5 1/2 In.	7.00 To 8.00
Bowl, 8 1/2 In........	10.00 To 22.00
Butter, Cover	22.00 To 47.00
Creamer.........	11.00 To 14.00
Cup	4.00 To 10.00
Cup & Saucer...............	13.50
Plate, 9 In........	10.00 To 15.00
Platter, Oval, 11 In.	22.00
Salt & Pepper....	35.00 To 43.00
Saucer..............	3.00 To 3.50
Sugar	14.00
Sugar, Cover...............	28.00
Tray, 2 Handles, 10 1/4 In.......	10.00 To 19.00

SMOCKING, see Windsor

SNOWFLAKE, see Doric

Spiral

It is easy to confuse Spiral and Twisted Optic patterns. Ask to be shown examples of each, because even a picture will not be much help. Most pieces of Twisted Optic spiral counterclockwise; most pieces of Spiral go clockwise. There are a few pieces that are exceptions. The spiral pattern was made from 1928 to 1930 in green and pink by Hocking Glass Company.

GREEN

Butter Tub.......	16.00 To 20.00
Creamer, Footed	6.00
Cup	4.00
Cup & Saucer................	7.00
Ice Bucket	35.00
Jam Jar, Cover	20.00
Pitcher, 7 5/8 In............	22.00
Plate, 6 In....................	1.00
Plate, 8 In...........	2.00 To 3.50
Sandwich Server, Center Handle.............	22.00

PINK

Platter, 12 In...............	15.00
Sherbet	3.00 To 4.00
Tumbler	6.00

Spiral Flutes

Duncan and Miller Glass Company, Washington, Pennsylvania, made Spiral Flutes pattern. It was made of amber, crystal, and green glass in 1924, pink in 1926. A few pieces are reported with gold trim and in blue or vaseline-colored glass.

SPIRAL OPTIC, see Spiral

AMBER

Cocktail, Crystal Footed,
3 3/8 In., 8 Piece.........60.00
Cup, Seafood Sauce Cup....12.50
Dish, Grapefruit, Footed....17.50
Goblet, 6 1/4 In............17.00
Plate, 6 In..................4.50
Plate, Torte, 13 3/4 In. 8.00
Saucer......................4.50
Sherbet, 3 3/4 In...........10.00
Soup, Cream, Footed,
4 3/4 In..................12.00
Sugar 4.00

CRYSTAL

Bowl, 4 3/8 In. 5.00
Candleholder, Low, Pair 35.00
Compote, 4 1/2 In...........9.50
Goblet, 6 1/4 In............12.00
Sherbet, 3 3/4 In. 8.00
Tumbler, 4 3/8 In...........6.50
Vase, 10 1/2 In.............30.00

GREEN

Bowl, 6 1/2 In. 10.00

Bowl, 7 1/2 In. 19.50
Bowl, Flanged, 8 1/2 In....17.50
Compote,
4 3/8 In........ 12.00 To 20.00
Cruet, Stopper 225.00
Cup & Saucer.... 10.00 To 11.00
Goblet, 6 1/4 In............12.00
Ice Tub 24.00
Plate, 6 In..................3.00
Plate, 7 1/2 In..............4.00
Plate, 8 3/8 In......4.50 To 8.00
Plate, 10 3/8 In. 15.00
Seafood Sauce Cup..........15.00
Sherbet,
3 3/4 In..........8.00 To 12.00
Soup, Cream, Footed,
4 3/4 In..................12.00
Sugar & Creamer, Oval.....25.00
Sweetmeat, Cover......... 125.00
Tumbler, Footed,
5 1/8 In..................17.50
Vase, 8 1/2 In..............30.00
Vase, 10 1/2 In.............40.00
Wine, 3 3/4 In. 14.50

PINK

Plate, 7 1/2 In..............8.00
Sherbet, 4 3/4 In. 9.00

SPOKE, see Patrician

Sportsman Series

Hazel-Atlas Glass Company made an unusual Depression glass pattern in the 1940s. It was made of cobalt blue, amethyst, or crystal with fired-on decoration. Although the name of the series was Sportsman, designs included golf, sailboats, hunting, angelfish, and a few strange choices like windmills. We list Windmill and White Ships separately, although they are sometimes considered part of this pattern.

COBALT BLUE

Cocktail Shaker,
Fish............. 16.00 To 25.00
Ice Bowl, Fish, Chrome
Holder & Spoon...........20.00
Pitcher, Hunter, Ice Lip,
Crystal Handle 85.00
Pitcher, Hunter,
No Ice Lip 65.00
Tumbler, Fish,
3 3/4 In...........7.00 To 8.00
Tumbler, Fish, 3 3/8 In. ...12.00
Tumbler, Golf, 4 3/4 In.....9.50
Tumbler, Golf, 5 In.........10.00
Tumbler, Hunter,
3 3/8 In...................16.00
Tumbler, Skier, Roly Poly...8.75

CRYSTAL

Cocktail Shaker,
Fish............. 30.00 To 55.00
Pitcher, Golf................70.00
Tumbler, Fish,
3 3/8 In........ 12.00 To 16.00
Tumbler, Fish, Roly Poly...14.00
Tumbler, Hunter,
4 5/8 In...................12.50

Square

Fire-King dinnerware by Anchor Hocking Glass Company, Lancaster, Ohio, was made in 5 patterns: Alice, Jane-Ray, Square, Swirl Fire-King, and Turquoise Blue. Square, named for its shape, was made in the 1940s-1960s and came in a variety of colors.

BLUE ──────────────

Bowl, 4 3/4 In. 8.00
Bowl, 5 In. 2.75
Bowl, 7 3/8 In. 13.00
Cup & Saucer.......2.00 To 4.50
Plate, 8 3/8 In......3.00 To 3.50
Saucer................ .50 To .75

JADITE ──────────────

Cup 2.00
Plate, 8 1/8 In.............. 3.00
Saucer........................ .50

Starlight

Starlight was made by the Hazel-Atlas Company of Wheeling, West Virginia, in the 1930s. Full table settings were made of cobalt blue, crystal, pink, and white. The pattern is pressed, not etched.

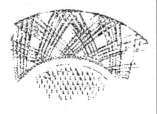

COBALT BLUE ──────────

Bowl, 8 1/2 In. 25.00

CRYSTAL ──────────────

Bowl, 5 1/2 In. ....3.00 To 4.00
Creamer......................3.00
Plate, 8 1/2 In.............. 2.50

STIPPLED ROSE BAND, see S Pattern

Strawberry

Strawberry and Cherry-Berry are similar patterns. The U.S. Glass Company made this pattern in the early 1930s with strawberry decoration. It was made in crystal, green, pink, and iridescent marigold.

STRAWBERRY, see also Cherry-Berry

GREEN ──────────────

Bowl, 4 In. 10.00
Bowl, 6 1/2 In. 35.00
Bowl,
  7 1/2 In........ 20.00 To 31.50
Dish, Olive, Handle,
  5 In........................30.00
Plate, Sherbet, 6 In. 6.00
Sugar, Small 17.50
Tumbler, 3 5/8 In..........24.00

PINK ──────────────

Bowl, 4 In. 9.50
Bowl, 7 1/2 In. 18.00
Butter, Cover 115.00

Compote, 5 3/4 In..........15.00
Dish, Olive, Handle,
  5 In........................32.00
Pitcher,
  7 3/4 In......100.00 To 145.00
Plate, 7 1/2 In.....8.50 To 11.00
Sherbet ....6.00 To 6.50

Sunburst

Crystal dinner sets were made in Sunburst pattern from 1938 to 1941 by Jeannette Glass Company of Jeannette, Pennsylvania.

CRYSTAL ──────────────

Candleholder, 2-Light....... 10.00
Plate, 6 In.................... 2.00
Plate, 8 1/2 In...............3.00
Plate, 11 In. 18.00
Relish, Oval 6.00
Sugar 4.00

Sunflower

Sunflower was made by Jeannette Glass Company, Jeannette, Pennsylvania, in the late 1920s and early 1930s. It is found in delphite, pink, and two shades of green.

GREEN ──────────────

Ashtray, 5 In.......7.00 To 12.00
Cake Plate,
  10 In. ....8.00 To 11.00
Cup & Saucer...............16.00
Plate, 9 In........ 10.00 To 15.00

Sugar .... 13.50 To 15.00
Trivet, 7 In. 215.00
Tumbler,
    4 3/4 In........ 21.00 To 23.00

PINK

Ashtray, 5 In................. 8.00
Cake Plate,
    10 In. ....9.00 To 11.00
Cup.................8.00 To 9.50
Cup & Saucer.... 11.00 To 13.00
Plate, 9 In..........9.00 To 12.50
Sugar 12.00
Sugar & Creamer 25.00
Tumbler,
    4 3/4 In........ 13.00 To 17.50

Swankyswigs

In October 1933, Kraft
Cheese Company began to
market cheese spreads in decorated, reusable glass tumblers. The tumbler was made
in a 5-ounce size. It had a
smooth beverage lip and a
permanent color decoration.
The designs were tested and
changed as public demand in-
dicated. Hazel-Atlas Glass
Company made the glasses,
which were decorated by
hand by about 280 girls,
working in shifts around the
clock. In 1937 a silk screen
process was developed and
the Tulip design was made by
this new, faster method. The
glasses were made thinner and
lighter in weight. The decorated Swankyswigs were discontinued from 1941 to 1946,
the war years. They were
made again in 1947 and were
continued through 1958.
Then plain glasses were used
for most of the cheese, although a few specially decorated Swankyswigs have been
made since that time.

ANTIQUE

Black................1.75 To 2.50
Blue 1.75
Brown 2.50
Green..............1.75 To 2.50
Orange......................1.75
Red..........................2.50

BAND NO.1

Red & Black.................1.50

BAND NO.2

Black & Red.................1.50

BAND NO.3

Blue & White...............3.00

BICENTENNIAL

Tulip, Yellow..............14.00

BUSTLIN' BETSY

Blue 2.00
Green........................2.00
Red..........................2.00
Yellow.......................2.00

CARNIVAL

Blue ....3.00 To 4.00
Green..............4.00 To 6.00
Orange......................2.50
Red..........................3.00

CHECKERBOARD

Red..........................2.00

CIRCLES & DOT

Black........................4.00
Green.......................4.00

DAISY

Red,
    White & Green....1.50 To 3.00

FORGET-ME-NOT

Dark Blue 1.75
Light Blue 1.75
Red..........................1.75
Yellow.......................1.75

KIDDIE CUP

Black........................2.00
Blue 2.00
Brown ....1.50 To 2.00
Green.......................2.00
Orange......................2.00
Red..........................2.00

POSY CORNFLOWER NO.1

Light Blue 2.00

POSY CORNFLOWER NO.2

Dark Blue ....1.75 To 2.00
Red..........................1.75
Yellow.......................1.75

POSY JONQUIL

Yellow.......................2.00

POSY TULIP

Red..........................2.00

POSY VIOLET

...........................2.00

SAILBOAT NO.1

Blue 12.00

SAILBOAT NO.2

Green.......................12.00

STARS NO.1

Blue 4.00
Black........................4.00

Green......................... 4.00
Red 4.00

TEXAS CENTENNIAL ——

Blue 23.00

TULIP NO.1 ——

Black................2.00 To 3.00
Blue ....2.00 To 3.00
Green, 3 1/2 In. ...2.00 To 3.00
Green, 4 1/2 In. 12.00
Red, 3 1/2 In.......2.00 To 3.00

TULIP NO.2 ——

Blue, Red...................18.00

TULIP NO.3 ——

Light Blue 2.00
Yellow...................... 2.00

SWEET PEAR, see
    Avocado

Swirl

Swirl, sometimes called Double Swirl or Petal Swirl, was made by Jeannette Glass Company during 1937 and 1938. It was made of amber, delphite, ice blue, pink, and a green-blue color called ultramarine.

DELPHITE ——

Bowl, 6 1/4 In. 8.00
Bowl, 9 In. 22.00
Cup & Saucer................ 9.00

Plate, 6 1/2 In............... 4.00
Plate, 9 1/4 In............... 8.00
Platter, Oval, 12 In. 24.00
Sugar 8.00
Sugar & Creamer 14.00

ICE BLUE ——

Bowl, 5 1/4 In. 8.00
Bowl, 9 In. 22.00
Cup & Saucer................ 9.00
Plate, 6 1/2 In............... 4.00
Plate, 9 1/4 In............... 8.00
Platter, Oval, 12 In. 24.00
Sugar & Creamer 30.00

PINK ——

Bowl, 6 1/4 In. 7.00
Candy Dish, 3-Footed,
    Open 6.00
Candy Dish, Cover 50.00
Coaster,
    1 X 3 1/4 In......5.50 To 9.00
Cup........................... 5.00
Plate, 9 1/4 In......7.00 To 8.00
Soup, Lug Handle 15.00
Sugar & Creamer 13.00
Tumbler, 4 5/8 In..........12.00

ULTRAMARINE ——

Bowl, 6 1/4 In. ....7.00 To 8.50
Bowl, 9 In. ...... 13.00 To 20.00
Bowl, 10 In.................13.00
Butter.......................45.00
Candleholder, Double,
    Pair........................22.00
Candy Dish, 3-Footed,
    Open 20.00
Candy Dish,
    Cover........100.00 To 110.00
Coaster, 1 X 3 1/4 In. 12.00
Console, Footed, Handle,
    10 1/2 In..................25.00
Creamer...........8.00 To 10.00
Cup ....7.00 To 9.00
Cup & Saucer...............12.50
Plate, 6 1/2 In......3.00 To 4.00
Plate,
    9 1/4 In........ 10.00 To 11.50
Plate, Sandwich,
    12 1/2 In....... 12.00 To 13.00

Salt & Pepper.... 19.00 To 21.00
Saltshaker .... 12.00 To 15.00
Saucer........................ 2.00
Sherbet ....8.00 To 10.00
Soup, Dish, Lug Handle 14.00
Sugar ....8.00 To 14.00
Sugar & Creamer... 19.00 To 20.00
Tumbler, 4 In...............13.50
Vase, Footed,
    8 1/2 In........ 15.00 To 18.00

Swirl Fire-King

Swirl Fire-King is named for its wide swirled border. It was made in blue, jadite, pink, white with gold trim, and ivory with trim from 1955 to the 1960s. Other related sections in this book are Alice, Fire-King, Jane-Ray, Square, and Turquoise Blue.

BLUE ——

Bowl, 4 7/8 In. 3.00
Creamer..................... 3.00
Cup......................... 2.50
Cup & Saucer................ 3.50
Plate, 9 1/8 In.............. 4.00
Saucer........................ .75

IVORY ——

Bowl, 4 7/8 In. 1.50
Platter, 12 In................ 5.00

JADITE ——

Bowl, 4 7/8 In. 3.00
Cup & Saucer................ 3.00

PINK ——

Creamer..................... 2.50
Plate, 6 7/8 In............... 3.50
Saucer........................ 1.00

WHITE ——

Bowl, 4 7/8 In. ....1.50 To 2.50
Creamer............2.00 To 3.00
Cup & Saucer................ 3.00
Plate, 6 7/8 In............... 1.50
Plate, 9 1/8 In......3.00 To 4.00

Sugar 3.00

**SWIRLED BIG RIB, see
Spiral**

**SWIRLED SHARP RIB,
see Diana**

Sylvan

Sylvan is often called Parrot or Three Parrot because of the center pattern on the plates. It was made by Federal Glass Company in 1931 and 1932 in amber, blue, crystal, and green.

AMBER

Bowl, 5 In. 10.00
Dish, Jam 48.00
Grill Plate .... 12.00 To 18.00
Sherbet 14.00
Soup, Dish................. 23.00

GREEN

Bowl, 5 In. 21.00
Bowl, 8 In. 55.00
Bowl, Vegetable, Oval,
10 In. 35.00
Butter...................... 15.00
Creamer..................... 25.00
Cup 30.00
Cup & Saucer............... 33.00
Grill Plate 25.00
Plate,
7 1/2 In........ 17.00 To 25.00
Plate, 9 In........ 32.00 To 35.00
Platter, Oval, 11 1/4 In. ...27.00

TASSELL, see Princess

Tea Room

The very Art Deco design of Tea Room has made it popular with a group of collectors; it is even called Moderne Art by some. The Indiana Glass Company, Dunkirk, Indiana, made it from 1926 to 1931. Dinner sets were made in amber, crystal, green, and pink glass.

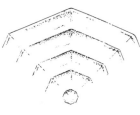

CRYSTAL

Dish, Sundae, Footed 30.00
Mustard,
Cover.......... 80.00 To 100.00
Sugar & Creamer 20.00
Sugar, Cover............... 33.00

Sherbet .... 10.00 To 17.00

Vase, 11 In. 125.00
Vase, Ruffled, 6 1/2 In.....24.00

GREEN

Bowl, Oval, 9 1/2 In.......50.00
Cake Plate, 2 Handles,
10 In. 65.00
Dish, Sundae,
Footed.......... 55.00 To 70.00
Ice Bucket 120.00
Lamp, Electric............. 115.00
Salt & Pepper.............. 45.00
Sugar & Creamer,
4 1/2 In........ 30.00 To 32.00
Sugar, 3 In.................. 10.00
Sugar, 4 In.................. 13.50
Vase, Ruffled, 6 1/2 In.....85.00
Vase, Ruffled,
9 1/2 In................. 195.00

PINK

Goblet, 9 Oz..... 40.00 To 50.00
Ice Bucket 90.00
Sugar & Creamer,
4 1/2 In................... 28.00
Sugar, 3 1/2 In............. 10.00
Sugar, 4 In....... 10.00 To 13.00
Tumbler, Footed, 12 Oz. ...35.00

Tear Drop

Tear Drop, a pattern available in full dinnerware sets, was made by Duncan and Miller Glass Company, Washington, Pennsylvania, from 1934 to 1955. It was made only in crystal.

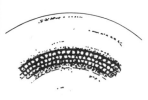

CRYSTAL

Ashtray, Individual, Round,
3 In........................9.00

Bowl, Flared, Flower,
11 1/2 In.................32.00

Bowl, Oval, 6 In...........20.00

Butter.......................18.50

Candleholder, 2-Light,
Pair.......................47.00

Candy Dish, Heart Shape,
7 1/2 In..................20.00

Champagne, 5 In............10.00

Compote, Cheese, 6 In......20.00

Cruet, 3 Piece 36.00

Cup & Saucer................7.50

Dish, Mayonnaise,
2 Piece 27.00

Dish, Nut, Individual,
6 In........................3.25

Goblet, 4 3/4 In............16.00

Goblet, 7 In................12.00

Ice Bucket, Footed..........37.00

Jam Jar, Cover 40.00

Lazy Susan, 16 In. 85.00

Pitcher, Amber Handle,
2 Qt. 95.00

Plate, 4 Handles, 7 In......50.00

Plate, 4 Handles,
13 In. .... 30.00 To 35.00

Plate, 6 1/4 In.............10.00

Plate, 7 1/2 In.............. 5.00

Plate, 15 In. 32.00

Relish, 2 Sections, Heart Shape,
7 1/2 In..................10.00

Relish, Divided, 6 In........15.00

Salt & Pepper..............12.50

Sugar & Creamer 12.00

Sweetmeat, Center Handle,
6 1/2 In..................30.00

Tumbler, 4 1/2 In..........7.50

Thistle

Thistle pattern was made by Macbeth-Evans Glass Company from 1929 to 1930. The pattern pictured large thistles on green, crystal, pink, and yellow dishes.

CRYSTAL

Bowl, 5 1/2 In. 6.00

Tumbler, 5 1/4 In..........22.00

GREEN

Cake Plate, 15 In. 50.00

Cup..........................18.00

Grill Plate, 10 1/4 In.......11.00

Plate, 8 In..................12.00

PINK

Bowl, 5 1/2 In. ...8.00 To 15.00

Cup..........................13.50

Plate, 8 In.................. 7.00

Saucer..............7.50 To 8.00

THREADING, see Old English

THREE PARROT, see Sylvan

THUMBPRINT, see Pear Optic

Tradition

Imperial Glass Company of Bellaire, Ohio, made Tradition pattern glass in the 1930s. It was made in amber, amethyst, blue, crystal, green, pink, and red.

AMBER

Sherbet 7.00

Tumbler, 12 Oz.....6.00 To 9.50

AMETHYST

Sherbet 4.00

BLUE

Goblet, 10 Oz.... 12.00 To 18.00

Pitcher,
Water.........145.00 To 175.00

Plate, 8 In..................20.00

Sherbet 19.00

Tumbler,
12 Oz.......... 22.00 To 30.00

CRYSTAL

Bowl, 6 In. 6.00

Plate, 8 In.................. 4.00

GREEN

Goblet, 10 Oz...............12.00

Pitcher, Water 125.00

Plate, 8 In..................14.00

Sherbet 8.00
Tumbler, 12 Oz. 18.00

PINK

Goblet, 10 Oz. . . . 15.00 To 18.00
Plate, 8 In. 19.00
Sherbet 13.00
Tumbler,
12 Oz. . . . . 12.00 To 20.00

RED

Goblet, 10 Oz. . . . . . . 4.00 To 9.50
Sherbet . . . . 12.00 To 15.00

Trojan

The Fostoria Glass Company made Trojan. The etched glass dishes were made in rose from 1929 to 1935, topaz from 1929 to 1938, and gold tint from 1938 to 1944. Crystal bases were used on some pieces from 1931 to 1944.

ROSE

Goblet, 5 1/4 In. 27.50
Ice Dish Liner, Tomato 37.00
Mayonnaise Set,
3 Piece 125.00
Plate, 6 In. 6.00
Sherbet, 4 1/4 In. 18.00
Soup, Cream 24.00
Sugar, Footed 27.50
Vase, 8 In. . . . . . 120.00 To 175.00

TOPAZ

Bonbon 29.50
Bowl, 2 Handles, 9 In. 35.00
Bowl, 5 In. 17.50
Bowl, Vegetable, Oval,
9 In. 75.00
Cake Plate, Handle,
10 In. 35.00
Candleholder, 2 In., Pair . . . 30.00
Candleholder, 5 In., Pair . . . 39.00
Candy Dish, Cover 150.00
Celery, 11 1/2 In. 32.50
Chop Plate, 13 In. 35.00
Compote, 5 In. 36.00
Compote, 6 In. 28.00
Console, 12 In. 25.00
Cruet, Stopper 350.00
Cup 12.00
Cup & Saucer. . . . 16.00 To 20.00
Cup & Saucer,
After Dinner 49.50
Dish, Sweetmeat 25.00
Finger Bowl, 6 1/4 In. 22.00
Goblet, 4 In. 33.00
Goblet, 5 1/2 In. 33.00
Goblet, 6 In. 31.00
Goblet,
8 1/4 In. . . . . 20.00 To 27.50
Ice Bucket, With Bail 65.00
Mayonnaise Set, 3 Piece . . . 95.00
Oyster Cocktail, Footed 22.50
Parfait. . . . . 33.00 To 49.50
Plate, 6 In. . . . . 2.00 To 7.50
Plate, 7 1/2 In. 8.00
Plate, 8 3/4 In. . . . . . 6.50 To 9.50
Platter, Oval, 12 In. 45.00
Relish, 2 Sections,
8 3/4 In. 35.00

Sherbet, 4 1/4 In. 14.00
Sherbet, 6 In. . . . . . 11.00 To 15.00
Soup, Cream 17.00
Tumbler, 5 1/4 In. 17.00
Tumbler, 6 In. 22.00
Tumbler, Footed,
4 1/2 In. 20.00
Tumbler, Footed,
5 1/4 In. . . . . 13.00 To 18.00
Tumbler, Footed,
6 In. . . . . 16.00 To 17.00

Tulip

Tulip pattern pictures the side of a tulip in a very stylized border. It was made by the Dell Glass Company of Millville, New Jersey, during the 1930s. Amber, amethyst, blue, crystal, and green pieces were made.

AMETHYST

Bowl, Oval, 13 In. 40.00
Console Set, 3 Piece 68.00
Plate, 10 1/2 In. 17.00
Whiskey 11.00

CRYSTAL

Juice Set 12.00

GREEN

Sugar 10.00

Turquoise Blue

Turquoise Blue, one of the patterns made by Anchor Hocking Glass Company, is a plain pattern named for its color. It was made in the 1950s. Related sections in this book are Alice, Fire-King, Jadite, Jane-Ray, Square, and Swirl Fire-King.

Bowl, 4 1/2 In. ....3.00 To 4.00
Bowl, 5 In. 4.50
Bowl, 8 1/4 In. 9.00
Bowl, 9 1/2 In. 12.00
Bowl, Vegetable, 8 In........9.00
Creamer...................... 3.50
Cup .... 1.50 To 3.00
Cup & Saucer.......2.50 To 5.00
Egg Plate 10.00
Mixing Bowl, 1 Qt.......... 7.00
Mixing Bowl,
  2 Qt. ....7.00 To 9.00
Mixing Bowl,
  3 Qt. ....8.00 To 15.00
Mug ....5.00 To 7.50
Plate, 6 1/8 In......2.50 To 4.00
Plate, 7 In...........3.50 To 4.50
Plate, 9 In...........4.00 To 7.00
Plate, 10 In. ..... 15.00 To 17.00
Relish, 3 Sections 8.00
Relish, 3 Sections,
  Gold Trim................15.00
Saucer................ .50 To 1.50
Sugar ....3.50 To 3.75
Sugar & Creamer 7.75

Twisted Optic

Twisted Optic is the pattern sometimes confused with Spiral. Be sure to look at the information about that pattern. Imperial Glass Company made Twisted Optic from 1927 to 1930 in amber, blue, canary yellow, green, and pink.

Bowl, 7 In. 18.00
Plate, 6 In...........2.00 To 4.00
Plate, Oval, 9 In. 4.00
Sherbet 5.00

GREEN

Bowl, 7 In. 17.50
Candleholder................. 5.00
Cup 5.00
Plate, 8 In.................... 2.00

PINK

Cup 5.00
Plate, 6 In.................... 2.00
Plate, 8 In.................... 3.00

YELLOW

Plate, 7 In.................... 2.00
Sherbet 4.00

V

VERNON, see No. 616

Versailles

Versailles by Fostoria Glass Company was made in many colors during the years of its production, 1928 to 1944. Azure blue, green, and rose were made from 1928 to 1944, topaz from 1929 to 1938, and gold tint from 1938 to 1944. Crystal bases were used with colored glass from 1931 to 1944.

BLUE

Baker, Oval, 9 In. 55.00
Bonbon 42.50
Bouillon 47.50
Bowl, 5 In. ...... 20.00 To 30.00
Bowl, 6 In. 60.00
Candleholder, 3 In., Pair ...60.00
Candleholder, 5 In.,
  Pair............. 35.00 To 50.00
Celery, 11 1/2 In...........75.00
Champagne, 6 In...........37.50
Cheese & Cracker Set,
  11 In. ....65.00 To 145.00
Compote, 6 In. 95.00
Compote, 7 In. 65.00
Creamer.....................35.00
Cup & Saucer...............27.00
Cup & Saucer,
  After Dinner 75.00
Dish, Sweetmeat 42.50
Finger Bowl 30.00
Goblet, 8 1/4 In...........42.00
Ice Bucket .....100.00 To 125.00
Mayonnaise Set,
  3 Piece 150.00
Oyster Cocktail 45.00
Pitcher.................... 350.00
Plate, 8 3/4 In.............12.50
Plate, 9 1/2 In.............20.00
Plate,
  10 1/4 In....... 45.00 To 75.00
Plate, 13 1/2 In. 125.00
Plate, Handle, 9 In. 125.00

Platter, 12 In.............. 125.00
Relish, Divided,
    8 1/2 In.................50.00
Salt & Pepper............. 225.00
Salt & Pepper, Footed 110.00
Sandwich Server,
    Center Handle.............75.00
Sherbet 27.50
Soup, Cream................25.00
Sugar 35.00
Sugar & Creamer,
    Individual............... 175.00
Sugar Pail................ 225.00
Tumbler, 4 1/2 In.........40.00
Tumbler, Footed,
    5 1/4 In.................29.50
Tumbler, Footed, 6 In. 37.50
Whipped Cream Pail........95.00
Wine.......................85.00

GREEN

Bowl, 9 In. 65.00
Candy Dish, Cover 125.00
Creamer....................35.00
Cup & Saucer..............25.00
Cup & Saucer,
    After Dinner 49.50
Finger Bowl, Underplate....38.00
Goblet, 4 In.................85.00
Plate, 10 1/4 In. 49.50
Sandwich Server,
    Center Handle.............55.00
Sugar Pail................ 150.00
Sugar, Cover, Flat Top.... 175.00
Sugar, Individual...........47.50

ROSE

Ashtray 45.00
Bouillon 29.50
Compote, 7 In. 47.50
Creamer, Individual........47.50
Dish, Grapefruit, Insert ... 125.00
Goblet, 5 1/4 In...........35.00
Gravy Boat,
    Underplate 175.00
Salt & Pepper, Footed 125.00
Saucer....................... 5.00
Sugar Pail................ 150.00
Sugar, Cover............. 135.00
Sugar, Individual...........30.00

TOPAZ

Bonbon 29.50
Bouillon 22.00
Bowl, 5 In. 18.00
Bowl, Lemon 19.50
Bowl, Vegetable, Footed, Oval,
    9 In.........................35.00
Candy Dish, Cover 185.00
Compote, 6 In. 35.00
Console 65.00
Cup & Saucer,
    After Dinner 49.50
Dish, Grapefruit, Liner ... 125.00
Finger Bowl 20.00
Finger Bowl, Underplate....27.50
Goblet, 4 In.................60.00
Goblet, 5 1/2 In...........45.00
Goblet, 6 In...... 42.00 To 45.00
Goblet, 8 1/4 In...........27.50
Ice Bucket .... 65.00 To 95.00
Mayonnaise Set,
    3 Piece 110.00
Oyster Cocktail 18.00
Plate, 6 In................... 5.00
Plate, 7 1/2 In.............. 7.50
Plate, 8 3/4 In.............. 9.50
Sherbet, 4 1/4 In. 18.00
Sugar, Individual...........47.50
Whiskey....................39.50

VERTICAL RIBBED, see Queen Mary

Vesper

Vesper was made by the Fostoria Glass Company of Ohio and West Virginia from 1926 to 1934. Dinner sets were made in amber, blue, crystal, and green.

• • • • • • • • • • • • • • •

If you discover a cache of very dirty antiques and you are not dressed in work clothes, make a temporary cover up from a plastic garbage bag.

• • • • • • • • • • • • • • •

AMBER

Bowl, 6 1/2 In. 24.00
Bowl, Oval, 11 In...........58.00
Butter......................40.00
Cake Plate 165.00
Candleholder, 2 In., Pair ...40.00
Candleholder, 4 In.,
    Pair............. 22.00 To 30.00
Candy Dish, Cover 145.00
Cocktail, 3 Oz.... 15.00 To 20.00
Compote, 7 In. 45.00
Compote, Rolled, 11 In.....35.00
Compote, Rolled, 13 In.....65.00
Cordial, 2 1/2 Oz...........85.00
Creamer,
    Footed.......... 15.00 To 20.00
Cup & Saucer.... 18.00 To 22.50
Cup & Saucer,
    After Dinner 30.00
Decanter, 30 Oz. 50.00
Dish,
    Grapefruit ...... 35.00 To 40.00
Dish, Grapefruit,
    Liner .... 45.00 To 60.00

Goblet, 9 Oz..... 17.00 To 22.00
Goblet, 12 Oz.... 15.00 To 27.50
Ice Bucket .... 37.50 To 75.00
Pitcher.................... 265.00
Plate, 6 In.................... 5.00
Plate, 7 1/2 In............... 7.50
Plate, 8 1/2 In.............10.00
Plate,
  10 1/2 In...... 30.00 To 35.00
Platter, Oval, 15 In. 150.00
Sherbet 15.00
Sugar & Creamer, Footed...35.00
Sugar, Footed...............17.50
Tumbler, Footed, 5 Oz.....18.00
Tumbler, Footed, 12 Oz. ...22.50
Urn, Small 150.00
Water Set, Footed,
  7 Piece 285.00

BLUE ───────────────

Bowl, 5 1/2 In. 15.00
Tumbler, Footed, 5 Oz......15.00
Vase, 8 In................. 130.00

CRYSTAL ───────────────

Parfait.......................25.00
Plate, 8 1/2 In............... 7.50
Sherbet 10.00

GREEN ───────────────

Boullion,
  Footed.......... 16.00 To 22.50
Bowl, 5 1/2 In. 14.00
Bowl, 6 1/2 In. 20.00
Candleholder, 2 In., Pair ...37.50
Candleholder, 3 1/2 In.,
  Pair.........................39.00
Candy Dish, Cover 125.00
Celery, 11 In................37.00
Chop Plate, Round,
  13 In. 55.00
Compote, 6 In. 16.00
Compote,
  8 In............. 37.00 To 45.00
Creamer......................18.00
Cup & Saucer.... 12.00 To 22.50
Finger Bowl 18.00
Goblet, 2 3/4 Oz...........37.50
Gravy Boat,
  Underplate 145.00

Ice Bucket 75.00
Plate, 6 In.................... 4.50
Plate, 7 1/2 In............... 6.50
Plate, 8 1/2 In.............10.00
Plate,
  9 1/2 In........ 12.00 To 17.50
Plate, 10 1/2 In. 29.50
Platter, 10 1/2 In...........47.00
Platter, 12 In................60.00
Platter, 15 In.............. 125.00
Sandwich Server, Center Handle,
  11 In. 35.00
Sherbet 18.00
Soup, Cream 17.50
Sugar & Creamer,
  Cover.................... 175.00
Sugar, Footed...............17.50
Tumbler, 5 Oz..............22.50
Tumbler, 12 Oz.............29.50
Vase, 8 In................. 125.00
Whiskey, 2 1/2 Oz. 45.00

Victory

The Diamond Glass-Ware Company, Indiana, Pennsylvania, made Victory pattern from 1929 to 1932. It is known in amber, black, cobalt blue, green, and pink. A few pieces have gold trim.

AMBER ───────────────

Bowl, 6 1/2 In. 7.00
Bowl, Vegetable, Oval,
  9 In............. 24.00 To 30.00
Creamer......................12.00
Cup & Saucer.......6.00 To 8.00

Sandwich Server,
  Center Handle.............20.00

BLACK ───────────────

Cup & Saucer...............26.00
Plate, 8 In...................11.00
Sandwich Server,
  Center Handle.............40.00
Sugar & Creamer 60.00

BLUE ───────────────

Cheese & Cracker Set.......50.00

GREEN ───────────────

Bowl, 6 1/2 In. 9.00
Creamer......................17.00
Cup & Saucer.......6.00 To 9.00
Plate, 6 In...........2.00 To 3.00
Plate, 8 In................... 5.50
Plate, 9 In........ 10.00 To 17.00
Sandwich Server,
  Center Handle.............21.00
Saucer........................ 1.50
Sugar, Footed...............15.00

PINK ───────────────

Bowl, 6 1/2 In. 9.50
Cup 7.00
Cup & Saucer................ 9.00
Dish, Mayonnaise, Liner 27.00
Plate, 8 In...........5.00 To 6.00
Plate, 9 In...................15.00
Platter, 12 In................22.00
Sandwich Server,
  Center Handle.... 18.00 To 24.00

Vitrock

Vitrock is both a kitchenware and a dinnerware pattern. It has a raised flowered rim and so is often called Floral Rim or Flower Rim by collectors. It was made by Hocking Glass Company from 1934 to 1937. It was made of white with fired-on colors, solid red, green, and decal-decorated centers.

WHITE

Bowl, 5 1/8 In.	3.00
Bowl, 6 In.	9.25
Bowl, 9 1/2 In.	15.00
Creamer.	2.25
Cup	3.25
Plate, 10 In.	9.50
Platter, 11 1/2 In.	19.00
Soup, Cream	9.50
Soup, Dish, 9 In.	15.00
Sugar	2.50

VIVID BANDS, see Petalware

WAFFLE, see Waterford

Waterford

Waterford, or Waffle, pattern was made by Anchor Hocking Glass Company from 1938 to 1944. It was made in crystal, pink, yellow, and white. In the 1950s some forest green pieces were made.

CRYSTAL

Ashtray	3.00
Bowl, 4 3/4 In.	3.00 To 6.00
Bowl, 5 1/2 In.	6.50 To 14.00
Bowl, 8 1/4 In.	7.00
Butter, Cover	20.00 To 25.00
Cake Plate, Handle, 10 1/4 In.	9.00
Coaster, 4 In.	1.00 To 4.00
Creamer.	3.50
Cup	6.00
Cup & Saucer	5.00 To 8.50
Goblet, 5 1/4 In.	9.00 To 12.00
Pitcher, 42 Oz.	12.00
Plate, 6 In.	1.50
Plate, 7 1/8 In.	2.00 To 4.50
Plate, 9 5/8 In.	5.00 To 8.50
Relish	12.00
Salt & Pepper, Bell	7.50
Salt & Pepper, Metal Tops	5.00
Salt & Pepper, Red Plastic Tops	5.00
Saucer.	1.00 To 2.50
Sherbet, Footed	3.00 To 6.50
Sugar & Creamer, Cover.	4.00 To 5.00
Tray, Handle	5.00
Tumbler, Footed, 4 7/8 In.	7.50 To 8.50
Water Set, 9 Piece	65.00

GREEN

Cup & Saucer	5.00

PINK

Ashtray	15.00
Bowl, 4 3/4 In.	8.00 To 9.00
Bowl, 5 1/2 In.	16.00
Butter, Cover	185.00
Cup & Saucer	14.00
Pitcher, 80 Oz.	110.00
Plate, 9 5/8 In.	14.00
Tumbler, Footed, 4 7/8 In.	12.00 To 15.00

WEDDING BAND, see Moderntone

WESTMORELAND SANDWICH, see Princess Feather

Whirly-Twirly

Anchor Hocking made Whirly-Twirly pattern in the 1940s. It was forest green or red.

GREEN

Pitcher, 3 Qt.	27.00
Tumbler, 12 Oz.	7.00
Water Set, 7 Piece	60.00

WHITE SAIL, see White Ship

White Ship

White Ship, also called Sailing Ship, Sail Boat, or White Sail, is really part of the Sportsman series made by Hazel-Atlas in

1938. The ships are enamel decorations on cobalt blue glass.

BLUE

Ashtray, Metal Sail.........52.00

Ashtray, Silver Boats,
Round....................20.00

Cocktail Shaker,
Stirrer .... 17.00 To 30.00

Ice Bowl....................23.00

Pitcher,
36 Oz.......... 40.00 To 45.00

Pitcher, Ice Lip, 80 Oz......32.00

Plate, 8 In........ 15.00 To 16.00

Plate, 9 In..................30.00

Tumbler,
3 3/4 In..........6.00 To 13.00

Tumbler,
3 3/8 In........ 10.00 To 16.00

Tumbler,
4 5/8 In.........6.00 To 12.50

Tumbler, 4 7/8 In..........10.00

Tumbler, Roly Poly,
6 Oz..............7.00 To 14.00

Water Set, 7 Piece........ 110.00

WILDFLOWER, see No. 618

WILDROSE, see Dogwood

WILDROSE WITH APPLE BLOSSOM, see Flower Garden with Butterflies

Windmill

Windmill, or Dutch, is a part of the Sportsman series made by Hazel-Atlas in 1938. Of course it pictures a landscape with a windmill.

BLUE

Cocktail Shaker..... 15.00 To 24.00

Ice Bowl......... 15.00 To 23.00

Tumbler, 3 3/4 In........... 8.00

Tumbler, 4 5/8 In........... 8.00

Tumbler, Roly Poly,
6 Oz....................... 7.00

Tumbler, Roly Poly,
8 Oz....................... 7.00

Windsor

Windsor pattern, also called Diamond, Smocking, or Windsor Diamond, was made by Jeannette Glass Company, Jeannette, Pennsylvania, from 1936 to 1946. The pattern is most easily found in crystal, green, and pink, although pieces were made of amberina, blue, delphite, and red.

• • • • • • • • • • • • • •

Check the metal strips holding any heavy wall-hung shelves. After a few years, the shelf holder may develop "creep" and gradually bend away from the wall.

• • • • • • • • • • • • • •

CRYSTAL

Bowl, 4 3/4 In. 6.75

Bowl, 8 1/2 In. 8.00

Butter, Cover .... 18.00 To 22.00

Candleholder, 3 In., Pair ...14.00

Chop Plate, 13 5/8 In......10.00

Creamer, Footed 5.00

Cup........................... 2.00

Cup & Saucer................ 4.50

Pitcher, 4 1/2 In............16.00

Plate, Closed Handle,
10 1/4 In................... 8.00

Relish, Divided,
11 1/2 In................... 8.00

Salt & Pepper...............12.00

Sherbet 6.00

Sugar & Creamer, Cover..... 7.50

Sugar, Cover........2.00 To 8.00

Tumbler, 3 1/4 In........... 6.50

Tumbler, Footed,
5 In................5.00 To 6.50

GREEN

Ashtray, 5 3/4 In..........42.50

Bowl, 5 3/8 In. 16.00
Butter......................30.00
Chop Plate, 13 5/8 In. 12.50
Coaster, 3 1/4 In. 15.00
Cup & Saucer.... 10.00 To 11.00
Salt & Pepper.... 30.00 To 34.50
Soup, Cream................30.00
Sugar & Creamer 18.00
Tray, Square,
  8 1/2 X 9 3/4 In. 35.00
Tumbler, 3 In...............25.00
Tumbler, 7 1/4 In..........22.00

PINK

Ashtray,
  5 3/4 In........ 28.00 To 35.00
Bowl, 12 1/2 In. 75.00
Bowl, 3-Footed,
  7 1/2 In...................20.00
Bowl, 4 3/4 In. 14.00
Bowl, 5 3/8 In. 17.00
Bowl, 8 1/2 In. 12.00
Bowl, Handle, 9 In. 13.00
Butter......................19.50
Butter, Cover .... 30.00 To 40.00
Cake Plate, Footed,
  10 3/4 In....... 11.50 To 15.00
Candleholder, 3 In., Pair ...85.00
Chop Plate,
  13 5/8 In....... 25.00 To 30.00
Coaster, 3 1/4 In. 13.50
Creamer............. 8.00 To 9.00
Cup ....6.00 To 8.00
Cup & Saucer...............11.00
Pitcher,
  6 3/4 In........ 18.00 To 25.00
Plate, 6 In...........2.50 To 3.00
Plate, 7 In..........9.00 To 15.00
Plate, 9 In..........9.00 To 11.50
Platter, Oval, 11 1/2 In. 9.00
Salt & Pepper.... 20.00 To 35.00
Sandwich Server, Handle,
  10 1/4 In...................9.00
Sherbet ....6.00 To 9.50

Soup, Cream..... 13.00 To 20.00
Sugar, Cover..... 17.50 To 18.00
Tray, 8 1/2 X 9 3/4 In. ...30.00
Tumbler,
  3 1/2 In........ 14.50 To 20.00
Tumbler, 4 In......8.50 To 10.00
Tumbler, 5 In.... 22.00 To 25.00
Tumbler, 7 1/4 In..........15.00

WINDSOR DIAMOND,
  see Windsor

WINGED MEDALLION,
  see Madrid

Woolworth

Woolworth was made by Westmoreland Glass Company, Grapeville, Pennsylvania, in the early 1930s. The design, showing bunches of grapes, was also called Oregon Grape, but it is not the same as the pattern just called Grape. It was made of crystal, blue, green, and pink glass.

GREEN

Pitcher......................25.00

PINK

Tumbler 11.00

 X

X Design

X Design, or Criss Cross, was a Hazel-Atlas pattern made from 1928 to 1932. The name indicates that the pattern has rows of X's in grids. It was made in crystal, green, pink, and white opaque glass. Only a breakfast set was made.

CRYSTAL

Bowl, 6 1/2 In. 8.00
Butter, Cover 15.00
Relish, 4 X 8 In. 8.00
Shaker, Malt,
  Embossed Baby's Face.....65.00

GREEN

Butter, 1 Lb.................25.00
Butter, Cover, 1/4 Lb. 40.00

PINK

Reamer, Orange 175.00

DEPRESSION GLASS
Reproductions

PATTERN	OBJECT	COLORS	DATES
Adam	Butter dish	Green, pink	1981
American	Two-piece candle night light		1987
Avocado	Cup and saucer, handled dish, nappy, pickle, pitcher, sugar and creamer	Blue, burnt honey, frosted pink, pink, red amethyst, yellow	1974
Avocado	Pitcher	Green	1979
Avocado	Berry, olive, 5 1/2-inch plate, relish, sundae, tumbler	Amber, amethyst, blue, frosted pink, green, pink, red amethyst, red-yellow	1974
Bubble	Ashtray, bowl, ivy ball, punch cup, vase	Red	1977-1978
Cameo	Children's dishes	Green, pink, yellow	1982
Cameo	Salt & pepper shakers	Green	1982
Cameo	Salt & pepper shakers	Pink	1989
Candlewick	Bowl, candelabra, cup & saucer, cream & sugar, 2-handled jelly, plate, basket	Alexandrite, blue, pink	1987
Cape Cod	Cruet		1986
Cape Cod	Dinner set		1978
Caprice	Butter, cream & sugar, footed juice, footed water glass, relish, square dish	Cobalt, light blue	1985
Cherry Blossom	Almost all items have been reproduced in various colors since 1972		
Diana	Bowl	Pink	1986
Early American Sandwich	Ashtray, berry set, bowl, bridge set, napkin holder, platter, pitcher, snack set, 3-part relish, tidbit, tumbler, vase, basket, boxes, candleholder	Amber, light green	1982
English Hobnail	18 pieces	Red	1980

PATTERN	OBJECT	COLORS	DATES
English Hobnail	26 pieces	Pink	1983
English Hobnail	Pedestal salt dip		1986
Floral	Shaker	Cobalt blue, dark green, pink	1989
Florentine No. 1	Shaker	Cobalt blue, pink	1989
Hazel Atlas Quilt	Kitchen shaker	pink	1987
Heritage	5-inch bowl	Amber, crystal	1987
Iris	Candy dish (bottom only), vase	Multicolored	1976
Iris	Various items	Crystal	1969
Iris	Various items	Milk glass and sprayed-on colors	1970
Madrid (called Recollection)	Various items	Blue, crystal, pink	1982
Madrid	Dinner set	Amber	1976-1979
Mayfair Open Rose	Cookie jar	Amethyst, green, pink	1982
Mayfair Open Rose	Cookie jar	Cobalt blue	1990
Mayfair Open Rose	Salt & pepper shakers	Green, pink	1989
Mayfair Open Rose	Shot glass	Blue, cobalt blue, green, pink	1977
Miss America	Butter dish	Amberina, crystal, green, ice blue, pink	1977
Miss America	Pitcher, tumbler	Crystal, green	1982
Miss America	Salt & pepper shakers	Crystal, green, pink	1977
Miss America	Various items	Cobalt blue	1987
No. 610	Berry bowl, relish, tray, tumbler	Black, blue	1974
Princess Feather	1- and 2-piece reamers, "Gillespie" measuring cup	Various colors	1986
Royal Ruby	Tumblers: 7-ounce, 9-ounce, 12-ounce, 16-ounce	Red	1977-1978
Sandwich Anchor Hocking	Covered cookie jar	Crystal	1977
Sandwich Indiana	Basket, bridge set, candleholder, goblets, napkin holder, nappy, punch set, snack set, tidbit, vase, wine set	Amber	1982
Sandwich Indiana	Basket, candleholder, snack set, wine set	Light green	1982

PATTERN	OBJECT	COLORS	DATES
Sandwich Indiana	Dinner set	Amber, crystal, dark blue, red	1969
Sandwich Indiana	Various items	Amber, blue, crystal, green, red	
Sharon	Butter dish	Amber, blue, dark green, light green, pink	1976
Sharon	Covered candy dish	Green, pink	1984
Sharon	Covered candy dish	Cobalt blue	1990
Sharon	Cheese dish	Blue, burnt umber, green, pink	1977
Sharon	Salt & pepper shakers	Green, pink, and other colors	1980
Sharon	Covered sugar & creamer	Pink, green	1982
Shirley Temple	Milk pitcher, mug	Cobalt blue	1982
Shirley Temple	6 1/2-inch bowl		1986

DEPRESSION GLASS
Factories

NAME	LOCATION	DATES	
Akro Agate	Clarksburg, West Virginia	1914–1951	
Bartlett-Collins	Sapulpa, Oklahoma	1914-present	
Belmont Tumbler Company	Bellaire, Ohio	c.1920–1952	
Cambridge Glass Company	Cambridge, Ohio	1901–1958	
Central Glass Works	Wheeling, West Virginia	1860s–1939	
Consolidated Lamp & Glass Company	Coraopolis, Pennsylvania	1894–1933; 1936–1967	
Co-Operative Flint Glass Company	Beaver Falls, Pennsylvania	1879–1934	
Dell Glass Company	Millville, New Jersey	1930s	
Diamond Glass-Ware Company	Indiana, Pennsylvania	1891–1931	
Dunbar Flint Glass Corporation/Dunbar Glass Corporation	Dunbar, West Virginia	1913–1953	
Duncan & Miller Glass Company	Washington, Pennsylvania	1893–1955	
Federal Glass Company	Columbus, Ohio	1900–1971	
Fenton Art Glass Company	Williamstown, West Virginia	1906–present	
Fostoria Glass Company	Fostoria, Ohio; Moundsville, West Virginia	1887–1986	
Hazel Atlas Glass Company	Washington, Pennsylvania; Zanesville, Ohio; Clarksburg, West Virginia; Wheeling, West Virginia	1902–1956	
A. H. Heisey & Company	Newark, Ohio	1893–1956	
Hocking Glass Company/Anchor Hocking Glass Corporation	Lancaster, Ohio	1905–present (Anchor Hocking from 1937)	
Imperial Glass Company	Bellaire, Ohio	1904–1982	

95

NAME	LOCATION	DATES	
Indiana Glass Company	Dunkirk, Indiana	1907–present	
Jeannette Glass Company	Jeannette, Pennsylvania	c.1900–present	
Jenkins Glass Company	Kokomo Indiana; Arcadia, Indiana	1901–1932	
Lancaster Glass Company	Lancaster, Ohio	1908–1937	
Libbey Glass Company	Toledo, Ohio	1892–present	
Liberty Works	Egg Harbor, New Jersey	1903–1932	
Louie Glass Company	Weston, West Virginia	1926–present	
Macbeth-Evans Glass Company	(several factories); Toledo, Ohio; Charleroi, Pennsylvania; Corning, New York	1899–1936 (acquired by Corning)	
McKee Glass Company	Jeannette, Pennsylvania	1853–1961	
Morgantown Glass Works	Morgantown, West Virginia	Late 1800s–1972	
New Martinsville Glass Manufacturing Company	New Martinsville, West Virginia	1901–1944	
Paden City Glass Manufacturing Company	Paden City, West Virginia	1916–1951	
Seneca Glass Company	Fostoria, Ohio; Morgantown, West Virginia	1891–present	
Silex (division of Macbeth-Evans)	Corning, New York	mid-1930s	
L. E. Smith Glass Company	Mt. Pleasant, Pennsylvania	1907–present	
Standard Glass Manufacturing Company (Subsidiary of Hocking/Anchor Hocking)		1924–present	
United States Glass Company	Pennsylvania (several factories); Tiffin, Ohio; Gas City, Indiana	1891–1966	
Westmoreland Glass Company	Grapeville, Pennsylvania	1890–1985	

Pattern List

Note: (R) = pattern has been reproduced
* = Prices & paragraph in body of book

PATTERN NAME	CROSS-REFERENCE	MANUFACTURER AND DATES	COLORS AND DESCRIPTION
ABC Stork		Belmont	Crystal, green; child's plate
Accordion Pleats	See Round Robin		
*Adam (R)	Chain Daisy; Fan & Feather	Jeannette, 1932-1934	Crystal, delphite, green, pink, yellow
Aero Optic		Cambridge, 1929	Crystal, emerald, Peach-blo, Willow Blue
Afghan & Scottie Dog		Hazel Atlas, 1938	Blue with white decorations
*Akro Agate		Akro Agate, 1932-1951	Marbleized colored glass
*Alice	See also Fire-King Oven Ware; Jadite; Jane-Ray; Square; Swirl Fire-King; Turquoise Blue	Anchor Hocking, 1940s	Jadite, opaque white; blue, pink borders
*Alpine Caprice	See also Caprice	Cambridge, 1936	Blue, crystal, pink; satin finish
*American (R)	Fostoria	Fostoria, 1915-1986	Amber, blue, crystal, green, milk glass, yellow
American Beauty	See English Hobnail		
*American Pioneer		Liberty Works, 1931-1934	Amber, crystal, green, pink
*American Sweetheart	Lily Medallion	Macbeth-Evans, 1930-1936	Blue, Cremax, Monax, pink, red; gold, green, pink, platinum, red, smokey black trim
Angel Fish	See Sportsman Series		
*Anniversary		Jeannette, 1947-1949; 1970s	Crystal, iridescent amber, pink
Apple-Blossom		Cambridge, 1930s	Amber, blue, crystal, dark green, light green, yellow
Apple Blossom	See Dogwood		
Apple Blossom Border	See Blossoms & Band		
April		Macbeth-Evans	Pale Pink
Aramis		Dunbar, 1936	Luster colors

PATTERN NAME	CROSS-REFERENCE	MANUFACTURER AND DATES	COLORS AND DESCRIPTION
Arcadia Lace		Jenkins, c.1930	Crystal
Arctic		Hocking, 1932	Red & white decorations
Art Moderne		Morgantown, 1929	Rose, green; black stem & foot
Artura		Indiana, c.1930	Crystal, green, pink
Athos		Dunbar, 1936	Colored stripes
*Aunt Polly		U.S. Glass, late 1920s	Blue, green, iridescent
*Aurora		Hazel Atlas, late 1930s	Cobalt blue, crystal, green, pink
Autumn		McKee, 1934	French ivory, jade green
*Avocado (R)	No. 601; Sweet Pear	Indiana Glass, 1923-1933	Crystal, green, pink
B Pattern	See Dogwood		
Ballerina	See Cameo		
*Bamboo Optic	See also Octagon Bamboo Optic	Liberty, 1929	Green, pink
Bananas		Indiana, c.1930	Green, pink
Banded Cherry	See Cherry Blossom		
Banded Fine Rib	See Coronation		
Banded Petalware	See Petalware		
Banded Rainbow	See Ring		
Banded Ribbon	See New Century		
Banded Rings	See Ring		
Barbra		Dunbar, 1928	Pink
*Baroque		Fostoria, 1936-1966	Azure, crystal, Gold Tint, ruby, topaz
Basket	See No. 615		
*Beaded Block	Frosted Block	Imperial, 1927-1930s	Amber, crystal, green, ice blue, pink, red, vaseline, white; iridescent (frosted) colors
Bee Hive	See also Queen Anne	U.S. Glass, 1926	Crystal; amber, green, pink trim
Belmont Ship Plate		Belmont	Amber, crystal, green, iridescent
Berwick	See Boopie		
Beverages with Sailboats	See White Ship		
Bibi		Anchor Hocking, 1940s	Forest green, red
Big Rib	See Manhattan		
Birch Tree	See Deerwood		
Blackberry Cluster	See Loganberry		
Blaise		Imperial, c.1930	Amber, crystal, green, Rose Marie

PATTERN NAME	CROSS-REFERENCE	MANUFACTURER AND DATES	COLORS AND DESCRIPTION
Blanche		Standard, c.1930	Crystal
Block	See Block Optic		
*Block Optic	Block	Hocking, 1929-1933	Blue, crystal, green, pink, yellow
Block with Rose	Rose Trellis	Imperial	Crystal, green, pink
Block with Snowflake	Snowflake on Block		Green, pink; plates only
Block with Windmill	See Windmill & Checkerboard		
*Blossoms & Band	Apple Blossom Border	Jenkins, 1927	Crystal, green, iridescent marigold, pink
*Boopie	Berwick	Anchor Hocking, late 1940s-1950s	Crystal, forest green, Royal Ruby; glasses
Bordette	See also Chinex Classic; Cremax Chinex, Cremax	Macbeth-Evans, 1930-1940	
Bouquet & Lattice	See Normandie		
*Bowknot		Late 1920s	Crystal, green
Bridal Bouquet	See No. 615		
Bridget		Jeannette, 1925	Green, topaz; bridge set
*Bubble (R)	Bullseye; Provincial	Anchor Hocking, 1934-1965	Crystal, dark green, milk white, pale blue, pink, ruby red, yellow
Bullseye	See Bubble		
*Burple		Anchor Hocking, 1940s	Crystal, forest green, ruby red; dessert sets, bowls
Butterflies & Roses	See Flower Garden with Butterflies		
Buttons & Bows	See Holiday		
*By Cracky		Smith, late 1920s	Amber, canary, crystal, green
Cabbage Rose	See Sharon		
Cabbage Rose with Single Arch	See Rosemary		
Camellia		Jeannette, 1947-1951	Crystal
*Cameo (R)	Ballerina; Dancing Girl	Hocking, 1930-1934	Crystal with platinum, green, pink, yellow
*Candlewick (R)		Imperial, 1937-1982	Black, blue, brown, crystal, green, lavender, pink, red, yellow; crystal with gold; fired-on gold, red, blue, green beading
*Cape Cod (R)		Imperial, 1932-1980s	Amber, azalea, cobalt blue, crystal, green, light blue, milk glass, ruby

PATTERN NAME	CROSS-REFERENCE	MANUFACTURER AND DATES	COLORS AND DESCRIPTION
*Caprice (R)	See also Alpine Caprice	Cambridge, 1936-1953	Amber, amethyst, cobalt blue, crystal, emerald green, light green, milk glass, Moonlight Blue, pink
Carolyn	See Yvonne		
*Caribbean	Wave	Duncan & Miller, 1936-1955	Amber, crystal, blue, red
Catalonian		Consolidated, 1927-1936	Amethyst, emerald green, Honey, jade, Spanish Rose
Centaur	Sphinx	Lancaster, 1930s	Green, yellow
*Century		Fostoria, 1926-1986	Crystal
Chain Daisy	See Adam		
Chantilly		Fostoria	Crystal
*Chantilly		Jeannette, 1960s	Crystal, pink
Charade			Amethyst, dark blue, pink
Chariot		Hocking, 1932	Red & white decorations
Chateau		Fostoria, 1933-1940	Crystal
*Cherokee Rose		Tiffin, 1940s-1950s	Crystal
Cherry	See Cherry Blossom		
*Cherry-Berry	See also Strawberry	U.S. Glass, early 1930s	Crystal, green, iridescent amber, pink
*Cherry Blossom (R)	Banded Cherry; Cherry; Paneled Cherry Blossom	Jeannette, 1930-1939	Crystal, delphite, green, jadite, pink
Chesterfield		Imperial, c.1930	Amber, green, Rose Marie; iced tea set
Chico		Louie, 1936	Black, green, pink, royal blue, ruby, topaz; crystal handles; beverage set
*Chinex Classic	See also Cremax; Bordette; Oxford; Pie-Crust; Sheffield	Macbeth-Evans, c.1938-1942	Ivory; decal decorated; colored edges
Chintz		Fostoria, 1940-1972	Crystal
*Chintz		Heisey, 1931-1938	Crystal, green, orchid, pink, yellow
*Christmas Candy	Christmas Candy Ribbon; No. 624	Indiana, 1937; 1950s	Crystal, emerald green, Seafoam Green, teal blue; luncheon sets
Christmas Candy Ribbon	See Christmas Candy		
*Circle	Circular Ribs	Hocking, 1930s	Crystal, green, pink
Circular Ribs	See Circle		
Classic	See Chinex Classic		

PATTERN NAME	CROSS-REFERENCE	MANUFACTURER AND DATES	COLORS AND DESCRIPTION
*Cleo		Cambridge, 1930	Amber, blue, crystal, green, pink, yellow
Clico		McKee, 1930	Crystal with black, green feet, jade green, transparent green, rose pink
*Cloverleaf	Shamrock	Hazel Atlas, 1930-1936	Black, crystal, green, pink, topaz
*Colonial	Knife & Fork	Hocking 1934-1938	Crystal, green, opaque white, pink
*Colonial Block		Hazel Atlas	1930s—green, pink; 1950s—white
*Colonial Fluted	Rope	Federal, 1928-1933	Crystal, green
*Colony	Elongated Honeycomb; Hexagon Triple Band	Hazel Atlas, 1930s	Crystal, green, pink
Colony		Fostoria, 1920s-1970s	Amber, blue, crystal, green, white, yellow
*Columbia		Federal, 1938-1942	Crystal, pink
Columbus		Anchor Hocking	Amber; plate only
Comet	Scroll	U.S. Glass, mid-1920s	Crystal, green, pink
Corded Optic		Federal, 1928	Crystal, green
Coronada	See Royal		
*Coronation	Banded Fine Rib; Saxon; see also Lace Edge	Anchor Hocking, 1936-1940	Crystal, dark green, pink, ruby red
*Cosmos		Jeannette, 1950s	Crystal, golden iridescent
*Cracked Ice		Indiana, 1930s	Green, pink
Crackled	See Craquel		
*Craquel	Crackled; Stippled; Tree of Life	U.S. Glass, 1924	Crystal with green trim, blue, yellow
*Cremax	See also Bordette; Chinex Classic; Ivex; Oxford; Pie-Crust; Sheffield	Macbeth-Evans, 1930s-1940s	Cream-colored opaque; decal decorated; colored edges
Criss Cross	See X Design		
Crossbar		Federal, mid-1930s	Crystal, Golden Glow, green, Rose Glow
Crystal Leaf		Macbeth-Evans, 1928	Crystal, green, pink
Crystolite		Heisey	Amber, crystal, Sahara, Zircon
Cube	See Cubist		

PATTERN NAME	CROSS-REFERENCE	MANUFACTURER AND DATES	COLORS AND DESCRIPTION
*Cubist	Cube	Jeannette, 1929-1933	Amber, blue, canary yellow, crystal, green, pink, ultramarine, white
*Cupid		Paden City, 1930s	Black, green, light blue, pink, yellow
Daisy	See No. 620		
Daisy J		Jeannette, 1926	Amber, green
Daisy Petals	See Petalware		
Daisy Spray & Lattice		Federal, 1928	Crystal, green
Dance of the Nudes		Consolidated, 1920s	Crystal, pink
Dancing Girl		Morgantown, 1920s-1930s	Blue, green, pink
Dancing Girl	See Cameo	Hocking	
D'Artagnan		Dunbar, 1936	Lusters
Debbra		Hocking, 1931-1933	Green, rose, topaz
*Decagon		Cambridge, 1930s	Amber, cobalt blue, green, Moonlight Blue, pink, red
Deerwood	Birch Tree	U.S. Glass, 1920s-1930s	Amber, green, pink
*Della Robbia		Westmoreland, 1920s-1930s	Amber, crystal, green, pink
*Dewdrop		Jeannette, 1954-1955	Crystal
Diamond	See Windsor		
Diamond Arch	Diamond Lattice	Federal, 1938-1940	Crystal, green, pink
Diamond Dart		Macbeth-Evans, 1928	Crystal, emerald green
Diamond Lattice	See Diamond Arch		
Diamond Panel	See Diamond Point Columns		
Diamond Pattern	See Miss America		
Diamond Point	See Petalware		
Diamond Point Columns	Diamond Panel	Hazel Altas, late 1920s-1930s	Crystal, green, iridescent, pink
*Diamond Quilted	Flat Diamond	Imperial, 1920s-1930s	Amber, black, blue, crystal, green, pink, red
Diamond Squat		Federal, 1928	Crystal; water set
*Diana (R)	Swirled Sharp Rib	Federal, 1937-1941	Amber, crystal, pink
Diane		Cambridge, 1934-1950s	Blue, crystal, heatherbloom, pink, yellow
Diner		U.S. Glass, 1927	Amber, green, pink
Dixie		Macbeth-Evans, 1931	Green, pink; water set

PATTERN NAME	CROSS-REFERENCE	MANUFACTURER AND DATES	COLORS AND DESCRIPTION
*Dogwood	Apple Blossom; B Pattern; Magnolia; Wildrose	Macbeth-Evans, 1929-1934	Cremax, crystal, green, Monax, pink, yellow
Doreen		Westmoreland, 1924	Amber, blue, crystal, green, rose
*Doric	Snowflake	Jeannette, 1935-1938	Delphite, green, pink, yellow
*Doric & Pansy	Doric with Pansy; Pansy & Doric; see also Pretty Polly Party Dishes	Jeannette, 1937-1938	Crystal, pink, ultramarine
Doric with Pansy	See Doric & Pansy		
Do-Si-Do		Smith, 1930s	Black, black with crystal
Double Shield	See Mt. Pleasant		
Double Swirl	See Swirl		
Drape & Tassel	See Princess		
Dutch	See Windmill		
Dutch Rose	See Rosemary		
Early American	See Princess Feather		
Early American Hobnail	See also Hobnail	Imperial, 1930s	Amber, black, blue, crystal, green, pink, red
Early American Lace		Duncan & Miller, 1932	Amber, crystal, green, rose, ruby
Early American Rock Crystal	See Rock Crystal		
Early American Sandwich (R)		Duncan & Miller, 1925-1949	Amber, chartreuse, crystal, green, pink, ruby
Early American Scroll		Heisey, 1932	Crystal
Early American Thumbprint		Heisey, 1932	Crystal, golden yellow, green, rose
Egg Harbor		Liberty, 1929	Green, rose
Elaine		Cambridge, 1934-1950s	Crystal
Elongated Honeycomb	See Colony		
Empress		Heisey, 1930-1938	Alexandrite, cobalt blue, crystal, Flamingo, Moongleam, Sahara, Tangerine
*English Hobnail (R)	American Beauty; Sawtooth; see also Miss America	Westmoreland, 1920-1970s	Amber, blue, cobalt blue, crystal, dark amber, green, pink, red, turquoise
Everglades		Cambridge, 1933-1934	Amber, Carmen, crystal, Eleanor Blue, forest green

PATTERN NAME	CROSS-REFERENCE	MANUFACTURER AND DATES	COLORS AND DESCRIPTION
*Fairfax		Fostoria, 1927-1960	Amber, black, blue, green, orchid, pink, ruby, topaz
Fan & Feather	See Adam		
Fanfare		Macbeth-Evans	Pale pink
Feather Scroll	See Scroll Fluted		
Fieldcrest		Jenkins	Crystal, green, iridescent amber
Fine Rib	See Homespun (Jeannette)		
Fire-King Dinnerware	See Alice; Jane-Ray; Jadite; Square; Swirl Fire-King; Turquoise Blue		
*Fire-King Oven Glass	See also Philbe	Anchor Hocking, 1942-1960s	Crystal, pale blue
*Fire-King Oven Ware	See also Alice; Jadite; Jane-Ray; Philbe; Square; Swirl Fire-King; Turquoise Blue	Anchor Hocking, 1950s	Opaque; blue, ivory with gold or colored trim, jadite, pink, white
*Flanders		U.S. Glass, 1914-1935	Crystal, pink, or yellow with crystal trim
Flat Diamond	See Diamond Quilted		
Flora		Imperial, c.1925	Amber, green, Rose Marie
Floradora	Floral Bouquet	Imported, 1929	Amber, amethyst, green
*Floragold	Louisa	Jeannette, 1950s	Crystal, ice blue, iridescent, red-yellow, shell pink
*Floral (R)	Poinsettia	Jeannette, 1931-1935	Amber, crystal, delphite, green, jadite, pink, red, yellow
*Floral & Diamond Band		U.S. Glass, 1920s	Black, crystal, green, pink
Floral Bouquet	See Floradora		
Floral Rim	See Vitrock		
Floral Sterling		Hazel Atlas, early 1930s	Black
Florentine		Fostoria, 1931-1944	Crystal; Gold Tint base; topaz base
*Florentine No. 1 (R)	Old Florentine; Poppy No. 1	Hazel Atlas, 1932-1935	Cobalt blue, crystal, green, pink, yellow; hexagonal plates
*Florentine No. 2	Oriental Poppy; Poppy No. 2	Hazel Atlas, 1932-1935	Amber, cobalt blue, crystal, green, ice blue, pink, yellow
Flower	See Princess Feather		
Flower & Leaf Band	See Indiana Custard		
Flower Band		McKee, 1934	French Ivory, jade green, Poudre Blue

PATTERN NAME	CROSS-REFERENCE	MANUFACTURER AND DATES	COLORS AND DESCRIPTION
Flower Basket	See No. 615		
Flower Garden	See Flower Garden with Butterflies		
*Flower Garden with Butterflies	Butterflies & Roses; Flower Garden; Wildrose with Apple Blossom	U.S. Glass, late 1920s	Amber, black, blue, crystal, green, pink, yellow
Flower Rim	See Vitrock		
Forest		Co-Operative Flint, 1928	Blue, green, pink
*Forest Green		Anchor Hocking, 1950-1957	Green
*Fortune		Anchor Hocking, 1937-1938	Crystal, pink
Fostoria	See American		
Fountain Swirl		Imperial, 1928-1930	Crystal, green, pink
Franklin		Fenton, 1934	Amber, crystal, ruby; beverage glasses
Frosted Block	See Beaded Block		
Frosted Ribbon		Anchor Hocking, 1940	Red
*Fruits		Hazel Atlas, 1931-1933	Crystal, green, iridescent, pink
Full Sail		Duncan & Miller, 1925	Amber, green
Fuschia		Fostoria, 1931-1944	Crystal; Wisteria base
Fuschia		U.S. Glass, 1930s-1940s	Crystal
Garland		Indiana	Crystal—1935; decorated milk glass—1950s
Georgian		Hocking, 1935	Crystal, green; beverage sets
*Georgian	Lovebirds	Federal, 1931-1935	Crystal, green
Georgian		Duncan & Miller, 1928	Amber, crystal, green, rose
*Georgian Fenton		Fenton, c.1930	Amber, black, cobalt blue, crystal, green, pink, ruby, topaz
Gladiola	See Royal Lace		
*Gloria		Cambridge, c.1930	Amber, crystal, emerald green, green, heatherbloom, pink, yellow
Gothic Arches	Romanesque	L. E. Smith, 1920s	Amber, crystal, green, yellow

PATTERN NAME	CROSS-REFERENCE	MANUFACTURER AND DATES	COLORS AND DESCRIPTION
Grand Slam		Federal, 1930	Crystal; bridge set
*Grape	See also Woolworth	Standard, 1930s	Green, rose, topaz
Greek Key		Heisey	Crystal, Flamingo
Groucho		Louie, 1936	Black, green, pink, royal blue, ruby, topaz; crystal handles; beverage set
Hairpin	See Newport		
*Hammered Band	Melba; Pebbled Band	L. E. Smith, early 1930s	Amethyst, black, green, pink
Hanging Basket	See No. 615		
*Harp		Jeannette, 1954-1957	Crystal, crystal with gold trim, light blue, pink
Harpo		Louise, 1936	Black, green, pink, royal blue, ruby, topaz; crystal handles; beverage set
Hazel Atlas Quilt (R)		Hazel Atlas, 1937-1940	Amethyst, cobalt blue, green, pink
Hazen		Imperial, c.1930	Crystal
*Heritage (R)		Federal, late 1930s-1960s	Crystal, blue, light green, pink
Hermitage		Fostoria, 1932-1945	Amber, azure, black, crystal, Gold Tint, green, topaz, Wisteria
Hex Optic	See Hexagon Optic		
*Hexagon Optic	Hex Optic; Honeycomb	Jeannette, 1928-1932; c.1960	Blue green, green, pink; iridized
Hexagon Triple Band	See Colony		
High Point		Anchor Hocking	Ruby; water set
Hinge	See Patrician		
Hob		Jenkins, 1927-1931	Crystal, green
*Hobnail	See also Early American Hobnail; Moonstone	Hocking, 1934-1936	Crystal, pink; red rims; black base
Hobstars Intaglio		Imperial, c.1930	Crystal, green, pink
*Holiday	Buttons & Bows; Russian	Jeannette, 1947-1949	Crystal, iridescent, pink, shell pink opaque
*Homespun	Fine Rib	Jeannette, 1939-1940	Crystal, pink
Homespun		Hazel Atlas	Cobalt blue, crystal
*Homestead		Smith, 1930s	Amber, black, green, pink
Honeycomb	See Hexagon Optic		
Horizontal Fine Rib	See Manhattan		
Horizontal Ribbed	See Manhattan		

PATTERN NAME	CROSS-REFERENCE	MANUFACTURER AND DATES	COLORS AND DESCRIPTION
Horizontal Rounded Big Rib	See Manhattan		
Horizontal Sharp Big Rib	See Manhattan		
Horseshoe	See No. 612		
Huck Finn		Jenkins, c.1930	Crystal
Huckabee		Imperial, c.1930	Crystal
Hughes		Morgantown, 1932	Black, crystal, green, Ritz Blue, ruby; beverage sets
Ida		Imperial, c.1930	Blue, crystal, green, ruby
Imperial Hunt		Cambridge, 1932	Crystal
*Imperial Optic Rib	Optic Rib	Imperial, 1927	Amberina, blue, crystal, green, iridescent
*Imperial Plain Octagon	Molly	Imperial, 1927	Crystal, green, pink
Indian		Federal, c.1930	Green
*Indiana Custard	Flower & Leaf Band; see also Orange Blossom	Indiana, 1930s-1950s	Custard, ivory, white; bands of pastel colors
Ipswich		Heisey, 1931-1946; 1951-1953	Alexandrite, cobalt blue, crystal, Flamingo, Moongleam, Sahara
*Iris (R)	Iris & Herringbone	Jeannette, 1928-1932, 1950s	Crystal, iridescent, pink
Iris & Herringbone	See Iris		
Ivex	See also Chinex Classic; Cremax	Macbeth-Evans, 1930-1940	Chinex, Cremax
Jack Frost		Federal, 1928	Crystal; crackled; water, iced tea & lemonade sets
*Jadite	See also Alice; Fire-King Oven Ware; Jadite; Jane-Ray; Philbe; Square; Swirl Fire-King; Turquoise Blue	Jeannette, 1936-1938	Jadite
Jamestown	See Tradition		
Jane		Lancaster, c.1930	Green, pink, topaz
*Jane-Ray	See also Alice; Fire-King Oven Ware; Jadite; Philbe; Square; Swirl Fire-King; Turquoise Blue	Anchor Hocking, 1945-1963	Jadite
Jenkins' Basket		Jenkins	Crystal, green, iridescent amber

PATTERN NAME	CROSS-REFERENCE	MANUFACTURER AND DATES	COLORS AND DESCRIPTION
John		Federal, mid-1930s	Crystal, Golden Glow, green, Rose Glow
*Jubilee		Lancaster, early 1930s	Pink, yellow
*June		Fostoria, 1928-1952	Azure blue, crystal, gold-tinted, green, rose, topaz
Kashmir		Fostoria, 1930-1934	Azure, crystal, green, topaz
Katy Blue	See Laced Edge		
Kimberly		Duncan & Miller, 1931	Amber, crystal, green, rose
King Arthur		Indiana, c.1930	Green, pink
Knife & Fork	See Colonial		
Krinkle		Morgantown, 1924	Crystal
*Lace Edge	Loop; Open Lace; Open Scallop; see also Coronation; Queen Mary	Hocking, 1935-1938	Crystal, pink
Laced Edge	Katy Blue	Imperial, early 1930s	Blue, green; opalescent edge
Lacy Daisy	See No. 618		
Lafayette		Fostoria, 1931-1960	Amber, blue, burgundy, crystal, Empire Green, Gold Tint, green, rose, ruby, topaz, Wisteria
*Lake Como		Hocking, 1934-1937	Opaque white with blue decoration
Langston		Morgantown, 1932	Black, crystal, green, Ritz Blue, ruby
Lariat		Heisey	Black, crystal
Lariette		U.S. Glass, 1931	Crystal, green, pink
*Laurel	Raspberry Band; see also Scottie Dog	McKee, 1930s	Ivory, jade, powder blue, white opal; child's set-colored rim
Leaf		Macbeth-Evans, early 1930s	Crystal, green, pink
Legion		Fostoria, 1931-1940	Crytal, rose, topaz
Lenox		McKee, 1930s	Crystal, green, Ritz Blue, Rose Pink
*Lido		Federal, mid-1930s	Crystal, Golden Glow, green, Rose Glow
Lily Medallion	See American Sweetheart		
Lily Pons		Indiana, c.1930	Green
Lincoln Drape	See Princess		

PATTERN NAME	CROSS-REFERENCE	MANUFACTURER AND DATES	COLORS AND DESCRIPTION
*Lincoln Inn		Fenton, 1928	Amber, amethyst, black, cobalt blue, crystal, green, jadite, light blue, pink, red
Lindburgh	Scalloped Panels	Imperial, c.1930	Crystal, green, rose pink
*Line 92	See Twitch		
Line 191	Party Line; Tiered Block; Tiered Semi-Optic	Paden City, 1928	Amber, blue, Cheri-Glo, crystal, green, mulberry
Line 300	See Peacock & Wild Rose		
Line 412	See Peacock Reverse		
Line 550	See Sheraton		
Line 994	See Popeye & Olive		
Little Bo Peep		Anchor Hocking, 1940	Green & orange on ivory; child's line
Little Hostess	See Moderntone Little Hostess		
Little Jewel	See also New Jewel	Imperial, late 1920s-1930	Crystal, green, pink, white
Loganberry	Blackberry Cluster	Indiana, c.1930	Green, pink
Lombardi		Jeannette, 1938	Light blue; bowl only
Loop	See Lace Edge		
Lorain	See No. 615		
Lorna		Cambridge, 1930	Amber, crystal, emerald, Gold Krystol, Peach-Blo
Lotus		Westmoreland, 1920s-1930s	Amber, blue, crystal, green, rose
Louisa	See Floragold		
Lovebirds	See Georgian		
Lydia Ray	See New Century		
*MacHOB		Macbeth-Evans, 1928	Crystal, Monax, pink
*Madrid (R)	Meandering Vine; Paneled Aster; Primus; Winged Medallion	Federal, 1932-1939	Amber, blue, crystal, green, pink
Magnolia	See Dogwood		
*Manhattan	Horizontal Fine Rib; Horizontal Ribbed; Horizontal Rounded Big Rib; Horizontal Sharp Big Rib, Ribbed	Anchor Hocking, 1938-1941	Crystal, green, pink, red
Manor		Fostoria, 1931-1944	Crystal, green, topaz
Many Windows	See Roulette		
Marguerite		Westmoreland, 1924	Amber, blue, crystal, green, rose

PATTERN NAME	CROSS-REFERENCE	MANUFACTURER AND DATES	COLORS AND DESCRIPTION
Marilyn		Morgantown, 1929	Green, pink
*Martha Washington		Cambridge, 1932	Amber, crystal, forest green, Gold Krystol, Heatherbloom, royal blue, ruby
Mary		Federal, mid-1930s	Crystal, Golden Glow, green, Rose Glow
Mayfair	See Mayfair Open Rose		
*Mayfair Federal		Federal, 1934	Amber, crystal, green
*Mayfair Open Rose (R)	Mayfair; Open Rose	Hocking, 1931-1937	Crystal, green, ice blue, pink, yellow
Meadow Flower	See No. 618		
Meandering Vine	See Madrid		
Melba	See Hammered Band		
Melon		Morgantown, 1932	Black, blue, green, ruby, opal with colors; beverage set
Memphis		Central, 1923	Amethyst, black, blue, canary, green
Midnight Rose		Fostoria, 1933-1957	Crystal
Millay		Morgantown, 1932	Black, blue, crystal, green, ruby; beverage set
Minuet		Heisey, 1939-1950s	Crystal
*Miss America (R)	Diamond Pattern; see also English Hobnail	Hocking, 1933-1936	Crystal, green, ice blue, pink, red, Ritz Blue
Moderne Art	See Tea Room		
*Moderntone	Wedding Band	Hazel Atlas, 1935-1942	Amethyst, cobalt blue, crystal, pink, Platonite with fired-on colors
*Moderntone Little Hostess	Little Hostess	Hazel Atlas, 1940s	Fired-on colors
Molly	See Imperial Plain Octagon		
Monarch		Anchor Hocking	Ruby
Monticello		Imperial	Crystal
*Moondrops		New Martinsville, 1932-1940s	Amber, amethyst, black, cobalt blue, crystal, Evergreen, ice blue, jade, light green, medium blue, pink, Ritz Blue, ruby, smoke
*Moonstone	Opalescent Hobnail; see also Hobnail	Anchor Hocking, 1941-1946	Crystal with opalescent hobnails, green

PATTERN NAME	CROSS-REFERENCE	MANUFACTURER AND DATES	COLORS AND DESCRIPTION
Morning Glory		Fostoria, 1931-1944	Crystal; amber base
*Mt. Pleasant	Double Shield	L. E. Smith, mid-1920s-1934	Black amethyst, cobalt blue, crystal, green, pink; gold trim
*Mt. Vernon		Cambridge, 1920s-1940s	Amber, blue, crystal, emerald green, Heatherbloom, red, violet
Mt. Vernon		Imperial, c.1930	Crystal
Mutt'N Jeff		Federal, 1928	Crystal, green; water set
Naomi		Seneca, mid-1930s	Blue, crystal
Nautilus		Cambridge, 1933-1934	Amber, crystal, royal blue
*Navarre		Fostoria, 1937-1980	Crystal
Nectar		Fostoria, 1934-1943	Crystal
*New Century	Banded Ribbon; Lydia Ray; see also Ovide	Hazel Atlas, 1930-1935	Amethyst, cobalt blue, crystal, green, pink
New Garland		Fostoria, 1930-1934	Amber, crystal, rose, topaz
New Jewel	See also Little Jewel	Imperial, 1931	Crystal, green, pink, white
*Newport	Hairpin	Hazel Atlas, 1936-1940	Amethyst, cobalt blue, fired-on Monax, pink, Platonite
No. 601	See Avocado		
*No. 610 (R)	Pyramid; Rex	Indiana, 1926-1932	Crystal, green, pink, white, yellow
*No. 612	Horseshoe	Indiana, 1930-1933	Green, pink, yellow; crystal sugar and creamer
*No. 615	Basket; Bridal Bouquet; Flower Basket; Hanging Basket; Lorain	Indiana, 1929-1932	Crystal, crystal with colored borders, green, yellow;
*No. 616	Vernon	Indiana, 1930-1932	Crystal, crystal with platinum trim, green, yellow
*No. 618	Lacy Daisy; Meadow Flower; Pineapple & Floral; Wildflower	Indiana, 1932-1937; 1960s	Amber, crystal, fired-on green, olive green, red

PATTERN NAME	CROSS-REFERENCE	MANUFACTURER AND DATES	COLORS AND DESCRIPTION
*No. 620	Daisy	Indiana	1933—crystal; 1940—amber; 1960s-1970s—dark green, milk glass
No. 622	See Pretzel		
No. 624	See Christmas Candy		
Nora Bird		Paden City, 1929-1930s	Crystal, green, pink
*Normandie	Bouquet & Lattice	Federal, 1933-1940	Amber, crystal, iridescent, pink
Oatmeal Lace	See Princess Feather		
Ocean Wave	Ripple	Jenkins, c.1930	
Octagon		Heisey, 1925-1937	Flamingo, Hawthorne, marigold, Moongleam, Sahara, Tangerine
*Octagon	Tiered Octagon; U.S. Octagon	U.S. Glass, 1927-1929	Green, pink
Octagon Bamboo Optic	See also Bamboo Optic	Liberty, 1929	Green, pink
Octagon Edge		McKee	Green, pink
*Old Cafe		Anchor Hocking, 1936-1938	Crystal, pink, red
Old Colony	See Victorian		
*Old English	Threading	Indiana, late 1920s-early 1930s	Amber, crystal, emerald green, light green, pink
Old Florentine	See Florentine No. 1		
Old Sandwich		1931-1956	Cobalt blue, Flamingo, Moongleam, Sahara, Tangerine, Zircon
Opalescent Hobnail	See Moonstone		
Open Lace	See Lace Edge		
Open Rose	See Mayfair Open Rose		
Open Scallop	See Lace Edge		
Optic Design	See Raindrops		
Optic Rib	See Imperial Optic Rib		
*Orange Blossom	See also Indiana Custard	Indiana, 1957	Milk glass
Orchid		Heisey, 1940-1957	Crystal
*Orchid		Paden City, early 1930s	Amber, black, cobalt blue, green, pink, red, yellow
Oregon Grape	See Woolworth		
Oriental Poppy	See Florentine No. 2		
Orphan Annie		Westmoreland, 1925	Amber, blue, crystal, green; breakfast set

PATTERN NAME	CROSS-REFERENCE	MANUFACTURER AND DATES	COLORS AND DESCRIPTION
*Ovide	See also New Century	Hazel Atlas, 1929-1935	Black, green, Platonite, white, trimmed with fired-on colors
Oxford	See also Chinex Classic; Cremax Chinex, Cremax	Macbeth-Evans, 1930-1940	
*Oyster & Pearl		Anchor Hocking, 1938-1940	Crystal, pink, red, white; fired-on green, pink
Palm Optic		Morgantown, 1929	Green, pink
Panel	See Sheraton		
Paneled Aster	See Madrid		
Paneled Cherry Blossom	See Cherry Blossom		
Panelled Ring-Ding		Hocking, 1932	Black, green, orange, red, yellow, painted bands
Pansy & Doric	See Doric & Pansy		
Pantryline		Hocking, 1920s-1930s	
Parrot	See Sylvan		
Party Line	See Line 191		
*Patrician	Hinge; Spoke	Federal, 1933-1937	Amber, crystal, green, pink, yellow
*Patrick		Lancaster, c.1930	Rose, topaz
Peacock & Rose	See Peacock & Wild Rose		
*Peacock & Wild Rose	Line 300; Peacock & Rose	Paden City, 1930s	Black, cobalt blue, green, pink, red
Peacock Optic		Morgantown, 1929-1930	Green, pink
Peacock Reverse	Line 412	Paden City, 1930s	Amber, black, cobalt blue, crystal, green, red, yellow
*Pear Optic	Thumbprint; see also Raindrops	Federal, 1929-1930	Green
Pebble Optic	See Raindrops		
Pebbled Band	See Hammered Band		
*Penny Line		Paden City, 1932	Amber, Cheri-Glo, crystal, green, royal blue, ruby
Petal	See Petalware		
Petal Swirl	See Swirl		
*Petalware	Banded Petalware; Daisy Petals; Diamond Point, Petal; Shell; Vivid Bands	Macbeth-Evans, 1930-1940	Cremax, crystal, Monax, pink; gold trim; red trim; hand-painted fruit designs; fired-on blue, green, red, yellow

PATTERN NAME	CROSS-REFERENCE	MANUFACTURER AND DATES	COLORS AND DESCRIPTION
*Philbe	Fire-King Dinnerware; see also Fire-King Oven Glass	Anchor Hocking, 1937-1940s	Blue, blue with platinum trim, crystal, green, pink
Pie-Crust	See also Chinex Classic, Cremax	Macbeth-Evans, 1930-1940	Chinex, Cremax
*Pillar Flute		Imperial, c.1930	Amber, blue, crystal, green, pink
Pillar Optic		Hocking, 1935	Green
Pineapple & Floral	See No. 618		
Pineapple Optic		Morgantown, 1929	Green, rose
Pinwheel	See Sierra		
*Pioneer		Federal, 1930s-1970s	Crystal, pink
Plantation		Heisey	Amber, crystal
Plymouth		Fenton, 1933	Amber, green, ruby
Poinsettia	See Floral		
Polar Bear		Hocking, 1932	Red & white decorations
Polo		Hazel Atlas, 1938	Blue with white decorations
*Popeye & Olive	Line 994	Paden City, early 1930s	Cobalt blue, crystal, green, red
Poppy No. 1	See Florentine No. 1		
Poppy No. 2	See Florentine No. 2		
Portia		Cambridge, 1932-1950s	Crystal, green, Heatherbloom, yellow
Pretty Polly Party Dishes	See also Doric & Pansy	Jeannette, 1937-1938	Children's dishes
*Pretzel	No. 622; Ribbon Candy	Indiana, 1930s-1970s	Crystal, teal
*Primo		U.S. Glass, 1932	Green, yellow
Primrose Lane		Morgantown, 1929	Green, pink
Primus	See Madrid		
*Princess	Drape & Tassell; Lincoln Drape; Tassell	Hocking, 1931-1935	Amber, blue, green, pink, topaz
*Princess Feather (R)	Early American; Flower; Oatmeal Lace; Scroll & Star; Westmoreland Sandwich	Westmoreland, 1939-1948; 1960s	Aqua, crystal, green, pink
Prismatic Line	See Queen Mary		
Provincial	See Bubble (Anchor Hocking)		
Provincial		Heisey	Crystal, Limelight
Punties		Duncan & Miller, 1931	Amber, crystal, green, rose

PATTERN NAME	CROSS-REFERENCE	MANUFACTURER AND DATES	COLORS AND DESCRIPTION
Puritan		Duncan & Miller, 1929	Crystal
Pyramid	See No. 610		
Pyramid Optic		Hocking	Crystal, green
Queen Anne	See also Bee Hive	Anchor Hocking, late 1930s	Crystal, pink; beverage set
*Queen Mary	Prismatic Line; Vertical Ribbed; see also Lace Edge	Anchor Hocking, 1936-1940	Crystal, pink, red
*Radiance		New Martinsville, 1936-1939	Amber, cobalt blue, crystal, green, ice blue, red
*Raindrops	Optic Design; Pebble Optic; see also Pear Optic	Federal, 1929-1933	Crystal, green
Rambler		Fostoria, 1935-1958	Crystal
Raspberry Band	See Laurel		
Rex	See No. 610		
Ribbed	See Manhattan		
Ribbed Octagon		Heisey, 1925-1936	Crystal, Flamingo, Hawthorne, Moongleam
*Ribbon		Hazel Atlas, 1930s	Black, crystal, green
Ribbon Candy	See Pretzel		
Ridgeleigh		Heisey, 1935-1957	Crystal, Sahara, Zircon
*Ring	Banded Rainbow; Banded Rings	Hocking, 1927-1932	Crystal, green, pink; rings of black, blue, orange, pink, platinum, red, yellow
*Ring-Ding		Hocking, 1932	Painted bands of green, orange, red, yellow
Ringed Target		Macbeth-Evans, 1931	Crystal, green, pink; iced tea set
Ripple	See Ocean Wave		
*Rock Crystal	Early American Rock Crystal	McKee, 1920s-1930s	Amber, blue-green, cobalt blue, crystal, green, pink, red, yellow
Romanesque	See Gothic Arches		
Rope	See Colonial Fluted		
Rosalie		Cambridge, 1920s-1930s	Amber, blue, green, Heatherbloom, pink, red
Rose		Standard, c.1930	Topaz
Rose & Thorn	See Thorn		
*Rose Cameo		Belmont Tumbler, 1933	Green
Rose Lace	See Royal Lace		
Rose Point		Cambridge	Crystal; gold trim
Rose Trellis	See Block with Rose		

PATTERN NAME	CROSS-REFERENCE	MANUFACTURER AND DATES	COLORS AND DESCRIPTION
*Rosemary	Cabbage Rose with Single Arch; Dutch Rose; see also Mayfair Federal	Federal, 1935-1937	Amber, green, pink
*Roulette	Many Windows	Anchor Hocking, 1935-1939	Crystal, green, pink
*Round Robin	Accordian Pleats	Late 1920s-1930s	Crystal, green, iridescent marigold
*Roxana		Hazel Atlas, 1932	Crystal, white, yellow
Royal	Coronada	Fostoria, 1925-1934	Amber, black, blue, crystal, green; blue trimmed in white and yellow gold
*Royal Lace	Gladioli; Rose Lace	Hazel Atlas, 1934-1941	Amethyst, cobalt blue, crystal, green, pink
*Royal Ruby (R)		Anchor Hocking, 1939-1960s	Red
Russian	See Holiday		
*S Pattern	Stippled Rose Band	Macbeth-Evans, 1930-1935	Amber, crystal, green, Monax, pink, red, ritz blue, topaz; trimmed in amber, blue, gold, green, pink, platinum, red, rose, silver, white
Sail Boat	See White Ship		
Sailing Ship	See White Ship		
*Sandwich Anchor Hocking (R)		Anchor Hocking, 1939-1964	Amber, crystal, forest green, opaque white, pink, red
Sandwich Duncan & Miller		Duncan & Miller, 1924-1955	Amber, cobalt blue, crystal, green, pink, red
*Sandwich Indiana (R)		Indiana, 1920s-1980s	Amber, crystal, light green, pink, red, teal blue
Saturn		Heisey, 1937-1957	Crystal, pale green
Sawtooth	See English Hobnail		
Saxon	See Coronation		
Scallop Edge		McKee	Green, pink
Scalloped Panels	See Lindburgh		
Scottie Dog	See also Laurel	McKee, 1930s	Children's set
Scrabble		Macbeth-Evans, 1931	Crystal, green, pink; iced tea set and tumblers
Scramble		Westmoreland, 1924	Amber, blue, crystal, green, rose
Scroll	See Comet		
Scroll & Star	See Princess Feather		
Scroll Fluted	Feather Scroll	Imperial, c.1930	Crystal, green, pink

PATTERN NAME	CROSS-REFERENCE	MANUFACTURER AND DATES	COLORS AND DESCRIPTION
Sea-Side		Jenkins	Crystal, green, iridescent amber
Semper		Louie, 1931	Green, pink, topaz; refreshment set
Shaffer		Imperial, c.1930	Amber, blue, crystal, green
Shamrock	See Cloverleaf		
*Sharon (R)	Cabbage Rose	Federal, 1935-1939	Amber, crystal, green, pink
Sheffield	See also Chinex Classic; Cremax	Macbeth-Evans, 1930-1940	Chinex, Cremax
Shell	See Petalware		
Sheraton	Line 550; Panel	Barlett Collins, 1930s	Crystal
*Shirley Temple (R)		Hazel Atlas, U.S. Glass, and others, 1934-1942	Cobalt blue and white
*Sierra	Pinwheel	Jeannette, 1931-1933	Green, pink
Simplicity		Morgantown	Green, pink
Smocking	See Windsor		
Snowflake	See Doric		
Snowflake on Block	See Block with Snowflake		
Soda Fountain		Indiana, c.1930	Green, pink
Soda Shop		Smith, mid-1920s	Crystal
Sommerset		Morgantown, 1932	Black, blue, crystal, green, ruby; beverage set
Spanish Fan	Spanish Lace		Crystal, green
Spanish Lace	See Spanish Fan		
Sphinx	See Centaur		
*Spiral	Spiral Optic; Swirled Big Rib; see also Twisted Optic	Hocking, 1928-1930	Green, pink
*Spiral Flutes		Duncan & Miller, 1924-early 1930s	Amber, crystal, crystal with gold trim, green, light blue, pink, vaseline
Spiral Optic	See Spiral		
Spoke	See Patrician		
*Sportsman Series	See also White Ship; Windmill	Hazel Atlas, 1940s	Amethyst, cobalt blue, crystal with fired-on decorations
Spring Flowers		Imperial, 1920s	Crystal; plate only
Springtime		Fostoria, 1933-1944	Crystal, topaz
Spun		Imperial, 1935	Aqua, crystal, fired-on orange, pastel colors, red

PATTERN NAME	CROSS-REFERENCE	MANUFACTURER AND DATES	COLORS AND DESCRIPTION
*Square	See also Alice; Fire-King Oven Ware; Jadite; Jane-Ray; Swirl Fire-King; Turquoise Blue	Anchor Hocking, 1940s-1960s	
Square		Morgantown, 1928	Crystal
Squat Optic		Federal, 1928	Crystal; water set
Squirt		Macbeth-Evans, 1931	Crystal, emerald green; water sets
*Starlight		Hazel Atlas, 1930s	Cobalt blue, crystal, pink, white
Stippled	See Craquel		
Stippled Rose Band	See S Pattern		
*Strawberry	See also Cherry-Berry	U.S. Glass, 1930s	Crystal, green, iridescent marigold, pink
Strawflower		Imperial, c.1930	Amber, crystal, green, Rose Marie
Stripe		Hocking, 1932	Red and white bands
*Sunburst		Jeannette, 1938-1941	Crystal
*Sunflower		Jeannette, late 1920s-early 1930s	Delphite, emerald green, light green, pink; opaque
Sunray		Fostoria, 1935-1944	Amber, azure, Gold Tint, green, ruby
*Swankyswigs		Hazel Atlas, 1933-1940; 1947-1958	5-oz. decorated tumblers
Sweet Pear	See Avocado		
*Swirl	Double Swirl; Petal Swirl	Jeannette, 1937-1938	Amber, delphite, ice blue, pink, ultramarine
*Swirl Fire-King	See also Fire-King Oven Ware; Alice; Jadite; Jane-Ray; Square; Turquoise Blue	Anchor Hocking, 1955-1960s	Blue, ivory with trim, jadite, pink, white with gold trim
Swirled Big Rib	See Spiral		
Swirled Sharp Rib	See Diana		
*Sylvan	Parrot; Three Parrot	Federal, 1931-1932	Amber, blue, crystal, green
Tall Boy		Federal, 1928	Green; iced tea sets
Tassell	See Princess		
*Tea Room	Moderne Art	Indiana, 1926-1931	Amber, crystal, green, pink
*Tear Drop		Duncan & Miller, 1934-1955	Crystal
Terrace		Duncan & Miller, 1935	Amber, blue, crystal, ruby

PATTERN NAME	CROSS-REFERENCE	MANUFACTURER AND DATES	COLORS AND DESCRIPTION
*Thistle		Macbeth-Evans, 1929-1930	Crystal, green, pink, yellow
Thorn	Rose & Thorn	U.S. Glass, 1930s	Black, crystal, green, pink
Threading	See Old English		
Three Bands		Hocking, 1930s	Opaque white with three enameled bands
Three Parrot	See Sylvan		
Thumbprint	See Pear Optic		
Tiered Block	See Line 191		
Tiered Octagon	See Octagon		
Tiered Semi-Optic	See Line 191		
Tom & Jerry		Hazel Atlas, 1930s	Opaque white, enameled decorations
Tom & Jerry		McKee, 1940s	Black, ivory, white with black, gold, green, red decorations
*Tradition	Jamestown	Imperial, 1930s	Amber, amethyst, blue, crystal, green, pink, red
Tree of Life	See Craquel		
*Trojan		Fostoria, 1929-1944	Gold Tint, green, rose, topaz
Trudy		Standard, c.1930	Green, pink
Truman		Liberty, 1930	Green, pink
Trump Bridge		Federal, 1928	Colored enamel decorations; luncheon set
Tudor Ring		Federal, 1928	Crystal, green; water set
*Tulip		Dell, 1930s	Amber, amethyst, blue, crystal, green
*Turquoise Blue	See also Alice; Fire-King Oven Ware; Jadite; Jane-Ray; Square; Swirl Fire-King	Anchor Hocking, 1950s	Turquoise
Twentieth Century		Hazel Atlas, 1928-1931	Crystal, green, pink
Twin Dolphin		Jenkins	Crystal, green, iridescent amber
Twist		Heisey, 1928-1937	Crystal, Flamingo, marigold, Moongleam, Sahara
*Twisted Optic	See also Spiral	Imperial, 1927-1930	Amber, blue, canary yellow, green, pink
Twitch	Line 92	Bartlett-Collins, early 1930s	Green
U.S. Octagon	See Octagon		
U.S. Swirl		U.S. Glass, late 1920s	Crystal, green, pink

PATTERN NAME	CROSS-REFERENCE	MANUFACTURER AND DATES	COLORS AND DESCRIPTION
Vernon	See No. 616		
*Versailles		Fostoria, 1928-1944	Azure, crystal bases with colored glass, gold tinted, green, rose, topaz
Verticle Ribbed	See Queen Mary		
*Vesper		Fostoria, 1926-1934	Amber, crystal, green, blue
Victorian	Old Colony; Waffle King; Wayside Inn	Heisey, 1933-1953	Cobalt blue, crystal, Flamingo, Moongleam, Zircon
*Victory		Diamond Glass, 1929-1932	Amber, black, cobalt blue, green, pink; gold trim
Victory Model		Silex, 1938-1942	Amber, cobalt blue, green, pink; coffeepot
*Viking		Imperial, 1929	Green, rose
*Vitrock	Floral Rim; Flower Rim	Hocking, 1934-1937	Green, red, white with fired-on colors; decal decorations
Vivid Bands	See Petalware		
Waffle	See Waterford		
Waffle Keg	See Victorian		
Wagner		Westmoreland, 1924	Amber, blue, green, rose
Wakefield		Westmoreland, 1933-1960s	Crystal
Washington Bi-Centennial		1932	Topaz; tumbler
*Waterford	Waffle	Anchor Hocking, 1938-1944; 1950s	Crystal, forest green, pink, white, yellow
Wave	See Caribbean		
Wayside Inn	See Victorian		
Weatherford		Cambridge, 1926	Amber-Glo, emerald, Peach-Blo
Wedding Band	See Moderntone		
Westmoreland Sandwich	See Princess Feather		
Wheat		Federal, early 1930s	Crystal, green, pink
*Whirly-Twirly		Anchor Hocking, 1940s	Forest green, red
White Sail	See White Ship		
*White Ship	Beverages with Sailboats; Sail Boat; Sailing Ship; White Sail	Hazel Atlas, 1938	Blue with white decorations

PATTERN NAME	CROSS-REFERENCE	MANUFACTURER AND DATES	COLORS AND DESCRIPTION
Wiggle		McKee, 1925	Amethyst, amber, blue, canary, green
Wildflower	See No. 618		
Wildrose	See Dogwood		
Wildrose with Apple Blossom	See Flower Garden with Butterflies		
*Windmill	Dutch; see also Sportsman Series	Hazel Atlas, 1938	Blue with white decorations
Windmill & Checkerboard	Block with Windmill		Crystal, green
*Windsor	Diamond; Smocking; Windsor Diamond	Jeannette, 1936-1946	Amberina, blue, crystal, delphite, green, pink
Windsor Diamond	See Windsor		
Winged Medallion	See Madrid		
Woodbury		Imperial, c.1930	Amber, crystal, green, Rose Marie
*Woolworth	Oregon Grape; see also Grape	Westmoreland, early 1930s	Blue, crystal, green, pink
Wotta Line		Paden City, 1933	Amber, amethyst, Cheri-Glo, crystal, ebony, green, royal blue, ruby, topaz
*X Design	Criss Cross	Hazel Atlas, 1928-1932	Crystal, green, pink, white; breakfast set
Yankee		Macbeth-Evans, 1931	Crystal, green, pink; water set
Yoo-Hoo		Jenkins, c.1930	
Yo-Yo		Jenkins, c.1930	
Yvonne	Carolyn	Lancaster, mid-1930s	Green, yellow
Zeppo		Louie, 1936	Black, green, pink, royal blue, ruby, topaz; crystal handles; beverage set

We welcome any additions or corrections to this chart. Please write to us c/o Crown Publishers, Inc., 201 E. 50th St., New York, NY 10022.

THE COLLECTOR'S SPEEDY GUIDE TO DEPRESSION GLASS AND AMERICAN DINNERWARE

Price Trends and How To Care for Glass and Pottery

INVESTING IN DEPRESSION GLASS

Depression glass is the 1970s name for the 1930s glassware gaining favor again in the 1990s. A full set of Depression glass dishes sold for $1.99 when it was first offered for sale in the late 1920s. No one could have imagined that in 1991 there would be pieces of Depression glass that sold for more than $1,000 each.

Delphite plate in the Cherry Blossom pattern.

Green Adam pattern plate, 12 inches long.

The first collectors to rediscover Depression glass in the 1970s had very little information to help with their search. The first commercial book listing prices was the 1971 edition of *The Complete Antiques Price List* by Ralph and Terry Kovel. There were nine pages listing 650 priced pieces of Depression glass. More than half the pieces were selling for less than $3. The most expensive piece at that time was a pink Mayfair wine decanter for $40. A child's set of delphite Cherry Blossom listed for $160 to $175. The least expensive piece was an amber Spoke (Patrician) creamer for $1. This year these pieces list at $115 for the decanter, $170 to $225 for the child's set, and $8 for the creamer.

Depression glass was a stepchild in the 1970s' world of collecting. The major newspapers and magazines rarely even mentioned it. Few pieces appeared at shows. Pioneer collectors went to flea markets, church rummage sales, and garage sales and began to assemble sets of dishes. Some were lucky enough to discover a set at Mother's house. One enterprising collector built shelves in the basement and began to search for the glass as an investment. He paid pennies for many of the pieces, kept careful records of each purchase, watched the market to see which patterns were going up in popularity and price. He wanted to make enough money for his young daughter's future college education. In 1985 he sold the collection and had the necessary tuition.

Although most collectors bought Depression glass to fill in an old set, to form a new set to use, or because of a love of the glass, it is reassuring to collectors to know that the value has increased.

DEPRESSION GLASS PRICE SURVEY

	1971	1975	1980	1985	1991
Adam, cake plate, 10 in., pink	$5	$6	$9	$12	$15
American Sweetheart, plate, 8 in., pink	$2	$2	$4.50	$6	$9
Cubist, creamer, 3 in., green	$2.75	$2.25	$3.50-5	$6	$7
Floral, creamer, pink	$1.75	$3-4.50	$7	$6-7	$8.50-10
Lace Edge, cup & saucer, pink	$4	$7.50	$14.50	$22	$27
Mayfair Open Rose, cup & saucer, pink	$4-4.50	$5.50	$14.50	$22.50	$20-25.50
Miss America, pitcher, water, 8 in., pink	$20	$35	$30	$90	—
Moonstone, goblet, 10 oz., crystal	—	$5	$8	$12.50	$16
No. 612, cup & saucer, green	$3.75	$4.75	$8.50	$8.50	$9-13
Patrician, creamer, amber	$1	$2-3	$5	$7	$8
Patrician, plate, 10½ in., amber	$2	$1.25-2.50	$4	$5.25	$5.50-8
Princess, cup & saucer, green	$2	$3.25-3.50	$9	$14.50	$10-15
Royal Lace, cookie jar, cover, blue	$45	$50-65	$145	$175	$230
Royal Lace, cup & saucer, blue	$15.50	$8-13	$14.50-19	$21	$33-35
Sharon, bowl, 5 in., pink	$2	$1.75-2	$5.50	$8	$6-8
Sharon, butter, cover, pink	$15	$20-30	$25-35	$30-40	$31-37

COLLECTING GLASS

The introductory paragraph in Kovels' 1971 price book said that the name *Depression glass* was a 1970s collector's term, a convenient name used by writers and dealers. Hazel Weatherman had written *Colored Glassware of the Depression Era* in 1970, the first of a series of privately printed books that became the recognized source of information about Depression glass for dealers and collectors. The well-researched books had pictures of the glass, old ads, factory histories, and prices. Sometimes, when factory names were unknown, patterns were named by the author. Other authors also gave names to patterns, usually basing the name on something in the design. That is why there are often several names for one pattern of glass, such as Adam, which is also known as Chain Daisy or Fan & Feather. More books and price guides appeared as interest grew, and in 1971 publication of a monthly newspaper began.

The meaning of *Depression glass* has changed since the 1970s. At first only the pressed pastel glassware was included, then the deep blue and red wares gained interest. Gradually, a wide assortment of glass products from the 1920s through the 1960s was called *Depression glass*. (See the Introduction to this book.) There were many kitchen pieces: storage jars for food, reamers to be used to make orange juice, mixing bowls, measuring glasses, water carafes or jugs to be kept in the refrigerator, metal-topped glass bottles for spices, cooking, baking, serving casserole dishes, and ice-water pitchers.

In 1933, when Prohibition was repealed, alcoholic beverages could be legally served. The glassmakers immediately made decanters, martini shakers, bar glasses of all sizes and shapes, even punch bowls, cups, and ice buckets. Many of these pieces were made in familiar patterns to match the dinnerware sets.

One other type of Depression glass is favored by some collectors. Special pieces were made as advertisements for food products or stores. The famous cobalt blue Shirley Temple cereal set was given away with cereal. Some fancy decanters held vinegar. Footed tumblers were packed with peanut butter. Many small pieces can be found with a company name as part of the pattern, either molded in the glass or enameled on the outside. Ashtrays, cups, mugs, plates, and mixing bowls are common.

A clear Cubist bowl and two Miss America plates, pink and green, 5½- and 6-inch diameter.

The Shirley Temple set included a bowl, plate, sugar and this creamer and milk mug. It was made in the Honeycomb pattern by the Hazel Atlas Glass Company in 1935.

CARE AND REPAIR OF GLASS

Depression glass is still plentiful. Perfect, "mint" pieces are available. A mint piece is undamaged, with no scratches on the surface. It should look as if it just came from a store. If the original box that held the glass is available, that adds to the value. Then it is known as "mint in the box," the best a collector can hope for.

But if you plan to use your dishes, here are a few helpful rules. Depression glass was made to be used every day. It was an inexpensive but sturdy dinnerware. Dishwashers and detergents were unknown when the dishes were made. Hot water and soap were used. The extra hot water of a dishwasher can harm dishes with an iridescent sheen, such as "Iris" or "Floragold," or with an enameled decoration, such as "White Sails" or "Stripes." A strong detergent may also cause discoloration. But it is safer to use a dishwasher than to handle the dishes in a sink filled with soapy water. Accidents do happen. It is fine to use the dishwasher for most of the glass. Be sure you do not put a very cold dish that held ice cream or a refrigerated salad in a hot dishwasher; it may crack.

Newly purchased, very dirty dishes can be soaked in ammonia and water or in a strong detergent solution. After soaking, scrub with a toothbrush to clean the crevices. This is not advised for iridescent pieces.

The microwave is another modern convenience that was unknown when Depression glass was made. Some of the kitchen bowls and casseroles can be put in the microwave with no problems. The leftover dishes with deeply molded fruit designs seem to have a structural weakness. When zapped in a microwave, they sometimes explode. It is especially dangerous to use the old glassware to cook frozen foods; the change in temperature often causes cracks.

Depression glass was inexpensive and many pieces had flaws. These will weaken the piece and sometimes even hot coffee will crack a cup. This will probably not be a major problem because most of the flawed cups have probably cracked in past years of use. To protect the cups — already in short supply for most patterns — try Ralph's mother's trick: Put a metal spoon in the cup before you pour the coffee or tea. The metal will help dissipate the heat.

Some Depression glass pieces, such as the tidbit server, are made with glass and chrome. These pieces are made to be taken apart so the chrome can be polished with the proper product and the glass can be washed. The chrome plating is very thin, so polish only when it is necessary.

If your Depression glass is damaged, there is some hope. It may still be used, even though the value is lowered by the damage. Permanent glue can be used to mend a broken handle or knob. A scratched plate cannot be polished; but if you want to display the piece,

An iridescent covered butter dish in the Iris pattern.

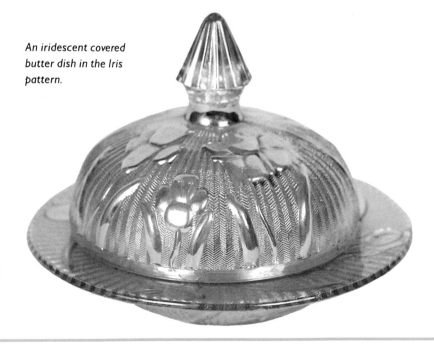

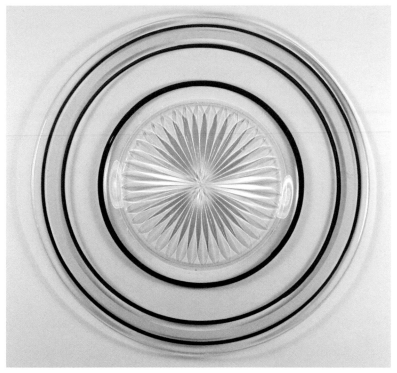

A pink Stripe pattern plate.

a little oil or hairspray may hide the scratches. Pieces that have lost some of the iridescence cannot be repaired. Chips can be filled with some of the new plastic materials. Bottle collectors often use these products, and bottle magazines list experts who do this type of restoration. But it is very expensive and is not suggested for any pieces that are not great rarities or of great sentimental value.

DISPLAYING GLASS

Depression glass should never be displayed in a sunny window. The ultraviolet rays and the heat can cause discoloration. We have heard of a few instances when a dish has exploded. If plates are hung on a wall, be sure the plate hangers are not too tight; a tight holder will chip the rim.

The best way to show off your dishes is to use them. Set the table for a party. Fill the vases with flowers. Mix-and-match sets of dishes are in fashion now and you can assemble a set in one pattern, one color, or mix several similar patterns and colors. One collector has shelves of light green Depression glass in the kitchen as a display. The twenty-four grill plates and other serving pieces are used at every picnic. Be sure to wash the dishes soon after dinner so acidic foods will not cause damage. Flower vases should be carefully emptied and filled every few days to avoid water marks inside the glass.

. . . .

INVESTING IN
AMERICAN DINNERWARE

The "look" of table settings changed dramatically in the twentieth century. New technology and the influence of modern design inspired designers. Potteries such as Wedgwood or Spode made dinner plates with raised rims and added colored decoration since the eighteenth century. Some patterns such as Blue Willow have remained popular. Others, such as Zeisel or American Modern, are innovations of the twentieth century, featuring rimless plates and free-form bowls. Inexpensive dinnerwares were made to be sold at the dimestore, through catalogs such as Sears, or to be given away as premiums for soap or groceries. Bright solid-colored pottery dishes, hand-painted flower-decorated wares, and decal-decorated pieces were made. Kovels' Antiques & Collectibles Price List first included prices for Fiesta, Harlequin, and the other solid-colored potteries in 1974, decal-decorated Autumn Leaf in 1977. By the 1980s, there were several books about the dish patterns, a newspaper, and a yearly pottery show.

Dinnerware and kitchenwares were made, sometimes in matching patterns. Autumn Leaf, the pattern sold by Jewel Tea Company, can be found on dinner plates, mixing bowls, glasses, even plastic tablecloths. Hall China Company made a line of teapots that matched kitchenwares or dinnerwares, or were just attractive novelties. Many exclusive patterns were made that were given away or sold at grocery stores. It is still possible to assemble and use a full dinner service of these dishes of the 1930–1970 period and the cost is usually less than that of a new set of dishes.

Harlequin pattern plates in Spruce green and gray. Cup and saucer in Russel Wright's famous American Modern pattern.

Assorted Fiesta pattern dishes, old and new issues of 1986.

THE HOMER LAUGHLIN CHINA CO., NEWELL, W. VA.

The cover of a Fiesta advertising pamphlet issued in 1962 by the Homer Laughlin Company. The full line of dinnerware is listed and priced.

Hacienda pattern bowl by Homer Laughlin.

Autumn Leaf dinner plate by the Hall China Company.

A child's tea set in the traditional Blue Willow pattern.

DINNERWARE PRICE SURVEY

	1975	1980	1985	1991
Autumn Leaf, cup & saucer	$3.75	$5-6	$7	$5-12
Autumn Leaf, gravy boat	$4-6	$10	$12-15	$20
Autumn Leaf, dinner plate	$2-3	$5	$5	$10
Autumn Leaf, Aladdin teapot	$12-15	$45	$42	$30-35
Fiesta, ashtray	$15-18.50	$12-13	$20-35	$35
Fiesta, cup & saucer	$6.50-9	$7-15	$11-25	$25-27
Fiesta, dessert plate	$.75-1.50	$2	$3.50-6	$2.50-8
Fiesta, grill plate	$10-12.50	$9	$12-20	$10-25
Harlequin, cream soup	$3	$3.50-5.50	$5-9	$10-16
Harlequin, cup & saucer	$2.75-4	$2.50-10	$7-12	$8.50-10
Harlequin, dessert plate	$1	$.50-3	$2	$2-3.50
Harlequin, gravy boat	$2.50-5	$4-10	$8	$8-17
Russel Wright, creamer	—	$7-8	$5.50	$8-12
Russel Wright, cup & saucer	—	$1.75-4	$6	$4-15
Russel Wright, dinner plate	—	$1.75	$5-7.50	$4-18
Russel Wright, salt & pepper	—	$4	$6.50	$8-13

CARE AND REPAIR OF DINNERWARE

Pottery dinnerwares were made to be used every day and will withstand normal use. Like all pottery, they will chip easily. Most of the dishes are dishwasher- and detergent-safe. Never put a dish with a crazed surface (covered with small lines) in a dishwasher. This may make the pieces of glaze pop off. Some of the decal decorations are not under the glaze and after repeated washings the decoration will fade or disappear. The Mexican-inspired designs such as Hacienda seem to have this problem.

Many dinnerware sets were made to be mixed and matched. Replacements for broken dishes can be found through the antiques shows and shops and the china matching services. (A list is available in Kovels' Guide to Selling Your Antiques & Collectibles.) Unless there is a very special sentimental reason, it is not practical to repair the dinnerware — buy replacements.

A COLLECTOR'S VOCABULARY LIST

Collectors need to know more than prices. They also need to understand the table settings of the past. The dinner sets of the 1930s had pieces that are unfamiliar today.

A *grill plate*, popular then, is an oddity today. The modern divided TV dinner tray was designed for the same purpose. Small ridges divided the plate so each food could be kept in a separate compartment. It kept the gravy away from the peas. A *berry bowl* is part of a set. Strawberries were put in a large master berry bowl about 6 to 8 inches in diameter. Each person took the berries and ate from a smaller, 3- to 4-inch-diameter berry bowl. A *bottom's-up* drinking glass is a 1930s joke. The glass was made without a flat base so it could not be put down until it was empty. The most popular form was a glass molded to resemble a woman draped around the glass. The rounded bottom was really a woman's rounded bottom.

A *butter dish* was a covered dish, round or rectangular, that held butter on the table or in the refrigerator. In the 1930s, butter was served at room temperature. A *console bowl* is a low oval bowl about 12 inches long. It was made with a matching pair of candlesticks so the set could be used in the center of a long table. An *ivy ball* is a simple round glass vase. Of course, it was made to hold ivy or flowers. A drinking glass is a *goblet* if it has a stem, a *tumbler* if it has no stem. There are also special names for stemmed glasses of various

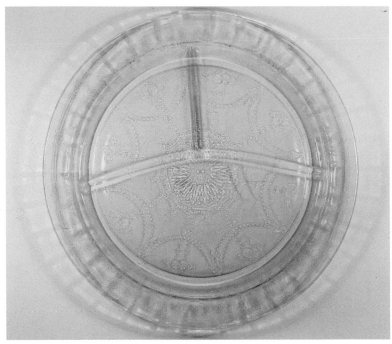

A yellow grill plate
in the Cameo pattern.

A green covered butter dish in
the Cubist pattern.

shapes and sizes, including *cordial*, *wine*, *cocktail*, *claret*, *champagne*, and *water*.

Every set of dinnerware had a *nappy* for each person. The nappy is a round or oval dish with a flat bottom and sloping sides. It is about 6 inches in diameter. The nappy is an all-purpose dish used for pudding, ice cream, peas, applesauce, or other juicy foods.

A set also had plates in a variety of sizes, ranging from a 6-inch *dessert plate* to 13 inches for a *chop plate* (serving dish). A complete set could also have a 7-inch *bread and butter plate*, 7½-inch *salad plate*, 8- to 9-inch *luncheon plate*, 9-inch *breakfast plate*, and 10-inch *dinner plate*.

A *tidbit* is a two- or three-layer serving piece with a metal upright and handle. Today it might be called an hors d'oeuvres plate or a cookie plate.

Pottery collectors need to know these terms plus a few others. A *ball jug* is a round pitcher first made by the Hall China Company in 1938. A *disk pitcher* is a water pitcher with flattened sides. This type of pitcher was often made for Fiesta sets. *Refrigerator sets* are specially designed containers for water, butter, or leftovers made specifically for a particular refrigerator manufacturer and included as part of the original equipment. A *coupe soup* is a special pottery bowl about 7 or 8 inches in diameter that has no handles and is used to serve soup. A *cream soup* holds bisque or creamed soup. It has two handles. A

A leftover dish made for Westing-house refrigerators.

A green Diamond Quilted cream soup with matching underliner plate.

Iroquois dishes designed by Russel Wright. These butter dishes are Oyster gray, Lettuce green, Forest green, and Irish red.

fluted baker or *French baker* is a dish with straight sides, now more commonly known as a soufflé dish. The small version holds a serving for one, larger versions serve eight. A *mixing bowl set* is a nest of bowls of graduated sizes made to fit inside each other. The bowls are numbered from 1 for the smallest.

Depression glass and American dinnerwares were first made in the 1930s. Customers wanted inexpensive, attractive, useful pieces to use in the kitchen or dining room. Styles have changed several times since then and today collectors recognize the good design and pleasing colors of these wares. There are many types of household wares from the past that can be collected but few are as useful as these glass or pottery dishes favored by our grandmothers. Search in the attics, the yard sales, and the shops and put together your own very special set of dishes to display and use.

AMERICAN DINNERWARE

AMERICAN DINNERWARE

Introduction

Many patterns of ceramic dinnerware were made in America from the 1930s through the 1960s. Some collectors refer to it as "Depression dinnerware," but the name used by the manufacturers was "American dinnerware," and that is the name used by most collectors and dealers.

Pottery, porcelain, semiporcelain, ironstone, and other ceramic wares are included in the category of dinnerware. Most were made in potteries located in Southern Ohio and in West Virginia near the Ohio River. Each factory made many patterns for sale to gift shops and department stores. The potteries also made special patterns for use as premiums and free giveaways or to sell for low prices as store promotions.

American dinnerware patterns fall into six categories. The first patterns to be rediscovered by collectors and the first to be reproduced have been the solid-colored pottery lines such as Fiesta or Harlequin. Some of this type of dinnerware was also made in California potteries before 1960.

Many manufacturers preferred hand-painted decorations on their dinnerware. Included in this group are the pieces made by Southern Potteries under the name Blue Ridge and the pottery by Stangl of New Jersey picturing fruit, flowers, or birds.

An unusual type of dinnerware made by Harker and others was Cameo Ware: a solid-colored plate embellished with a white decoration that appears to be cut into the colored glaze.

Realistically shaped pieces resembling corn were produced by several makers. The most important was Corn King by the Shawnee Pottery Company. Green and yellow dishes were made in full sets. Other dishes in three-dimensional shapes include the Red Riding Hood line, many figural cookie jars, a few figural teapots, and salt and pepper shakers.

Some of the dishes were made in very modern shapes with solid-colored decorations. The innovative shapes and subtle earth-tone colorings made them a favorite in the 1940s and 1950s. Examples of these are wares designed by Russel Wright for several firms and the Lu-Ray pattern by Taylor, Smith, and Taylor.

Most of the dinnerware was decorated with decal designs: colored, printed patterns applied to the dishes. The most famous of these designs, Autumn Leaf, was made for and sold by the Jewel Tea Company. Mexican-inspired designs such as Mexicana by Homer Laughlin were popular during the late 1930s. The Hall China Company made many decal-decorated wares, including Poppy, Red Poppy, and Crocus. Black silhouette designs against light-colored dishes were popular in the 1930s, and included Silhouette by the Crooksville China Company and Taverne by the Hall China Company.

Because dishes were made by so many manufacturers, there is a problem with variations in vocabulary. Most sugar bowls made for these dinnerware sets had covers. Today many have lost the original cover and are sold as open sugars. We do not include the word "open" in the description, but we do indicate if there is a cover.

The terms "kitchenware" and "dinnerware" are used in the original sense. A dinnerware set includes all the pieces that might have been used on a dinner table, including dishes, bowls, platters, tumblers, cups, pitchers, and serving bowls. A kitchenware set has bowls and storage dishes of the type used in a kitchen and does not include dinner plates or cups. Kitchenwares include rolling pins, pie servers, and other kitchen utensils.

Colors often were given romantic names; and, whenever necessary, we have used more ordinary language. So although we may describe a set as "Surf Green" or "Persian Cream," we will list it as green or ivory. Some colors, such as Camellia (rose), Cadet (light blue), Indian Red (orange), or Dresden (deep blue), are explained in the paragraph descriptions.

It is important to remember that the descriptions of dinnerware may include many strange names. Some are the factory names, some names refer to the pattern (decorations applied to the piece), and many of the names were used by the factory to describe the shape. For example, Taverne is a pattern, Laurel is the shape of the dish used to make that pattern, and Taylor, Smith, and Taylor is the name of the company that made the dinnerware. Sometimes a name refers to both a pattern and a shape.

Pieces of American dinnerware are constantly being discovered in attics, basements, garage sales, flea markets, and antiques shops. The publications that offer them through the mail use descriptions that often include both the pattern and the shape name. Learn to recognize the shapes that were used by each maker. Authors of some of the other books about dinnerwares have arbitrarily named the pieces. Sometimes these names, although referring to the same piece, are different in different books. We have tried to cross-reference these names so you can locate them in any of the books. A list of known patterns of dinnerware, shapes, and makers is included at the end of this section.

Although hundreds of patterns are included in this book, many patterns were not seen at sales this year and were not included. Prices listed in this book are actual prices asked by dealers at shows, shops, and through national advertising. It is not the price you would pay at a garage sale or church bazaar. Prices are not estimates. If a high and low are given, we have recorded several sales. There is a regional variation in the prices, especially for the solid-colored wares. In general, these pieces are high-priced in the East and West, lower in the center of the country.

There have been a few reissues of dinnerwares. Harlequin was put back into production in 1979 for the Woolworth Company, the sole distributor. Complete dinner sets were made in the original colors, except that the salmon is a deeper color than the original. The sugar bowls were made with closed handles. A Fiesta look-alike has been made by Franciscan since 1978 under the name Kaleidoscope. Fiesta was reissued by Homer Laughlin China Company in 1986. The original molds and marks were used. The new Fiesta has a china body that shrinks a little more than the semi-vitreous clay body used before. This means that most pieces are slightly smaller than the old ones. Dinner plates and soup-cereal bowls, however, were made slightly larger to accommodate modern tastes. New molds were made for these pieces. The dinner plates are 10 1/2 inches. The new dishes were first made in cobalt blue (darker than the original), black, white, apricot, and rose. Other colors have been added. A few of the pieces have been slightly redesigned since 1986 and there are variations in handles and bases.

If you plan to collect dinnerwares, be sure to do further research into your patterns in the books listed in the Bibliography that follows.

Particular patterns can be found by using either the Depression Glass or American Dinnerware main listings, both of which are arranged alphabetically. Depression Glass begins on page 11 and American Dinnerware on page 132. There is no index of pattern names in this book because it would only duplicate the main listings. However, we have compiled lists of known Depression glass and American Dinnerware patterns along with information on manufacturers, dates, alternate names, and descriptions. These can be found at the end of each section.

Patterns listed in the main sections of the book are those most popular with collectors. This book is a report of prices for pieces offered for sale during the past year. Most of the patterns included in earlier books are still to be found here because the collectors still buy these patterns. Many newly popular patterns are also included.

AMERICAN DINNERWARE
Bibliography

Bess, Phyllis and Tom. *Frankoma Treasures.* Privately printed, 1983 (14535 E. 13th St., Tulsa, OK 74108).

Bess, Phyllis and Tom. *Suggested Values for Frankoma Treasures.* Privately printed, 1990 (14535 E. 13th St., Tulsa, OK 74108).

Bougie, Stanley J. and David A. Newkirk. *Red Wing Dinnerware.* Privately printed, 1980 (Rte. 3, Box 141, Monticello, MN 55362).

Catalina Art Pottery Price List and General Sales Instructions, 1942 (catalog reprint). Privately printed, 1982 (Delleen Enge, 912 N. Signal, Ojai, CA 93023).

Chipman, Jack and Judy Stangler. *Bauer Pottery 1982 Price Guide.* Privately printed, 1982 (16 East Holly Street, Pasadena, CA 91003).

Cox, Susan N. *Collectors Guide to Frankoma Pottery,* Book Two. Privately printed, 1982 (P.O. Box 2674, La Mesa, CA 92041).

Cunningham, Jo. *Autumn Leaf Story Price Guide, 1979/1980.* Privately printed, 1979 (Box 4929, Springfield, MO 65808).

Cunningham, Jo. *Collector's Encyclopedia of American Dinnerware.* Paducah, Kentucky: Collector Books, 1982.

Cunningham, Jo. *Hall China Price Update.* Privately printed, 1982 (Box 4929, Springfield, MO 65808).

Derwich, Jenny and Mary Latos. *Dictionary Guide to United States Pottery & Porcelain (19th and 20th Century).* Privately printed, 1984 (P.O. Box 674, Franklin, MI 48025).

Dole, Pat. *Purinton Pottery.* Privately printed, 1984 (P.O. Box 4782, Birmingham, AL 35206).

Duke, Harvey. *Official Identification and Price Guide to Pottery and Porcelain,* 7th edition. New York: House of Collectibles, 1989.

Duke, Harvey. *Superior Quality Hall China: A Guide for Collectors.* Privately printed, 1977 (Box HB, 12135 N. State Road, Otisville, MI 48463).

Enge, Delleen. *Franciscan Ware.* Paducah, Kentucky: Collector Books, 1981.

Eva Zeisel: Designer for Industry. Chicago: University of Chicago Press, 1984.

Farmer, Linda D. *Farmer's Wife's Fiesta Inventory & Price Guide.* Privately printed, 1984 (P.O. Box 10371, Pittsburgh, PA 15234).

Fridley, A. W. *Catalina Pottery: The Early Years 1927-1937.* Privately printed, 1977 (P.O. Box 7723, Long Beach, CA 90807). *From Kiln to Kitchen: American Ceramic Design in Tableware.* Springfield, Illinois: Illinois State Museum, 1980.

Hayes, Barbara and Jean Bauer. *California Pottery Rainbow.* Privately printed, 1975 (1629 W. Washington Boulevard, Venice, CA 90291).

Homer Laughlin China Company: A Fiesta of American Dinnerware. Newell, West Virginia: Homer Laughlin China Co., 1985.

Hull, Joan Gray. *Hull: The Heavenly Pottery.* Privately printed, 1990 (173 Second S.W., Huron, SD 57350).

Huxford, Sharon and Bob. *Collectors Encyclopedia of Fiesta,* 6th Edition. Paducah, Kentucky: Collector Books, 1987.

Huxford, Sharon and Bob. *Collectors Encyclopedia of Roseville Pottery.* Paducah, Kentucky: Collector Books, 1976.

Keillor, Winnie. *Dishes What Else? Blue Ridge of Course!* Privately printed, 1983 (5731 Gorivan Road, Frankfort, MI 49635).

Kerr, Ann. *Collector's Encyclopedia of Russel Wright Designs.* Paducah, Kentucky: Collector Books, 1990.

Kerr, Ann. *Russel Wright and His Dinnerware.* Privately printed, 1981 (P.O. Box 437, Sidney, OH 45365).

Kerr, Ann. *Russel Wright Dinnerware: Designs for the American Table.* Paducah, Kentucky: Collector Books, 1985.

Kerr, Ann. *Steubenville Sage.* Privately printed, 1979 (P.O. Box 437, Sidney, OH 45365).

Klein, Benjamin. *Collector's Illustrated Price Guide to Russel Wright Dinnerware.* Smithtown, New York: Exposition Press, Inc., 1981.

Kovel, Ralph and Terry. *Kovels' Antiques & Collectibles Price List,* 23rd Edition. New York: Crown Publishers, 1990.

Kovel, Ralph and Terry. *Kovels' Guide to Selling Your Antiques & Collectibles,* Updated Edition. New York: Crown Publishers, 1990.

Kovel, Ralph and Terry. *Kovels' Know Your Collectibles.* New York: Crown Publishers, 1981.

Kovel, Ralph and Terry. *Kovels' New Dictionary of Marks Pottery & Porcelain 1850 to the Present.* New York: Crown Publishers, 1986.

Lehner, Lois. *Complete Book of American Kitchen and Dinner Wares.* New York: Wallace-Homestead Book Co., 1980.

Lehner, Lois. *Lehner's Encyclopedia of U.S. Marks on Pottery, Porcelain & Clay.* Paducah, Kentucky: Collector Books, 1988.

Nelson, Maxine Feek. *Versatile Vernon Kilns.* Privately printed, 1978 (P.O. Box 1686, Huntington Beach, CA 92647).

Nelson, Maxine. *Versatile Vernon Kilns Book II.* Paducah, Kentucky: Collector Books, 1983.

Newbound, Betty. *Gunshot Guide to Values of American Made China & Pottery.* Privately printed, 1981 (4567 Chadsworth, Union Lake, MI 48085).

Newbound, Betty. *Gunshot Guide to Values of American Made China & Pottery.* Privately printed, 1984 (4567 Chadsworth, Union Lake, MI 48085).

Newbound, Betty and Bill. *Southern Potteries Inc. Blue Ridge Dinnerware,* 3rd Edition. Paducah, Kentucky: Collector Books, 1989.

Newkirk, David A. *Guide to Red Wing Prices.* Privately printed, 1982 (Rte. 3, Box 146, Monticello, MN 55362). *Pottery 1880-1960.* Encino, California: Orlando Gallery, 1973.

Rehl, Norma. *Abingdon Pottery.* Privately printed, 1981 (P.O. Box 556, Milford, NJ 08848).

Rehl, Norma. *Collectors Handbook of Stangl Pottery.* Privately printed, 1979 (P.O. Box 556, Milford, NJ 08848).

Rehl, Norma. *Stangl Pottery Part II.* Privately printed, 1982 (P.O. Box 556, Milford, NJ 08848).

Riederer, LaHoma and Charles Bettinger. *Fiesta III, A Collector's Guide to Fiesta Dinnerware.* Privately printed, 1980 (P.O. Box 2733, Monroe, LA 71201).

Roberts, Brenda. *Collectors Encyclopedia of Hull Pottery.* Paducah, Kentucky: Collector Books, 1980.

Schneider, Robert. *Coors Rosebud Pottery.* Privately printed, 1984 (Box 10382S Pike Place Station, Seattle, WA 98101).

Simon, Dolores. *Red Wing Pottery with Rumrill.* Paducah, Kentucky: Collector Books, 1980.

Simon, Dolores. *Shawnee Pottery.* Paducah, Kentucky: Collector Books, 1977.

Supnick, Mark E. *Collecting Shawnee Pottery,* Revised Edition. Gas City, Indiana: L-W Book Sales, 1989.

Teftt, Gary and Bonnie. *Red Wing Potters & Their Wares.* Privately printed, 1981 (W174 N9422 Devonwood Road, Menomonee Falls, WI 53051).

Whitmyer, Margaret and Kenn. *Collector's Encyclopedia of Hall China.* Paducah, Kentucky: Collector Books, 1989.

AMERICAN DINNERWARE

Clubs and Publications

CLUBS

Abingdon Pottery Collectors Club, *Abingdon Pottery Collectors Newsletter*, Route 1, Box 29-A, Altoona, IL 61414.

Blue & White Pottery Club, *Blue & White Pottery Club* (newsletter), 224 12th Street NW, Center Point, IA 52405.

International Willow Collectors, *American Willow Report* (newsletter), P.O. Box 900, Oakridge, OR 97463.

Novelty Salt & Pepper Shakers Club, *Novelty Salt & Pepper Shakers Club Newsletter*, R.D. 2, Box 2131, Stroudsburg, PA 18360.

Red Wing Collectors Society, *Red Wing Collectors Newsletter*, Route 3, Box 146, Monticello, MN 55362.

Shawnee Pottery Collector's Club, *Exclusively Shawnee* (newsletter), P.O. Box 713, New Smyrna Beach, FL 32170-0713.

PUBLICATIONS

Antique Trader Weekly (newspaper), P.O. Box 1050, Dubuque, IA 52001.

Daze (newsletter), Box 57, Otisville, MI 48463.

Hall China Encore (newsletter), 317 North Pleasant Street, Oberlin, OH 44074.

Hot Tea (newsletter), Handle on the Teapot Enthusiast Association, 882 South Mollison Avenue, El Cajon, CA 92020.

Kovels on Antiques and Collectibles (newsletter), P.O. Box 22200, Beachwood, OH 44122.

Matching Services: China, Silver, Crystal (leaflet), Ralph and Terry Kovel (P.O. Box 22900, Beachwood, OH 44122).

National Blue Ridge Newsletter, 144 Highland Drive, Blountville, TN 37617.

New Glaze (newsletter), P.O. Box 4782, Birmingham, AL 35206.

"Our McCoy Matters" (newsletter), 12704 Lockleven Lane, Woodbridge, VA 22192.

Vernon Views (newsletter) (Vernon Kilns pottery), P.O. Box 945, Scottsdale, AZ 85252.

Willow Word (magazine), P.O. Box 13382, Arlington, TX 76094-0382.

A

Amberstone

Fiesta is a popular dinnerware pattern found in solid colors. In 1967 Amberstone was made by the Homer Laughlin China Company of Newell, West Virginia, using the Fiesta shapes. The pieces were glazed a rich brown. Some pieces ·had black machine-stamped underglaze patterns. The pieces were used for supermarket promotions and were called Genuine Sheffield dinnerware. Full sets of dishes were made.

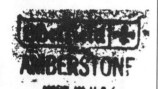

Bowl, 5 1/2 In.	3.00
Bread Plate	2.50
Cup & Saucer	7.50
Plate, 10 In.	6.00
Salt & Pepper	6.00

American Modern

Russel Wright was a designer who made dinnerware in modern shapes for many companies, including Iroquois China Company, Harker China Company, Steubenville Pottery, Paden City (Justin Tharaud and Sons), Sterling China Company, Edwin M. Knowles China Company, and Bauer Company. American Modern was made by the Steubenville Pottery Company, Steubenville, Ohio, from 1939 to 1959. The original dishes were made in Bean Brown (a shaded brown), chartreuse, Coral, Granite Gray, Seafoam (blue-green), and white. The brown was replaced with Black Chutney (dark brown) during World War II. Canteloupe, Cedar Green, and Glacier Blue were added in the 1950s. Matching linens and glassware were made.

Russel Wright
MFG. BY
STEUBENVILLE

. . . .

China can be washed in warm water with mild soap suds. The addition of ammonia to the water will add that extra sparkle.

. . . .

BEAN BROWN ————

Bowl, Salad	40.00
Creamer	10.00
Cup & Saucer, Demitasse	20.00
Pitcher	45.00
Plate, 10 In.	10.00
Platter	24.00
Salt & Pepper	8.00
Sauce Boat	16.00

BLACK CHUTNEY ————

Cup	4.00
Dish, Pickle	7.50
Plate, 10 In.	10.00
Sugar & Creamer	23.00

CANTELOUPE ————

Plate, 6 1/4 In.	6.00
Platter	45.00
Sauce Boat	35.00

CEDAR GREEN ————

Baker, Small	30.00
Bowl, Soup	12.00
Bowl, Vegetable	12.00
Creamer	12.00
Cup	4.00
Cup & Saucer	10.00
Plate, 6 1/4 In.	6.00
Plate, 10 In.	10.00
Sugar, Cover	20.00

CHARTREUSE ————

Ashtray	12.00 To 15.00
Bowl, Salad	40.00
Bowl, Vegetable	8.00 To 10.00
Casserole, Cover, 12 In.	40.00
Celery, 12 In.	25.00

Coffeepot, After Dinner 55.00
Cup & Saucer............... 4.00
Cup & Saucer,
   After Dinner 15.00
Plate, 10 In. 10.00
Sugar, Cover................ 6.00
Teapot .... 30.00 To 37.50

CORAL

Ashtray 11.00
Baker, Open 12.00
Bowl, Vegetable, 10 In. 18.00
Creamer....................10.00
Gravy Boat 15.00
Pitcher .... 45.00 To 60.00
Plate, 6 1/4 In.............. 4.00
Plate, 8 In................... 6.00
Plate, 10 In. 8.00
Plate, 13 In. 26.00
Salt & Pepper..............13.00
Tumbler 45.00

GLACIER BLUE

Baker 45.00
Celery......................45.00

GRANITE GRAY

Bowl, Vegetable, 10 In. 14.00
Coffeepot 40.00
Cup & Saucer.......4.00 To 6.00
Cup & Saucer,
   After Dinner 20.00
Gravy Boat,
   Underplate ..... 20.00 To 30.00
Pitcher......................67.50
Plate, 8 In................... 6.00
Plate, 10 In. ....4.00 To 7.50
Salt & Pepper......8.00 To 10.00
Saucer....................... 1.00

SEAFOAM

Bowl, Vegetable 19.00
Creamer..................... 8.00
Cup 8.00
Gravy Boat ...... 15.00 To 22.00
Plate, 6 1/4 In.............. 4.00
Plate, 10 In. 8.00
Saltshaker 4.00
Saucer...................... 3.00

Sugar, Cover................10.00

WHITE

Bowl, Vegetable 28.00
Casserole...................45.00
Coaster.....................20.00
Cup & Saucer...............15.00
Gravy Boat 22.00
Pitcher......................65.00
Plate, 8 In..................18.00
Plate, 10 In. 18.00
Plate, 13 In. 35.00

Americana

Americana (pattern A2000) was made by Stangl Pottery of Trenton, New Jersey, in the 1930s. The pieces were modern in shape and glazed with solid colors, including Colonial Blue, green, tangerine, and yellow.

STANGL 2000

Plate, 7 In................... 7.00
Plate, 8 In................... 8.00
Saucer, 5 3/4 In. 6.00
Saucer, 6 1/2 In. 5.00
Soup, Liner 8.00

Apple & Pear

Apple & Pear was made by Blue Ridge in the 1950s. The Woodcrest shape was decorated with red apples, yellow pears, and green leaves.

Bowl, 5 In. 6.00
Bowl, 6 In. 10.00
Cookie Jar 18.50
Pitcher, 1 Qt................12.00
Plate, Salad, Square......... 5.00
Salt & Pepper..............12.50
Soup, Dish..................10.00
Water Set, 7 Piece..........95.00

Apple Blossom

Two companies made patterns called Apple Blossom. Crooksville China of Crooksville, Ohio, made a pink flowered pattern. The pattern listed here was made by Homer Laughlin China Company of Newell, West Virginia, from 1935 to 1955. It has a flowered border and gold trim.

Bowl, 5 In. 2.00
Plate, 6 In.................. 1.50
Plate, 10 In. 3.50
Soup, Dish.................. 4.00

Apple Delight

Apple Delight was made by Stangl from 1965 to 1974. The pattern featured red and yellow apples as a center design and a dark border.

Ashtray ....5.00 To 7.50
Pitcher Set,
  4 Short Mugs..............35.00
Pitcher, 2 Qt................27.50
Saucer, 6 In..................3.00

Apple Franciscan

Gladding, McBean & Company made Apple pattern dishes, one of its Franciscan Ceramics "Classics" designs, beginning in 1940. The pattern is still being made, but Franciscan Ceramics is now part of Wedgwood Inc.

• • • • • • • • • • • • • • • •
When stacking dinner plates put a piece of felt or paper between each plate. Never put more than 24 in one stack.
• • • • • • • • • • • • • • • •

Ashtray, Individual..........12.50
Baker, 7 In....... 19.00 To 25.00
Bowl, 5 1/4 In. 4.00
Bowl, 6 In. ....8.00 To 15.00
Bowl, 9 In. 20.00
Bowl, Fruit ....3.50 To 7.00
Bowl, Vegetable 25.00
Bowl, Vegetable,
  Divided....................32.00
Butter, Cover,
  1/4 Lb.......... 22.50 To 25.00
Casserole, Cover,
  2 1/2 Qt. 45.00
Casserole, Individual........25.00
Chop Plate, Round,
  12 In. 50.00
Clock, Battery Operated,
  10 In. 35.00
Coaster......................22.00
Coffeepot, 8 Cup 25.00
Cookie Jar, Cover........ 100.00
Creamer.......... 10.00 To 14.00
Cup & Saucer......8.00 To 15.00
Eggcup......................15.00
Gravy Boat,
  Attached Plate .... 23.00 To 30.00
Marmalade,
  Cover........... 48.00 To 65.00
Mug, 12 Oz.................18.00
Pitcher, 32 Oz. 38.00
Plate, 6 In..........3.00 To 4.00
Plate, 8 In..........7.00 To 12.00
Plate, 9 1/2 In...............9.00
Plate,
  10 1/2 In....... 10.00 To 15.00
Platter, 12 In..... 20.00 To 24.00
Platter, 14 In..... 20.00 To 38.00
Relish,
  3 Sections ...... 20.00 To 22.50
Salt & Pepper...... 15.00 To 22.00
Saucer...............1.50 To 3.00

Saucer, Demitasse............ 4.00
Sherbet .... 15.00 To 27.00
Soup, Dish..................12.00
Sugar, Cover..... 15.00 To 20.00
Teapot, 6 Cup 55.00
Tidbit, 2 Tiers 30.00
Tumbler, 6 Oz..............16.00

Apple Watt

The Watt Pottery Company was incorporated in Crooksville, Ohio, in 1922. Watt made a variety of hand-decorated potteries. The most popular is Apple pattern. It was made from the 1930s as dinnerware sets and also in kitchenwares. The company burned to the ground in 1965.

Baker, No.96...............18.50
Bean Pot, No.76............55.00
Bowl Set, No.5, 6, 7, 8 ....95.00
Bowl Set, No.63, 64,
  65 .... 100.00
Bowl, No. 5 ....35.00
Bowl, No. 7 ....35.00
Bowl, No.14................22.00
Bowl, No.64................18.00
Bowl, No.65................35.00
Bowl, No.73..... 40.00 To 45.00
Bowl, No.74................15.00
Casserole, No. 96,
  Cover........... 35.00 To 65.00
Casserole, No.110 ....40.00
Cookie Jar, No.76, Cover...50.00
Creamer,
  No.62 .... 35.00 To 45.00
Ice Bucket, No.59 ....95.00
Mug, No.501 .... 100.00

Nappy, No.7 . . . . .32.00

Pie Plate,
  Advertising . . . . . 65.00 To 95.00

Pitcher, No. 6 . . . . .32.50

Pitcher, No.16 . . . 25.00 To 45.00

Pitcher, No.17 . . . . .95.00

Pitcher, No.62 . . . 15.00 To 38.00

Salt & Pepper . . . .125.00 To 225.00

Sugar, No.98 . . . . .70.00

Arcadia

Arcadia pattern was made by
Vernon Kilns of Los Angeles,
California, about 1947.

Plate, 7 1/2 In 2.50

Salt & Pepper 11.00

Arlington Apple

Arlington Apple is a Blue
Ridge pattern made in the
1950s. Two red apples are
painted on pieces in the Skyline shape.

Cup & Saucer 6.50

Plate, 10 In. . . . . .2.00 To 6.00

Platter, 12 In. 7.50

Saucer. 2.00

Autumn Apple

Autumn Apple is another
Blue Ridge pattern featuring
apples. This pattern, on the
Colonial shape, pictures small
apples on branches surround-
ing the center of the plate.
Red swatches of paint decorate the rim.

Bread Plate 2.50

Pie Plate 6.00

Platter, 12 In. 7.50

Soup, Dish 6.00

Autumn Leaf

One of the most popular
American dinnerware patterns,
Autumn Leaf was made for
the Jewel Tea Company, a
grocery chain, beginning in
1936. Hall China Company of
East Liverpool, Ohio; Crooks-
ville China Company of
Crooksville, Ohio; Harker
Potteries of Chester, West
Virginia; and Paden City Pot-

tery of Paden City, West Virginia, made dishes with this
design. The Autumn Leaf pattern always has the same
shades of dark yellow and rust
leaves. The shape of the dish
varied with the manufacturer.
Several special terms are used
to describe these shapes, such
as "bud-ray," which describes a
bowl lid with a knob sur-
rounded by raised rays. Collectors can find Autumn Leaf
pattern tinware, plastic tablecloths, glassware, clocks, even
painted furniture. There are
several books about Autumn
Leaf and a collectors club
listed in other sections of this
book.

Baker, French,
  3 Sections . . . . . . 10.00 To 12.00

Bowl, 5 1/2 In. . . . .4.00 To 6.00

Bowl, 6 1/2 In. 10.00

Bowl, Vegetable, Cover, Oval,
  10 In. .42.00

Bowl, Vegetable, Oval,
  10 1/2 In. . . . . . . 12.00 To 15.00

Butter, 1 Lb. 325.00

Butter, 1/4 Lb. 155.00

Cake Plate . . . . .8.00 To 10.00

Cake Stand, Metal Base . . . 125.00

Cannister Set, Cover, Round, 6,
7 & 8 1/4 In.,
3 Piece 55.00
Casserole, Cover,
2 Qt. .... 12.00 To 18.00
Coffee Server, 9 Cup 45.00
Coffeepot, 8 Cup 30.00
Coffeepot, 9 Cup 37.00
Cookie Jar 130.00
Creamer, Rayed.............11.00
Creamer,
Ruffled ....4.00 To 10.00
Cup ....4.00 To 6.00
Cup & Saucer......5.00 To 12.00
Gravy Boat 20.00
Jar, Drip 16.00
Jug, Beverage,
Ball............. 14.00 To 20.00
Marmalade, 3 Piece.........30.00
Mixing Bowl Set, 3 1/2 Qt.,
2 Qt, 1 Qt, 3 Piece.......95.00
Mixing Bowl, 1 Qt...........8.00
Mustard, Cover, Underplate,
3 Piece .... 30.00 To 40.00
Pepper Shaker, Range 9.00
Pitcher, Ball,
Ice Lip.......... 22.00 To 28.00
Plate, 6 In...........2.00 To 5.00
Plate, 8 In....................5.00
Plate, 9 In....... 10.00 To 16.00
Plate, 10 In. 10.00
Platter,
11 1/2 In...... 10.00 To 12.00
Platter,
13 1/2 In...... 14.00 To 25.00
Salt & Pepper,
Range .... 12.00 To 18.00
Saltshaker 5.00
Saucer...............1.50 To 2.00
Soup, Cream 23.00
Soup, Dish....... 10.00 To 15.00
Stack Set,
4 Piece .... 47.00 To 95.00
Sugar & Creamer, Cover,
Rayed 30.00
Sugar & Creamer, Cover,
Ruffled 18.00
Sugar, Cover, Ruffled........9.00
Teapot,
Aladdin......... 30.00 To 35.00
Tidbit, 3 Tiers 75.00

Tray, Rectangular...........75.00
Tumbler, Frosted,
3 3/4 In........ 17.00 To 20.00
Tumbler, Frosted,
5 1/2 In....... 12.00 To 22.00
Vase, Bud, Crimped 195.00
Warmer, Round 125.00

B

Ballerina

Solid-colored pottery was
popular in the 1950s. Universal Potteries of Cambridge,
Ohio, made Ballerina from
1947 to 1956. Ballerina was
very modern in shape and had
solid-colored glazes. A later
line was decorated with abstract designs. The original
solid-colored Ballerina dinnerware was offered in Dove
Gray, Jade Green, Jonquil
Yellow, and Periwinkle Blue.
In 1949 chartreuse and forest
green were added. By 1955
burgundy, charcoal, and pink
were added, while some other
colors had been discontinued.
There was also a line called
Ballerina Mist, which was a
pale blue-green with decal
decorations.

BLUE ────────────
Saucer......................1.00

BURGUNDY ────────────
Plate, 6 In....................2.00

CHARTREUSE ────────────
Chop Plate, 11 1/2 In.......2.00

DOVE GRAY ────────────
Cup 3.00
Gravy Boat 4.00
Plate, 9 In....................3.00
Plate, Handle, 10 In. 4.50
Salt..........................3.00
Saucer.......................1.00

FOREST GREEN ────────────
Bowl, 5 1/2 In. 2.00
Cup & Saucer................3.00
Gravy 4.00
Plate, 6 In..........1.50 To 2.00
Plate, 7 1/2 In................3.00
Plate, 9 In....................3.00
Plate, 10 In. 4.00
Sugar, Cover.................3.50

JONQUIL YELLOW ────────────
Plate, 6 In....................2.00
Plate, 9 In....................3.00
Plate, 10 In. 4.00

PINK ────────────
Salt..........................3.00

Bamboo

Bamboo was a pattern name
used by several firms. Pieces
listed here were made by
Blue Ridge in the 1950s.

Cup & Saucer................4.00
Plate, 8 1/2 In................3.00
Plate, 10 In. ....4.00 To 5.00
Plate, Fruit..................2.50
Soup, Dish, 5 3/4 In. 3.50

Sugar 4.00

BEEHIVE, see Ring

Betty

Betty is a Blue Ridge pattern made on the Candlewick shape. It features a red flower, a yellow flower, and green leaves.

Creamer..................... 3.50
Cup & Saucer................ 4.50
Plate, 9 In.................. 3.00
Platter, 15 In...............10.00

Bittersweet

Blue Ridge, Hall, Universal, and Stangl potteries made patterns named Bittersweet. Listed here is the Stangl Bittersweet pattern.

Bowl, Vegetable, 8 In.......10.00
Coaster..................... 5.50
Cup & Saucer.......5.50 To 8.00
Plate, 5 In.................. 5.00
Plate, 6 In.................. 3.00
Plate, 7 In.................. 4.00
Plate, 10 In. 4.50

Blossom Time

Blossom Time by Red Wing Pottery was made in 1947. It is a dinnerware with modern shapes, red flowers, and green leaves. Yellow and green accessory pieces were made.

Bowl, 5 In. 3.00
Cup & Saucer................ 5.50
Plate, 9 In.................. 5.00
Plate, 10 1/2 In. 5.00

Blue Blossom

Blue Blossom is a kitchenware made by the Hall China Company about 1939. It is a cobalt blue glazed ware with floral decal decoration.

Bean Pot, Cover, New England
..............100.00 To 125.00

Casserole, Cover,
  Thick Rim.................40.00
Cookie Jar, Five Band 75.00
Jug, Ball, Five Band,
  7 In............ 50.00 To 55.00

Blue Bouquet

Standard Coffee of New Orleans, Louisiana, gave Blue Bouquet pattern dinnerware and kitchenware as a premium from the early 1950s to the early 1960s. Although it was made by the Hall China Company, East Liverpool, Ohio, it is most easily found in the South. The pattern is very plain with a thin blue border interrupted by roses.

Casserole, Big Lip 25.00
Mixing Bowl, No.3.........16.00
Sugar & Creamer, Boston...20.00

Blue Daisy

Stangl pottery made Blue Daisy pattern from 1963 to 1974. As you might guess, the pieces were decorated with blue daisies.

Cup 8.00
Cup & Saucer...............11.00
Mug, Coffee 8.00
Plate, 6 In...................6.00
Plate, 10 In. 10.00

BLUE PARADE, see Rose
  Parade

Blue Willow

Willow pattern pictures a bridge, three figures, birds, trees, and a Chinese landscape. The pattern was first used in England by Thomas Turner in 1780 at the Caughley Pottery Works. It was inspired by an earlier Chinese pattern. The pattern has been copied by makers in almost every country. Many pieces of Blue Willow were made by Homer Laughlin, Sebring, and other American makers, but we list dishes here from these and foreign firms.

Bowl, 5 3/4 In., Japan	4.50
Bowl, 6 In., Homer Laughlin	4.50
Bread Plate, Royal	4.00
Creamer, Royal	5.00
Cruet, Stopper	18.00
Cup & Saucer, Demitasse	20.00
Cup & Saucer, Homer Laughlin	5.50
Cup & Saucer, Japan	7.00
Cup & Saucer, Royal	4.50
Cup, Royal	4.00
Grill Plate, Japan	9.00 To 13.00
Grill Plate, Royal	15.00
Plate, 6 In.	1.25
Plate, 6 In., Allerton	2.00
Plate, 6 In., Homer Laughlin	2.00
Plate, 6 In., Royal	2.00
Plate, 7 In., Royal	4.00
Plate, 9 In., Homer Laughlin	5.00
Plate, 9 3/4 In., Allerton	12.00 To 18.00
Plate, 10 In., Allerton	18.00
Plate, 12 In., Royal	15.00
Platter, 15 X 12 In., Allerton	70.00
Salt & Pepper, Wooden Base	9.00
Saucer, Royal	2.00 To 4.00
Soup, Dish, Allerton	16.00
Tumbler, 5 In.	12.00
Tumbler, 5 1/2 In.	14.00

Blueberry

Stangl Pottery of Trenton, New Jersey, made Blueberry (pattern No. 3770) before 1942. The heavy red pottery dishes were glazed with a yellow border and a sgraffito decoration of blueberries in the center.

Pitcher, 1 Qt.	10.00
Plate, 6 In.	3.50
Plate, 9 In.	7.50
Plate, 10 In.	9.50

Bob White

Bob White was made by Red Wing Potteries from 1956 to 1967. It was one of the most popular dinnerware patterns made by the factory. The pattern, a modern hand-painted design, shows a stylized bird and background.

Bowl, Salad	22.50 To 28.00
Bowl, Vegetable, 2 Sections	20.00 To 25.00
Casserole, 2 Handles	30.00
Cruet	150.00
Cup	4.00 To 6.00
Cup & Saucer	10.00 To 15.00
Gravy Boat, Cover, Handle	32.00
Pitcher, 12 In.	22.50 To 28.00
Pitcher, Small	15.00 To 20.00
Plate, 6 1/2 In.	2.00 To 4.00
Plate, 10 1/2 In.	6.00 To 7.00
Platter, Small	20.00
Relish, 3 Sections, Handle	25.00 To 30.00
Salt & Pepper, Short	15.00 To 20.00
Server, Center Metal Handle	9.00
Shaker, 6 1/2 In.	7.00 To 11.00

Sugar 12.00
Teapot .... 30.00 To 50.00
Tray, French Bread 75.00

Brittany

Brittany is a pattern made by Red Wing in 1941. It pictures a yellow rose and a yellow band on the rim of the plates.

Bowl, 9 1/2 In. 12.00
Plate, 10 In. 7.00
Shaker 4.50

Brown-Eyed Susan

Brown-Eyed Susan was first made by Vernon Kilns, Vernon, California, in the 1940s.

Bowl, Chowder 5.00
Creamer......................8.00
Creamer, Cover.............12.00
Mug 13.00
Plate, 7 In....................3.50
Plate, 10 1/2 In. 4.50
Salt & Pepper......8.00 To 12.00

C

Calico

Calico is one of the plaid designs made by Vernon Kilns of Vernon, California. The design was pink and blue with a blue border. Other related plaids are Coronation Organdy (gray and rose), Gingham (green and yellow), Homespun (cinnamon, yellow, and green), Organdie (brown and yellow), Tam O'Shanter (green, lime, and cinnamon), and Tweed (gray and blue).

Carafe.......................25.00
Pitcher, 11 In. 22.50
Plate, 9 In....................6.00
Saucer....................... 1.00

Calico Fruit

Dinnerware and kitchenware were made in Calico Fruit pattern in the 1940s. The pattern was made by Universal Potteries, Cambridge, Ohio; matching tinware and glass pieces were also made by other firms. The design of the fruit is a vivid red and blue on a plain white dish. Unfortunately, the decals often fade.

Bowl, 6 In. 10.00
Bowl, Cover, 5 1/4 In......14.00
Jug, Refrigerator...........18.00
Pitcher, Utility, 6 1/2 In....32.00

Caliente

Every pottery company, it seemed, made a solid-colored dinnerware in the 1940s. Paden City Pottery Company, Paden City, West Virginia, made Caliente, a semi-porcelain, in blue, green, tangerine, and yellow. There is also matching ovenproof cooking ware.

BLUE ───────────

Plate, 9 In.	10.00
Salt & Pepper	10.00

GREEN ───────────

Bowl, 4 In.	3.00
Cup & Saucer	8.00
Plate, 9 In.	10.00

TANGERINE ───────────

Bowl, 10 In.	20.00
Teapot, Cover	35.00

YELLOW ───────────

Plate, 9 In.	10.00
Plate, Bread	4.00

California Ivy

California Ivy was one of the most popular patterns made by the Metlox Potteries of Manhattan Beach, California. It was introduced in 1946. The pattern was named for its ivy vine border.

POTTERY

Bowl, Cereal	8.00

Bowl, Round, 9 1/4 In.	15.00
Butter, Cover	20.00
Casserole, Cover	30.00
Coffeepot	45.00
Cup & Saucer	8.00
Gravy Boat, Underplate	10.00 To 25.00
Pitcher, Ice Lip	28.00
Plate, 6 In.	2.00
Plate, 8 In.	4.50
Plate, 10 1/4 In.	5.00 To 10.00
Platter, Oval, 13 In.	20.00
Salt & Pepper, Handle	8.00
Sugar & Creamer, Cover	15.00
Teapot	22.00 To 30.00

California Provincial

California Provincial dinnerware pictures a rooster in the center. The rooster is maroon, green, and yellow. The border is green and coffee brown. It was made by Metlox beginning in 1950.

Bowl, 6 In.	7.00 To 8.00
Bowl, Round, 10 In.	25.00
Bowl, Vegetable, Divided	14.00 To 25.00
Butter Pat	8.00

Casserole, Cover	45.00
Chop Plate, Round, 12 In.	25.00
Coffee Server, Wooden Handle	40.00
Creamer	9.00
Cup & Saucer	6.00 To 10.00
Gravy Boat	16.00 To 25.00
Mug	12.50 To 15.00
Pitcher, Milk	30.00
Plate, 6 In.	2.00
Plate, 7 In.	5.00
Plate, 9 In.	5.00
Plate, 10 In.	6.00 To 10.00
Plate, Bread	4.00
Salt & Pepper	12.00
Soup, Dish	10.00
Sprinkler, Water	25.00
Sugar	11.00
Sugar & Creamer, Cover	20.00

Cameo Rose Hall

Cameo Rose made by Hall China Company has gray and white decal decorations and a gold trim. It was not made by the cameo process used for cameo shellware and other designs.

Bowl, 5 In.	4.00 To 7.00

Bowl, Handles, 9 In. 14.00
Bowl, Vegetable,
    8 3/4 In. 15.00
Bowl, Vegetable,
    Oval .... 10.00 To 14.00
Creamer............. 6.00 To 8.00
Cup 4.00
Cup & Saucer 7.00
Gravy Boat, Underplate 22.00
Plate, 6 1/4 In. 3.00
Plate, 8 In. 5.00
Plate, 9 In. 6.00
Plate, 10 In. .... 6.00 To 7.00
Platter, Oval, 13 1/4 In. ... 14.00
Salt & Pepper 16.00
Sugar, Cover 14.00
Tidbit, 3 Tiers 27.50

Cameo Rose Harker

The names of the various cameo ware shapes and designs are confusing. One pattern is Cameo Rose, made by Harker China Company, Chester, West Virginia, from about 1940. The design is of solid white roses against a blue, gray, pink, or yellow background.

CAMEO ROSE HARKER,
    see also Cameo
    Shellware; White Rose

BLUE ————————————

Beanpot 24.00
Cup 4.00
Plate, 9 In. 27.00
Plate, Sandwich 3.00
Sugar & Creamer 27.00

PINK ————————————

Bowl, Serving, 9 In. 27.50
Dish, Cover, 7 In. 27.50
Plate, 9 In. 3.00
Sugar & Creamer, Cover 27.50

Cameo Shellware

Another Harker cameo pattern, Cameo Shellware, has the same design as Cameo Rose, but the dishes are fluted.

· · · · · · · · · · · · · · · · ·
Stains on porcelains can be removed by soaking in a mixture of two tablespoons of Polident denture cleaner in a quart of tepid water.
· · · · · · · · · · · · · · · · ·

BLUE ————————————

Cake Plate 8.00
Mug, Child's 25.00
Pie Baker 10.00
Plate, 9 In. 5.00

Capistrano

Capistrano is a design picturing modern yellow-breasted swallows flying near black foliage. It was made by the Red Wing Pottery from 1953 to 1967.

Console Set, 10-
    In. Flower Frog 23.00
Plate, Dinner 4.00
Platter, 13 1/2 In. 13.00
Platter, 15 In. 15.00

Caprice

Caprice is a streamlined pattern made by Hall China Company from 1952 to 1957. The dishes have a leaf and floral design in pink, gray, or yellow. The designs on the smaller pieces are not the same as those on the full-sized plates.

Baker, 11 Oz.................. 7.50
Cup & Saucer................ 4.00
Gravy Boat, Ladle 12.50
Plate, 6 In................... 1.50

Carnival Blue Ridge

Blue Ridge made one of the patterns called Carnival. It is decorated with a red, yellow, and blue flowered border. Stangl's Carnival pieces are listed separately. Homer Laughlin China Company of Newell, West Virginia, also made a solid-colored pattern named Carnival, which was distributed as a premium by the Quaker Oats Company sometime during the 1940s.

Plate, 6 In................... 1.50
Plate, 9 1/2 In.............. 6.00
Saucer....................... 2.00

Carnival Stangl

One pattern named Carnival was made by Stangl Pottery, Trenton, New Jersey, from 1954 to 1957. It is decorated with abstract star patterns.

Bowl, 9 In. 7.00
Butter, Corn Shape 10.00
Eggcup...................... 10.00
Platter 15.00
Teapot 35.00

Casual California

Vernon Kilns made Casual California, a very popular solid-color dinnerware, from 1947 to 1956. It was made in Acacia Yellow, Dawn Pink, Dusk Gray, Lime Green, Mahogany Brown, Mocha Brown, Pine Green, Snowhite, and Turquoise Blue.

GRAY —————————————

Salt & Pepper................ 5.00

LIME —————————————

Butter, Cover 10.00

YELLOW ———————————

Salt & Pepper................ 5.00

Casualstone

Casualstone is another in the family of Fiesta dinnerware. Homer Laughlin China Company, Newell, West Virginia, made the dishes for supermarket promotions under the trade name Coventry in 1970. Antique Gold Fiesta Ironstone dishes were decorated with a gold-stamped design on some pieces. Small, deep dishes were left in solid colors.

Bowl, 15 1/2 In. 4.00
Cup & Saucer................ 6.50
Plate, 6 In................... 2.00
Plate, 9 In................... 5.00

Cat-Tail

Cat-Tail pattern dishes must have been found in most homes in America in the 1940s. Sears, Roebuck and Company featured the pattern from 1934 to 1956. It was made by the Universal Potteries of Cambridge, Ohio. The red and black cat-tail design was used for dinnerware and matching tinware, kitchenware, glassware, furniture, and table linens.

• • • • • • • • • • • • • • • •
Some tea and coffee stains on dishes can be removed by rubbing them with damp baking soda.
• • • • • • • • • • • • • • • •

Batter Set, 3 Piece........ 250.00

Bowl, 5 1/4 In. 6.50

Bowl, Berry.................. 3.00

Bowl, Vegetable, Cover,
10 In. 18.50

Cake Plate, Handle,
12 1/2 In..................12.00

Casserole, Cover,
8 1/4 In..................18.00

Creamer...................... 7.50

Cup.......................... 3.00

Cup & Saucer.......4.50 To 9.50

Grill Plate 12.00

Jug, Canteen,
Tilt Top .... 13.00 To 18.00

Jug, Stopper 30.00

Pie Plate, 10 In. 12.00

Pie Server 20.00

Plate, 6 In...........2.00 To 3.75

Plate, 10 In. 8.00

Platter, Oval,
11 1/2 In.........8.50 To 10.00

Platter, Oval, 13 1/2 In. ...13.00

Saucer....................... 1.50

Soup, Dish, 7 5/8 In. 8.50

Tumbler, Glass,
4 3/4 In........ 17.00 To 25.00

Water Set, 7 Piece..........65.00

Champagne Pinks

Blue Ridge made a pattern called Champagne Pinks in the 1940s and 1950s. It had light pink and blue flowers.

Bowl, 5 1/4 In. 3.00

Bowl, 6 In. 5.00

Cup & Saucer............... 8.00

Plate, 6 In................... 2.00

Plate, 9 1/2 In.............. 7.00

Platter, 14 In...............15.00

Pitcher 45.00

Plate 15.00

Chatelaine

Vernon Kilns of Los Angeles and Vernon, California, introduced the solid-colored Chatelaine pattern in 1953. Pieces were square with leaf handles. It was made in bronze, topaz, jade with a leaf decoration, and platinum with a leaf decoration.

Chatelaine
a Sharon Merrill Design
a Vernonware
California USA
Jade

JADE ─────────

Cup & Saucer,
Pedestal .... 14.00 To 18.00

Plate, 6 1/2 In......5.00 To 7.00

Plate, 7 1/2 In.....8.00 To 10.00

Saucer........................ 3.00

Sugar, Cover................. 7.50

Chesterton

Chesterton was a pattern produced by Harker Pottery Company of Chester, West Virginia, from 1945 to 1965. The pieces had a gadroon border. They were made in blue, gray, green, pink, or yellow.

GRAY ─────────

Bowl, 5 1/2 In. ....2.00 To 2.25

Bowl, 6 1/4 In. 2.75

Creamer...................... 6.00

Cup & Saucer............... 3.00

Plate, 6 1/4 In......2.25 To 3.00

Plate, 9 1/4 In.............. 3.00

Plate, 10 In. ....4.00 To 6.00

Platter, 13 1/2 In...........15.00

Saucer........................ 2.00

Chinese Red

Chinese Red is a color used by Hall China Company, East Liverpool, Ohio. This bright red was used on many shapes of dishes. A few are listed here that are not included in the more recognizable sets.

Casserole, Saf-Handle,
8 In......................40.00

Beanpot, Cover,
Ribbed .... 30.00 To 40.00

Casserole, French,
7 In............. 35.00 To 50.00

Casserole, French, Ribbed,
9 1/2 In..................48.00

Chintz

Chintz is a floral decorated pattern made by Vernon Kilns in about 1942 and again in 1950. The pattern in red, blue, yellow, green, and maroon resembled the English dinnerware patterns of the early nineteenth century. Another pattern named Chintz was made by Blue Ridge.

VERNON KILNS

Cake Plate, Floral	45.00
Cake Plate, Maple Leaf	45.00
Plate, 6 1/2 In.	2.50 To 6.00
Plate, 9 1/2 In.	6.00 To 10.00
Saltshaker	6.00
Soup, Dish	10.00

Chrysanthemum

Blue and red flowers and buds and yellow and black leaves decorate Colonial-shaped dinnerware to create the Chrysanthemum pattern. It was made by Blue Ridge.

Bowl, 5 1/4 In.	4.00
Plate, 6 In.	2.50
Plate, 9 1/2 In.	6.00

Colonial

Colonial, also called Medallion, was the first kitchenware line made by Hall China Company, East Liverpool, Ohio. It was first made in 1932. The first pieces were made in ivory or ivory with lettuce-colored exteriors. Later pieces were made in Chinese Red, Delphinium (blue), Golden Glo, or with decal decorations. Some are still being made. The Stangl Colonial pattern is also listed here.

HALL'S SUPERIOR QUALITY KITCHENWARE MADE IN U. S. A.

BLUE

Drip Coffee, Hall	75.00
Leftover, Square, Hall	40.00
Plate, 7 In., Stangl	2.50
Sugar & Creamer, Open, Stangl	6.25
Sugar, Cover, Hall	10.00

GOLDEN GLO

Cup, Hall	3.00
Plate, 6 In., Hall	2.00

IVORY

Bowl, No.2, Hall	2.50
Drip Jar, Hall	10.00
Jug, 6 1/2 In., Hall	18.00

LETTUCE GREEN

Baker, French, Hall	18.00
Bowl, 9 1/4 In., Hall	30.00
Bowl, No.2, Hall	4.00
Bowl, No.3, Hall	6.00

Casserole, Cover, Hall	10.00 To 20.00
Custard, Hall	6.00
Drip Jar, Hall	10.00
Jug, No. 3, 5 In., Hall	10.00
Teapot	45.00

Colonial Homestead

Colonial Homestead was one of many patterns made by Royal China Company of Sebring, Ohio. The dinnerware was made in the 1940s and 1950s.

MADE IN U. S. A.

Bowl, 5 In.	1.25 To 3.00
Bowl, 9 In.	6.00
Bowl, 10 In.	7.00
Chop Plate, 12 In.	7.00
Cup	2.00
Plate, 6 1/2 In.	2.00
Plate, 9 In.	3.00
Plate, 10 In.	3.00 To 6.00
Saucer	1.50
Soup, Dish	3.00

Conchita

Mexican-inspired designs became the rage for dinnerwares in the late 1930s. Conchita was one of several made by Homer Laughlin Company, Newell, West Virginia. The dinnerware was a decal-decorated ware made on the Century shape line. The decoration pictured three pots of cacti in one corner, and on large flat pieces, like plates, a group of hanging gourds and peppers. There is a thin red border trim. Conchita decals were also used on kitchenwares made on the Kitchen Kraft shapes.

HOMER LAUGHLIN

Bowl, 5 1/2 In. 5.00
Bowl, 6 1/2 In. 7.00
Creamer 5.00
Cup......................... 5.00
Cup & Saucer................ 7.00
Plate, 7 1/4 In.............. 3.00
Platter, 13 In...............13.00

Conchita Kitchen Kraft

Conchita pattern decals of three pots of cacti were used to decorate the Oven Serve and Kitchen Kraft oven-to-table kitchenwares made by Homer Laughlin China Company, Newell, West Virginia, in the 1930s.

GENUINE
OVEN SERVE
WARE
U·S·A

Mixing Bowl, 9 In. 20.00
Mixing Bowl, 10 In.........25.00

COORS, see Rosebud

Corn King

Dishes shaped like ears of corn? This novel idea became a popular reality when Corn King pattern was sold by Shawnee Pottery Company, Zanesville, Ohio, before 1954. The green and yellow pieces, three-dimensional representations of ears of corn, ranged from dinner plates to small salt and pepper shakers. Corn King has darker yellow corn kernels and lighter green leaves than a later pattern called Corn Queen.

Shawnee
U.S.A.

Bowl, No.5 ...... 22.00 To 25.00
Bowl, No.6 ...... 15.00 To 20.00
Butter, Cover .... 30.00 To 65.00
Casserole, Cover,
  11 In. .... 42.00 To 50.00
Casserole, No.73 ....28.00
Creamer 25.00
Mug 25.00
Pitcher, No.70..............22.00
Pitcher, No.71..............50.00
Plate 15.00

Relish.......................22.50
Salt & Pepper,
  3 1/4 In........ 10.00 To 15.00
Salt & Pepper, 5 1/4 In. ...22.00
Sugar, Cover................22.00
Teapot 42.00

Corn Queen

Corn King was redesigned slightly by Shawnee Pottery Company, Zanesville, Ohio, and continued to be marketed from 1954 to 1961. The kernels of the new line were lighter yellow and the foliage was a deeper green. It was called Corn Queen.

Shawnee
U.S.A.

Bowl, 8 In. 16.00
Cookie Jar 65.00
Plate, 10 In. 19.00
Salt & Pepper, 4 In. 6.00
Sugar, Cover................16.00

Coronado

Franciscan dinnerware was made by Gladding, McBean in Los Angeles, California. Coronado was a popular plain-colored art ware made from 1935 to 1942. Fifty different shapes and fifteen different colors were made. Another pattern called Coronado was made by Vernon Kilns. The Franciscan pieces are listed in this book.

CORAL

Bowl, 7 1/2 In. ....7.50 To 8.50
Casserole, Cover............25.00
Cup & Saucer..............11.00
Gravy Boat 12.00
Plate, 9 1/4 In...............9.50
Plate, 10 1/2 In. 12.00

IVORY

Chop Plate, 14 In...........10.00
Cup..........................7.00
Cup & Saucer..............10.00
Plate, 6 1/2 In...............7.00
Plate, 9 1/2 In...............9.50
Plate, 10 1/2 In. 12.50
Platter, 13 In...............27.50
Relish, Leaf, 9 1/4 In........7.50
Soup, Dish..................23.00

MAROON

Ashtray, Shell Shape 10.00
Bowl, 11 In.................35.00
Cup..........................8.00
Plate, 6 1/2 In...............6.00

TURQUOISE

Bowl, 13 X 9 In............28.00
Chop Plate, 12 1/2 In. 18.00
Creamer.....................7.50
Cup..........................8.00
Gravy Boat,
   Attached Plate .... 25.00 To 29.00
Pepper Shaker 6.00
Plate, 8 In....................4.00
Plate, 8 1/2 In..............10.00

WHITE

Sugar & Creamer 32.00

YELLOW

Bowl, Vegetable, Oval,
   13 In. 15.00
Chop Plate, 12 1/2 In. 15.00
Creamer.............5.00 To 8.00
Cup..........................5.00
Dish, Crescent Shape 7.00
Plate, 6 1/2 In...............4.50
Plate, 9 1/2 In...............6.00
Saltshaker 6.00
Soup, Cream 9.00
Soup, Dish..................15.00
Sugar, Cover...............12.00

COTTAGE, see Petit Point House

Country Garden

Three raised flowers are pictured on the Country Garden dinnerware. The pattern was made by Stangl Pottery of Trenton, New Jersey, from 1956 to 1974.

Cup & Saucer..............13.00
Plate, 6 In...................5.00
Server, Handle, 10 In.......15.00
Tidbit, 3 Tiers ... 10.00 To 12.00

Crab Apple

One of the most popular dinnerware patterns made by Southern Potteries, Inc., of Erwin, Tennessee, under the name Blue Ridge was Crab Apple. This brightly colored hand-painted dinnerware was decorated with red apples and green leaves. A thin red spatter border was used. Matching glassware was made. The pattern was in production after 1930 and was discontinued when the factory went out of business in 1957.

Bowl, 5 1/2 In. 3.00
Bowl, Tab Handle...........4.50
Bowl, Vegetable, Oval,
   9 In......................10.00
Plate, 6 In..........2.25 To 3.00
Plate, 9 1/2 In...............8.50
Plate, 10 In. ....6.00 To 10.00

Crocus

Crocus was a popular name for dinnerware patterns. Prices listed are for the Crocus pattern by Hall China Company of East Liverpool, Ohio, in the 1930s. The decal-decorated dinnerware was sometimes called Holland. The design was a border of oddly shaped crocuses in black, lavender, red, green, and pink. Most pieces have platinum trim. Other firms, including Stangl Pottery and Blue Ridge, had very different-looking dinnerwares called Crocus.

Baker, French Flute.........22.00
Bowl, Berry..................3.50
Casserole....................10.00
Cup..........................7.00
Cup & Saucer...............12.00
Plate, 7 In...................6.00
Plate, 8 In........10.00 To 11.00
Plate, 9 In...................8.00
Plate, 10 In..................9.00
Platter, 11 In...............18.00
Saucer.......................2.00

Cumberland

Large hand-painted blue and white flowers with green leaves and reddish flowerlets are centered on the plates of Cumberland pattern. The pattern was made by Southern Potteries, Inc., Erwin, Tennessee, about 1948.

Never stack cups or bowls inside each other.

Bowl, 5 1/2 In. 5.00
Cup & Saucer................5.00
Plate, 9 In...................7.00

CURIOSITY SHOP, see Old Curiosity Shop

Currier & Ives

Currier & Ives was made by the Royal China Company of Sebring, Ohio, from the 1940s. It is a blue and white pattern that was popular as a store premium. The pattern is still being made.

Ashtray ....5.00 To 8.00
Baker, Divided, Oval,
    12 In. 12.00
Bowl, 5 1/2 In. ....1.50 To 2.00
Bowl, 6 In. 4.00
Bowl, 9 In. 7.00

Bowl, Vegetable, 10 In. 9.00
Butter, Cover...............15.00
Cake Plate, 2 Handles,
    10 1/2 In.........7.00 To 9.00
Casserole, Cover............35.00
Creamer.............1.50 To 3.50
Cup & Saucer.......2.00 To 4.00
Gravy Boat, Underplate 20.00
Pepper Shaker 5.00
Pic Plate, 9 In. ....5.50 To 12.00
Pie Plate, Deep, 10 In......13.00
Pie Server,
    Christmas Scene 3.00
Pie Server, Metal Handle...18.50
Pie Server, Tulip............10.00
Pie Server,
    Victorian Couple 5.00
Plate, 6 In..........2.00 To 4.00
Plate, 10 In. ....2.50 To 3.25
Platter, 13 In...............13.00
Salt & Pepper......8.50 To 10.00
Soup Dish ....3.50 To 5.00
Sugar, Cover................10.00
Teapot, Cover 43.00
Tidbit, 3 Tiers 20.00
Tumbler, 4 3/4 In...........5.00
Tumbler, 5 1/2 In...........6.00

D

Daffodil

Daffodil is a pattern made by Southern Potteries, Inc., Erwin, Tennessee, under the trademark Blue Ridge. It pictures a large single yellow and orange daffodil realistically painted on each plate. The dinnerware shape has a pie-crust edge.

• • • • • • • • • • • • • • • •
Cups are best stored by hanging them on cup hooks. Stacking cups inside each other can cause chipping.
• • • • • • • • • • • • • • • •

Bowl, 5 1/2 In. 4.00

Bowl, Salad 5.00

Cup & Saucer 5.00

Plate, 10 In. 6.00

Desert Rose

Desert Rose by Franciscan is a popular pattern with today's collectors. It was introduced in 1942 by Gladding McBean's Franciscan Ceramics. The pattern is still being made by Wedgwood, which purchased Franciscan Ceramics in 1979. The flowers on the dishes are a soft pink.

Ashtray ....9.00 To 10.00

Bowl, 5 1/4 In. ...5.00 To 12.00

Bowl, 5 3/4 In. ...8.00 To 14.00

Bowl, 9 In. ...... 25.00 To 28.00

Bowl, Divided, Oval,
   10 3/4 In................32.00

Bowl, Serving..............12.00

Bowl, Vegetable,
   Divided...................32.00

Bread Plate ....3.00 To 4.00

Butter, Cover,
   1/4 Lb.......... 12.00 To 27.00

Candleholder, Pair..........30.00

Casserole...................28.00

Creamer .... 14.00 To 19.00

Cup & Saucer......6.00 To 15.00

Cup & Saucer, Jumbo.......22.00

Eggcup.....................15.00

Gravy Boat,
   Liner .... 32.00 To 37.50

Gravy Boat, Stand 25.00

Mug 15.00

Napkin Ring................12.00

Pepper Shaker 8.00

Pickle, 10 In. 35.00

Plate, 6 1/4 In......4.50 To 6.00

Plate, 8 In. ....8.00 To 12.00

Plate, 9 1/4 In..............15.00

Plate,
   10 1/2 In....... 12.00 To 18.00

Platter, 12 1/2 In...........25.00

Platter, Turkey, 19 In......135.00

Relish, 3 Sections, 12 In....30.00

Salt & Pepper,
   Rosebud........ 15.00 To 18.00

Salt & Pepper, Tall 30.00

Soup, Dish....... 14.00 To 15.00

Sugar & Creamer 57.00

Sugar, Cover..... 20.00 To 24.00

Teapot, Cover 40.00

Tumbler, 5 1/2 In..........16.00

Dolores

Dolores is a Vernon Kilns pattern made in the 1940s. It has a floral border.

Bowl, 5 1/2 In. 4.00

Bowl, 5 3/4 In. 4.00

Creamer 6.00

Plate, 7 In. 4.00

Plate, 10 1/2 In. 7.50

Platter, 14 In...............12.00

E

Early California

In the late 1930s Vernon Kilns of Vernon, California, made a solid-color line of dinnerware called Early California. The dishes, in blue, brown, green, orange, pink, turquoise, or yellow, were made to be used as mix-and-match sets. The dishes are marked with the name of the pattern.

• • • • • • • • • • • • • • • •

Rubber cement solvent, available at art supply and office supply stores, has many uses. Put a few drops on a paper towel and rub off ink smudges, adhesive tape glue, and label glue from glass or porcelains.

• • • • • • • • • • • • • • • •

BLUE ─────────────

Bowl, 5 3/4 In. 2.50
Candleholder, Round 25.00
Cup & Saucer, Demitasse ... 20.00

BROWN ─────────────

Cup 12.00
Salt & Pepper............... 16.00

GREEN ─────────────

Bowl, 5 In. 1.50

ORANGE ─────────────

Compote 22.00

PINK ─────────────

Bowl, 5 In. 1.50

TURQUOISE ─────────────

Chop Plate, 16 1/4 In. 10.00
Cup & Saucer............... 12.00

YELLOW ─────────────

Cup & Saucer............... 12.00
Sugar, Cover............... 12.00

Eggshell Polka Dot

Eggshell Polka Dot was a buffet service made by Hall China Company of East Liverpool, Ohio, in 1934. The dishes were made of matte white or ivory glaze, decorated with blue, green, or red dots. Some pieces had floral decorations.

Cocotte, Green Dot
  Handle .... 2.00 To 7.00

El Patio

El Patio is one of many solid-color dinnerware patterns made by Franciscan from 1936 to 1956. It comes in twenty colors.

BLUE ─────────────

Plate, 8 1/2 In............... 6.00
Plate, 9 1/2 In............... 8.00

BROWN ─────────────

Cup 6.00

CHARTREUSE ─────────────

Bowl, 9 In. 15.00

DESERT ROSE ─────────────

Cup & Saucer............... 10.00

GOLDEN GLOW ─────────────

Cup 2.50
Sugar, Cover............... 6.00

GREEN ─────────────

Bowl, 5 1/2 In. 8.00
Cup & Saucer............... 9.50

Plate, 6 In................. 2.50
Plate, 8 1/2 In............. 8.00
Plate, 9 1/4 In............. 9.00
Platter, Oval, 13 In. 22.00
Salt & Pepper............... 18.00
Soup, Cream, Handle 10.00
Sugar, Cover............... 13.00

IVORY ─────────────

Cup 1.50

MAROON ─────────────

Plate, 6 In................. 2.50

ORANGE ─────────────

Chop Plate.................. 13.00
Plate, 6 1/4 In............. 2.50
Plate, 8 1/4 In............. 6.00
Plate, 9 1/2 In............. 8.00

REDWOOD ─────────────

Cup 2.50

TURQUOISE ─────────────

Dish, Baking, Handle,
  Cover...................... 5.00

YELLOW ─────────────

Cup 1.50
Plate, 6 /4 In............... 2.50

F

Fantasia

Fantasia is an abstract leaf pattern made by Blue Ridge on the Skyline shape. It is brown, blue, and yellow.

Cup.........................3.50
Plate, 6 In...................2.00
Plate, 9 In...................9.00
Salt & Pepper...............8.00

Festival

Festival is a Stangl pattern made from 1961 to 1967. Varicolored fruit are pictured in the center. The rim has a wide yellow band.

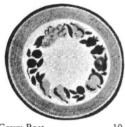

Gravy Boat 10.00
Plate, 6 In....................6.00
Plate, 9 In...................10.00
Saucer.......................4.00

FESTIVE FRUIT, see Fruit (Stangl)

Fiesta

Fiesta ware was introduced in 1936 by the Homer Laughlin China Company, Newell, West Virginia. It was originally designed by Frederick Rhead. The line was redesigned in 1969 and withdrawn in 1973. The design was characterized by a band of concentric circles, beginning at the rim. The complete Fiesta line in 1937 had 54 different pieces. Rarities include the covered onion bowl, the green disk water jug, the 10-inch cake plate, and the syrup pitcher. Cups had full-circle handles until 1969, when partial-circle handles were made. The original Fiesta colors were dark blue, Fiesta red, light green, Old Ivory, and yellow. Later, chartreuse, forest green, gray, medium green, rose, and turquoise were added. From 1970 to 1972 the redesigned Fiesta Ironstone was made only in Antique Gold, Mango Red, and Turf Green. Homer Laughlin reissued Fiesta in 1986 using new colors but the original marks and molds. The new colors were apricot, black, cobalt blue, rose (pink), and white. In 1989 the company added three other colors—periwinkle blue, turquoise, and yellow. See American Dinnerware Introduction for more information. Most Fiesta ware was marked with the incised word *Fiesta*. Some pieces were hand-stamped before glazing. The word *genuine* was added to the mark in the 1940s. The Fiesta shape was also made with decal decorations, but these are not considered Fiesta by collectors; instead they are collected by the pattern names. There is also a Fiesta Kitchen Kraft line, a group of kitchenware pieces made in the early 1940s in blue, green, red, or yellow. These were bake-and-serve wares. Glassware and linens were made to match the Fiesta colors.

FIESTA, see also Amberstone; Casualstone; Fiesta Ironstone; Fiesta Kitchen Kraft

BLUE

Bowl, 5 1/2 In. 15.00
Candleholder, Bulb, Pair....45.00
Casserole, Cover 80.00
Cup 18.00
Gravy Boat 40.00
Mug 45.00
Pitcher, Disk...............65.00
Plate, 9 In...................10.00
Plate, 10 In. 20.00
Relish......................25.00
Soup, Cream 30.00
Syrup, Cover.............. 175.00
Teapot, Small 75.00

Tray, Utility 22.00
Tumbler, Juice.............20.00
Tumbler, Water............35.00

CHARTREUSE

Bowl,
  4 3/4 In....... 18.00 To 20.00
Bowl, 5 1/2 In. 18.00
Bowl, 6 In. 30.00
Creamer....................15.00
Cup & Saucer.... 25.00 To 27.00
Jug, 2 Pt. 40.00
Pitcher, Disk...............55.00
Plate, 6 In..........4.50 To 7.00
Plate, 7 In..................8.00
Plate, 9 In.................17.00
Plate, 10 In. 15.00
Saucer......................4.00
Soup, Cream 35.00
Teapot, Medium 145.00

DARK BLUE

Plate, Chop, 13 In. 20.00
Saucer......................2.50
Soup, Cream 25.00
Tumbler, 5 Oz. 22.00

FOREST GREEN

Bowl, 4 1/2 In. 18.00
Bowl, 5 1/2 In. 18.00
Bowl, 6 In. 25.00
Cup & Saucer..............27.00
Mug 55.00
Nappy, 8 1/2 In...........32.00
Pitcher, Water, Disk 12.00
Plate, 6 In..................6.00
Plate, 7 In..................8.00
Plate, 9 In.........9.00 To 17.00
Plate, Deep, 8 In. 20.00
Sauce Boat.................30.00
Soup, Cream 35.00
Teapot 12.00

GRAY

Bowl, Large............... 120.00
Jug, 2 Pt. 65.00
Plate, Chop, 13 In. 40.00
Teapot 145.00

LIGHT GREEN

Bowl, 4 3/4 In. 15.00
Bowl, 6 In. 22.00
Bowl, Nesting, No.7 ....70.00
Butter, Cover 45.00
Candleholder, Bulb,
  Pair............. 35.00 To 45.00
Carafe......................95.00
Coffeepot,
  After Dinner....100.00 To 150.00
Compote, Sweet,
  10 1/4 In.................30.00
Mustard, Cover 85.00
Pitcher, Disk...............80.00
Pitcher, Ice Lip,
  2 Qt. .... 55.00 To 60.00
Pitcher, Juice...............25.00
Plate, 6 In..................3.00
Plate, 9 In..................6.00
Plate, 10 In. ..... 15.00 To 20.00
Plate, Chop,
  13 In. .... 18.00 To 22.00
Plate, Deep, 8 In. 20.00
Platter, Oval, 12 In. 28.00
Relish Tray 40.00
Relish Tray,
  5 Colored Sections 95.00
Saltshaker 7.00
Saucer......................2.00
Syrup 100.00
Teapot, Small 65.00
Tumbler,
  5 Oz. .... 18.00 To 20.00
Vase, 12 In. ...375.00 To 385.00
Vase, 8 In................. 200.00
Vase, Bud..................60.00

MEDIUM GREEN

Bowl, 6 In. 18.00
Creamer....................30.00
Cup 15.00
Mug 35.00
Pitcher, Ice Lip 55.00
Plate, 6 In..........6.00 To 8.00
Plate, 9 In.................12.00
Plate, 10 1/2 In. 15.00
Sugar 19.00
Teapot 125.00
Tumbler, 8 Oz. 35.00

OLD IVORY

Bowl,
  4 3/4 In........ 15.00 To 17.00
Bowl, 7 In. 25.00
Bowl, No.5, 9 In. 40.00
Coffeepot, After Dinner 95.00
Compote, 10 1/2 In. 25.00
Compote, 12 In. 65.00
Creamer....................12.00
Nappy, 9 1/2 In............25.00
Pitcher, Disk, 2 Qt..........65.00
Plate, 6 In..................2.50
Plate, 9 In..................7.00
Plate, 10 In. 20.00
Plate, Deep, 8 In. 20.00
Relish, Turquoise &
  Yellow Inserts 75.00
Saucer...............2.00 To 3.00
Syrup 110.00
Teapot, Small 75.00
Tidbit, 3 Tiers 65.00
Tumbler, 5 Oz. 18.00
Tumbler, 8 Oz. 35.00
Vase, 10 In. 210.00

RED

Ashtray 35.00
Bowl, 5 1/2 In. 20.00
Bowl, No.5, 9 In. 60.00
Candleholder, Bulb, Pair....45.00
Carafe, 3 Pt............... 145.00
Coffeepot, Cover............45.00
Creamer....................20.00
Mixing Bowl, No.1,
  5 In......................65.00
Mustard................... 100.00
Pitcher, Disk...............75.00
Pitcher, Ice Lip, 2 Qt. 110.00
Plate, 6 In..................4.50
Plate, 7 In.................10.00
Plate, 10 In. ..... 10.00 To 25.00
Plate, Chop, 13 In. 22.00
Plate, Deep, 8 In. 30.00
Platter, Oval, 12 In. 30.00
Relish, 5 Inserts........... 130.00
Salt & Pepper..............20.00
Saucer......................2.50
Sugar, Cover...............35.00
Teapot, Large............. 145.00

Tumbler, 5 Oz. 25.00

ROSE ————————

Bowl, 4 3/4 In. 18.00
Bowl,
5 1/2 In. .... 18.00 To 22.00
Bowl, 6 In. 30.00
Casserole, Cover 130.00
Creamer. 17.00
Cup & Saucer 27.00
Mug 55.00
Plate, 6 In. 7.00
Plate, 7 In. 8.00
Plate, 9 In. .... 13.00 To 20.00
Plate, Chop, 13 In. 23.00
Plate, Chop, 15 In. 45.00
Plate, Deep, 8 In. 30.00
Soup, Cream 35.00

TURQUOISE ————————

Ashtray .... 25.00 To 30.00
Bowl, 4 3/4 In. 15.00
Bowl, 5 1/2 In. 15.00
Bowl, 11 3/4 In. 90.00
Compote, 10 1/4 In. 35.00
Cup 18.00
Eggcup. 25.00
Jug, 2 Pt. .... 35.00 To 40.00
Mug 35.00
Nappy, 8 1/2 In. 22.00
Pitcher, Disk. 50.00
Plate, 6 In. 3.00
Plate, 7 In. 5.00
Plate, 9 In. 6.00
Plate, 10 In. 20.00
Plate, Compartment,
10 1/2 In. 20.00
Plate, Deep, 8 In. 20.00
Platter, Oval, 12 In. 15.00
Saucer. 2.00
Sugar 10.00
Sugar, Cover 20.00
Teapot, Medium 75.00
Tray, Figure 8 Shape 100.00
Tumbler, 5 Oz. 18.00

YELLOW ————————

Bowl, 4 3/4 In. 15.00
Bowl, 5 1/2 In. 15.00

Bowl, 7 5/8 In. 45.00
Casserole, Cover 50.00
Casserole, French,
Cover. 110.00
Coffeepot,
After Dinner 150.00
Compote, 10 1/4 In. 30.00
Compote, 12 In. 55.00
Creamer. 12.00
Creamer, Stick 24.00
Cup 16.00
Gravy Boat 22.00
Marmalade 50.00
Mustard 75.00
Nappy, 8 1/2 In. 22.00
Nappy,
9 1/2 In. .... 17.50 To 25.00
Pitcher, Disk, 2 Qt. 40.00
Pitcher, Disk, 30 Oz. 25.00
Plate, 6 In. .... 3.00 To 6.00
Plate, 9 In. 6.00
Plate, 10 In. 20.00
Plate, Chop, 13 In. 20.00
Plate, Deep, 8 In. 20.00
Relish, Base. 40.00
Saltshaker 7.00
Saucer. 2.00
Tumbler, 5 Oz. 18.00
Vase, 8 In. 200.00

Fiesta Ironstone

Fiesta Ironstone by Homer
Laughlin China Company, Newell, West Virginia, was made
from 1970 to 1972. It was
made in Antique Gold,
Mango Red, and Turf Green.

ANTIQUE GOLD ————————

Cup 5.00
Plate, 9 In. 7.00

TURF GREEN ————————

Bowl, 5 1/2 In. 15.00
Cup 5.00
Plate, 9 In. 7.00

Fiesta Kitchen Kraft

Fiesta Kitchen Kraft was a
bake-and-serve line made in
the early 1940s by Homer
Laughlin China Company, Newell, West Virginia. It was
made in red, yellow, green,
and blue.

BLUE ————————

Casserole, Individual 110.00
Jar, Cover, Large. 190.00

GREEN ————————

Cake Plate, 11 In. 35.00
Casserole, Holder,
7 1/2 In. 75.00
Jug, Cover 95.00

IVORY ————————

Blue, Green, Stack Set,
Red Cover. ...200.00 To 290.00

RED ————————

Blue, Green, Stack Bowl, Refrig.,
Yellow Cover 95.00
Cake Plate, 11 In. 40.00
Casserole, Cover,
Individual. .....85.00 To 110.00
Casserole, Holder,
7 1/2 In. 90.00
Casserole, Holder,
8 1/2 In. 80.00
Jug, Cover 200.00
Pie Plate, 10 In. 45.00

YELLOW ————————

Cake Plate, 11 In. 35.00
Casserole, Cover,
7 1/2 In. 45.00
Pie Plate, 10 In. 40.00

Flower Ring

Flower Ring is another of the many Blue Ridge patterns made on the Colonial shape. A red, a yellow, and a blue flower are pictured near the border. Green leaves and a green rim finish the decoration.

Bowl, Individual, 5 In.	4.00
Creamer	5.00
Cup	6.00
Plate, 10 1/2 In.	8.00
Saucer	1.00
Sugar	5.00

Frageria

Blue Ridge made Frageria pattern in the 1950s. The center design was red strawberries. The border was green.

Bowl, Vegetable, Oval	7.00
Gravy, Boat	10.00
Plate, 9 1/2 In.	4.00
Platter, 12 In.	8.00
Salt & Pepper	8.00
Soup, Dish	4.00

French Peasant

French Peasant is a Blue Ridge pattern of dishes made to resemble the French Quimper pottery. The pattern is in reds and blues.

Plate, 8 1/2 In.	35.00
Plate, 10 1/2 In.	40.00
Shell, Deep	95.00
Shell, Flat	75.00
Soup, Dish, 8 In.	30.00
Tumbler, Frosted, 8 Piece	35.00

Frontenac

Frontenac is a modern-looking pattern made by Red Wing Potteries on the Futura shape about 1960. It has an abstract border design of yellow and turquoise.

Bowl, 5 In.	5.00
Butter, Cover	15.00
Creamer	7.00
Plate, 7 In.	5.00
Plate, 8 In.	3.00
Plate, 10 1/2 In.	7.00
Saucer	2.00
Trivet	45.00

Fruit

Stangl Pottery, Trenton, New Jersey, made Fruit pattern from 1942 to 1974. The dishes had center designs that were different fruits. Some pictured apples, some pears, grapes, or other fruit. This pattern, No. 3697, was sometimes called Festive Fruit. It was marked Terra Rose. Also listed here are Fruit pattern dishes made by Franciscan Ceramics from 1949 and by Red Wing from 1947.

Bowl, 6 In., Franciscan	15.00
Cup & Saucer, Franciscan	18.00
Cup & Saucer, Stangl	9.50
Cup, Stangl	9.00
Gravy Boat, Stangl	15.00
Plate, 6 In., Red Wing	2.00
Plate, 7 In., Red Wing	3.00
Plate, 8 In., Franciscan	16.00
Plate, 8 In., Stangl	5.50 To 7.00
Plate, 9 In., Stangl	6.00
Plate, 10 In., Red Wing	5.00
Plate, 10 In., Stangl	10.00 To 15.00
Plate, 10 1/2 In., Franciscan	20.00
Platter, 11 1/2 In., Stangl	8.00
Platter, 14 1/2 In., Franciscan	45.00
Relish, 3 Sections, Stangl	10.00
Salt & Pepper, Stangl	9.00
Saucer, Stangl	5.00
Server, Center Handle, Stangl	12.50
Sherbet, Stangl	16.00
Sugar & Creamer, Stangl	18.00

Teapot, 2 Cup, Stangl......18.00
Tray, Condiment, Stangl....25.00

Fruit & Flowers

Fruit & Flowers pattern, No. 4030, was made by Stangl Pottery, Trenton, New Jersey, from 1957 to 1974. The design shows a mixed grouping of flowers, leaves, grapes, and fanciful shapes. Pieces have a colored border.

Butter.......................9.50
Cup...........................6.00
Cup & Saucer......8.00 To 15.00
Mug 8.50
Pitcher, 2 Qt................27.50
Plate, 6 In...................4.00

G

Gingham

Vernon Kilns, Vernon, California, made six different plaid patterns. Each plaid was given a special name. Gingham is the pattern with a dark green border and green and yellow plaid. Other related plaids are Calico (pink and blue), Coronation Organdy (gray and rose), Homespun (cinnamon, yellow, and green), Organdie (brown and yellow), Tam O'Shanter (green, lime, and cinnamon), and Tweed (gray and blue).

Bowl, 5 1/2 In. 3.00
Bowl, Vegetable, Divided,
  10 In. ....9.00 To 15.00
Carafe.......................20.00
Casserole, Cover,
  8 In............. 20.00 To 25.00
Creamer.............4.00 To 5.00
Cup & Saucer...............7.00
Mixing Bowl,
  7 In..............8.00 To 12.50
Mixing Bowl, 8 In. 12.50
Pepper Shaker 3.50
Pitcher, 1 Pt. ......8.00 To 12.00
Pitcher, 2 Qt................25.00
Plate, 6 In...................2.00
Plate, 7 1/2 In......2.50 To 3.00
Plate, 9 1/2 In......4.50 To 5.00
Plate, Chop,
  12 In. ....7.50 To 12.50
Platter, 12 In...............12.50
Platter, 14 In...............10.00
Salt & Pepper...............7.00
Sugar, Cover.................6.00
Tumbler, 8 Oz. 15.00

Golden Harvest

Golden Harvest was made by Stangl Pottery from 1953 to 1973. The pattern pictured yellow flowers on a gray background.

. . . .
Glue broken china with any invisible mending cement that is waterproof.
. . . .

Creamer......................9.00
Cup 8.00
Plate, 6 In...................6.00
Plate, 8 In...................8.00
Plate, Chop, 12 1/2 In. 20.00
Saucer.......................6.00
Sugar 9.00

Golden Wheat

Golden Wheat was a popular pattern name. It was used for dishes by Edwin M. Knowles and Homer Laughlin. The patterns pictured wheat stalks. Prices listed here are for the dinnerware by Knowles made about 1936.

Bowl, 5 1/2 In. 1.25
Creamer......................2.00
Cup & Saucer...............1.50
Gravy Boat 5.00
Plate, 7 In..................1.75
Plate, 9 In..................2.25
Soup, Dish..................3.00

H

Hacienda

Another Mexican-inspired pattern, Hacienda was made by Homer Laughlin China Company, Newell, West Virginia, in 1938. The dinnerware was made on the Century shape. A decal showed a bench, cactus, and a portion of the side of a Mexican home. Most pieces have red trim at the handles and at the edge of the plate well.

HOMER LAUGHLIN

Bowl, 5 In.	5.00
Creamer	4.00
Cup & Saucer	8.00
Plate, 6 In.	2.50
Plate, 9 In.	4.00
Platter	15.00

Hall Teapot

Teapots of all sizes and shapes were made by the Hall China Company of East Liverpool, Ohio, starting in the 1920s. Each pot had a special design name such as Airflow or Boston. Each shape could be made in one of several colors, often with names like Cadet (light blue), Camellia (rose), Delphinium (purple blue), Dresden (deep blue), and Indian Red (orange). Coffeepots were also made.

Cadet Label GROUP FOR HALL CHINA DECORATED TEAPOTS

AIRFLOW

Cobalt & Gold	30.00
Cobalt Blue	40.00

ALADDIN

Crocus	100.00
Green	26.00

BALTIMORE

Maroon, Gold Label	45.00

BELLEVUE

Cadet Blue	25.00
Maroon	10.00
Pink	25.00

BIRDCAGE

Red	350.00

BOSTON

Crocus, Metal Lid & Dripper	65.00
Green	17.00
Maroon & Gold	32.00
Yellow & Gold	18.00

CLEVELAND

Emerald & Gold	30.00
Turquoise & Gold	35.00
Warm Yellow & Gold	35.00

COLONIAL

Crocus	30.00

CONNIE

Celadon Green	20.00

DISRAELI

Pink	20.00

DONUT

Chinese Red	250.00
Green	135.00
Orange Poppy	250.00

FRENCH

Blue	25.00
Brown	15.00
Maroon & Gold	28.00

GLOBE

Cadet Blue & Gold	45.00
Dripless, Yellow & Gold	39.00

HOLLYWOOD

Maroon & Gold	22.00 To 39.00

HOOK COVER

Blue & Gold	25.00
Emerald & Gold	24.00
Yellow & Gold	25.00

LIPTON

Brown	95.00
Stock Green	25.00
Yellow	15.00 To 25.00

LOS ANGELES

Stock Brown	15.00

MCCORMICK

Blue & Green	27.50
Marine Blue	20.00
Maroon	25.00
Pink, Infusor	20.00

MELODY

Chinese Red	100.00
Ivory	65.00
Yellow	95.00

MODERNE

Canary 30.00
Green.......................20.00

NEW YORK

Crocus 50.00
Red Poppy.................40.00
Serenade 45.00
Stock Brown................25.00
Yellow & Gold 30.00

PARADE

Yellow & Gold 27.50

PHILADELPHIA

Delphinium & Gold 30.00
Old Rose, Gold Looping ...20.00

RONALD REAGAN

.... 65.00 To 75.00

RUTHERFORD

Eggshell, Buffet Swag.......75.00
Pastel Morning Glory.......70.00

SAF-HANDLE

Canary & Gold 40.00

STREAMLINE

Chinese Red ..... 35.00 To 55.00
Delphinium,
   Gold Handle 45.00
Yellow & Silver.............25.00

T-BALL

Maroon, Square.............55.00

TWINSPOUT

Turquoise...................50.00

WINDSHIELD

Cadet Blue & Gold 37.00
Ivory, Gold Dot 30.00

Harlequin

Harlequin, a solid-color dinnerware made by Homer
Laughlin China Company of
Newell, West Virginia, was
less expensive than Fiesta. It
was made from 1938 to 1964
and sold unmarked in Woolworth stores. The rings
molded into the plate were at
the edge of the plate well and
the rim was plain. Dishes
were made in blue, yellow,
turquoise, gray, rose, forest
green, dark blue, light green,
chartreuse, maroon, mauve
blue, spruce green, ivory, and
tangerine (red).

BLUE

Cup, After Dinner 3.50
Eggcup.....................14.00
Plate, 7 In.................. 5.00

CHARTREUSE

Bowl, Salad, Individual,
   7 In.......................15.00
Cup & Saucer...............9.00
Eggcup, Double.............16.00
Plate, 6 In..................2.50
Plate, 7 In..................4.50
Plate, 9 In..................9.50
Platter, 11 In...............12.00
Sugar, Cover................12.00

DARK GREEN

Eggcup.....................15.00
Plate, 6 In..................3.50
Plate, 7 In..................5.50
Saucer......................3.00

FOREST GREEN

Cup........................ 7.00
Plate, 9 In..................9.50
Teapot, Cover 20.00

GRAY

Bowl, 7 In. 17.50
Cup........................ 7.50
Cup & Saucer...............9.00
Jug, 22 Oz. 19.00
Plate, 6 In.................. 3.50
Plate, 9 In..........6.50 To 10.00
Plate, 10 In. 20.00
Platter, 13 In...............18.00
Soup, Cream 15.00
Sugar, Cover...............15.00

LIGHT GREEN

Bowl, 6 In. 9.00
Bowl, 7 In. 23.00
Creamer, Novelty...........17.00
Cup & Saucer...............8.50
Gravy Boat ...... 15.00 To 17.00
Jug, 22 Oz. 15.00
Plate, 6 In.................. 2.50
Plate, 7 In.................. 4.00
Saucer...................... 2.00

MAROON

Ashtray 48.50
Candleholder...............42.00
Casserole...................95.00
Creamer, Individual.........15.00
Creamer,
   Novelty......... 22.00 To 30.00
Cup & Saucer,
   After Dinner ... 65.00 To 75.00
Dish, Nut 8.00
Eggcup, Double.............25.00
Pitcher, Water ... 50.00 To 75.00
Plate, 9 In..................10.50
Platter, 13 In...............30.00
Sugar & Creamer 45.00

MAUVE BLUE

Ashtray, Basketweave 30.00
Bowl, 9 In. 10.00
Casserole, Cover 45.00
Creamer....................10.00
Cup........................ 4.50
Cup & Saucer............... 5.50
Dish, Nut.................. 6.50
Jug, 22 Oz.................40.00
Pepper Shaker 7.00

Pitcher, Ball 25.00
Plate, 6 In.................. 2.50
Plate, 9 In.................. 6.50
Platter, 13 In...............10.00
Soup, Cream...............15.00
Sugar & Creamer, Cover....18.50
Sugar, Cover...............11.00
Teapot.....................60.00
Tumbler .... 25.00 To 40.00

MEDIUM GREEN ————

Bowl, 6 1/2 In. 13.00
Bowl, 9 In. 20.00
Cup........................13.00
Plate, 7 In.................. 6.00
Plate, 10 In. 20.00
Plate, Deep, 8 In. 42.00
Saucer...................... 3.00

ROSE ————

Bowl, 5 1/2 In. 6.00
Bowl, 6 1/2 In. ....6.50 To 9.00
Bowl, 9 In. 15.00
Casserole, Cover 50.00
Creamer...................... 6.00
Cup.................4.50 To 6.00
Cup & Saucer.......6.00 To 8.50
Cup, After Dinner 15.00
Eggcup........... 13.00 To 15.00
Gravy Boat 15.00
Jug, 22 Oz. .... 25.00 To 30.00
Pepper Shaker 6.00
Plate, 6 In.................. 2.50
Plate, 7 In..........4.00 To 5.00
Plate, 9 In..........8.00 To 9.50
Plate, 10 In. 8.00
Platter, 11 In................ 9.00
Saltshaker 6.00
Saucer...................... 2.00

SPRUCE GREEN ————

Ashtray, Basketweave 35.00
Cup........................ 9.00
Dish, Nut................... 8.00
Eggcup........... 12.00 To 18.00
Pepper Shaker 7.00
Plate, 6 1/2 In............... 2.50
Plate, 9 In.................10.50

Plate, Deep, 8 1/2 In.......12.50
Saucer...................... 3.50
Soup, Cream...............15.00
Teapot.....................75.00
Tumbler 40.00

TANGERINE ————

Ashtray,
  Basketweave.... 30.00 To 38.00
Baker, Oval.................14.00
Bowl, 5 1/2 In. ...6.50 To 10.00
Bowl,
  6 1/2 In........ 14.00 To 20.00
Casserole, Open.............30.00
Creamer, Individual.........12.00
Cup........................ 7.00
Cup & Saucer............... 7.50
Cup & Saucer,
  After Dinner 30.00
Dish, Nut................... 7.00
Eggcup.....................15.00
Jug, 22 Oz. 35.00
Marmalade 95.00
Pitcher, Water ... 38.00 To 50.00
Plate, 7 In..........6.00 To 6.50
Plate, 10 In. 12.00
Platter, 11 In.......9.00 To 11.00
Platter, 13 In..... 15.00 To 18.50
Salt & Pepper...............15.00
Saucer...................... 3.00
Soup, Cream...............16.00
Sugar & Creamer, Cover....18.00
Sugar, Cover...............12.00
Teapot.....................25.00

TURQUOISE ————

Ashtray,
  Basketweave.... 19.00 To 35.00
Bowl, 5 1/2 In. ....4.00 To 5.50
Bowl,
  6 1/2 In........ 10.00 To 14.00
Bowl, 9 In. 10.00
Casserole, Cover 45.00
Creamer....................12.00
Creamer, Novelty...........15.00
Cup.................2.50 To 4.50
Cup & Saucer............... 7.50
Cup & Saucer,
  After Dinner ... 23.00 To 25.00
Eggcup, Double............. 9.00

Eggcup, Single... 12.00 To 18.00
Jar, Jam 95.00
Jug, 22 Oz. 20.00
Pitcher, Water 25.00
Plate, 6 In..........2.00 To 2.50
Plate, 7 In..........3.00 To 4.00
Plate, 9 In..........5.50 To 6.50
Plate, 10 In. 10.00
Plate, Deep, 8 In. 10.00
Platter, 11 In................ 9.00
Platter, 13 In..... 12.00 To 14.00
Salt & Pepper............... 7.50
Saucer...................... 2.00
Soup, Cream...............10.00
Sugar & Creamer, Cover....14.00
Sugar, Cover...............15.00

YELLOW ————

Ashtray, Basketweave 25.00
Bowl, 5 1/2 In. 4.75
Bowl, 6 1/2 In. ...9.00 To 12.00
Bowl, 9 In. 12.00
Creamer,
  Individual....... 11.00 To 13.00
Creamer, Novelty...........13.00
Cup........................ 2.50
Cup & Saucer......5.50 To 10.00
Cup & Saucer,
  After Dinner 25.00
Dish, Nut..........5.00 To 7.00
Eggcup, Double....8.00 To 12.00
Eggcup, Single... 12.00 To 18.00
Gravy Boat ....8.00 To 15.00
Jug, 22 Oz. 25.00
Pitcher, Water ... 27.00 To 50.00
Plate, 6 In..........2.00 To 2.50
Plate, 7 In..........3.00 To 3.50
Plate, 9 In..........5.00 To 6.50
Plate, Deep, 8 In. 10.00
Platter, 11 In.......8.50 To 12.00
Platter, 13 In..... 12.50 To 16.00
Salt & Pepper...............10.00
Saltshaker 5.50
Saucer...................... 2.00
Soup, Cream...............15.00
Soup, Dish, 2 Handles......10.00
Sugar, Cover.......6.00 To 12.00
Tumbler 24.00

Hawaiian Flowers

Hawaiian Flowers was a well-known Vernon Kilns, Vernon, California, tableware designed by Don Blanding. It was first made in 1939.

MAROON

Bowl, 6 In.	13.50
Bowl, 9 In.	15.00
Creamer	14.50
Cup & Saucer	14.00 To 16.50
Gravy Boat	20.00
Plate, 6 1/2 In.	6.50 To 12.00
Plate, 9 1/2 In.	16.50
Plate, Chop, 12 In.	60.00
Salt & Pepper	15.50
Saucer	6.50
Sugar, Individual	18.50

PINK

Plate, 6 1/2 In.	6.50
Saucer	6.50

Heather Rose

Heather Rose is a decal-decorated Hall Pottery pattern. Both dinnerware and utility ware pieces were made with this decoration. It pictures a realistic-looking pale pinkish purple rose on a stem with many leaves.

Bowl, 5 1/4 In.	4.50
Bowl, 9 In.	12.00
Bowl, Vegetable, Cover	30.00
Cup	3.50
Cup & Saucer	7.50
Jug, Rayed	15.00
Plate, 7 1/4 In.	8.50
Plate, 9 1/4 In.	4.50
Saucer	1.50
Soup, Coupe, 8 In.	12.75

HOLLAND, see Crocus

Homespun

Homespun, a yellow, green, and reddish brown plaid pattern, was made by Vernon Kilns, Vernon, California. Other related plaids are Calico (pink and blue), Coronation Organdy (gray and rose), Gingham (green and yellow), Organdie (brown and yellow), Tam O'Shanter (green, lime, and cinnamon), and Tweed (gray and blue).

Bowl, 5 1/2 In.	3.00
Casserole, Cover	23.00
Cup & Saucer	5.00
Gravy Boat	7.50
Pitcher, 2 Qt.	20.00
Plate, 6 In.	2.00
Plate, 7 1/2 In.	4.00
Plate, 9 1/2 In.	6.00
Plate, 10 1/2 In.	8.00
Salt & Pepper	6.00 To 7.00
Saucer	2.50
Soup, Dish, 8 1/2 In.	5.00
Teapot	23.00

Homestead Provincial

Homestead Provincial is one of the Poppytrail patterns by Metlox.

Bowl, Salad	15.00
Bowl, Vegetable, Round	20.00
Box, Cover, Rectangular	25.00
Coffeepot	30.00
Creamer	7.00
Cup	7.00
Cup & Saucer	8.00
Match Holder	30.00
Salt & Pepper	12.00
Sugar & Creamer, Cover	20.00
Sugar, Cover	9.00

HOUSE, see Petit Point House

I

Iroquois

Russel Wright was an important industrial designer. His dinnerwares were made by at least four companies. Iroquois Casual China was à Russel Wright modern design made by Iroquois China Company, Syracuse, New York. The dinnerware was less expensive than American Modern, heavier and less breakable. It was advertised as cook-and-serve. The first pieces were marked China by Iroquois with the signature of Russel Wright. In the 1950s the ware was redesigned and the mark was changed to Iroquois Casual China by Russel Wright. The dishes were made in a number of colors, designed to be mixed and matched. Sets were often sold with pieces in several colors. The original Iroquois was glazed Avocado Yellow, Ice Blue, Lemon Yellow, Nutmeg Brown, Parsley Green, or Sugar White. In 1951 more colors were added, including aqua, Brick Red, Canteloupe, Charcoal, Lettuce Green, Oyster Gray, Pink Sherbet, or Ripe Apricot. In 1959 some Iroquois pieces were decorated with patterns and sold under other names. Glass tumblers were made in matching colors.

IROQUOIS
CASUAL
CHINA
by
Russel
Wright

AVOCADO YELLOW

Cup & Saucer, After Dinner	50.00
Butter	20.00
Butter, Cover	50.00
Casserole, Cover	35.00
Casserole, Divided	20.00
Creamer	8.00
Cup	10.00
Cup, Redesigned	6.00
Pitcher, Cover	50.00
Plate, 6 In.	2.50
Plate, 6 1/2 In.	4.00
Plate, 10 In.	5.00

CANTELOUPE

Coffeepot	45.00

ICE BLUE

Bowl, 5 1/2 In.	7.00
Bowl, Vegetable	15.00
Butter, Cover	50.00
Creamer, Stacking	10.00
Cup	5.00 To 10.00
Mug	35.00
Plate, 6 1/2 In.	5.00
Saucer	3.00
Soup, Dish, 8 1/2 In.	11.00

LEMON YELLOW

Creamer, Stacking	9.00
Cup & Saucer	10.00
Mug, Redesigned	55.00
Pitcher, Cover	60.00

Platter	22.00
Teapot, Redesigned	70.00 To 95.00

NUTMEG

Bowl, 5 1/2 In.	8.00
Butter	65.00
Carafe	60.00 To 115.00
Casserole, Cover, 8 In.	40.00
Casserole, Divided, Cover, 10 In.	40.00
Mug	45.00
Mug, Redesigned	55.00
Plate, 6 In.	3.00
Plate, 7 In.	4.50
Plate, 10 In.	8.00
Salt & Pepper, Stacking	22.00
Soup, Gumbo	20.00
Sugar & Creamer, Stacking	18.00 To 25.00

OYSTER

Platter, Oval, 12 In.	9.00

PINK SHERBET

Bowl, 5 1/2 In.	6.00
Carafe	60.00
Cup & Saucer	15.00 To 18.00
Mug, Redesigned	35.00
Pitcher, Cover	65.00
Plate, 10 In.	10.00 To 12.00

RIPE APRICOT

Butter, Cover	50.00
Carafe	60.00

SUGAR WHITE

Butter, Cover	50.00
Coffeepot, Redesigned	95.00
Platter, 14 In.	11.00

Ivy

Ivy is a hand-painted pattern made by Franciscan Ceramics from 1948.

Ashtray, Leaf.................25.00
Batter Set....................65.00
Bowl, 5 1/4 In. ....5.00 To 7.00
Bowl, 6 In. 8.50
Bowl, 7 1/2 In. 19.00
Bowl, 11 In..................25.00
Bowl, 12 In..................20.00
Bowl, Oval, 8 In.............8.00
Bowl, Round, 8 In..........27.00
Bowl, Vegetable, Divided,
   12 In. 40.00
Carafe, Water, Cover 115.00
Coffeepot 110.00
Creamer......................8.00
Cup.........................5.00
Cup & Saucer.......6.00 To 9.00
Cup & Saucer, 14 Oz. 16.00
Goblet 15.00
Gravy Boat,
   Attached Underplate... 28.00 To
   35.00
Jug, Cover 10.00
Plate, 6 In...........2.00 To 6.00
Plate, 8 1/2 In...............7.00
Plate, 9 In..................10.00
Plate, 10 In. ..... 12.00 To 15.00
Plate, Chop, 11 3/4 In. 25.00
Platter, Oval,
   13 In. .... 25.00 To 35.00
Platter, Round, 12 In. 55.00
Salt & Pepper...............22.00
Saucer......................5.00
Soup, Dish,
   8 1/2 In........ 12.00 To 20.00
Sugar & Creamer,
   Cover........... 30.00 To 40.00
Sugar, Cover...............18.00
Tidbit, 2 Tiers 5.00
Tumbler, 6 Piece 90.00

K

Kitchen Kraft

Kitchen Kraft oven-to-table
pieces were made by Homer
Laughlin China Company, Newell, West Virginia, from the
early 1930s. The pieces were
made in plain solid colors or
with decals. If decorated with
decals, they are listed in this
book under the decal's name.
If solid colors, they are listed
here.

BLUE

Cake Plate 40.00
Casserole, Cover,
   Individual.................85.00
Creamer.....................5.00

GREEN

Cake Server................45.00
Mixing Bowl, 8 In. 45.00
Pie Baker 4.00
Spoon.......................45.00

RED

Cake Plate, 11 In. 30.00
Fork 40.00
Stack Set, Cover 90.00

YELLOW

Casserole, Cover,
   Individual....... 55.00 To 60.00
Fork 45.00
Spoon.......................45.00

L

La Linda

La Linda is a solid-colored
California dinnerware made
by the Bauer Pottery Com-
pany of Los Angeles. It was
first offered in 1939 in matte
glazes, later in glossy glazes.
Early colors in matte were
blue, dusty pink, green, and
ivory. In 1945 glossy colors
of chartreuse, dark brown,
gray, green, ivory, light
brown, olive green, pink, turquoise, and yellow were used.

BLUE

Plate, 9 In...................7.00

CHARTREUSE

Salt & Pepper, 2 1/4 In. 6.00

YELLOW

Bowl, 5 In. 3.00
Plate, 9 1/2 In...............6.00

Lei Lani

Lei Lani was made by Vernon
Kilns from 1938 to 1942 and
again from 1947 to 1955.
The pattern was a maroon
printed lotus flower.

CALIFORNIA
ULTRA VERNON KILNS AUTHENTIC CALIFORNIA POTTERY MADE IN U.S.A.

Cup & Saucer.... 12.00 To 15.50
Cup & Saucer,
After Dinner 32.50
Eggcup......................25.00
Mug, 8 Oz. 36.50
Plate, 7 1/2 In.............15.00
Plate, 8 In.................15.00
Plate, 10 In. ..... 12.00 To 25.00
Plate, Chop, 17 In. 110.00
Saucer......................6.00
Soup, Coupe 20.00
Sugar & Creamer... 22.00 To 32.50
Sugar & Creamer,
Individual.................48.50

**LITTLE RED RIDING
HOOD, see red riding
hood**

Lu-Ray

The characteristic slightly
speckled glaze of the solid-
colored Lu-Ray makes it easy
to identify. Taylor, Smith, and
Taylor of Chester, West Virginia, made this pattern after
1938. Pastel colors include
Chatham Gray, Persian
Cream, Sharon Pink, Surf
Green, and Windsor Blue.

T.S.&T. Lu-Ray PASTELS U.S.A

BLUE

Bowl, 5 1/2 In. ....3.50 To 5.00
Creamer.............4.00 To 5.00
Cup & Saucer.......5.00 To 7.50
Cup & Saucer,
After Dinner ... 12.00 To 20.00
Eggcup, Double............12.00
Plate, 6 In..........1.25 To 3.00
Plate, 7 In...................4.00
Plate, 8 In....... 15.00 To 18.00
Plate, 9 In..........2.00 To 5.00
Plate, 10 In. 10.00
Plate, Chop, 14 In. 15.00
Plate, Sections 16.00
Platter, 11 1/2 In...........12.00
Saltshaker 4.00
Saucer.......................2.00
Soup, Cream 9.00
Teapot .... 45.00 To 75.00
Tumbler, Juice 35.00

CREAM

Plate, Chop, 14 In. 12.00
Teapot 65.00

GREEN

Bowl, 5 1/2 In. 5.00
Bowl, Berry.................4.00
Butter, 1/4 Lb. 11.00
Creamer, Ovoid.............19.00
Cup & Saucer.................4.00
Epergne......................85.00
Grill Plate 18.00
Plate, 6 In...................3.00
Plate, 7 In...................4.00
Plate, 8 In...................18.00
Plate, 9 In...................12.00
Plate, 10 In..................15.00
Plate, Chop, 14 In. 16.00
Platter, 13 In................14.00
Saltshaker 6.00
Saucer.......................2.00
Saucer, After Dinner.........3.00
Soup, Dish...................6.00

PINK

Bowl, 5 1/2 In. ....3.50 To 5.00
Bowl, Berry.................4.00

Bowl, Vegetable,
9 In............. 12.50 To 14.00
Creamer.............4.00 To 5.00
Cup & Saucer.......4.00 To 7.50
Cup, After Dinner 20.00
Eggcup, Double.............12.00
Gravy Boat 15.00
Pitcher, Water,
Footed.......... 35.00 To 45.00
Plate, 6 In...................3.00
Plate, 7 In...................4.00
Plate, 8 In...................5.00
Plate, 9 In..........2.00 To 5.00
Plate, 10 In. ..... 10.00 To 13.00
Platter, 11 3/4 In...........12.00
Saltshaker ....4.00 To 6.00
Saucer.......................2.00
Soup, Cream, Liner 10.00
Soup, Dish...................10.00
Soup, Lug....................10.00
Sugar, Cover.................3.50
Teapot 35.00

YELLOW

Bowl, 5 1/2 In. ....3.50 To 4.00
Bowl, Vegetable, Oval......15.00
Casserole,
Cover........... 45.00 To 70.00
Creamer......................4.00
Cup & Saucer.......4.00 To 6.00
Cup & Saucer,
After Dinner 10.00
Eggcup......................15.00
Epergne......................70.00
Gravy Boat,
Attached Underplate... 15.00 To
20.00
Grill Plate 13.00
Jug, Flat....................35.00
Pickle 13.00
Plate, 6 In...................3.00
Plate, 9 In...................5.00
Plate, 10 In. ..... 10.00 To 13.00
Plate, Chop, 14 In. 15.00
Platter, 11 3/4 In...........12.00
Platter, 13 1/2 In...........13.50
Saucer.......................2.00
Soup, Dish, 8 In. 9.00
Soup, Lug...................10.00

Sugar & Creamer,
After Dinner 85.00

Lute Song

Red Wing Potteries made
many dinnerware sets in modern forms with stylized designs in the 1950s and 1960s.
Lute Song is a typical pattern
with pictures of musical
instruments.

Bowl, 5 In. 6.00
Bowl, 6 3/8 In. 8.00
Bowl, Vegetable, Divided,
Oval.......................12.00
Cup & Saucer................ 4.00
Plate, 5 In.................... 2.50
Plate, 10 1/4 In. ...4.00 To 6.00
Salt & Pepper...............10.00
Saucer....................... 1.00
Tidbit, 2 Tiers 18.00

M

Magnolia

A wide, bright, cranberry-red
band borders Magnolia pattern by Stangl Pottery, Trenton, New Jersey. The pattern,
No. 3870, was made from
1952 to 1962. Another version of Magnolia by Red
Wing does not have the
banded edge. It was made in
1947. Both are listed here.

Bowl, 8 1/2 In.,
Red Wing 9.00
Bowl, Vegetable, 8 In.,
Stangl......................12.00
Butter, Cover, Red Wing...12.00
Casserole, Cover, Individual,
4 1/4 In., Stangl 15.00
Creamer, Red Wing 5.00
Cup & Saucer,
Stangl..............4.50 To 7.50
Eggcup, Stangl..............12.50
Gravy Boat, Stangl..........10.00
Pepper Shaker, Red Wing ... 5.00
Plate, 6 In., Stangl...........6.00
Plate, 7 1/4 In.,
Red Wing 3.00
Plate, 8 In., Stangl...........6.00
Plate, 10 In., Red Wing 9.00
Plate, 10 In., Stangl........10.00
Plate, Chop, 12 1/2 In.,
Red Wing 20.00
Plate, Chop, 13 In.,
Stangl......................17.50
Platter, 13 In., Stangl.......13.00
Relish, Tray, Red Wing 16.00
Salt & Pepper, Stangl 15.00
Saucer, Stangl...............1.50
Soup, Lug, Stangl............ 9.00
Sugar, Cover, Stangl 8.00
Sugar, Stangl................. 4.00
Teapot, 6 1/2 In., Stangl...45.00

Mar-Crest

Mar-crest is a dark brown pottery pattern made by Western
Stoneware in the 1950s. It
was made as a premium to be
sold at a low price or given
away at gasoline stations and
grocery stores.

Bean Pot, Cover............28.00
Bean Pot,
Warming Stand............22.00
Bowl, 5 1/2 In. 3.00
Bowl, Cover, Individual 4.00
Bowl, Divided 9.00
Bowl, Soup ....5.00 To 6.00
Bowl,
Stick Handle.......3.00 To 4.00
Bowl, Vegetable,
Divided....................20.00
Casserole, Cover,
Large .... 18.00 To 25.00
Casserole, Cover,
Medium 14.00
Cookie Jar .... 20.00 To 22.00
Creamer....................10.00
Cup ....2.00 To 3.00
Cup & Saucer.......3.50 To 4.00
Jar, Cover, 5 In. 21.00
Jug, Water 12.00
Lazy Susan 35.00
Mixing Bowl, Large.........15.00
Mixing Bowl, Medium......12.00
Mixing Bowl, Small.......... 9.00
Mug ....3.75 To 5.00
Pitcher, 4 In. 4.00
Pitcher, 6 In. 15.00
Pitcher, 8 1/2 In............22.75
Plate, 10 In. ....4.00 To 10.00
Salt & Pepper......6.00 To 17.50
Saucer....................... 3.50

Mardi Gras

Southern Potteries, Inc.,
Erwin, Tennessee, made
Mardi Gras, a hand-painted
dinnerware. A large blue
daisy and a large pink-petaled
flower are surrounded by
leaves and buds. The design is

placed so that only parts of the flowers are seen on the plate.

Bowl, 9 1/2 In.	9.00
Creamer.	6.50
Plate, 8 In.	7.00
Plate, Handle, Round	8.00
Platter, 11 1/2 In.	9.00
Platter, 13 In.	9.00 To 10.00
Punch Cup	6.00
Teapot, Square	80.00

Mayflower

Mayflower is a Blue Ridge pattern by Southern Potteries, Inc. Two large soft-pink flowers on a leafy stem grace the left side of a Skyline-shape plate.

Bowl, 5 3/4 In.	4.00
Cup & Saucer	6.00
Cup, After Dinner	10.00
Dish, 6 1/2 In.	5.00
Platter, 13 1/2 In.	12.50

MEDALLION, see Colonial

Mexicana

The first of the Mexican-inspired patterns that became popular as a dinnerware in the 1930s was Mexicana. This decal-decorated set, designed by Frederick Hurten Rhead, was first offered in 1938. The design shows a collection of orange and yellow pots with a few cacti. The edge of the dish well is rimmed with red or occasionally blue, green, or yellow. Almost all of the pieces are Century line, a popular Homer Laughlin dinnerware shape.

Kitchen Kraft OVENSERVE U.S.A.

Cake Server, Spoon, Fork, 3 Piece	150.00
Casserole, Cover, 8 1/2 In.	23.00
Cup & Saucer, Red Trim	12.00
Cup, Blue Ring	2.50
Jar, Cover, Medium	72.00
Mixing Bowl, 6 & 8 In., 2 Piece	60.00
Pie Plate, Red Trim, 9 In.	15.00
Plate, Red Trim, 7 In.	8.00
Platter, Square Well, 11 1/2 In.	24.00
Salt & Pepper	65.00
Tumbler, 14 Oz.	7.50

Modern California

Modern California was made in the 1930s by Vernon Kilns, Vernon, California. Colors include azure blue, orchid, pistachio, straw, sand, and gray.

MODERN CALIFORNIA VERNON KILNS LOS ANGELES AUTHENTIC CALIFORNIA POTTERY MADE IN USA

AZURE

Bowl, 9 In.	9.00
Bowl, Chowder	6.00
Cup	4.00
Cup & Saucer	5.00
Plate, 6 In.	2.00
Plate, 7 1/2 In.	3.50
Plate, 10 In.	6.00

ORCHID

Bowl, Chowder	6.00
Cup & Saucer	5.00
Cup & Saucer, After Dinner	10.00
Plate, 6 In.	2.00
Plate, 7 1/2 In.	3.50
Plate, 10 In.	6.00
Salt & Pepper	9.00

PISTACHIO

Bowl, Chowder	6.00
Creamer	4.00
Plate, 6 In.	2.00
Plate, 7 1/2 In.	3.50
Plate, 10 In.	6.00
Platter, 12 In.	9.00
Sugar	3.00

STRAW

Bowl, 9 In.	9.00
Bowl, Chowder	6.00
Cup & Saucer	5.00
Plate, 6 In.	2.00
Plate, 7 1/2 In.	3.50
Plate, 10 In.	6.00

Monterey

J. A. Bauer made a solid-color pottery line from 1934 to the early 1940s. The Los Angeles, California, pottery sold full dinnerware sets with matching serving pieces. It was a mix-and-match set made in black, brown, burgundy, canary yellow, chartreuse, gray, ivory, Monterey blue, olive green, orange, pink, turquoise blue, and white. A series of molded rings was used on plates, vases, cups, pitchers, and bowls.

BAUER POTTERY
LOS ANGELES

Bowl, 9 In. 7.00
Plate, 10 In. . . . . 4.50 To 6.00
Salt & Pepper. 10.00

Monterey Moderne

The name Monterey must have been a selling feature, because in 1948 Bauer made a different style of dinnerware and named it Monterey Moderne. It stayed in production until 1968. The mix-and-match dishes were made of glossy black, burgundy, chartreuse, dark brown, gray, olive green, pink, and yellow.

· · · · · · · · · · · · · · · · ·
For emergency repairs to chipped pottery, try coloring the spot with a wax crayon or oil paint. It will look a little better.
· · · · · · · · · · · · · · · · ·

BAUER

CHARTREUSE

Bowl, Vegetable, Round,
  8 1/2 In. 10.00
Mug 4.00
Sugar, Cover. 6.00

Monticello

Sears, Roebuck often had special dinnerware made for its stores. Monticello was made by Hall China Company from 1941 to 1959 for the exclusive use of Sears. Blue, green, pink, and yellow flower sprigs were scattered as a border.

Plate, 6 1/2 In. 2.00
Plate, 8 In. 2.50
Plate, 9 In. 4.00
Platter, 13 In. 9.00
Platter, Oval, 15 1/2 In. . . . 12.00

Morning Glory

From 1942 to 1949 the Hall China Company, East Liverpool, Ohio, made a dinnerware called Morning Glory. The outside of the pieces was Cadet Blue, the inside had a Morning Glory decal decoration.

Bowl, 6 In. 7.00
Casserole. 5.00
Pepper Shaker 6.00
Soup, Dish. 10.00

Mt. Vernon

Mt. Vernon is a pattern made by the Hall China Company for Sears, Roebuck and Company in the 1940s. It has pink and green flowers in the design.

Bowl, 5 In. . . . . 2.50 To 3.00
Bowl, 9 In. . . . . . . 11.00 To 12.00
Bowl, Lug, 6 In. 5.00
Cup . . . . 2.50 To 4.00
Gravy Boat, Underplate 10.00

Plate, 6 In.................... 2.00
Plate, 8 In........... 2.00 To 3.00
Plate, 10 In. 5.00
Soup, Dish, 8 In. ... 3.00 To 5.00

N

Native California

Vernon Kilns of Vernon, California, made a pastel-colored dinnerware called Native California from 1942 to 1947. The dishes had a leaf border on the plates. Colors used were aqua, blue, green, pink, and yellow.

GREEN ─────────

Plate, Chop, 14 In. 28.00

PINK ─────────

Plate, Chop, 14 In. 20.00

YELLOW ─────────

Bowl, Vegetable 10.00
Cup 4.00
Plate, 6 1/4 In............... 4.00
Plate, 7 1/2 In............... 5.00
Plate, 12 In. 10.00
Saucer....................... 2.00

• • • • • • • • • • • • • • • •
Dental wax (ask your dentist about it) is a good adhesive to keep figurines on shelves or lids on teapots
• • • • • • • • • • • • • • • •

O

Old Curiosity Shop

The Old Curiosity Shop is one of many patterns made by Royal China Company of Sebring, Ohio, in the 1940s. It pictures a view of the shop and an elaborate border.

GREEN ─────────

Ashtray 3.00
Bowl, 5 1/2 In. 1.25
Bowl, 10 In. 7.00
Creamer...................... 1.50
Cup & Saucer................. 2.00
Plate, 6 In.................... 1.25
Plate, 7 In.................... 3.00
Plate, 10 In. 12.00
Plate, Chop 7.00
Plate, Handle 5.00
Salt & Pepper................ 6.50
Soup, Dish................... 3.00
Soup, Lug.................... 4.00
Sugar, Cover................. 3.00
Teapot, Cover 18.00

PINK ─────────

Bowl, 5 1/2 In. 1.25
Bowl, 10 In. 7.00
Creamer...................... 1.50
Cup & Saucer................. 2.00
Plate, 7 In.................... 3.00
Plate, 10 In. 2.00
Platter 7.00
Soup, Dish................... 3.00
Sugar, Cover................. 3.00

ORANGE POPPY, see
Poppy

Orchard Song

Orchard Song was made by Stangl Pottery, Trenton, New Jersey, from 1962 to 1974.

Cup & Saucer............... 18.00
Plate, 8 In................... 8.00
Plate, 10 In. 10.00
Server,
Center Handle..... 7.50 To 9.00
Tray 20.00

Organdie

Organdie is one of six different plaid patterns made by Vernon Kilns, Vernon, California. It is an overall brown pattern with a yellow and brown plaid border. Other related plaids are Calico (pink and blue), Coronation Organdy (gray and rose), Gingham (green and yellow), Homespun (cinnamon, yellow, and green), Tam O'Shanter (green, lime, and cinnamon), and Tweed (gray and blue).

Bowl, 5 1/2 In. .... 3.00 To 6.00
Bowl, 9 In. 9.00
Bowl, Chowder,
6 1/4 In......... 7.00 To 10.00
Bowl, Divided,
11 1/2 In................. 12.00
Bowl, Vegetable, Round,
9 In.............. 8.00 To 10.00
Carafe, Cover .... 20.00 To 25.00
Casserole, 8 In. 25.00
Creamer............ 4.00 To 5.00

Cup & Saucer	5.00 To 8.00
Eggcup	7.50
Gravy Boat	5.00 To 9.00
Mixing Bowl, 8 In.	21.00
Mug	7.00
Pitcher, 1 Qt.	13.00 To 16.00
Plate, 6 1/2 In.	1.50
Plate, 7 1/2 In.	3.00
Plate, 9 1/2 In.	4.00 To 5.00
Plate, 10 1/2 In.	6.00
Plate, Chop, 12 In.	10.00
Plate, Chop, 14 In.	15.00
Platter, 12 In.	9.00
Platter, Round, 14 In.	21.00
Salt & Pepper	6.00 To 10.00
Soup, Dish	6.00
Sugar & Creamer, Cover, Ice Lip	10.00
Sugar, Cover	6.00 To 10.00
Teapot, Cover	20.00 To 30.00
Tidbit, 2 Tiers	15.00

Organdy

Organdy by Homer Laughlin is very different from the Organdie pattern by Vernon Kilns. Homer Laughlin made a plain, pastel-bordered, semiporcelain set with very clean, modern shapes. Colors included green, yellow, blue, and pink. Each set had green handles.

Bowl, Vegetable, Round	7.00
Cup	5.00
Cup & Saucer	7.00
Plate, 6 In.	2.00
Plate, 9 1/2 In.	5.00
Plate, Chop, 12 In.	12.50
Platter, 12 In.	12.50
Salt & Pepper	8.00
Soup, Dish	6.00
Sugar	8.00

P

Painted Daisy

Red, blue, yellow, and green were the colors used to hand paint the flowers on the Painted Daisy pattern by Blue Ridge. It is on the Colonial shape.

Bowl, 5 In.	3.00
Plate, 9 In.	10.00
Platter, 13 1/2 In.	9.00

Pastel Tulip

Pastel Tulip is a decal-decorated dinnerware with pale tulips. It was made by Harker Pottery Company. The tulip decal was used on several different shapes, so you may find variations in the size and border molding of plates with the same tulip decorations.

Casserole, Cover	22.00
Jug, Cover	32.00
Pie Plate, 10 In.	18.00
Plate, 9 In.	4.50
Soup, Dish	8.50
Sugar & Creamer, Cover	18.00

Pate Sur Pate

Pate Sur Pate is a solid color Harker pattern. It has a scalloped border.

TEAL

Ashtray	3.00
Ashtray, Individual	1.50
Bowl, 5 1/2 In.	2.00
Bowl, Round, 9 In.	5.00
Bowl, Vegetable	12.00
Luncheon Set, 8 Piece	20.00
Plate, 6 In.	1.25
Sugar, Cover	3.00

Pepe

Pepe is a dinnerware made by Red Wing. It is hand painted and was advertised in 1963 as colorfast, ovenproof, and detergent-safe. The design is very simple and modern in shades of bittersweet, green, and dark bluish purple.

Coffeepot, Tall..............25.00
Cup..........................3.00
Plate, 6 1/2 In...............3.00

Petalware

Petalware is a solid-color dinnerware made in the late 1930s by W. S. George Company of Kittanning, Pennsylvania. It was made in black, blue, coral, ivory, pink, red, and turquoise.

DARK GREEN

Plate, 9 In...................5.00

LIGHT BLUE

Creamer......................3.00
Soup, Dish...................5.00

LIGHT GREEN

Bowl, 6 In. 4.00
Cup..........................2.50
Plate, 7 In...................2.50
Plate, 9 In...................3.00
Saucer.......................4.00

PINK

Cup..........................2.50
Plate, 5 1/2 In..............4.00
Plate, 9 In...................3.00

YELLOW

Gravy........................5.00
Plate, 6 In...................1.50
Platter 6.00

Petit Point House

Petit Point House, sometimes called Cottage or House, is another pattern made with a design that looks like a series of small stitches. It was made by Crooksville China Company.

Bowl, 11 In.................16.00
Coffeepot, After Dinner 45.00
Jug, Cover 15.00

Petit Point Rose

Petit point designs were very popular. This pattern has a decal picturing a wreath or a grouping of stitched roses. Collectors refer to the patterns as Petit Point Rose I, II, or III, each having a slightly different decal. There is also a pattern called Petit Point Rose that was made by W. S. George. Listed here are the Harker pieces.

Pie Baker, 9 In. 5.00
Cake Server.................16.00
Jug, Cover 20.00
Pie Baker, 9 In. 16.00
Server, Center Handle,
6 In..............6.00 To 9.00
Utility Set, 3 Bowls........42.00

Plantation Ivy

Blue Ridge made several ivy patterns. Plantation Ivy is decorated with a stylized hand-painted ivy vine in yellow and green. It was made in the 1950s.

. . . .
Don't store dishes for long periods of time in old newspaper wrappings. The ink can make indelible stains on the china.
. . . .

Cup & Saucer................7.00
Gravy Boat 14.00
Plate, 6 In...................2.50
Saucer.......................2.00

Plum Blossom

Plum Blossom was made by Red Wing in 1949. The pattern had scalloped dishes with a stylized Oriental plum blossom of pink or yellow. Plates and cups were six-sided.

YELLOW

Bowl, 5 1/2 In. 4.00
Cup..........................4.00
Plate, 10 In. 6.00
Soup, Dish...................7.00
Sugar, Cover................7.00

Poppy

Poppy, sometimes called Orange Poppy by collectors, was made by the Hall China Company, East Liverpool, Ohio, from 1933 through the 1950s. The decals picture realistic groups of orange poppies with a few leaves. Another Hall pattern called Red Poppy has bright red stylized flowers with black leaves and trim.

Baker, French.............14.00
Bean Pot, Silver Trim 45.00
Bowl, 5 1/2 In. 6.00
Bowl, 9 1/8 In. 15.00
Cake Keeper...............12.50
Cake Plate,
  9 1/2 In.........7.00 To 10.00
Canister Set.................47.00
Coffee Dispenser, Wall 55.00
Coffeepot, Drip, Cover 18.00
Coffeepot, Golden Key 35.00
Cup & Saucer...............17.50
Custard ....3.50 To 5.50
Dispenser, Waxpaper 20.00
Jar, Drip, Cover 15.00
Jar, Pretzel....... 55.00 To 85.00
Jug, Ball 35.00
Jug, Radiance,
  No.4 .... 20.00 To 27.50
Jug, Radiance,
  No.5 .... 18.00 To 20.00
Leftover, Loop Handle......45.00
Match Holder..............48.00
Mixing Bowl,
  7 1/2 In..........7.00 To 10.00
Mustard, Liner 20.00
Pitcher.....................18.50
Plate, 7 In.................. 3.00
Platter, 11 1/2 In............ 8.00
Recipe File, Metal 25.00
Salt & Pepper,
  Loop Handle 12.00
Salt & Pepper, Range,
  Handle 34.00
Shaker, Canister-Style,
  Radiance.................50.00
Sifter......................43.00

Poppy & Wheat

Poppy & Wheat is a design that seems to have been made in the 1930s. It was made by Hall China Company, East Liverpool, Ohio. The design shows a realistic spray of orange flowers and wheat heads. It is sometimes called Wheat or Wild Poppy.

Creamer....................20.00
Jug, Sunshine, Cover,
  No.3 ....60.00
Mixing Bowl, 7 3/8 In. 15.00
Pitcher.....................35.00

Poppy Trail

Metlox Potteries of California made many dinnerwares marked with the word Metlox or Poppytrail (Poppy Trail). Solid-colored wares and hand-decorated pieces were made. Listed here are solid mix-and-match pieces marked Metlox Poppy Trail. Colors include delphinium blue, canary yellow, ivory, old rose, poppy orange, rust, and turquoise blue.

IVORY ─────────────

Bowl, 5 1/4 In. 3.00
Butter, Cover 29.00
Coffeepot 34.00
Cup 5.00
Cup & Saucer..............10.00
Gravy Boat, Underplate,
  9 1/2 In........ 20.00 To 28.00
Plate, 6 In...........4.00 To 5.00

Plate, 8 In.................... 6.00
Plate, 9 1/4 In.............. 7.00
Plate,
  10 1/4 In........9.00 To 10.00
Platter, 13 In..............18.00
Salt & Pepper..............12.00
Saucer...................... 2.00
Sugar & Creamer 15.00

ORANGE ─────────────

Cup........................ 3.00
Cup & Saucer............... 5.00
Plate, 6 In.................. 3.00

TURQUOISE ────────────

Bowl, 5 1/4 In. 4.00
Cup........................ 5.00
Cup & Saucer............... 6.50

Prelude

Prelude is a pattern with a stylized flower design. It was made by Stangl Pottery, Trenton, New Jersey, from 1949 to 1957.

Butter, Cover 22.00
Compote 30.00
Cup & Saucer..............12.00
Plate, 6 In.................. 6.00
Plate, 8 In.................. 8.00
Plate, 10 In. 10.00

Priscilla

Priscilla was made by Homer Laughlin China Company, Newell, West Virginia. It is a decal-decorated ware with pale pink roses and sprigs of flowers.

Bowl, 5 In.	2.50
Cake Plate	4.00 To 7.00
Mixing Bowl, 6 3/8 In.	15.00
Mixing Bowl, 8 1/2 In.	17.50
Mixing Bowl, 10 1/2 In.	20.00
Plate, 6 In.	1.75
Plate, 8 In.	3.00
Platter, 13 1/2 In.	10.00
Underplate, For Gravy	5.00

Provincial Fruit

Metlox made Provincial Fruit pattern in 1965. It is part of the Poppytrail line.

Bowl, 6 1/4 In.	2.50
Creamer	3.00
Plate, 7 1/2 In.	3.00
Plate, 10 1/2 In.	3.00
Saucer	.50

Teapot, Cloverleaf Finial, Dull Finish	15.00
Teapot, Fruit Finial, High Glaze	15.00

R

Rancho

French Saxon China of East Liverpool, Ohio, started working in 1935. Rancho is the solid-color line they made as mix-and-match sets. Pieces were made in dark colors, including chartreuse, dark green, gray, and maroon. Plates had a molded band of rings near the slightly scalloped the edge.

DARK GREEN

Bowl, 5 1/2 In.	2.50 To 3.00
Cup & Saucer	4.00 To 5.00
Plate, 9 In.	4.00 To 4.50
Soup, Dish	4.00 To 5.00

GRAY

Bowl, 5 1/2 In.	2.50 To 3.00
Cup & Saucer	4.00 To 5.00
Plate, 9 In.	4.00 To 6.00
Soup, Dish	4.00

MAROON

Bowl, 5 1/2 In.	2.50 To 3.00
Cup & Saucer	4.00 To 5.00
Plate, 7 In.	2.00
Plate, 9 In.	4.00 To 4.50
Soup, Dish	4.00 To 5.00

Random Harvest

Random Harvest is a Red Wing dinnerware pattern that is colorfast and ovenproof. It was made in the 1960s. The design is hand painted in brown, copper, coral, green, and turquoise on a flecked dish.

Bowl, 5 In.	4.00
Casserole, Cover	25.00
Celery	10.00
Plate, 6 In.	2.00 To 3.50
Plate, 8 1/2 In.	4.00
Plate, 10 In.	5.00 To 7.00
Platter, 13 In.	12.00
Relish, Divided	7.00

Raymor

Many collectors search for pieces in the Raymor pattern. It is a stoneware made by Roseville Pottery Company of Zanesville, Ohio, in 1952 and 1953. It was designed by Ben Siebel. One advertisement claimed the textured glaze was offered in Autumn Brown, Avocado Green, Beach Gray, Contemporary White, and Terra Cotta (rust). There were also pieces made in mottled green and black.

BROWN

Bowl, 9 In.	16.00
Celery	22.50
Cup & Saucer	16.00
Plate, 6 In.	6.00
Saucer	3.00
Sugar & Creamer, Cover	40.00

DARK GREEN

Bowl, Fruit, Lug	8.50
Plate, 6 In.	6.00
Plate, 10 In.	14.00
Sugar & Creamer, Cover	40.00
Teapot	75.00

IVORY

Cup & Saucer...............16.00
Gravy Boat 14.00
Plate, 10 In. 14.00

RUST

Tumbler, Set of 6........ 300.00

Red Poppy

Bright red flowers and black leaves were used on this popular Hall pattern called Red Poppy. The pattern, made in East Liverpool, Ohio, from 1930 through 1950, was a premium item for Grand Union Tea Company. Matching metal pieces, such as wastebaskets and bread boxes, were made, and glass tumblers are known.

Bowl, 5 1/2 In. ....3.75 To 4.00
Bowl, 8 1/2 In.............. 9.75
Bowl, 8 1/2 In. 12.50
Cake Safe 30.00
Coffeepot, Drip, Cover 16.00
Jug, 4 In. .... 15.00 To 17.50
Salt & Pepper,
  Handle .... 16.00 To 17.00
Saltshaker, Handle 8.00
Tumbler,
  Frosted .... 15.00 To 20.00

Red Riding Hood

One of the easiest patterns of American dinnerware to recognize is Red Riding Hood. Three-dimensional figures of the little girl with the red hood have been adapted into saltshakers, teapots, and other pieces. The pattern was made by the Hull Pottery Company, Crooksville, Ohio, from 1943 to 1957.

Hull Ware
Little Red Riding Hood
Patent Applied For
U.S.A.

Cookie Jar 95.00
Creamer, Side Pour.........65.00
Matchbox 525.00
Pitcher, Side Pour,
  6 3/4 In................. 135.00
Salt & Pepper, Large........50.00
Salt & Pepper, Small........25.00
Saltshaker, 5 1/2 In.........19.00
Sugar & Creamer,
  Head Pour 185.00
Sugar & Creamer,
  Open Side.................95.00
Teapot.........150.00 To 165.00

Red Rooster

Red Rooster by Metlox is one of the Poppytrail lines and was made beginning in 1955. It is easy to identify because the center design is a large red rooster. Accessory pieces may be all red. A Blue Ridge dinnerware is also known as Red Rooster (see Rooster). Metlox pieces are listed here.

Bowl, 8 In. 15.00
Bowl, 10 In...... 18.00 To 20.00
Bowl, Vegetable,
  Rooster Cover.............75.00
Bread Server, 9 1/2 In. 28.00
Canister Set, 4 Piece...... 150.00
Canister, All Red, Large 25.00
Canister, All Red,
  Medium 22.00
Canister, All Red, Tea......20.00
Canister, Tea................25.00
Casserole, Cover,
  1 1/4 Qt. 20.00
Coffeepot .... 20.00 To 30.00
Creamer.....................12.00
Cup 6.00
Cup & Saucer...............12.00
Mug, 8 Oz. ...... 15.00 To 18.00
Pitcher, Milk, 1 Qt..........15.00
Plate, 6 3/8 In............... 4.00
Plate, 7 1/2 In............... 5.00
Plate, 10 In. ....6.00 To 10.00
Platter, 13 1/2 In...........20.00
Salt & Pepper.... 10.00 To 12.00
Soup, Dish.........8.00 To 10.00
Sugar & Creamer,
  Cover........... 10.00 To 20.00
Teapot,
  Rooster......... 35.00 To 45.00
Wall Pocket...... 25.00 To 45.00

Refrigerator Ware

Refrigerator sets were made by the Hall China Company, East Liverpool, Ohio, from the late 1930s. For Westinghouse, the company made Patrician in 1938, Emperor in 1939, Aristocrat in 1940-1941, and Prince in 1952.

Hall also made King and Queen ovenware to match the Refrigerator Ware. Sears, Roebuck, Montgomery Ward, Hotpoint, and General Electric also used Hall Refrigerator Ware. In addition, the company made some pieces sold with the Hall name: Bingo in the late 1930s, Plaza in the 1930s to the 1960s, and Norris.

Made Exclusively for WESTINGHOUSE By The Hall China Co.
MADE IN U.S.A.

BINGO

Leftover, Red 8.00

COLDSPOT

Leftover, Blue & White,
    Cover 15.00

FRIGIDAIRE

Ice Tea Server, Green 37.00
Water Bottle,
    Frosted Green 15.00

G.E.

Butter, Dark Green,
    Cover .... 9.00 To 16.00
Leftover Set, Yellow & Gray,
    Cover, 5 Piece 35.00
Leftover, Cover, Yellow 6.00
Leftover, Crystal,
    4 X 8 In. 10.00
Leftover, Crystal,
    8 X 8 In. 16.00
Leftover, Prince, Oblong 6.00
Leftover, Prince, Round 6.00
Salt & Pepper 25.00
Sugar, Cover 45.00
Water Bottle,
    Dark Green 22.00

Water Server, Prince,
    Turquoise & Daffodil 45.00

HOTPOINT

Leftover, No.1, Green Luster,
    Round 18.50
Leftover, No.2, Garden 8.00

MONTGOMERY WARD

Bowl, Blue, Medium,
    Cover 12.50
Leftover, Blue 8.50
Water Server, Blue,
    Cover .... 25.00 To 45.00

WESTINGHOUSE

Butter, Aristocrat, Yellow ... 17.00
Butter, Green 8.00
Butter, Hercules, Cover 9.00
Casserole, Cover, Yellow,
    Rack 32.50
Casserole, Yellow 18.00
Leftover, Aristocrat,
    Canary 20.00
Leftover, Aristocrat, Green,
    Round 6.00
Leftover, Cover, Aristocrat, Ivory,
    Oval 15.00
Leftover, Emperor, Red 6.00
Leftover, Emperor,
    Sunset 25.00
Leftover, Hercules,
    Turquoise 16.00
Pitcher, Blue 8.00
Water Server, Aristocrat,
    Blue 95.00
Water Server, Aristocrat,
    Tan 115.00
Water Server, Patrician,
    Delphinium 45.00

Rhythm Rose

Rhythm Rose was made by Homer Laughlin China Company, Newell, West Virginia, from the mid-1940s to the mid-1950s. The pattern featured a center rose decal.

Bowl, 5 In. 2.00
Bowl, Flat, 5 1/2 In. 13.00
Bowl, Vegetable, 8 In. 2.00

Cake Plate 6.00
Creamer 3.00
Pitcher, 5 1/2 In 9.00
Plate, 6 In .... 1.25 To 1.50
Plate, 7 In 2.25
Plate, 9 In 3.00
Platter, 12 In 7.00
Soup, Dish 4.00
Sugar, Cover 4.50

Rhythm

Rhythm is a solid-color dinnerware made by Homer Laughlin from about 1951 to 1958. It is a pattern with simple, modern shapes. The dishes were made in many of the Harlequin colors, including chartreuse, forest green, gray, maroon, and yellow.

CHARTREUSE

Plate, 9 In .... 2.50 To 4.00

FOREST GREEN

Bowl, 5 1/2 In. 3.00
Bowl, 8 In. 8.00

GRAY

Bowl, 5 1/2 In. 3.00
Sugar 4.00

MAROON

Bowl, 8 In. 9.00
Creamer 5.00
Plate, 9 In. 4.00
Saucer 1.50

YELLOW

Bowl, 8 1/2 In. 7.00

Cup & Saucer................ 7.00
Gravy Boat 8.00
Plate, 9 In.................. 4.00
Platter, 11 1/2 In........... 5.00
Sugar 4.00

Ring

Ring, sometimes called Bee-hive, was made by J. A. Bauer Company, Los Angeles, California, from 1932 to 1962. It was made in many colors. Bright shades include black, burnt orange, green, ivory, maroon, orange, and yellow. Pastel shades are chartreuse, gray, green, light yellow, olive, pale blue, pink, turquoise, and white.

BURGUNDY

Teapot, 6 Cup 40.00

DARK BLUE

Ashtray Set, Yellow, Orange,
  Green, Square, 3 In.,
  4 Piece 80.00
Ashtray, Square, 4 In. 32.50
Carafe...................... 38.00
Mixing Bowl, 1 1/2 Pt. 17.50
Pie Baker, 9 In. 25.00
Platter, 9 In................ 22.00
Saucer...................... 6.00
Tumbler, 12 Oz............. 20.00

GREEN

Ashtray, 4 In............... 22.50
Bowl, 5 X 2 In. 6.50
Bowl, Nesting, 6 In......... 16.00
Candlestick................. 15.00

Custard Cup 4.00
Mixing Bowl, 1 Qt......... 30.00
Plate, 9 In................. 10.00
Tumbler, 6 Oz. 15.00

ORANGE

Bowl, Nesting, 6 In........ 15.00
Carafe, Wooden Handle 40.00
Mixing Bowl, 1 Qt......... 38.00
Pitcher, Ice Lip, 1/2 Gal.... 49.00
Plate, 10 In. 25.00
Plate, Chop, 12 In. 30.00
Teapot, 2 Cup 30.00
Teapot, 6 Cup 60.00

YELLOW

Ashtray, 4 In............... 27.50
Cup 15.00
Pie Plate, 9 In. 12.50
Plate, 7 1/2 In............. 10.00
Plate, 9 1/2 In............. 10.00
Plate, 10 In. 20.00
Plate, Chop, 12 In. 25.00
Saucer...................... 6.00
Teapot, 2 Cup 35.00
Tumbler, 3 Oz............. 15.00

Riviera

Riviera was solid-color ware made by Homer Laughlin China Company, Newell, West Virginia, from 1938 to 1950. It was unmarked and sold exclusively by the Murphy Company. Plates and cup handles were squared. Colors were ivory, light green, mauve blue, red, yellow, and, rarely, dark blue.

IVORY

Casserole, Cover 80.00
Gravy...................... 12.00
Jug, Open.................. 65.00
Saltshaker 5.00
Tumbler, Handle 45.00

LIGHT GREEN

Bowl, 5 1/2 In. 6.00
Butter, 1/4 Lb. 95.00
Casserole, Cover 55.00
Cup & Saucer............... 9.50
Jug, Cover .... 75.00 To 80.00
Saltshaker .... 5.00 To 14.00
Soup, Dish....... 11.00 To 12.50
Sugar & Creamer, Cover.... 20.00
Sugar, Cover................ 14.00
Teapot 55.00
Tumbler, Handle 38.00

MAUVE BLUE

Bowl, 5 1/2 In. 6.00
Cup 7.50
Jug, Disk.......120.00 To 185.00
Plate, 6 1/2 In.............. 3.50
Plate, 7 In.................. 2.50
Saltshaker 5.00
Sugar, Cover................ 13.00
Tumbler, Handle 35.00

RED

Butter, 1/4 Lb. 75.00
Casserole, Cover 60.00
Creamer..................... 8.00
Gravy Boat 15.00
Jug, Open.................. 75.00
Plate, 9 In.........8.00 To 13.00
Salt & Pepper............... 8.00

Saltshaker 8.00

Soup, Dish 11.00

Tumbler, Handle 38.00

YELLOW ───────────

Bowl, 5 1/2 In. 8.00

Butter,
1/4 Lb. .... 65.00 To 85.00

Butter, 1/2 Lb. 25.00

Creamer. 6.00

Jug, Open. 65.00

Plate, 6 1/2 In. 13.00

Plate, 9 In. 6.00

Teapot, Cover 65.00

Tumbler, Handle 38.00

Rooster

Roosters of many sorts were used as decorations on Southern Potteries pieces. The Rooster crowing from the fence top with a sun and a barn in the distance is a pattern called Cock o' the Morn. Another pattern was known as Cock o' the Walk. Most other patterns picturing the bird are called Rooster by collectors, although Rooster was a giftware line and the dinnerware with the same design, on the Clinchfield shape, was known as Game Cock. These pieces have a rooster center and a series of red three-line designs as the border. Another Blue Ridge pattern, on the Skyline shape, shows a rooster standing in front of a fence. This pattern may be called Rooster or Red Rooster by collectors. Stangl also made a pattern called Rooster, but only Blue Ridge is listed here.

Bowl, 5 1/2 In. 7.00

Bowl, Vegetable, Divided,
9 1/2 In. .... 17.00 To 25.00

Bowl, Vegetable, Round 12.00

Butter, Cover 25.00

Carafe. 18.00

Creamer. 8.00

Creamer, After Dinner. 10.00

Cup & Saucer 6.00

Eggcup. 9.00

Gravy Boat 18.00

Plate, 6 In. 3.00

Plate, 10 In. 6.00

Plate, Snack 10.00

Platter, 13 1/2 In. 40.00

Relish, 3 Sections 35.00

Salt & Pepper, Figural 35.00

Soup, Dish 8.00

Sugar 9.00

Sugar & Creamer 20.00

Rose Parade

The Hall China Company, East Liverpool, Ohio, sometimes made surprising color- and decal-decorated wares. Rose Parade has a solid Cadet Blue body with contrasting Hi-white knobs and handles. A rose decal was added to the white spaces. Sometimes the flower is pink, sometimes blue. The pattern was made from 1941 through the 1950s. Serving pieces, not dinnerware sets, were made.

Rose Parade

Bowl, 9 In. 12.00

Bowl, Deep, 6 In. 10.00

Bowl, Deep, 7 In. 11.00

Bowl, Deep, 9 In. 16.00

Creamer. 12.00

Drip Jar, Cover 18.00

Salt & Pepper. 16.00

Teapot, 6 Cup 30.00

Rose White

Rose White, first made in 1941 by Hall China Company, is similar to Rose Parade. The same shapes were used, but the pieces were all white with a slightly different rose-decal decoration. There is silver trim on many pieces.

Casserole,
Cover. .... 26.00 To 28.00

Salt & Pepper. 5.00

Salt & Pepper, Sani-Grid 13.00

Rosebud

Rosebud was made by Coors Pottery, Golden, Colorado, from 1934 to 1942. It is a solid-colored ware with a stylized flower and leaves on the edge of plates or sides of cups. It was made in blue, green, ivory, maroon, turquoise, and yellow.

COORS
ROSEBUD
U.S.A.

BLUE ────────────

Cup & Saucer	5.00
Plate, 7 In.	4.50
Plate, 10 In.	7.00
Saucer	3.00

GREEN ────────────

Cup & Saucer	5.00
Plate, 10 In.	6.50

MAROON ────────────

Cup & Saucer	5.00
Plate, 7 In.	4.50
Plate, 10 In.	8.00

Royal Rose

Royal Rose is a Hall China Company pattern that can confuse you. It is Cadet Blue with Hi-white handles and knobs. The floral decal is the one used on Rose White. Pieces have silver trim. The shapes are different from those used for Rose Parade.

HALL'S
SUPERIOR
QUALITY
KITCHENWARE

MADE IN
U. S. A.

Casserole, Cover	23.50
Jug, Ball, No.3	30.00
Pepper Shaker, Handle	8.00
Saltshaker, Handle	8.00 To 9.00

RUSSEL WRIGHT, see American Modern; Iroquois; White Clover

Rustic Plaid

Rustic Plaid was made on the Skyline shape by Blue Ridge in the 1950s. Black lines and rim decorate a sponged background.

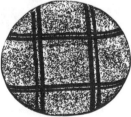

Bowl, 5 1/2 In.	3.00
Creamer, Cover	4.00 To 6.00
Cup & Saucer	5.00
Gravy Boat	15.00
Pepper Shaker	8.00

Plate, 9 1/2 In.	4.00
Plate, 10 In.	8.50
Plate, Handle, 12 1/2 In.	10.00
Platter, Oval, 13 1/2 In.	10.00
Salt & Pepper, Handle	10.00
Saucer	2.00

S

Salamina

Salamina is an important pattern made by Vernon Kilns in 1939. The pattern pictures a girl from Greenland. Each piece had a different scene. The designs were adapted from the drawings in a book by Rockwell Kent. The dinnerware was hand tinted.

VERNON KILNS
Made in U.S.A.

Cup & Saucer	50.00
Plate, 6 1/2 In.	22.00
Plate, 9 1/2 In.	60.00 To 75.00
Plate, 10 In.	75.00
Plate, Pickle, 6 In.	30.00
Saltshaker	45.00
Saucer	10.00 To 12.50

Serenade

There were at least three patterns named Serenade, one by Hall, another by Homer Laughlin, and still another by Edwin M. Knowles China Company. The Homer Laughlin dishes listed here were plain, made in blue, green, pink, or yellow. The Hall dishes are decorated with sprigs of orange flowers (see Serenade Hall).

GREEN

Bowl, 6 In. 5.00
Gravy Boat 10.00
Plate, 9 1/2 In. 6.00
Saucer. 2.00

PINK

Plate, 9 1/2 In. 6.00
Soup, Dish 7.00
Teapot, Sugar & Creamer,
3 Piece 95.00

YELLOW

Plate, 9 1/2 In. 6.00
Sugar & Creamer 18.00

Serenade Hall

Hall China Company made a pattern called Serenade on its D-shape dishes. The dishes were decorated with sprigs of orange flowers.

Casserole, Rayed 18.00
French Baker 10.00

SHELLWARE, see Cameo Shellware

Sherwood

Vernon Kilns made Sherwood pattern on beige dishes of the Anytime shape from 1955 to 1958. The decoration was several clusters of brown, bronze, and gold leaves.

Butter Pat, 2 1/2 In. 5.00
Gravy Boat 5.00
Pitcher, 1 Pt. 5.00
Plate, Chop, 12 3/4 In. 5.00
Relish, Divided 6.00

Silhouette

Silhouette looks just like its name. The 1930s pattern shows a black silhouette of two people eating at a table and a dog begging for food in front of the table. The plates are trimmed in platinum. The pattern, made by Crooksville China Company, Crooksville, Ohio, is similar to Taverne,

but Taverne has no dog. Matching metal pieces and glasswares were made.

Bowl, 5 5/8 In. 9.50
Bowl, 9 In. 12.00
Bowl, Vegetable 20.00
Creamer. 15.00
Cup. 8.00
Gravy Boat 15.00
Pie Baker 25.00
Plate, 7 In. 4.00
Saucer. 3.00
Soup, Dish 7.00

Skytone

Skytone is both a pattern and a shape. The pattern made by Homer Laughlin is plain and light blue colored. When decals were added to the dishes, the pieces are known by the name of the decal.

• • • • • • • • • • • • • • • •
Put a rubber collar on the faucet spout over the sink. This may save you from breaking a piece of glass or china you are washing.
• • • • • • • • • • • • • • • •

Berry Bowl 1.00
Bowl, Vegetable, Round,
   8 In. 3.00
Creamer. 3.00
Cup & Saucer 3.75
Plate, 6 In. 1.00
Plate, 10 In. 2.00

Springtime

Springtime is a dinnerware made by Hall China Company, East Liverpool, Ohio. It has a pink floral arrangement.

Bowl, 5 1/2 In. 2.80
Bowl, Round, 9 In. 12.00
Bowl, Vegetable, Oval 11.00
Cake Plate 5.00
Cup & Saucer 6.50
Gravy Boat 14.00
Plate, 6 In. 1.50
Plate, 7 1/4 In. 3.50
Plate, 9 1/4 In. ...... 5.00 To 6.00
Platter, 13 1/2 In. 10.00
Service For 8 .... 350.00
Soup, Dish .... 7.25 To 12.00

Stanhome Ivy

Stanhome Ivy is a Blue Ridge pattern made on the Skyline shape after 1954. It is decorated with a stylized green ivy sprig.

Bowl, 5 1/4 In. 4.00
Cup 5.00
Plate, 6 In. 2.50
Plate, 9 1/2 In. ...... 3.75 To 6.00
Platter, 11 In. 4.00

Star Flower

Star Flower is a pattern of dinnerware made by Stangl Pottery from 1952 to 1957.

Cup & Saucer 18.00
Cup Plate, 5 In. 5.00
Mug 40.00
Pitcher, 1 Qt. 18.00
Plate, 6 In. 6.00
Plate, 10 In. 10.00
Saucer. 5.00
Tray, Bread 20.00

Starburst

Franciscan Ceramics of Los Angeles, California, started in 1934 and since 1979 has been part of the English Wedg-wood Group. Starburst pattern was made by the company in 1954.

Bowl, 4 3/4 In. 4.00
Bowl, Vegetable,
   Divided .... 12.00 To 14.00
Butter. 25.00
Casserole. 36.00
Coffeepot,
   Cover. .... 65.00 To 60.00
Cruet, Oil & Vinegar 50.00
Cup & Saucer ...... 5.00 To 8.00
Gravy Boat ...... 20.00 To 22.00
Ladle. .... 16.00 To 25.00
Mug, Large 22.00
Mustard & Cruet Set,
   Tray 165.00
Plate, 6 In. .... 2.00 To 3.00
Plate, 7 In. 4.50
Plate, 10 In. 6.00
Platter, 13 In. 15.00
Salt & Pepper, Short 10.00
Soup, Dish 9.00
Sugar 4.00

Sunny

Sunny is a pattern of Blue Ridge pottery. It has a center design of yellow flowers and dark green leaves.

Bowl, Vegetable, Round,
   9 In. 9.00
Creamer. 5.00
Cup & Saucer ...... 5.00 To 6.00
Gravy Boat 9.00
Plate, 9 1/2 In. ..... 5.00 To 6.50
Platter, 11 In. 7.00
Platter, 14 In. 9.00
Saucer. 2.00

Soup, Coupe.................. 5.00
Teapot 45.00

Tam O'Shanter

Tam O'Shanter is one of the many plaid patterns made by Vernon Kilns, Vernon, California. It is a forest green, lime, and reddish brown plaid with forest green border. Other related plaids are Calico (pink and blue), Coronation Organdy (gray and rose), Gingham (green and yellow), Homespun (cinnamon, yellow, and green), Organdie (brown and yellow), and Tweed (gray and blue).

Bowl, 5 1/2 In. 5.00
Bowl, 8 1/2 In. 5.00
Bowl, Chowder 10.00
Bowl, Vegetable,
    8 3/4 In........ 10.00 To 12.00
Bowl, Vegetable, Divided, Oval,
    11 1/2 In..................15.00
Butter, Cover 10.00
Cup..........................5.00
Cup & Saucer.......6.00 To 7.00
Gravy Boat 10.00
Mug 13.00
Pitcher, 2 Qt.................17.50
Plate, 6 In....................3.00
Plate, 9 1/2 In................5.00
Plate, 10 1/2 In. 8.00
Plate, Chop, 12 In. 18.00
Platter,
    12 3/4 In....... 12.50 To 15.00

Platter, 14 In................12.00
Salt & Pepper..............12.00
Saltshaker 4.00
Water Set, 2-Qt.Pitcher,
    9 Piece 125.00

Tampico

Tampico, a brown, green, and watermelon-colored pattern on a Futura shape, was made by Red Wing Pottery of Red Wing, Minnesota. This modern design was introduced in 1955. Many other patterns were also made on the Futura bodies.

Console, Low 12.00
Cooler, Water............. 450.00
Gravy Boat ....6.00 To 7.50
Salt & Pepper...............6.00

Taverne

Taverne pattern was made in the 1930s by the Hall China Company of East Liverpool, Ohio, and Taylor, Smith, and Taylor of Chester, West Virginia. A rolling pin was made by Harker Potteries. The silhouetted figures eating at a table are very similar to those seen on the pattern Silhouette, but there is no dog in this decal. In some of the literature, Taverne is called Silhouette.

Baker, French, Fluted.......12.00
Cake Safe 27.00
Casserole, Cover 30.00
Coffeepot, Electric,
    Glass Infuser............. 160.00
Coffeepot, Medallion,
    Drip 175.00
Creamer....................10.00
Cup & Saucer...............10.00
Drip Jar, Cover 16.00
Gravy Boat 20.00
Jar, Pretzel..................50.00
Jug, No.3, Medallion 17.00
Mug .... 29.00 To 44.00
Plate, 7 1/4 In...............8.00
Plate, 9 In...................10.00
Salt & Pepper, Ball 16.00
Salt & Pepper,
    Loop Handle 75.00
Salt & Pepper, Medallion ...27.00
Sifter.......................26.00
Soup, Dish,
    8 1/2 In........ 10.00 To 12.00
Sugar, Cover, Medallion 12.00
Teapot 30.00

Thistle

Thistle, or No. 3847, is a pattern made by Stangl Pottery, Trenton, New Jersey. The hand-painted decoration is a purple thistle and green spiked thistle leaves. The dishes were made from 1951 to 1967.

Cup	2.00
Cup & Saucer	11.00
Eggcup	12.50
Plate, 5 In.	5.00
Plate, 6 In.	2.50 To 4.00
Plate, 10 In.	8.00
Sugar, Cover	4.00

Tickled Pink

The Tickled Pink pattern listed here is a Blue Ridge design on the Colonial shape. Pink leaves and soft gray dots fill the center of the plate, which has a pink rim. Vernon Kilns also made a pattern called Tickled Pink.

Bowl, Vegetable	18.00
Cup & Saucer	2.50
Pitcher, Small	18.00
Plate, 10 In.	2.50 To 4.50
Platter, 11 In.	5.00
Relish, Divided, 13 In.	7.50 To 18.00
Salt & Pepper	12.00
Sugar & Creamer	20.00

Tom & Jerry

Tom & Jerry sets were made to serve the famous Christmas punch. A set was usually a punch bowl and six matching cups.

Cup	8.00
Punch Cup Set, 16 Piece	65.00

Town & Country

Stangl Pottery made Town & Country pattern in a variety of colors in the 1970s. The design looks like the sponged stoneware made in the nineteenth century, but the pattern was not made just in blue. Black, green, honey beige, and yellow were also used.

BLACK

Bean Pot	50.00
Ladle	15.00
Salt & Pepper, Handle, 3 1/2 In.	15.00

BLUE

Bowl & Pitcher, 2 Piece	150.00

GREEN

Ashtray, Bathtub	15.00
Butter, Cover	40.00
Coffeepot	30.00 To 38.00
Pitcher, 2 1/2 Qt.	37.50

YELLOW

Bowl & Pitcher, 2 Piece	65.00
Bowl, 5 1/2 In.	8.00
Candlestick, Pair	35.00

Tulip

Tulip is a 1930s pattern made by Hall China Company, East Liverpool, Ohio. It remained popular until the 1950s. Most of the pieces were distributed by Cook Coffee of Cleveland, Ohio. Pale yellow and purple tulips were applied by decal. The ware is trimmed with silver. The same design is found on a Harker Pottery pattern called Pastel Tulip. Other patterns called Tulip were made by Stangl Pottery; Edwin M. Knowles; Paden City Pottery; Universal Pottery; Leigh Pottery and Crescent China Co.; and Royal Pottery. Other patterns called Tulips were made by Homer Laughlin China Company; Pottery Guild; Taylor, Smith, and Taylor; and Blue Ridge. Listed here are the Hall and Stangl Tulip patterns.

Creamer, 4 1/2 In., Hall	17.00
Cup, Stangl	5.00
Drip Jar, Jug, Hall	22.00
Gravy Boat, Hall	15.00
Plate, 9 In., Hall	6.00
Plate, Chop, 12 1/2 In., Stangl	22.00
Plate, Chop, 14 In., Stangl	25.00
Salt & Pepper, Handle, Hall	17.00
Saucer, Hall	2.50
Sugar, Cover, Stangl	8.00 To 12.00

Two Step

Two step is a Red Wing pattern made in the 1960s. The pattern has a wide border in blue, green, or pink.

Casserole, Cover, 1 Qt......20.00
Creamer......................3.00
Cup & Saucer.................5.00
Gravy Boat, Tray...........14.00
Plate, 10 In........4.50 To 5.00
Platter, 13 In...............12.00
Platter, 15 In...............14.00

V

Virginia Rose

Virginia Rose is the name of a shape of dishes made by Homer Laughlin China Company, Newell, West Virginia. The shapes were decorated with a variety of decal decorations. The dishes with a design of a spray of roses and green leaves is the pattern most often called Virginia Rose by collectors.

Dinner Set, 4-Place Setting,
    29 Piece..................90.00
Butter, Cover..............45.00
Cup & Saucer...............6.00
Plate, 6 In..................3.00
Plate, 9 In..................5.00
Plate, 10 1/2 In. 8.00

Plate, Deep, 9 1/4 In.......10.00
Platter, 11 1/2 In...........11.00
Sugar & Creamer.... 8.00 To 12.00
Tureen, Cover..............35.00

Vistosa

Taylor, Smith, and Taylor of Chester, West Virginia, made a solid-colored dinnerware about 1938 called Vistosa. The plates had piecrust edges and the other pieces had some bands or ridges. The glaze colors were cobalt blue, deep yellow, light green, and mango red. Pieces were marked with the name Vistosa and the initials T.S. & T. Co. U.S.A.

BLUE ───────────

Saucer.......................2.00

GREEN ───────────

Bowl, 2 Handles, 9 In. 15.00
Bowl, 6 In. 3.00
Saucer.......................2.00

RED ───────────

Saucer.......................2.00

YELLOW ───────────

Plate, 6 In..................3.00
Saucer.......................2.00

W

WHEAT, see Poppy & Wheat

White Clover

White Clover is a dinnerware that was designed by Russel Wright for Harker Pottery Company of East Liverpool, Ohio. It had the very sleek modern shapes inspired by his other design, American Modern, but a sprig of clover decoration was added. It was made in four colors-Charcoal, Coral Sand, Golden Spice, and Meadow Green. The dinnerware was advertised as oven-proof, chip-resistant, and detergent-resistant. The pattern was discontinued in 1955.

CHARCOAL ───────────

Bowl, 5 In. 3.00
Cup & Saucer...............15.00

CORAL ───────────

Cup & Saucer...............18.00
Plate, 6 In..................7.00
Plate, 7 In.................10.00
Plate, 10 In. 18.00
Plate, Chop, 11 In. 45.00
Plate, Cover 125.00

White Rose

White Rose is a cameo ware made by Harker China Company of Chester, West Virginia, in the 1940s. The rose pattern is cut into the glaze. It has white leaves and an outline of a single rose. The background is blue, pink, or yellow. The pieces are marked White Rose, Carv-Kraft by Harker. Both dinnerware and kitchenware were made in this pattern for Montgomery Ward.

BLUE ────────────

Jug, 5 1/2 In. 12.00
Jug, Sani-Grid, Large 27.50
Pitcher.....................15.00
Platter, 14 In...............26.00

WILD POPPY, see Poppy & Wheat

Wildfire

Great American Tea Company gave Wildfire pattern as a premium. This Hall Pottery pattern of the 1950s has a Hi-white body and flower garland decal decoration.

Bowl, 9 1/4 In. 18.00
Bowl, Vegetable, Oval.......7.00
Cup.........................5.00
Plate, 9 In. ....3.00 To 4.00
Platter, 11 In......8.00 To 10.00
Platter, 13 In..............12.00
Salt & Pepper, Teardrop....10.00
Saltshaker, Handle..........9.00

Wildflower

Wildflower was made by Edwin M. Knowles, Newell, West Virginia.

Bowl, 5 1/2 In. 5.00
Casserole, Tab 45.00
Cornucopia, 7 1/2 In. 30.00
Jug.........................12.00
Plate, 9 In. 10.00

Platter, 11 In................8.00

Woodfield

Woodfield was a dinnerware made by the Steubenville Pottery, Steubenville, Ohio. The dishes were shaped like leaves and were colored in many of the shades used for American Modern dishes, also made by the same pottery. Full dinner sets were made.

CHARTREUSE ───────

Cup........................4.00
Salt & Pepper...............9.00

CORAL ────────────

Cup........................4.00
Plate, 6 3/4 In..............2.50
Plate, 10 1/2 In. 5.00
Sugar & Creamer, Cover ...15.00

GRAY ─────────────

Plate, 10 1/2 In. ...5.00 To 6.00
Teapot, Cover 20.00

Woodvine

Woodvine was made by Universal Pottery as a premium to be used in grocery stores. The design pictured small red flowers and large leaves.

Bowl, 6 1/2 In. 5.00
Bowl, Oval, 9 In............. 4.00
Cup & Saucer................ 5.50
Plate, 8 In................... 4.00
Plate, 10 In. ....4.50 To 5.00
Salt & Pepper...............12.00

Y

Yorktown

Edwin M. Knowles, Newell, West Virginia, manufactured the Yorktown pattern in 1936. The solid-colored, Deco-shaped dishes were made in light yellow, maroon, periwinkle blue, and terra cotta.

MADE IN U.S.A.

• • • • • • • • • • • • • • • •
Don't put crazed pottery or porcelain in the dishwasher. It will often break even more.
• • • • • • • • • • • • • • • •

BLUE

Creamer..................... 4.00
Cup....................... 4.00
Plate, 9 In................... 3.00
Soup, Dish.................. 6.50

MAROON

Casserole, Cover 35.00
Creamer, Flower Pot......... 3.00
Cup 4.00
Plate, 9 In...........3.00 To 5.00
Plate, 12 In. 10.00
Plate, Handle, 12 In. 9.00
Soup, Dish.................. 6.50
Sugar, Cover................. 5.00

TERRA COTTA

Plate, 9 In.........5.00 To 10.00

YELLOW

Plate, 9 In................... 3.00
Soup, Dish.................. 6.50

Z

Zeisel

Eva Zeisel designed the Century and Tomorrow's Classic shapes for Hall China's Hallcraft line in 1952. Both designs remained popular until the 1960s. The solid white dinnerwares, sometimes decorated with decals, are marked with her name.

• • • • • • • • • • • • • • • •
Don't put china with gold designs in the dishwasher. The gold will wash off.
• • • • • • • • • • • • • • • •

HALLCRAFT

Eva Zeisel

Cookie Jar, Cover, Blue, Gold, Star......................42.50
Creamer..................... 7.00
Cup 5.00
Gravy Boat, Flair 9.50
Jug, Milk....................15.00
Plate, 6 In..........2.50 To 4.00
Plate, 10 In. 4.00
Platter, Sun Glow, 14 In....16.50
Salt & Pepper, Bird, Monmouth, 6 1/2 In...................25.00

• • • • • • • • • • • • • • •
Good tips for care of Bauer pottery—and, probably, for Fiesta and any other heavy, color-glazed dishes of the 1930s. Bauer is oven safe for baking—up to 350 degrees. Do not use in a microwave. Do not use on a direct flame. Do not wash in an automatic dishwasher. The detergent may discolor the glaze. Do not scour. Store with felt between stacked plates to avoid scratching. Early 1930 to 1942 dishes used a lead in the glazing, so do not use scratched dishes with acidic foods. Lead poisoning is possible with prolonged use.
• • • • • • • • • • • • • • • •

A M E R I C A N   D I N N E R W A R E
Factories

NAME	LOCATION	DATES
Abingdon Potteries	Abingdon, Illinois	1908-1951
American Pottery	Byesville, Ohio	1942-1965
Bauer Pottery Company	Los Angeles, California	1905-c.1958
Blair Ceramics	Ozark, Missouri	1946-1950s
Blue Ridge, see Southern Potteries		
Brusche Ceramics	Whittier, California	c.1950
Brush-McCoy	Roseville and Zanesville, Ohio	1911-1925 (Combined firm of Brush Pottery and J. W. McCoy Company)
Brush Pottery	Roseville and Zanesville, Ohio	1907-present (Brush-McCoy 1911-1925)
California Ceramics	Los Angeles, California	c.1948-1954
Caribe-Sterling	Vega Baja, Puerto Rico	early 1950s-1977
Catalina Pottery	Catalina Island, California	c.1927-1947 (name purchased by Gladding McBean Company in 1937; Catalina name remained in use until 1947)
Continental Kilns	East Liverpool, Ohio	1944-1954
H. F. Coors Company	Inglewood, California, and Golden, Colorado	1925-present
Crescent China Company	Alliance, Ohio	1920-1930 (Associated with Leigh Pottery after 1926)
Crooksville China Company	Crooksville, Ohio	1902-c.1960
Crown Pottery	Evansville, Indiana	1882-1962
Flintridge China Company	Pasadena, California	1945-present
Franciscan Ceramics	Los Angeles, California	1934-present (Wedgwood Group after 1979)
Frankoma Pottery	Sapulpa, Oklahoma	1936-present
French Saxon China Company	East Liverpool, Ohio	1935-present
W. S. George Company	Kittanig, Pennsylvania	1880-1959
Gladding, McBean & Co.	Los Angeles, California	1875-1986 (Wedgwood Group after 1979)
Gonder Ceramic Art Company	Zanesville, Ohio	1941-1957

NAME	LOCATION	DATES
Haeger Potteries	Dundee, Illinois	1914-present
Hall China Company	East Liverpool, Ohio	1903-present
Harker Pottery Company	Chester, West Virginia, and East Liverpool, Ohio	1890-1972
Harmony House	Mark used by Sears, Roebuck and Co.; various manufacturers	
Homer Laughlin China Company	Newell, West Virginia, and East Liverpool, Ohio	1877-present
A. E. Hull Pottery Company	Crooksville, Ohio	1905-present
Iroquois China Company	Syracuse, New York	1905-1969
James River Potteries	Hopewell, Virginia	1922-1938
Edwin M. Knowles China Company	Chester and Newell, West Virginia, and East Liverpool, Ohio	1900-1963, 1975-present
Leigh Pottery	Alliance, Ohio	1926-1938 (Crescent China Company before 1926)
J. W. McCoy Company	Zanesville, Ohio	1899-1925 (Brush-McCoy Pottery Company from 1911-1925)
Metlox Potteries	Manhattan Beach, California	1935-1989
Montgomery Ward	Sold variety of patterns under their own name, various manufacturers	
Paden City Pottery	Paden City, West Virginia	1914-1963
Pickard, Inc.	Chicago, Illinois	1893-present
Pope-Gosser China Company	Coshocton, Ohio	1902-1958
Pottery Guild	New York, New York	1937-1946
Purinton Pottery	Shippenville, Pennsylvania	1941-1951
Red Wing Potteries	Red Wing, Minnesota	1878-1967
Roseville Pottery Company	Zanesville, Ohio	1892-1954
Royal China Company	Sebring, Ohio	1933-1986
Sabin Industries	McKeesport, Pennsylvania	1946-present
Salem China Company	Salem, Ohio	1898-1967
Scio Pottery Company	Scio, Ohio	1932-1985
Sears, Roebuck and Company	Sold variety of patterns under their own name, various manufacturers	
Sebring-Limoges	Sebring, Ohio	1887-1955 (Sebring Pottery Company and Limoges China Company combined under same management c.1940)
Shawnee Pottery Company	Zanesville, Ohio	1936-1961

NAME	LOCATION	DATES
Southern Potteries (Blue Ridge)	Erwin, Tennessee	1917-1957
Standard Pottery Company	East Liverpool, Ohio	1886-1927
Stanford Pottery	Sebring, Ohio	1945-1961
Stangl Pottery	Flemington and Trenton, New Jersey	1930-1978
Stetson China Company	Lincoln, Illinois	1919-1965
Steubenville Pottery Company	Steubenville, Ohio	1879-c.1960
Syracuse China Corporation	Syracuse, New York	1871-present
Taylor, Smith, and Taylor	Chester, West Virginia, and East Liverpool, Ohio	1901-present
Terrace Ceramics	Marietta, Ohio	1961-1975
Universal Potteries	Cambridge, Ohio	1934-1956
Vernon Kilns	Los Angeles and Vernon, California	1912-1958 (name purchased by Metlox Potteries)
Watt Pottery Company	Crooksville, Ohio	1922-1965

AMERICAN DINNERWARE
Pattern List

Note: * = prices and paragraph in body of book

PATTERN	SHAPE	MAKER	DATE	DESCRIPTION
ABC	Kiddieware	Stangl	Mid-1940s-1974	Solid colors
Abingdon	Square	Abingdon	1935	
Abundance	Colonial	Blue Ridge		Pear and cherries; broken green rim
Abundance	Ultra	Vernon Kilns	1939	Maroon fruit and floral border
Acacia	Kitchenware	Hall		Pastel flowers; decal
Acacia Flowers	Shellcrest	Paden City		
Acorn		Harmony House		Blue, pink; cameoware
Adam	Antique	Steubenville		Rich ivory glaze; heavily embossed
Adobestone	Ceramastone	Red Wing	1967	
Adonis, see Prince				
Adrian		Stangl	1972-1974	
After Glow	Montecito	Vernon Kilns	1935-1937	Yellow with ivory bottom and interior
*Airflow	Teapot	Hall	1940	Canary, Chinese Red, cobalt, turquoise, and other colors
Al Fresco	Al Fresco	Franciscan	1952	Coffee Brown, Hemlock Green, Misty Gray, Olive Green
*Aladdin	Teapot	Hall	1939	Variety of colors; decals
Albany	Teapot	Hall	1930	Solid colors; gold decorations
Albert	Teapot	Hall	1940s	Celadon only; Victorian style
Alexandria	Candlewick	Blue Ridge		Red, yellow, and blue flowers; green leaves
Alia Jane	Round	Taylor, Smith, and Taylor	1933-1934	Decal
All Apple		Purinton		Hand painted; large apple
Alleghany	Colonial	Blue Ridge		Blue, red, yellow flowers; red rim
Allure	Classique	E. M. Knowles	1960	
Aloaha	Skyline	Blue Ridge	1950s	Gray, green, white; large leaves
Aloha		French Saxon		
Amapila	Amapila	Franciscan		Hand painted

PATTERN	SHAPE	MAKER	DATE	DESCRIPTION
Amarylis	Colonial	Blue Ridge		Red flowers, border, and rim
Ambassador	Regent	E. M. Knowles	1948	
Amber Glo		Stangl	1954-1962	
*Amberstone	Fiesta	Homer Laughlin	1967	Solids; brown designs
American Beauty	Minion	Paden City		Large pink rose
American Beauty		Stetson		
*American Modern	American	Steubenville (Russel Wright)	1939-1959	Bean Brown, Black Chutney, Canteloupe, Cedar Green, chartreuse, coral, Glacier Blue, Granite Gray, Blue, white
American Provincial		Homer Laughlin		Pennsylvania Dutch designs
*Americana	A2000	Stangl	1930s	Colonial Blue, green, tangerine, yellow
Amhurst	Colonial	Blue Ridge		Pink flowers; center and line border
Amy		Harker		Gold trim; multicolored flowers
Anemone	Piecrust	Blue Ridge		Red flowers; two-tone green leaves
Anniversary		Salem China	1943	
Antiqua		Stangl	1972-1974	Stylized flower, gold background, brown and black border
Antique Leaf	Lace Edge	Blue Ridge		Red, green, black leaf border
Anytime	Anytime	Vernon Kilns	1955-1958	Bands of gray, mocha, yellow
Appalachian Spring	Candlewick	Blue Ridge		Stylized red tulip and red border
*Apple	Apple	Franciscan	1940-present	Apples and leaves border
Apple		Purinton	1936-1959	Large center apple; scalloped rim
*Apple	Watt Ware	Watt	1930s-1965	
*Apple and Pear	Woodcrest	Blue Ridge	1950s	Red apple, yellow pear, green leaves
Apple Blossom		Crooksville		Pink flowers
*Apple Blossom	Nautilus Eggshell	Homer Laughlin	1935-1955	Flowered border; gold trim
Apple Crisp	Skyline	Blue Ridge	1950s	Three red apples, red rim
Apple Crunch	Piecrust	Blue Ridge	1948	Red and white apple, green leaves and border
*Apple Delight		Stangl	1965-1974	Red and yellow apples, dark border
Apple Jack	Skyline	Blue Ridge	1950s	Two apples; sponged yellow background
Apples		Pottery Guild		Apple tree branch

PATTERN	SHAPE	MAKER	DATE	DESCRIPTION
April		Homer Laughlin		Flowered border
Aquarium	Ultra	Vernon Kilns	1938	Tropical fish
Arabesque	Arabesque	Catalina	1935	Solids
Arabian Night		Paden City		
*Arcadia	Melinda	Vernon Kilns	1942; 1950-1955	Brown laurel wreath border
Ardennes	Provincial	Red Wing	1941	Laurel leaf band
Argosy		W. S. George	1930	Ivory body
Aristocrat	Refrigerator ware	Hall	1940-1941	Westinghouse; Arctic Blue, canary, Garden, Sunset; also called Hercules; Peasant Ware label
Aristocrat		Homer Laughlin		Flowered border
Aristocrat	Century	Salem		Delphinium blue; black and platinum band
Arlene	Trellis	Blue Ridge		Pink tulip, blue daisy, wide blue rim
*Arlington Apple	Skyline	Blue Ridge	1950s	Two red apples
Art Deco	Art Deco	Catalina	Early 1930s	Solids
Asbury	Pegasus	Sebring	1940s	
Ashland	Colonial	Blue Ridge		Red, light blue flowers; green rim
Astor Fruit	Astor	Blue Ridge		Aqua fruit; aqua and orange rim
Atlanta	Skyline	Blue Ridge	1950s	
Aurora	Candlewick	Blue Ridge		Two large pink flowers
Automobile	Teapot	Hall	1938	Canary, Chinese Red, maroon, common colors; sometimes with gold or silver trim
Autumn		Franciscan	1934	Leaves
*Autumn Apple	Colonial	Blue Ridge	1941	Apples border; broken red rim
Autumn Ballet	Ultra	Vernon Kilns	1940	Maroon floral and leaf
Autumn Breeze	Skyline	Blue Ridge	1950s	Stylized leaves, gray, green, and rust
Autumn Fancy		Universal		Decals
Autumn Foliage		Watt	1959-1965	Brown leaves on brown stems; also called Brown Leaves
Autumn Harvest	Versatile	Taylor, Smith, and Taylor		
Autumn Laurel	Colonial	Blue Ridge		Yellow berries, green leaves, border
Autumn Leaf		Blair		Floral decals
Autumn Leaf		Crooksville China		Floral decals
Autumn Leaf		Crown		Floral decals

PATTERN	SHAPE	MAKER	DATE	DESCRIPTION
*Autumn Leaf		Hall	1936-present	For Jewel Tea Co.; floral decals of dark yellow and rust leaves
Autumn Leaf		Harker Potteries		Floral decals
Autumn Leaf		Paden City		Floral decals
Avenue	Coupe, LaGrande	Crooksville		Reddish-brown plant sprigs
Aztec		Stangl	1967-1968	
Aztec	Citation	Steubenville		
Aztec on Desert Sand	Citation	Steubenville		
Bachelor's Button		Stangl	1965	
*Ballerina	Ballerina	Universal Potteries	1947-1956	Solids; burgundy, charcoal, chartreuse, Dove Gray, Forest Green, Jade Green, Jonquil Yellow, Periwinkle Blue, pink; abstract designs
*Baltimore	Teapot	Hall	1930s	Emerald and marine common colors
Bamboo		Blair		Stylistic bamboo design
*Bamboo	Woodcrest	Blue Ridge	1950s	
Banana Tree	Montecito	Vernon Kilns	1937	Tree on ivory ground
Banded	Kitchenware	Hall	1937	Kitchenware; floral decals; solid colors: Cadet, canary, Chinese Red, cobalt, Indian Red, ivory, marine, maroon; also called Five Band
Barbara	Colonial	Blue Ridge		Blue flowers and leaves
Bardstown	Skyline	Blue Ridge	1950s	Red flowers, outlined
Barkwood	San Marino	Vernon Kilns	1953-1958	Beige and brown; like tree bark
Basket	Decal	Hall	1932-1960	Small flower basket and diamond-shaped designs
Basket	Teapot	Hall	1938	Embossed flower; canary, Chinese Red, marine common colors
Basket	Harker			Flower basket border
Basket		Leigh/Crescent		Flower basket and individual small flowers
Basket		Salem		Center flower basket; border of leaves and individual flowers
Basket of Tulips	Bonjour	Salem		Various colored tulips; platinum rim
Basket Petit Point	Victory	Salem		Decals
Basketball	Teapot	Hall	1938	
Basketweave	Skyline	Blue Ridge	1950s	Black cross-hatch on beige background

PATTERN	SHAPE	MAKER	DATE	DESCRIPTION
Bauer, see Ring				
Beaded Apple	Colonial	Blue Ridge		Apple border, broken red rim
Beatrice	Skyline	Blue Ridge	1950s	Black-haired girl
Becky	Colonial	Blue Ridge		Large red flowers
Becky		Harker		Blue and red flowers
Beehive, see Ring				
Beige	Montecito	Vernon Kilns	1935-1937	Solid beige
Bel Air	San Marino	Vernon Kilns	1940; 1955	Three lines crossing three lines; green and brown on ivory
Bella Rosa		Stangl	1960-1962	Spray of roses and lily of the valley; pale gray background
Belle Haven	Woodcrest	Blue Ridge	1950s	Plaid tree, farm, rooster at sunrise; green rim
*Bellevue (or Bellvue)	Teapot	Hall	1920s-present	Six sizes; brown, green most common colors; some decorated with gold or decals
Bellemeade	Astor	Blue Ridge		Yellow flowers, blue and green leaves; brown line border
Bench	Deanna	E. M. Knowles		Mexican-styled jugs and cactus
Benjamin	Teapot	Hall	Early 1940s	Victorian style; see also Birch, Bowknot, Connie, Murphy, Plume
Berea Blossom	Colonial	Blue Ridge		Pastel flowers
Berkeley	Williamsburg	E. M. Knowles	1955	
Bermuda		Homer Laughlin	1977-1978	
Berry Patch	Skyline	Blue Ridge	1950s	Golden berries
Berryville	Colonial	Blue Ridge		Strawberry border; red rim
Bethany Berry	Moderne	Blue Ridge	1950s	Orange berries; gray, green, brown leaves
*Betty	Candlewick	Blue Ridge		Red and yellow flowers; green leaves
Beverly	Melinda	Vernon Kilns	1942	Rose blossom border
Big Apple	Colonial	Blue Ridge		
Big Boy	Coffeepot	Hall		Maroon with silver trim
Bimini		Homer Laughlin	1977-1978	
Bingo	Refrigerator ware	Hall	Late 1930s	Chinese Red; also called Zephyr
Birch	Teapot	Hall	Early 1940s	Victorian style; see also Benjamin, Bowknot, Connie, Murphy, Plume
Bird	Derwood	W. S. George		Red and brown bird on border
Bird		Blair		Sgraffito bird; also called Primitive Bird

PATTERN	SHAPE	MAKER	DATE	DESCRIPTION
*Birdcage	Teapot	Hall	1939	Maroon most common color; embossed birds
Bird in the Heart		Universal Cambridge		
Bird Pottery		Vernon Kilns	Early 1930s	
Birds and Flowers		Harker		Multicolored flowers, small birds
Bird's Eye	Montecito	Vernon Kilns		Floral
Bit Series	Kiddieware	Stangl	Mid-1940s-1974	
Bittersweet		Hall		Flowers
Bittersweet	Skyline	Blue Ridge	1950s	Red berries
*Bittersweet		Stangl		Sgraffito decoration
Bittersweet		Universal Potteries	1942-1949	Decals; orange and yellow
Black Beauty		Hall	1935	Red flowers and leaves, black shadows
Black-Eyed Susan	Forcast	E. M. Knowles	1959	
Black Ming	Skyline	Blue Ridge	1950s	Black tree
Black Tulip		Crooksville	1950s	Hand painted; black on pink
Blackberry Lily	Colonial	Blue Ridge		Dots on pink flowers
Bleeding Heart	Candlewick	Blue Ridge		Pink flowers; blue leaves, border, and rim
Blend No. 4	Montecito	Vernon Kilns	1938	Concentric rings in browns and greens
Blend No. 10	Montecito	Vernon Kilns	1938	Concentric rings in pinks and greens
Blossom Ring		Stangl	1967/68-1970	
Blossom Time	Coupe	Crooksville		Off-center decoration; branch of pink flowers
*Blossom Time	Concord	Red Wing	1947	Modern shapes; red flowers, green leaves, yellow and green accessory pieces
Blossom Time	Melinda	Vernon Kilns	1942	Blue blossoms
Blossom Tree	Skyline	Blue Ridge	1950s	Stylized tree; green leaves and yellow flowers
Blossoms	Shellcrest	Paden City		Large flower spray
Blossoms	Fruits	Crooksville		Red and pink flowers
Blossoms	Montecito	Vernon Kilns	1937	Blue blossom border on cream ground
Blossoms	Lido	W. S. George		Pink blossoms border
Blossomtime	Bolero	W. S. George		
Blossomtime	Accent	E. M. Knowles	1958	
Blue Bell		Stangl	c.1942	
Blue Bells	Accent	E. M. Knowles	c.1954	

PATTERN	SHAPE	MAKER	DATE	DESCRIPTION
Blue Bird		Crown	1941	Blue birds perched on pink apple blossoms; turquoise blue rim
*Blue Blossom	Kitchenware	Hall	c.1939	Cobalt blue background, floral decals
Blue Blossoms		Crooksville		Flowers in shades of blue
Blue Bonnett	Accent	E. M. Knowles	1954	
Blue Bouquet	Candlewick	Blue Ridge		Red flowers
*Blue Bouquet	D-Line	Hall	1950-1960s	Premium for Standard coffee; thin blue border with roses
Blue Carousel	Kiddieware	Stangl	Mid-1940s-1974	
*Blue Daisy		Stangl	1963-1974	Blue daisies
Blue Dresden	Virginia Rose	Homer Laughlin	1949	
Blue Elf	Kiddieware	Stangl	Mid-1940s-1974	
Blue Flower	Colonial	Blue Ridge		Large blue off-center flower
Blue Garden	Kitchenware	Hall	1939	Cobalt blue background, floral decals
Blue Heaven	Colonial	Blue Ridge		Blue flowers, gray leaves
Blue Medallion		Homer Laughlin	1920	Decals
Blue Moon	Candlewick	Blue Ridge		Blue flowers and leaves
Blue Parade, see Rose Parade				
Blue Rhythm		Harker	1959	Cameoware
Blue Shadows	True China	Red Wing	1964	
Blue Star	Montecito	Vernon Kilns	1938	Blue stars on blue ground
Blue Symphony		Homer Laughlin		
Blue Tango	Colonial	Blue Ridge		Floral design
Blue Tulip		Stangl		Terra Rose mark
Blue Willow	Trellis	Blue Ridge		Blue oriental scene, rim
*Blue Willow		Homer Laughlin	1942	Blue and pink
*Blue Willow	Cavalier	Royal	Late 1940s-1980s	Overall oriental design; also pink, green
Blue Willow		Sebring-Limoges		
Bluebell		Paden City		Floral sprig
Bluebell Bouquet	Candlewick	Blue Ridge		
Blueberry		Sold by Montgomery Ward	1921	Decals
*Blueberry		Stangl	c.1940	Red with yellow border; blueberries in center
Blueberry Hill	Year 'Round	Vernon Kilns	1957-1958	Blue and brown floral abstract
Bluebird		Salem		Small bluebirds on border

PATTERN	SHAPE	MAKER	DATE	DESCRIPTION
Bluebird	Derwood	W. S. George		Bluebird on border; thin blue rim
Bluefield	Colonial	Blue Ridge		Blue flowers; red, green leaves
Blushing Rose, see Lido Dalyrymple				
Bo Peep	Kiddieware	Stangl	Mid-1940s-1974	
*Bob White		Red Wing	1956-1967	Hand painted; stylized bird; figurals
Bolero		Homer Laughlin	1977-1978	
Bonita		Caribe-Sterling	1950s-c.1963	Modernistic flowers
Bonita		Stangl		Della-Ware mark
Boncai	Skyline	Blue Ridge	1950s	Gnarled tree
Bouquet	Astor	Blue Ridge		Pink and yellow flowers, pink border
Border Bouquet	LaGrande	Crooksville		Border of small flowers
Border Rim		E. M. Knowles		Border design of flowers
Border Rose		Crooksville		Continuous border design
Bosc	Colonial	Blue Ridge		Red pear, blue leaves, broken red border
*Boston	Teapot	Hall	1920	Variety of colors; gold decorated line
Botanica	Esquire	E. M. Knowles	1957-1966	Abstract decal; Russel Wright
Bountiful	Colonial	Blue Ridge		Fruit; broken green rim
Bouquet		Crown		Multicolored flowers and bow
Bouquet	Hallcraft	Hall	1950s-1960s	Random flower sprays; designed by Eva Zeisel
Bouquet		Harker		
Bouquet	Ultra	Vernon Kilns	1938	Floral; yellow rim
Bourbon Rose	Colonial	Blue Ridge		Two roses, leaves allover design
Bow Knot	Piecrust	Blue Ridge		Chartreuse and brown variation of Whirligig
Bowknot	Teapot	Hall	Early 1940s	Victorian style; see also Benjamin, Birch, Connie, Murphy, Plume
Bowling Ball	Teapot	Hall	Late 1930s	Cobalt, turquoise
Boyce		Harker		Flowers in shades of pink
Bramwell	Colonial	Blue Ridge		Yellow, red, and blue flowers
Breakfast Nook		W. S. George		Open windows with flower trellis
Breath O'Spring	Classique	E. M. Knowles	1960	
Breckenridge	Colonial	Blue Ridge		Red flowers and leaves
Breeze	Bountiful	Salem China; French Saxon	1948	

PATTERN	SHAPE	MAKER	DATE	DESCRIPTION
Brentwood	Cavalier	Royal		Ironstone; bold flower center design
Briar Patch	Colonial	Blue Ridge		Red flowers, green leaves, allover pattern
Briar Rose	Century	Homer Laughlin	1933	Sprays of wild roses, platinum edge
Bridal Bouquet	Colonial	Blue Ridge		Pink flowers, yellow and green leaves
Bridal Flower		Taylor, Smith, and Taylor		
Bridge	Tricorne	Salem		Decals
Bridle Rose		W. S. George		
Brilliance	Coupe	Crooksville		Multisized pink flowers
Brim		Harker		Bold-colored flower border
Bristol Bouquet	Astor	Blue Ridge		Centered red, yellow, blue flowers; red border
Bristol Lily	Candlewick	Blue Ridge		Two yellow flowers and birds; red border
Brittany	Clinchfield	Blue Ridge		Centered woman and flowers; stylized red border
*Brittany	Provincial	Red Wing	1941	Yellow rose; yellow band on rim
Brocade	True China	Red Wing	1964	
*Brown-Eyed Susan	Montecito; Ultra	Vernon Kilns	c.1938-1958	Yellow daisies on ivory ground
Brown Leaf	Accent	E. M. Knowles	1954	
Brown Leaves, see Autumn Foliage				
Brown Satin		Stangl		
Brownie	Candlewick	Blue Ridge		Edge design of three stylized flowers with brown center
Brunswick	Candlewick	Blue Ridge		Red, yellow, and blue flowers; green rim
Brushes	Al Fresco	Bauer		
Bryn-Mawr	Symphony	Salem		Floral sprays in brown, lavender, and gray
Bud	Concord	Red Wing	1947	
Buddah	Corinthian	Sebring		
Bunny Lunch	Kiddieware	Stangl	Mid-1940s-1974	
Buttercup	Colonial	Blue Ridge		
Buttercup		E. M. Knowles	1948	
Butterfly and Leaves	Trellis	Blue Ridge		Red, yellow flowers; two-tone green leaves
Cabaret	Cabaret	Franciscan		
Cactus		Blue Ridge		
Cactus	Banded; Kitchenware	Hall	1937-1940s	Decal; cactus in flowerpots
Cactus and Cowboy, see Ranger				

PATTERN	SHAPE	MAKER	DATE	DESCRIPTION
Cactus Banded, see Cactus (Hall)				
Cadenza	Piecrust	Blue Ridge	1948	Red and yellow flowers
Cadet Series		Salem		Fluted edge; thin bands of color
Caladium	Skyline	Blue Ridge	1950s	Yellow flower; yellow and red leaf
Calais	Astor	Blue Ridge		Center pattern of male, female, and ducks; leaf and flower border
Cal-Art		Bauer		
Calico	Colonial	Blue Ridge		Red and yellow flowers; allover pattern
*Calico	Montecito	Vernon Kilns	1949-1955	Blue border; pink and blue plaid; see also Coronation Organdy; Gingham; Homespun; Organdie; Tam O'Shanter; Tweed
Calico Chick	Coupe	Crooksville		Calico-print chickens
Calico Farm	Skyline	Blue Ridge	1950s	Red and green plaid forming scene
Calico Flower		Pottery Guild		Red band; calico-print flowers
Calico Flowers	Dartmouth	Crooksville		Calico-print tulips
Calico Fruit		Pottery Guild		Red band; calico-print fruits
*Calico Fruit		Universal	1940s	White background; bright red and blue fruits
Calico Tulip		Harker		Tulip-shaped decal of calico print
*Caliente		Paden City	1940s	Solids: blue, green, tangerine, yellow
California Casual, see Casual California				
California Heritage, see California Originals				
*California Ivy	Poppytrail line	Metlox	1946-1980	White, green ivy
California James Poppy	LaGrande	Crooksville		Large sprays of pastel flowers
California Originals	San Marino	Vernon Kilns	1947; 1954	Drip glaze border; Almond Yellow, Raisin Purple, Redwood Brown, Vineyard Green; also called California Heritage
California Poppy	Candlewick	Blue Ridge		Two large center flowers
California Pottery		Bauer		Solid Colors
*California Provincial	Poppytrail line	Metlox	1950-1980	Green, maroon, and yellow rooster in center; green and brown border
California Series		Vernon Kilns	1930s	Red, brown, green, blue

PATTERN	SHAPE	MAKER	DATE	DESCRIPTION
California Shadows	San Marino	Vernon Kilns	1953; 1955	Drip glaze border; Antique Gray, Cocoa Brown
California Strawberry	Poppytrail line	Metlox	1961-1980	Red strawberries on avocado green vines
Call Rose	Century	Homer Laughlin		Floral decal
Callaway	Piecrust	Blue Ridge	1948	Large blue and yellow and small pink flowers
Camelot	Piecrust	Blue Ridge	1948	Light blue, purple, red, and yellow flowers
*Cameo Rose	E-Shape	Hall	1970s	Gray and white leaf decorations
*Cameo Rose		Harker	1940s	Solid white roses; blue, pink, gray, yellow background
*Cameo Shellware	Shell	Harker	1940s	White, blue, pink, gray, yellow background; same cameo flower design as Cameo Rose; fluted plate edge
Candied Fruit	Candlewick	Blue Ridge		Different fruits; two yellow bands
Cantata	Piecrust	Blue Ridge	1948	Red and blue flowers
Canton	Encanto	Franciscan	1953	
*Capistrano	Anniversary	Red Wing	1953-1967	Yellow-breasted swallow, black foliage
Capri		Paden City	1933	
Capri	Rhythm Coupe	Homer Laughlin		
*Caprice	Tomorrow's Classic	Hall	1952-1957	Designed by Eva Zeisel; Pink, gray; yellow leaf and floral design
Caprice	Accent	E. M. Knowles	c.1954	
Caribe Casual		Caribe-Sterling	1950s-c.1963	
Carlise	Colonial	Blue Ridge		Blue leaves, tiny pink berries, blue rim
Carlton	Heritage	E. M. Knowles	1955	
Carmen	Accent	E. M. Knowles	1958	
Carnation Beauty		Homer Laughlin	1920	Decal
*Carnival	Candlewick	Blue Ridge		Red, yellow, and blue flowered border
Carnival	Fruits	Crooksville		Abstract
*Carnival		Stangl	1954-1957	Pink, green and black abstract starlike pattern
Carnival		Homer Laughlin	late 1930s-early 1940s	Light green, red, turquoise, yellow; later dark green and gray
Caroline	Skyline	Blue Ridge	1950s	Brown flowers
Carraway	Coffeepot	Hall		

PATTERN	SHAPE	MAKER	DATE	DESCRIPTION
Carretta Cattail	Woodcrest	Blue Ridge	1950s	Three cross-hatched cattails and leaves
Carriage		Crown		Coach and horses, manor
Casa California	Montecito	Vernon Kilns	1938	Blue; green leaves; pink flowers; yellow border
Casa del Sol	Cavalier	Royal		Indian-style design
Casablanca	Cavalier	Royal		Ironstone; large center sunflower design
Cascade		Sold by Montgomery Ward	1936	White with red lines; solids
Cashmere		Homer Laughlin		Border of small sprays of flowers
Cassandra	Waffle Edge	Blue Ridge		Wide blue, pink border; center flowers
Casual California	San Marino	Vernon Kilns	1947-1956	Acacia Yellow, Dawn Pink, Dusk Gray, Lime Green, Mahogany Brown, Mocha Brown, Pine Green, Sno-white, Turquoise Blue
*Casualstone	Fiesta	Homer Laughlin	1970	Gold and yellow, plain or with design; marked Coventry
Cat and the Fiddle	Kiddieware	Stangl	Mid-1940s-1974	
*Cat-Tail	Camwood; Old Holland; Laurelle	Universal	1934-1956	For Sears, Roebuck and Co.; red and black decals
Cattail		Hall	1927	
Cattails	Trailway	Blue Ridge	1950s	Brown cattails, light blue leaves and border, brown rim
Cattails	Accent	E. M. Knowles	1955	
Celeste	Tempo	E. M. Knowles	1961-1963	
Celestial	Criterion	E. M. Knowles	1955	
Century		Homer Laughlin		Floral decals; ivory
Chalet	Accent	E. M. Knowles	1955	
*Champagne Pinks	Colonial	Blue Ridge	1940s-1950s	Overall large floral, light pink and blue
Chanticleer	Skyline	Blue Ridge	1950s	Rooster; green stylized border
Charstone Bleu	Ceramastone	Red Wing	1967	
Chartreuse		Sold by Montgomery Ward	1936	Decals; green; green border
Chateau		Homer Laughlin		
Chateau-France		Sebring-Limoges		
*Chatelaine	Chatelaine	Vernon Kilns	1953	Bronze, jade, platinum, topaz

PATTERN	SHAPE	MAKER	DATE	DESCRIPTION
Cheerio	Skyline	Blue Ridge	1950s	Brown and green flowers; yellow dappled background
Cherokee Rose	Rope Handle	Blue Ridge	1950s	
Cherries Jubilee	Colonial	Blue Ridge		Bold cherries and leaves
Cherry		Harker		Brightly colored fruits
Cherry		Salem China	1951	
Cherry		Stangl	1940	Brown band with tan glaze and blue lines; blue band with tan glaze and yellow lines; blue band with blue glaze and green lines; cherry stems in center
Cherry Blossom	Colonial	Blue Ridge		Red and yellow cherries; pink flower; border
Cherry Blossom		Harker		Sprig of cherries and flowers
Cherry Cobbler	Colonial	Blue Ridge		Pink cherries, rim
Cherry Coke	Colonial	Blue Ridge		Red cherries, border, green rim
Cherry Trim		Harker		Border of groups of cherries
*Chesterton	Royal Gadroon	Harker	1945-1965	Gray, green, blue, pink, yellow
Chevron	Gypsy Trail	Red Wing	1935	Blue, ivory, orange, turquoise, yellow
Chicken Feed	Skyline	Blue Ridge	1950s	Girl feeding chickens; green rim
Chicken Pickins	Skyline	Blue Ridge	1950s	Hen and rooster; pink and green stylized border
Chickory	Colonial	Blue Ridge		Small yellow and blue flowers
Chicory		Stangl	1961	
Children's Plates		Harker		Blue and pink cameoware; duck, teddy bear, dog
*Chinese Red (color used by Hall), see also individual pattern names				
Chinling	Lotus	Vernon Kilns	1950	Oriental floral spray
Chintz	Colonial	Blue Ridge		Allover flower pattern
*Chintz	Melinda	Vernon Kilns	1942; 1950	Floral design
Choreography	Criterion	E. M. Knowles	1955	
Christmas Doorway	Skyline	Blue Ridge	1950s	
Christmas Tree	Colonial	Blue Ridge		
*Chrysanthe-mum	Colonial	Blue Ridge		Blue and red flowers, yellow and black leaves
Chrysanthe-mum	Concord	Red Wing	1947	
Cinnabar	Colonial	Blue Ridge		Bold pink and yellow flowers, green leaves

PATTERN	SHAPE	MAKER	DATE	DESCRIPTION
Circus Clown	Kiddieware	Stangl	Mid-1940s-1974	
Clairborne	Colonial	Blue Ridge		Centered pink and black flowers; border
Classic	Essex	E. M. Knowles	1954-1955	
Clear Day	Cavalier	Royal		Ironstone
*Cleveland	Teapot	Hall	1930s	
Clio	Corinthian	Leigh		Floral
Clive	Brittany	Homer Laughlin		Border of maroon panels and floral sprays
Clover	Clinchfield	Blue Ridge	1947-1954	Pink flowers with green clover; blue and black rim
Clover	Kitchenware	Hall	1940-1960	Bright colors; Impressionistic design
Cloverleaf, see Clover				
Coastline	Montecito	Vernon Kilns	1937	Map of Pacific Coast; blue, black on ivory ground
Cock-a-Doodle	Skyline	Blue Ridge	1950s	Rooster in center; blue rim
Cock o' the Morn	Skyline	Blue Ridge	1950s	Crowing rooster
Cock-o-the-Morn (Harker), see Engraved Rooster				
Cock O' Walk	Candlewick	Blue Ridge	1948	Center rooster; red and cream flowered border; broken green rim
Cocky-Locky	Clinchfield	Blue Ridge		Rooster; red stylized border
Cocolo	Cocolo	Franciscan		
Coffee Queen	Coffeepot	Hall		Chinese red and olive green common colors; also called Duchess
*Colonial	Kitchenware	Hall	1932	Chinese Red, Daffodil, Delphinium, Golden Glo, Hi-white, ivory, Lettuce Green; decals; also called Medallion
Colonial		Salem		Red and green stencil-like decorations
*Colonial		Stangl	1926	Aqua, Colonial Blue, brown, Persian Yellow, rust, silver-green, Surf White, tangerine
Colonial Birds No. 1	Colonial	Blue Ridge		Centered bird
Colonial Birds No. 2	Colonial	Blue Ridge		Centered bird
Colonial Dogwood		Stangl		Marked Prestige
*Colonial Homestead		Royal	1940s-1950s	
Colonial Lady		Harker		

PATTERN	SHAPE	MAKER	DATE	DESCRIPTION
Colonial Rose	Colonial	Blue Ridge		Red rose, green leaves, red border, green rim
Colonial Rose		Stangl	1970-1974	
Colonial Silver		Stangl	c.1970	
Colonnes	Futura	Red Wing	1960	Pillars
Color Stitch	Colonial	Blue Ridge		Red, blue, gray border
Colorado				Brown
Columbia	Teapot	Hall		
Columbia	Williamsburg	E. M. Knowles	1948	
Columbine	Skyline	Blue Ridge	1950s	Red and white flowers; red line border
Columbine	Century	Homer Laughlin		Floral decal; off-center
Commodore		Salem		Gold medallions and trim
*Conchita	Century	Homer Laughlin	1938	Mexican-inspired decal
*Conchita Kitchen Kraft		Homer Laughlin	1930s	Ovenwares; Mexican-inspired decal
Concord		Continental Kilns	1944-1957	
Concord		Stangl	1957	
Concorde	Astor	Blue Ridge		Centered grapes; blue line border; brown edge
Confetti	Candlewick	Blue Ridge		Red, yellow, and blue flower border; gray rim
*Connie	Teapot	Hall	Early 1940s	Victorian style; see also Benjamin, Birch, Bowknot, Murphy, Plume
Constance	Colonial	Blue Ridge		Centered red and yellow flowers; small flowers on border; pink rim
Contempo	Al Fresco	Bauer	1950s	
Contemps		Brusche	1952	Champagne White, Desert Beige, Indigo Brown, Pumpkin, Slate, Spicy Green
Cookie Twins	Kiddieware	Stangl	Mid-1940s-1971	
Coors, see Rosebud				
Coral Pine	Criterion	E. M. Knowles	1954	
Coral Reef	Ultra	Vernon Kilns	1938	Tropical fish in blue, mustard, maroon on cream ground
Coreopsis	Colonial	Blue Ridge		Yellow flowers; thin yellow border
Corn		American Pottery		
Corn		Brush-McCoy		
Corn		Paden City		
Corn		Standard Pottery		
Corn		Stanford Pottery	1946-1961	

PATTERN	SHAPE	MAKER	DATE	DESCRIPTION
Corn Gold		Sold by Montgomery Ward	1921	Decals
Corn Is Green		Paden City		Cornstalk center design
*Corn King	Corn King	Shawnee	c.1950	Yellow and green; three-dimensional
*Corn Queen	Corn Queen	Shawnee	1954-1961	Three-dimensional; lighter kernel than Corn King; dark foliage
Cornflower Blue		E. M. Knowles	1930s	Decals
*Coronado	50 different shapes	Franciscan	1935-1942	15 solid colors
Coronado		E. M. Knowles	1948	
Coronado	Coronado, Montecito	Vernon Kilns (grocery promotion)	1935-1939	Blue, brown, dark blue, light green, orange, pink, turquoise, yellow
Coronado Swirl		Franciscan	1936-1956	
Coronation Organdy	Montecito	Vernon Kilns	1937	Gray and rose plaid; see also Calico; Gingham; Homespun; Organdie; Tam O'Shanter; Tweed
Corsage	Astor	Blue Ridge		Pastel flowers, blue leaf border
Corsage	Lyric	E. M. Knowles	1954	
Cosmos	Skyline	Blue Ridge	1950s	Large yellow flowers
Cosmos		Stangl		Marked Prestige, cosmos flower border
Cosmos	Melinda	Vernon Kilns	1942	Red allover floral
Cottage		Harker		Flowered path leading to red-roofed cottage
Cottage (Crooksville), see Petit Point House				
Cottage Window	Montecito	Vernon Kilns	1937	Window with curtain
Country Classics		Haeger		
Country Cousin	Year 'Round	Vernon Kilns	1957-1958	People and flowers with geometric border
Country Fair	Colonial	Blue Ridge		Fruit; green rim
Country Fair	Criterion	E. M. Knowles	1955	
Country Fruit	Trailway	Blue Ridge	1950s	Plaid fruit, wide yellow border
Country Garden	Candlewick	Blue Ridge		Pink and purple flowers
Country Garden	Anniversary	Red Wing	1953	Floral
*Country Garden		Stangl	1956-1974	Three realistic flowers
Country Garden	Anniversary	Red Wing	1953	

PATTERN	SHAPE	MAKER	DATE	DESCRIPTION
Country Gentleman		W. S. George		Fruit
Country Home	Fruits	Crooksville		Cottage with mountains in background
Country Life		Stangl	1956-1967	
Country Road	Colonial	Blue Ridge		Yellow flowers; orange rim
Country Road		Homer Laughlin	1977-1978	
Countryside		Harker		Cottage with smoking chimney
Country Side	Montecito	Vernon Kilns	1950	Rural farm scene; marked "da Bron"
County Fair	Colonial	Blue Ridge		
Coverlet, see Cozy Cover				
Cowboys and Cactus, see Ranger				
Cowslip	Colonial	Blue Ridge		Yellow flowers
Cozy Cover	Teapot	Hall		Fleece-lined aluminum cozy to fit pot
*Crab Apple	Colonial	Blue Ridge	c.1930-1957	Hand-painted red apples with green leaves; red spatter border
Crab Orchard	Candlewick	Blue Ridge		Two apples; green rim
Cradle	Square	Blue Ridge		Blue flowers and leaves
Cranberry		Stangl		
Crazy Quilt		Homer Laughlin	1977-1978	
Crazy Rhythm	Futura	Red Wing	1960	Abstract; hand painted
Crestone		Hull		Turquoise
Crocus	Colonial	Blue Ridge		
*Crocus	D-Line	Hall	1930s	Floral decals; black, green, lavender, pink, red; platinum trim
Crocus	True China	Red Wing	1960	Floral
Crocus		Stangl		
Cross Stitch		Blue Ridge		Black X's and dots; red and green leaves
Croydon	Sovereign	Crown	1941	Black trellis border with multicolored flowers
Cube	Teapot	Hall		Also coffeepot, creamer, and tea tile
Cumberland	Astor	Blue Ridge	1948	Hand-painted blue and white flowers
Curiosity Shop, see Old Curiosity Shop				
Currier & Ives		Homer Laughlin	Present	Blue decal on white
*Currier & Ives	Cavalier	Royal	1940s-1980s	Ironstone; scenic center design in blue and white
Currier & Ives	Coupe	Scio		
Cut-A-Way		Hall	1930	Multicolored flowers
Cynthia		Blue Ridge	1949	

PATTERN	SHAPE	MAKER	DATE	DESCRIPTION
Cynthia	Lido	W. S. George		Sprigs of small pink flowers (Peach Blossom has same decal on Bolero shape)
*Daffodil	Piecrust	Blue Ridge	1948	Single flower
Dahlia	Candlewick	Blue Ridge	1948	Large red flower
Dahlia by Harker, see Deco-Dahlia				
Dahlia		Stangl	1970-1974	Blue flowered border; marked Prestige
Dainty	Montecito	Vernon Kilns	1935-1947	Dark pink leaves and flowers
Daisies	Deanna	E. M. Knowles		Field of flowers
Daisy	Fiesta	Homer Laughlin	1962-1968	Turquoise band; turquoise and brown daisies; Casual pattern; see also Yellow Carnation; also called Hawaiian Daisy and Hawaiian 12 Point Daisy
Daisy		Stangl	1936-1942	
Daisy	Versatile	Taylor, Smith, and Taylor		
Daisy	True China	Red Wing	1960	Floral
Daisy Wreath	Daisy Wreath	Franciscan		
Damask	True China	Red Wing	1964	
Damask Rose	Accent	E. M. Knowles	1954	
Dandridge Dogwood	Skyline	Blue Ridge	1950s	Single flower
Dawn Rose	Americana	E. M. Knowles	1958	
Daydream	Colonial	Blue Ridge		Gray flowers
Deanna		E. M. Knowles		
Debussy	Tempo	E. M. Knowles	1961-1963	
Deca-Flip	Coffeepot	Hall		
Deco-Dahlia		Harker		Stylized red flowers, red and black leaves
Deco-Delight		Stangl		Deco shaped; Colonial Blue, silver-green
Deep Purple		Blue Ridge		Purple flower and leaves
Del Mar	Del Mar	Franciscan		
Delft	Americana	E. M. Knowles	1957	Purple flower; wide yellow rim
Delft Rose	Colonial	Blue Ridge		
Delicious	Candlewick	Blue Ridge		Two painted apples with green and yellow leaves
Delight	Ultra	Vernon Kilns	1938	Blue and yellow peonies and gardenias
Della Robbia	Piecrust	Blue Ridge	1948	Border of variety of fruit
Della Robbia	Vernonware	Metlox	1965	
Delmar		Stangl	1972-1974	Gold background; brown and blue border

PATTERN	SHAPE	MAKER	DATE	DESCRIPTION
Delta Blue	Village Green	Red Wing	1954	Light blue with flowers
Desert Bloom	San Fernando	Vernon Kilns	1944; 1955	Small flowers on wide border
Desert Flower	Skyline	Blue Ridge	1950s	One yellow and one brown flower
Desert Mallow	Montecito	Vernon Kilns		Yellow and orange flowers
*Desert Rose	Desert Rose	Franciscan	1941-present	Border of large pink flowers and green leaves
Desert Sun	New Shape	Red Wing	1962	Geometric
Design 69		Taylor, Smith, and Taylor		Pale blue and brown
Dewberry	Colonial	Blue Ridge		Green leaves; white berry border
Dewdrop Fairies	Ultra	Vernon Kilns	1940	Blue print border on cream ground
Diana		Stangl	1972-1974	Light blue flowers and rim
Dick Tracy	Century	Homer Laughlin	1950	Decal; child's set
Dinner Rose, see Queen Rose				
Dis 'N Dot	Anytime	Vernon Kilns	1957-1958	Blue, green, and mustard off-center lines and dots
Disney	Ultra most common	Vernon Kilns	1940-1941	Various patterns based on *Fantasia*
*Disraeli	Teapot	Hall	1940s	Pink only; Victorian style
Dixie Harvest (No. 3913)	Piecrust	Blue Ridge	1949	
D-Line		Hall	1936	Plain; round; floral decals
Dogwood	Skyline	Blue Ridge	1950s	Large yellow flowers
Dogwood	Dogwood	Franciscan		
Dogwood	Bolero	W. S. George		
Dogwood	Century	Homer Laughlin	1960s	Pink and white floral decals
Dogwood		Stangl	1965	Della-Ware mark; raised border of pink flowers and pale green leaves
Dogwood		Taylor, Smith, and Taylor	1942	Underglaze pattern; overall flowers
*Dolores	Melinda	Vernon Kilns	1942-1947	Floral border
Dominion	Victory	Salem		Poppies, wheat, blue flowers; decal
Dorset		Scio		
*Donut	Teapot	Hall	1938	Ivory with orange poppy decal common; Chinese Red, cobalt, Delphinium
Dragon Flower		Winfield	1940s-1950s	Stylized brown plant
Drape, see Parade				
Dream Flower	Colonial	Blue Ridge		Red, blue, and yellow flowers; dot border
Dreambirds	Colonial	Blue Ridge		Birds kissing; red rim

PATTERN	SHAPE	MAKER	DATE	DESCRIPTION
Dresden		Crown	1941	Sprays of assorted flowers; gold rim
Dresden Doll	Colonial	Blue Ridge		
Driftwood	Anniversary	Red Wing	1953	Tree branch design
Dubarry	Regent	E. M. Knowles	1948	
Duchess, see Coffee Queen				
Duchess		Paden City	1942	Small flowers and scrolls
Ducky Dinners	Kiddieware	Stangl	Mid-1940s-1974	
Duet		Franciscan	1956	
Duet	Tempo	E. M. Knowles	1961-1963	
Dubonnet	Criterion	E. M. Knowles	1955	
Duff	Candlewick	Blue Ridge		Eight different fruits; gray and rust stylized background
Dutch Bouquet	Candlewick	Blue Ridge		Red tulip decoration
Dutch Iris	Candlewick	Blue Ridge		Two red and blue iris; red border
Dutch Petit Point	Tricorne; Bonjour	Salem		Decals; Dutch boy and girl in stitched pattern
Dutch Tulip	Candlewick	Blue Ridge		Centered yellow-orange tulip, green leaves
Dynasty	Cavalier	Royal		Ironstone
Early American		Homer Laughlin	1960s	Floral
Early California	Montecito	Vernon Kilns	1935-1947	Blue, dark blue, brown, green, ivory, maroon, orange, peach, pink, turquoise, yellow
Early Days	San Fernando	Vernon Kilns	1944; 1950-1955	1860s scene with wide floral border
Ebonite	Criterion	E. M. Knowles	c.1954	
Ecstasy	Ultra	Vernon Kilns	1938	Light brown peonies and gardenias
Edgemont	Colonial	Blue Ridge		Yellow and red flowers
Edmonton		Syracuse		
*Eggshell Polka Dot		Hall	1934	Matte white; ivory glaze; blue, green, red dots; floral decals
Eggshell Theme		Homer Laughlin	1940s	English look; decals; floral border
Eglantine	Clinchfield	Blue Ridge		Pink flower, red border
El-Chico		Bauer		
Eldorado		E. M. Knowles	1948	
*El Patio		Franciscan	1934-1954	20 different solid colors
El Rosa				Della-Ware mark; pink rose and lavender flowers; border of dark green, white, and yellow

PATTERN	SHAPE	MAKER	DATE	DESCRIPTION
El Vuelo		Caribe-Sterling	1950s-c.1963	Modernistic swirls
Elegant Modern		Homer Laughlin		Hotel dinnerware; decals on white
Emerald		Sold by Montgomery Ward	1921	Decals
Emma Susan	Washington Square	Taylor, Smith, and Taylor	1933-1934	Decals
Emperor	Refrigerator ware	Hall	1939	Westinghouse; Canary,
Delphinium, Garden, Sunset; also called General				
Enchantment		Harker		
Enchantment	Ultra	Vernon Kilns	1940	Blue print border
English Countryside		Hall		
English Garden	Century	Homer Laughlin	1933	Landscape design
Engraved Rooster		Harker		Cameoware; rooster standing in center; also called Cock o' the Morn
Epicure		Homer Laughlin	1955	Solid; Charcoal Gray, Dawn Pink, Snow White, turquoise blue; highly sculptured
Equation	Criterion Antiques	E. M. Knowles	1955	
Eureka Homewood		Hall (made for Eureka Co.)		Decal
Evening Flower	Skyline	Blue Ridge	1950s	
Evening Song	Classique	E. M. Knowles	1960	
Evening Star	Montecito	Vernon Kilns	1935-1937	Blue and ivory
Eventide	Woodcrest	Blue Ridge	1950s	Log cabin and tree in center; brown rim
Fairlawn		Stangl	1959-1962	
Fairmede Fruits	Clinchfield	Blue Ridge		Centered fruit, four-line border
Fairmount	Skyline	Blue Ridge	1950s	Brown and green leaves on partially brown background
Fairy Bells	Colonial	Blue Ridge		Red and purple flower bells, tan ground
Fairy Tale	Astor	Blue Ridge		Pink flowers, blue leaves, pink border
Fairyland	Ultra	Vernon Kilns	1940	Blue floral and leaf design
Falling Leaves	Colonial	Blue Ridge		Multicolored leaves; orange rim

PATTERN	SHAPE	MAKER	DATE	DESCRIPTION
Falmouth	Skyline	Blue Ridge	1950s	Blue and red outlined flowers; yellow swirled background
*Fantasia	Skyline	Blue Ridge	1950s	Abstract leaf pattern; brown, blue, yellow
Fantasia	Ultra	Vernon Kilns	1940	Brown floral and leaf pattern
Fantasy	Kitchenware	Hall	1930s-1940s	Decal; Swedish modern bright flowers on ivory
Fantasy	Accent	E. M. Knowles	1955	
Fantasy	Concord	Red Wing	1947	Abstract
Fantasy Apple	Skyline	Blue Ridge	1950s	Stylized apples; gray rim
Far East	Shellcrest	Paden City		Oriental design
Farmer Takes a Wife	Colonial	Blue Ridge		Figures in center; yellow flowers border; green rim
Farmhouse	Woodcrest	Blue Ridge	1950s	Large scenic design
Farmyard	Skyline	Blue Ridge	1950s	Barn, farmer, tree
Fashion White		Sold by Montgomery Ward	1936	Decals
Fayette Fruit	Candlewick	Blue Ridge		Apple, pear; series of three slashes on border
Feather Fantasy	Criterion	E. M. Knowles	1955	
Feathered Friends	Skyline	Blue Ridge	1950s	Cardinal, bluejay; gray background
Federal		Sebring-Limoges	1942	
Festival	Williamsburg; Forcast	E. M. Knowles	1955; 1957	
*Festival		Stangl	1961-1967	Yellow band, Della-Ware mark
Festive	Skyline	Blue Ridge	1950s	Black and yellow crepe paper
Festive Fruit, see Fruit (Stangl)				
Field Daisy	Colonial	Blue Ridge		Red and yellow flowers, brown leaves; broken rim
Field Daisy		Stangl	1941-1942	White daisies on blue; yellow background
*Fiesta	Fiesta	Homer Laughlin	1936-1972	Antique Gold, Bright Green, Chartreuse, Dark Blue, Forest Green, Gray, Light Green, Mango Red, Old Ivory, Red, Rose, Turf Green, Turquoise, Yellow; see also Amberstone; Casualstone; Daisy; Fiesta Ironstone; Fiesta Kitchen Kraft; Yellow Carnation
Fiesta Casual, see Daisy; Yellow Carnation				
*Fiesta Ironstone	Fiesta	Homer Laughlin	1970-1972	Antique Gold, Mango Red, Turf Green

PATTERN	SHAPE	MAKER	DATE	DESCRIPTION
*Fiesta Kitchen Kraft		Homer Laughlin	1939-early 1940s	Bake and serve line; blue, green, red, yellow
Fiesta Wood	Fiesta	Homer Laughlin		Colored border stripes; sleeping Mexican
Fireside	Skyline	Blue Ridge	1950s	Hearth and rocker; brown rim
First Love		Stangl	1968-1973	
Fisherman	Square	Blue Ridge		Man fishing; broken black rim
Five Band, see Banded				
Five Fingers	Ultra	Vernon Kilns	1938	Autumn leaves on ivory
Five Little Pigs	Kiddieware	Stangl	Mid-1940s-1974	
Fjord	Americana	E. M. Knowles	1959	
Flaming Rose		Paden City		Brightly colored floral design
Flamingo	Gray Lure	Crooksville		Sprig of delicate flowers
Flamingo		Hall		
Flare Ware Gold Lace		Hall	1960s	Overall stars and scalloped border
Fleur de Lis	Kitchen Kraft	Homer Laughlin		
Fleur de Lis		Vernon Kilns		Large pastel center design
Fleur de Lis	Criterion	E. M. Knowles	1955	
Fleur de Lis Iris, see Iris (Universal)				
Fleurette	Tempo	E. M. Knowles	1959	
Flight	Skyline	Blue Ridge	1950s	Centered flying birds
Flight	Forcast	E. M. Knowles	1957	
Flight	New Shape	Red Wing	1962	Birds
Flight of the Swallows	New Art	Homer Laughlin	1930s	Foliage spray and group of flying birds
Flirt	Piecrust	Blue Ridge	1950s	Red flowers; green leaves and rim
Flora	Williamsburg	E. M. Knowles	1948-1955	
Flora		Stangl	1941	Yellow band with pink, blue, and yellow flowers; Terra Rose mark
Flora	Ultra	Vernon Kilns	1938	Floral spray
Floral	Floral	Franciscan		
Floral	Lido	W. S. George		Decal of multicolored small flowers
Floral		Paden City		
Floral		Stangl	1941-1942	
Floral		Watt		Charcoal, pinkish-blue floral
Floral Bird-song	Sabina II	Sabin	c.1946	
Floral Border		Sold by Montgomery Ward	1936	Decals

PATTERN	SHAPE	MAKER	DATE	DESCRIPTION
Floral Bouquet	Fairway	Taylor, Smith, and Taylor	Early 1930s	
Floral Lattice	Five Band	Hall		
Floral Plaid		Stangl	1940-1942	
Florence	Squared-Off Edges	E. M. Knowles	1933-1934	Decals
Florence		Pope-Gosser	1940s	Border of small flowers
Florentine		Stangl	1958	
Floret	Ultra	Vernon Kilns	1939	Red floral
Florette		Stangl	1961-1962	
Florida	Williamsburg	E. M. Knowles	1948	
Flounce	Colonial	Blue Ridge		Red, pink, and blue cut-off flowers around edge
Flower Ballet	Ultra	Vernon Kilns	1940	Maroon border print
Flower Basket	Yorktown	E. M. Knowles		
Flower Bowl	Colonial	Blue Ridge		Flowers in bowl; green and yellow border
Flower Fair	Coupe	Crooksville		Muted flowers
Flower Fantasy		Blue Ridge	1954	
Flower Power		Homer Laughlin	1977-1978	
Flower Rim	Lido	W. S. George		Bands of small flowers
*Flower Ring	Colonial	Blue Ridge		Red, blue, and yellow flowers; green leaves and rim
Flower Wreath	Candlewick	Blue Ridge		Purple and pink flowers and border
Floweret	Skyline	Blue Ridge	1950s	Red flowers, black rim
Flowering Berry	Candlewick	Blue Ridge		Pink and red flower border
Flowerpot	Banded	Hall		Early decal
Flowers of the Dell	New Art	Homer Laughlin	1930s	Two floral sprays
Fluffy Ruffles	Astor	Blue Ridge		Large blue flowers
Flute	Kitchenware	Hall	1935	Kitchenware; Chinese Red, Hi-white Marine, Russet; also called Ribbed
Flying Bluebird	Empress	Homer Laughlin	1920	Decal
Foliage	Tempo	E. M. Knowles	1961-1963	
Fondoso	Gypsy Trail	Red Wing	1938	Pastels; blue, turquoise, yellow
Football	Teapot	Hall	1938-1940	
Forest Flower	Shellridge	Harker		Light brown and yellow
Forest Fruits	Skyline	Blue Ridge	1950s	Yellow fruit, dark border
Forever Yours	Shellridge	Harker		Rosebud garland
Formal		Salem		Rust and gold rim; gold border design
Forman		Hall		
Fountain	Ballerina	Universal	1950	Abstract

PATTERN	SHAPE	MAKER	DATE	DESCRIPTION
Four Seasons White	Four Seasons	E. M. Knowles	1959-1963	
Four Winds	Melinda	Vernon Kilns	1950	Yacht; maroon and blue border
Fox Grape	Colonial	Blue Ridge		Green leaves, dark grapes, broken rim
Foxfire	Skyline	Blue Ridge	1950s	Red leaf-shaped flowers
Frageria	Skyline	Blue Ridge	1950s	Red strawberries; green border
*French	Teapot	Hall	1920	Gold-decorated line
*French Peasant	Colonial	Blue Ridge		Light blue rim; pink and green floral border; peasant in center
French Provincial				Silhouette decal
Frolic	Anytime	Vernon Kilns	1955	Aqua, gold, and purple abstract floral
*Frontenac	Futura	Red Wing	1960	Abstract flowers
Frontier Days	Montecito	Vernon Kilns	1950; 1954	Western scene
Frosted Fruit		Stangl	1957	
Frosted Leaves	Mayfair	E. M. Knowles	1955	
*Fruit		Franciscan	1949	
Fruit		Purinton	1936-1959	Four fruits; brown X
*Fruit	Concord	Red Wing	1947	
*Fruit		Stangl	1942-1974	Center designs of fruit; also called Festive Fruit
*Fruit & Flowers		Stangl	1957-1974	Center design; colored border
Fruit & Flowers		Universal		Subdued colors; large center design
Fruit Basket		Homer Laughlin	1977-1978	
Fruit Basket		Salem		Narrow checkerboard band; border of fruit baskets
Fruit Cocktail	Astor	Blue Ridge		Different fruits; black and yellow border
Fruit Fantasy	Colonial	Blue Ridge		Painted fruits, green rim
Fruit Punch	Colonial	Blue Ridge		Various fruits; allover pattern
Fruit Ring	Clinchfield	Blue Ridge		Fruit border
Fruit Salad	Colonial	Blue Ridge		Yellow pear, red apple, blueberries; red rim
Fruit Sherbet	Colonial	Blue Ridge		Pastel fruit; broken blue rim
Fruitdale	Melinda	Vernon Kilns	1942-1947	Flower and fruit center
Fruitful	Colonial	Blue Ridge		Painted fruit
Fruits	Utility ware	Harker		Large stem of fruit—apple and pear
Fruits		E. M. Knowles		Brightly colored individual fruit
Fuchsia	Colonial	Blue Ridge		

PATTERN	SHAPE	MAKER	DATE	DESCRIPTION
Fuchsia		Leigh/Crescent		Predominately orange and green floral spray
Fuji		Hall		Oriental-styled flower
Full Bloom	Candlewick	Blue Ridge		Two large purple and red center flowers
Futura		Red Wing	1961	Hand painted
Fuzz Ball		Hall	1930s	Pink and green
Gaity	Skyline	Blue Ridge		Red flowers
Galaxy		Stangl	1963-1970	
Game Cock, see Rooster by Blue Ridge				
Garden Design		Salem China	1940s	
Garden Flower		Stangl	1947-1957	
Garden Flowers	Colonial	Blue Ridge		Eight different flowers
Garden Lane	Colonial	Blue Ridge		Hand-painted tulips, daisies, and roses
Garden Magic	Classique	E. M. Knowles	1960	
Garden Party	Garden Party	Franciscan		
Garden Pinks	Skyline	Blue Ridge	1950s	Pink flower
Garden Trail	Shellridge	Harker		Center bouquet; floral border
Garland	Colonial	Blue Ridge		Black leaves; pastel flower border
Garland	Monarch	Crown	1941	Garland of small roses
Garland	Williamsburg	E. M. Knowles	1948	
Garland		Pickard		
Garland		Stangl	1957-1967	
Gascon		W. S. George		Bright blue flowers, gray leaves; sold by Sears, Roebuck and Co.
Gay Plaid		Blair		Yellow, green, and brown; large plaid
Gayety	San Marino	Vernon Kilns	1948; 1954	Green and rose stripes on ivory
General, see Emperor				
General Electric	Refrigerator ware	Hall		G.E. logo on lid; Addison (blue) and yellow
Ginger Boy	Kiddieware	Stangl	Mid-1940s-1974	
Ginger Cat	Kiddieware	Stangl	Mid-1940s-1974	
Ginger Girl	Kiddieware	Stangl	Mid-1940s-1974	
Gingersnap	Gingersnap	Franciscan		
*Gingham	Montecito	Vernon Kilns	1949-1958	Green and yellow plaid; dark green border; see also Calico; Coronation Organdy; Homespun; Organdie; Tam O'Shanter; Tweed

PATTERN	SHAPE	MAKER	DATE	DESCRIPTION
Gingham Fruit	Trailway	Blue Ridge	1950s	Fruit with plaid leaves; gray swirled border
Gladstone	Teapot	Hall	1940	Pink/gold only; Victorian style
Glamour gardenias	Ultra	Vernon Kilns	c.1938	Blue, maroon peonies and
Glencoe	Thermal Porcelain	Coors	1920s	Brown, green, yellow, and other colors
Glenedon		Leigh		
Glenwood	Cavalier	Homer Laughlin	1961-1968	
*Globe	Teapot	Hall	Early 1940s	
Gloria		Blue Ridge	1949	
Gloriosa	Skyline	Blue Ridge	1950s	Yellow flowers
Glorious	Candlewick	Blue Ridge		One red and two blue morning glories, centered
Gloucester Fisherman	Ballerina	Universal Potteries	1950	
Godey Ladies		Salem		
Godney Prints	Victory	Salem		Decals; service plates
Gold & Cobalt	Empress	Homer Laughlin	1920	Decal
Gold Band		Sold by Montgomery Ward	1920-1936	Decals

Gold-decorated line of Hall teapots, see Airflow; Aladdin; Albany; Automobile; Baltimore; Basket; Basketball; Birdcage; Boston; Cleveland; Donut; Football; French; Globe; Hollywood; Hook Cover; Illinois; Los Angeles; Manhattan; Melody; Moderne; Nautilus; New York; Parade; Philadelphia; Rhythm; Saf-Handle; Sani-Grid; Star; Streamline; Surfside; Windshield; World's Fair

Gold Drape		Crooksville		Floral design; gold border, draped effect
Gold Floral Band		Homer Laughlin	1920	Decal
Gold Garland		Homer Laughlin	1920	Decal
Gold Initial		Sold by Montgomery Ward	1921	Decal
Gold Label	Kitchenware	Hall	1950s	Gold stamped decorations
Gold Lace over Cobalt Blue		Homer Laughlin	1920	Decal
Gold Stripe		Sold by Montgomery Ward	1936	Decals
Golden		Coors	1930s	Blue, green, ivory, orange, rose, yellow
Golden Blossom		Stangl	1964-1974	Brown blossoms, orange leaves
Golden Crown	Queen Anne	Sabin		
Golden Foliage	Four Seasons	E. M. Knowles	1960-1963	
Golden Grape		Stangl	1963-1972	

PATTERN	SHAPE	MAKER	DATE	DESCRIPTION
*Golden Harvest	Coupe	Stangl	1953-1973	Yellow flowers, gray background
Golden Laurel		E. M. Knowles	1930	Decals
Golden Maple	Montecito	Vernon Kilns	1935-1937	Pumpkin and ivory
Golden Viking	Futura	Red Wing	1960	Geometric; gold
Golden Wheat	Rhythm Coupe	Homer Laughlin	1953-1958	
*Golden Wheat	Yorktown	E. M. Knowles	1936	Decals
Golden Wreath	Accent	E. M. Knowles	1960	
Goldtrim	Briar Rose	Salem	1952	Gold rim; gold border design
Gooseberry	Candlewick	Blue Ridge		Yellow fruit and rim
Gourmet	Accent	E. M. Knowles	1956	
Granada		French Saxon	1939-1940	Solids: blue, green, tangerine, yellow
Granada	True China	Red Wing	1960	Floral
Grandfather's Clock	Square	Blue Ridge		Clock in hallway; broken black rim
Grandiose	Coupe	Paden City	1952	Muted large flowers
Grandmother's Garden	Colonial	Blue Ridge		
Granny Smith Apple	Skyline	Blue Ridge	1950s	Two red apples on yellow center
Grape	Teapot	Hall		Grape clusters in relief; decal decorations and/or embedded rhinestones
Grape		Stangl	1973-1974	
Grape Salad	Candlewick	Blue Ridge		Grapes with large green leaves; border and rim
Grass	Esquire	E. M. Knowles	1957-1962	Abstract decal; Russel Wright
Grass Flower	Moderne	Blue Ridge	1950s	Black and yellow flowers; green leaves and rim
Greenbriar	Forcast	E. M. Knowles	1959	
Green Briar	Piecrust	Blue Ridge	1948	
Green Dots	Avona	Taylor, Smith, and Taylor	Early 1930s	Wide border of dots
Green Eyes	Skyline	Blue Ridge	1950s	
Green Grapes		Stangl		
Green Valley		Homer Laughlin	1977-1978	
Green Wheat	Yorktown	E. M. Knowles		Decals
Green Wheat		Leigh/Crescent		Separate wheat stalks
Greensville	Skyline	Blue Ridge	1950s	Cream and brown flower
Greenwich-stone	Ceramastone	Red Wing	1967	
Gumdrop Tree	Candlewick	Blue Ridge		Red, yellow, and red with green leaves
Gypsy	Colonial	Blue Ridge		Red, orange, and yellow flowers

PATTERN	SHAPE	MAKER	DATE	DESCRIPTION
Gypsy Dancer	Colonial	Blue Ridge		Red and yellow flowers; red and green border
Gypsy Trail		Red Wing	1930s	
Hacienda	Hacienda	Franciscan		Hacienda green
*Hacienda	Century	Homer Laughlin	1938	Decal; cactus, bench, side of Mexican house; red trim
Hall teapots, see individual names				
Hallcraft, see Bouquet; Caprice; Harlequin; Peach Blossom; Zeisel				
Ham 'n Eggs	Candlewick	Blue Ridge		Pig, hen; wide green and thin red border
Happy Days	Forcast	E. M. Knowles	1957	
Harlequin	Fantasy/Hall craft	Hall		Designed by Eva Zeisel
*Harlequin	Harlequin	Homer Laughlin	1938-1964; 1979	Ironstone; chartreuse, cobalt blue, dark blue, forest green, gray, ivory, light green, maroon, mauve blue, rose, spruce green, tangerine, turquoise; 1979—deep coral, green, turquoise, yellow
Harvest	Concord	Red Wing	1947	
Harvest		Stangl		
Harvest	Ultra	Vernon Kilns	1938	Fruits in center: pears, green apples, plum, cherries, and a peach
Harvestime	Skyline	Blue Ridge	1950s	Wheat tied with bow
Hawaii	Melinda	Vernon Kilns	1942	Maroon lotus flower
Hawaiian Coral	San Marino	Vernon Kilns	1952; 1956	Spatter edge; brown, yellow, and green on cream
Hawaiian Daisy, see Daisy (Homer Laughlin)				
*Hawaiian Flowers	Ultra	Vernon Kilns	1938	Lotus in blue, maroon, mustard, pink
Hawaiian Fruit	Cinchfield; Piecrust	Blue Ridge	1948	Hand painted pineapple and two other fruits in blue, yellow, and brown; colors repeated in border
Hawaiian 12 Point Daisy, see Daisy (Homer Laughlin)				
Hawthorne	Quena	Crown		Pastel pink and blue flowers; gold rim
Hawthorne	Hawthorne	Franciscan		
Hazel	Ranson	Scio		
Hazelnut		Universal		Decals
Hearthstone	Casual	Red Wing	1961	Solids; beige, orange
*Heather Rose	E-Style	Hall		Pale pinkish-purple rose on a stem with many leaves
Heavenly Days	Anytime	Vernon Kilns	1956-1958	Aqua, mocha, and pink geometric designs

PATTERN	SHAPE	MAKER	DATE	DESCRIPTION
Heirloom	Candlewick	Blue Ridge		Blue, yellow, and red flowers; green rim
Heirloom	Corinthian	Sebring		Wide gold floral border; garland and bouquet in center
Hen Party	Lyric	E. M. Knowles	1954	Green
Hercules, see Aristocrat (Hall)				
Heritage		Stangl		
Heritance		Harker		
Heyday	San Marino	Vernon Kilns	1954-1958	Geometric circles in green and brown
Hibiscus (Crooksville), see Flamingo				
Hibiscus	San Fernando	Vernon Kilns	1944; 1954	Yellow flowers and brown print
Hidden Valley	Cavalier	Royal		Ironstone; colored band and large center stencil-like flowers
Hi-Fire		Bauer	1930s	
High Sierra	Accent	E. M. Knowles	1955	
High Stepper	Square	Blue Ridge		Rooster stepping
Highland Ivy	Piecrust	Blue Ridge	1949	Dark and light green ivy
Highlands	Criterion	E. M. Knowles	1957	
Highlight		Paden City	1948	Heavy quality oven- and craze-proof colors: Blueberry, Citron, Dark Green, Nutmeg, Pepper, White; Russel Wright; distributed by Justin Tharaud and Son
Hilda	Candlewick	Blue Ridge		Large red flower and smaller blue and yellow flowers
Hilo	Ultra	Vernon Kilns	1938	Light brown lotus flower
Holland, see Crocus (Hall)				
Holly		Stangl	1967-1972	
Hollyberry	Colonial	Blue Ridge		Traditional Christmas plant; green rim
Hollyhock	Colonial	Blue Ridge		Pink flowers; yellow line border
Hollyhock	New Art	Homer Laughlin		Decal; pink flowers on stem
Hollyhock		Universal		Multicolored flowers
*Hollywood	Teapot	Hall	Late 1920s	Variety of colors; three sizes
Homesplace	Skyline	Blue Ridge	1950s	Tree, fence, and house
*Homespun	Montecito	Vernon Kilns	1949-1958	Brown, green, and yellow plaid; see also Calico; Coronation Organdy; Gingham; Organdie; Tam O'Shanter; Tweed
Homestead	Skyline	Blue Ridge	1950s	Farm scene

PATTERN	SHAPE	MAKER	DATE	DESCRIPTION
Homestead	Iva-Lure	Crooksville		Winter scene
Homestead in Winter, see Homestead (Crooksville)				
*Homestead Provincial	Poppytrail line	Metlox	1952-1980	Early American folk art themes in red and green
Honolulu	Candlewick	Blue Ridge		Different fruits; green rim
Honolulu	Ultra	Vernon Kilns	1938	Yellow and blue lotus flower
*Hook Cover	Teapot	Hall	1940	Cadet, Chinese Red, Delphinium, emerald common colors
Hopscotch	Astor	Blue Ridge		Centered yellow and orange flower; cross-hatched border
Hors-d'oeuvres	Accent	E. M. Knowles	1955	
Hostess Pantry Ware		Pottery Guild	1954	Hand painted
Hotpoint	Refrigerator ware	Hall		Addison, Chinese Red, Dresden, Green Lustre, Indian Red, maroon, Sandust, Warm Yellow Daffodil
House, see Petit Point House				
Housetops		Leigh/Crescent		Variety of buildings
Humpty Dumpty	Kiddieware	Stangl	Mid-1940s-1974	
Hunting	Iva-Lure	Crooksville		Scenic
Illinois	Teapot	Hall	1920s-early 1930s	Cobalt and emerald common colors
Imperial	Anytime	Vernon Kilns	1955-1956	Sgraffito; white lines on black ground
Indian Campfire	Kiddieware	Stangl	Mid-1940s-1974	
Indian Tree		Leigh/Crescent		Large floral spray; pink and blue
Indian Tree	Victory	Salem		Decals; Minton-style floral
Indiana	Teapot	Hall		Warm yellow
Ingrid	Regent	E. M. Knowles	1954	
Inspiration		Stangl	1967-1968	Marked Prestige
Intaglio		Purinton	1936-1959	Dark swirling background; white etched flower
Iris	Concord	Red Wing	1947	Brown, turquoise-green
Iris		Universal		Pastel pinks; also called Fleur de Lis Iris
Iris Bouquet		Leigh/Crescent		Brightly colored flowers
Irongate	Teapot	Hall		Made for Irongate Products Co. of New York; black

PATTERN	SHAPE	MAKER	DATE	DESCRIPTION
*Iroquois	Casual	Iroquois China	1959-mid 1960s	Aqua, Avocado Yellow, Brick Red, Canteloupe, Charcoal, Ice Blue, Lemon Yellow, Lettuce Green, Nutmeg, Oyster, Parsley, Pink Sherbet, Ripe Apricot, Sugar White
Iroquois Red	Ranchero	W. S. George		Red banded design
Isle of Palms	Common-wealth	James River Pottery		
Isobella		E. M. Knowles	1948	
*Ivy	Ivy	Franciscan	1948	Hand painted
Ivy	Regal	Harker		Fall colors
Ivy		Paden City		
Ivy Vine	Coupe	Crooksville		Pastel greens
Ivy Vine		Harker		Border of ivy
Jack in the Box	Kiddieware	Stangl	Mid-1940s-1974	
Jacobean	Queen Anne	Sabin	c.1946	
Jade Ware		Sebring	1940s	
Jamestown	Tempo	E. M. Knowles	1961-1963	
Jamoca	Jamoca	Franciscan		
Jan	Candlewick	Blue Ridge		Red, yellow, purple, and pink flower border
Jane Adams	Victory	Salem	1950s	Yellow and green floral sprays
Jean		Nancy	Steubenville	
Jeanette	New Yorker	Salem		Flowerpot center design
Jellico	Skyline	Blue Ridge	1950s	Two-tone red and yellow flowers
Jessamine	Piecrust	Blue Ridge	1948	Red flowers, multicolored leaves, green border
Jessica	Colonial	Blue Ridge		Red, pink, and blue flowers; pink line border
Jessica		Harker		Brightly colored flowers
Jessie		Crooksville		Pastel pink; floral sprays on border and center
Jigsaw	Skyline	Blue Ridge	1950s	Rooster
Joan of Arc	Diana	Sebring-Limoges		
Joanna	Colonial	Blue Ridge		Red and yellow flowers
Jonquil	Astor	Blue Ridge		Yellow flowers, red border
Jonquil		Paden City		Pastel flowers, border of yellow sprays
Jonquil	Tricorne	Salem		Decals
Jonquil		Stangl		
Joy	Ultra	Vernon Kilns	1938	Yellow peonies and gardenias on brown
Joyce	Colonial	Blue Ridge		Red, light blue, and dark blue flowers

PATTERN	SHAPE	MAKER	DATE	DESCRIPTION
J-Sunshine		Hall		Floral decals
Jubilee		Homer Laughlin	c.1948; 1977-1978	Pastel; Celadon Green, Cream Beige, Mist Gray, Shell Pink; solids
June Apple	Woodcrest	Blue Ridge	1950s	Broken line outlining red apples and leaves
June Bouquet	Colonial	Blue Ridge		Pink, purple, and yellow flowers
June Bride	Colonial	Blue Ridge		Pink and yellow flowers; yellow centered border
June Rose	Colonial	Blue Ridge		Pink flowers, dark leaves
Kaleidoscope	Birds	Crooksville		Floral pattern with green divider
Karen	Colonial	Blue Ridge		Pink, purple, and red flowers
Karen		Sebring-Limoges	1940	
Kashmir	True China	Red Wing	1964	
Kate	Colonial	Blue Ridge		Red flower and rim
Kimberly	Moderne	Blue Ridge	1950s	
King	Refrigerator ware	Hall		Westinghouse ovenware; canary
Kingsport	Astor	Blue Ridge		Centered pink flower; inner and outer leaf border
Kitchen Bouquet	Century-Kitchen Kraft	Homer Laughlin		Floral decals
*Kitchen Kraft	Kitchen Kraft	Homer Laughlin	1930s	Red, blue; also decals under pattern name
Kitchen Shelf	Astor	Blue Ridge		Kitchenware; centered light blue and yellow borders

Kitchenware, see Acacia; Banded; Blue Blossom; Blue Garden; Cactus; Clover; Colonial; Fantasy; Flute; Gold Label; Meadow Flower; Morning Glory; No. 488; Plum Pudding; Provincial; Radiant Ware; Red Dot; Rose Parade; Rose White; Royal Rose; Saf-Handle; Sani-Grid; Shaggy Tulip; Sunshine; Thorley

Kitten Capers	Kiddieware	Stangl	Mid-1940s-1974	
Kitty	Harker			Blue and pink cameoware
Knowles	Esquire	E. M. Knowles	1955	Russel Wright
Kumquat		Stangl		
La Gonda		Gonder	1950s	Modern shapes; aqua, pink, yellow
Lacquer Blossom	Accent	E. M. Knowles	1957	
Lady Alice	Brittany	Homer Laughlin		Maroon border; bluebells and roses
Lady Greenbriar	Liberty	Homer Laughlin		Green border
Lady Stafford	Liberty	Homer Laughlin		Maroon border

PATTERN	SHAPE	MAKER	DATE	DESCRIPTION
La Linda		Bauer	1939-1940s	Solid colors; smooth (no ridges)
Landscape		Salem	1940s	
Language of Flowers	Candlewick	Blue Ridge		Blue basket, red flowers, blue rim, writing
Lanterns	Concord	Red Wing	1947	Abstract
Largo		Universal		Border of fall leaves; small center decal
Laura	Colonial	Blue Ridge		Red flowers, red and yellow leaves
Laurel	Monarch	Crown	1941	Black and gold wreath border
Laurel		Stangl	c.1942	
Laurelton		Harker		Green, beige
Laurie	Colonial	Blue Ridge		Large pink flowers, small blue flowers
Laurita		Stangl		Della-Ware mark
Lavalette	Moderne	Blue Ridge	1950s	Pink flower; green border
Lavender Fruit	Colonial	Blue Ridge		
Lazybone		Frankoma	1953	Solids
Leaf		Taylor, Smith, and Taylor		Coral
Leaf and Flower		Harker		Cameo-type design
Leaf Ballet	Accent	E. M. Knowles	1953-1954	
Leaf Dane	Four Seasons	E. M. Knowles	1960-1963	
Leaf Spray		E. M. Knowles		Muted colors
Leaf Swirl	Shellridge	Harker		Fall colors
Leaves of Fall	Trailway	Blue Ridge	1950s	Centered leaves with outline; wide yellow border
Ledford	Candlewick	Blue Ridge		Mostly pink flowers
Lei Lani	Ultra; San Marino	Vernon Kilns	1938-1942; 1947-1955	Maroon lotus flower
Lenore	Candlewick	Blue Ridge		Pink and red tulip; red border
Lenore	Monticello; Olivia	Steubenville		
Lexington	Colonial	Blue Ridge		Gray flowers; blue leaves and rim
Lexington	Concord	Red Wing	1947	Rose
Lexington		Homer Laughlin		Wide solid-colored border
Lexington Rose		Red Wing		Large flowers
Lido		Homer Laughlin	1977-1978	
Lido	Regent	E. M. Knowles	1948	
Lido Dalyrymple		W. S. George		Tiny buds
Lime		Stangl	1950	

PATTERN	SHAPE	MAKER	DATE	DESCRIPTION
Linda	Montecito	Vernon Kilns	1940	Burgundy border; pink and blue flowers
*Lipton	French; Boston	Hall		Teapots, sugars and creamers; marked Lipton Tea; maroon and warm yellow most common colors
Little Bo Peep, see Bo Peep				
Little Bouquet	LaGrande	Crooksville		Small flower grouping
Little Boy Blue	Kiddieware	Stangl	Mid-1940s-1974	
Little Mission	Montecito	Vernon Kilns	1937	Mission house
Little Quackers	Kiddieware	Stangl	Mid-1940s-1974	
Little Red Riding Hood, see Red Riding Hood				
Little Violet	Astor	Blue Ridge		Centered bunch of violets; border
Liz	Colonial	Blue Ridge		Pink and yellow flowers; red rim
Lollipop Tree	Year 'Round	Vernon Kilns	1957-1958	Abstract pastel lollipops
Los Angeles		Bauer		
*Los Angeles	Teapot	Hall	1926	Variety of colors; three sizes
Lotus		Harker	1960s	Cameoware
Lotus	Concord	Red Wing	1947	
Lotus	Lotus	Vernon Kilns	1950	Red and yellow lotus flower
Louise	Virginia Rose	Homer Laughlin		
Louisiana Lace	Candlewick	Blue Ridge		
Love Song	Astor	Blue Ridge		Centered male, female, and leaves; yellow and double black border
Lucerne	Classique	E. M. Knowles	1960	
Lupine	Futura	Red Wing	1960	Floral
*Lu-Ray	Laurel (1932); Empire (1936)	Taylor, Smith, and Taylor	1930s-1950s	Pastels: Chatham Gray, Persian Cream, Sharon Pink, Surf Green, Windsor Blue
Lute Song	True China	Red Wing	1960s	Musical instruments
Lyric		Stangl	1954-1957	Black and brown freeform shapes; white background
Madison		Leigh		
Madras	Square	Blue Ridge		Bold geometric
Madrid		Homer Laughlin	1977-1978	
Magic Flower	Candlewick	Blue Ridge		Red and blue flower; green border
Magnolia	Piecrust	Blue Ridge	1948	White and red flowers; green leaves; dark stems
Magnolia	Liberty	Homer Laughlin		Decal
*Magnolia	Concord	Red Wing	1947	

PATTERN	SHAPE	MAKER	DATE	DESCRIPTION
*Magnolia		Stangl	1952-1962	Red border
Majestic	True China	Red Wing	1960	White
Mallow		Harker		Pastel flower arrangements
Manassas	Colonial	Blue Ridge		Red leaves; green leaf border
Mandarin Red		Salem		Solid colored; bright red and white
Mandarin Tricorne	Tricorne	Salem		Red borders, white interiors
Mango	Mango	Franciscan		
Manhattan	Teapot	Hall		Stock Brown; side handle
Manhattan		Leigh/Crescent		Bordered with rings of gold
Mantilla	Tempo	E. M. Knowles	1961-1963	
Maple Leaf	Woodcrest	Blue Ridge	1950s	Stylized leaves with outlines
Maple Leaf		Salem		Fall leaf design
Maple Whirl		Stangl	1965-1967	
*Mar-Crest		Western Stoneware	1950s	Dark brown, many different designs; wholesaled by Marshall Burns
*Mardi Gras	Colonial	Blue Ridge	1943	Blue daisy and pink flower; flowers cut off on plates
Mardi Gras Variant	Colonial	Blue Ridge		Red cut-off flowers
Margaret Rose		Homer Laughlin		Thick colored border; floral center
Mariner	Candlewick	Blue Ridge		Center sailboat; blue rope border; Mariner written on plate
Marines	Montecito	Vernon Kilns	1937	Anchor and ships
Mariposa Tulip	Montecito	Vernon Kilns		Yellow flowers
Mary	Astor	Blue Ridge		Fruit and flowers, border
Mary Quite	Kiddieware	Stangl	Mid-1940s-1974	
Marylou		Hall		Floral decals; creamer and sugar
Max-i-cana	Yellowstone	Homer Laughlin	1930s	Mexican decal; man, cactus, pots; octagonal plates
May and Vieve Hamilton		Vernon Kilns		
May Flower	Melinda	Vernon Kilns	1942-1955	Large floral spray
Mayan Aztec		Frankoma		Solids
Mayfair	Esquire	E. M. Knowles	1957	
Mayfair		Leigh/Crescent		Bold flower decal
*Mayflower	Skyline	Blue Ridge	1950s	
Mayflower		E. M. Knowles	1957-1963	

PATTERN	SHAPE	MAKER	DATE	DESCRIPTION
Maypole	Maypole	Franciscan	1977	
Maywood		Purinton	1936-1959	Gray-blue background; white flower
*McCormick	Teapot	Hall	1907	Golden brown oldest color; made for McCormick Tea Co.
Meadow Beauty	Colonial	Blue Ridge		Brightly colored floral border
Meadow Bloom	Montecito	Vernon Kilns	1947	Blue flowers and rose; brown border
Meadow Flowers	Kitchenware	Hall	1938	Flowers in meadow on ivory; teapot
Meadow Flowers	Coupe	Crooksville		Brightly colored floral border
Meadow Gold	Criterion	E. M. Knowles	1954	
Meadow Rose	Meadow Rose	Franciscan	1977	
Meadowlea	Skyline	Blue Ridge	1950s	White flowers, brown leaves, outlined
Mealtime Special	Kiddieware	Stangl	Mid-1940s-1974	
Medallion, see Colonial				
Medallion		Crooksville		Small floral border
Medici	Cavalier	Royal		Ironstone; wide, elaborate scroll border
Mediterranean	True China	Red Wing	1960	Floral
Mediterranean		Stangl	1965-1974	Dark blue and black
Medley	Colonial	Blue Ridge		Blue flower and rim
Melinda	Melinda	Vernon Kilns	1942	Solid colors
Mello-Tone		Coors	Late 1930s	Pastels: aqua blue, canary yellow, coral pink, spring green
*Melody	Teapot	Hall	1939	Canary, cobalt common colors
Memory Lane	Astor	Blue Ridge		Pink, deep red, and yellow flowers
Memory Lane		Royal		
Memphis	Colonial	Blue Ridge		Pastel flowers, brown and black leaves, hatch-mark border
Mermaid	Ballerina	Universal	1950	Abstract
Merrileaf	True China	Red Wing	1960	Floral
Mesa	Encanto	Franciscan		
Metlox Poppy Trail, see Poppy Trail				
*Mexicana	Century	Homer Laughlin	1930s	Decal; orange and yellow pots of cacti
Mexicana	Montecito	Vernon Kilns	1950; 1954	Dark brown, rust, and yellow bands on border
Mexicana		W. S. George		Colored rim

PATTERN	SHAPE	MAKER	DATE	DESCRIPTION
Mexicana Kitchen Kraft		Homer Laughlin	1938	Mexican decals, scenes with different colored bands
*Mexi-Gren		W. S. George	1930s	Mexican-style archway, pots, blanket; green rim
Mexi-Lido		W. S. George		Mexican-style pots
Meylinda	Colonial	Blue Ridge		Red, yellow, and blue flowers; gray leaves
Michigan Coastline	Montecito	Vernon Kilns	1937	Lake Michigan coast; blue and black on ivory ground
Mickey	Colonial	Blue Ridge		Red and pink flowers; green and gold leaves
Middlebury	Cavalier	Royal		Ironstone; large flower-burst center design
Midnight Rose	Anniversary	Red Wing	1953	Rose
Midsummer	Victory	Salem		Decals
Midsummer		Sebring-Limoges	1940	
Milkweed Dance	Montecito; Ultra	Vernon Kilns	1940	Floral pattern in blue, maroon
Ming Blossom	Woodcrest	Blue Ridge	1950s	Oriental motif; pink flowers, brown rim
Ming Tree (No. 4387)	Woodcrest	Blue Ridge	1950s	Gnarled tree; yellow dappled background
Ming Tree	Accent	E. M. Knowles	c.1954	
Mini Flowers	Deanna	E. M. Knowles		Small red flowers
Mirador		Homer Lauglin	1977-1978	
Mirasol	Mirasol	Franciscan		
Miss Terry	Teapot	Hall		H/3 mark; gold dots; also called Ohio
Moby Dick	Ultra	Vernon Kilns	1939	Blue, brown, maroon, and orange; whaling scene
Mod Tulip	Colonial	Blue Ridge		Two red and yellow striped tulips with green leaves
Modern		J. A. Bauer	1935	Solids
*Modern California	Montecito	Vernon Kilns	1937-1947	Azure, gray, ivory, orchid, Pistachio, Sand, Straw
Modern Classic	Four Seasons	E. M. Knowles	1960-1963	
Modern Orchid	Round; Trend	Paden City		Large center orchid; gold border
Modern Tulip	Plymouth	Harker	1930s	Stencil-type tulip design; muted colors
*Moderne	Teapot	Hall	1930s	Gold foot, knob, and inside of spout
Mojave	San Marino	Vernon Kilns	1955	Brown, green, yellow bands on rim
Monk's Head	Tankard/ flagon	Hall		Decal of friar's head
Monogram		Salem		Gold initialed
Montecito	Montecito	Vernon Kilns	1935	

PATTERN	SHAPE	MAKER	DATE	DESCRIPTION
*Monterey		J. A. Bauer	1934-early 1940s	Burgundy, ivory, light blue, orange-red, turquoise, red-brown, yellow, white
Monterey		Stangl	1967-1968; 1970	
Monterey	Melinda	Vernon Kilns	1942; 1950-1954	Red and blue leaf border
*Monterey Moderne		J. A. Bauer	1948-1962	Black, burgundy, chartreuse, dark brown, gray, olive green, pink, yellow
Montgomery Ward	Refrigerator ware	Hall	Early 1940s	Delphinium, Mid-white
*Monticello	E-Shape	Hall	1941-1959	Border; small, individual, pale flowers (made for Sears)
Monticello		Steubenville		
Montmartre	Futura	Red Wing	1960	French street scene
Moon Flower		Salem		
Moon Song		J. A. Bauer		
Morning	Teapot	Hall		Solid colors or decals; sets with matching sugar and creamer
Morning Blue		Stangl	1970	
*Morning Glory	Kitchenware	Hall	1942-1949	Cadet Blue with Hi-white features and morning glory; decal
Morning Glory	Concord	Red Wing	1947	
Morning Glory	Shenandoah	Paden City		Floral sprays
Morning Glory	Montecito	Vernon Kilns		Turquoise and blue flowers
Morningside	Delphian	Taylor, Smith, and Taylor	Late 1920s	Flower garden scene
Moss Rose (No. 4486)	Trailway	Blue Ridge	1950s	Hand painted
Moss Rose	Criterion	E. M. Knowles	1954	
Moss Rose		Universal Potteries	1953-1955	Decals
Mother Hubbard	Kiddieware	Stangl	Mid-1940s-1974	
Mountain Aster	Colonial	Blue Ridge		Pink and blue flowers
Mountain Bells	Colonial	Blue Ridge		Pink flowers
Mountain Cherry		Blue Ridge	1951	
Mountain Flower		Hall	1940	Cobalt; floral design; red line treatment
Mountain Ivy	Candlewick	Blue Ridge	1951	Two-tone green leaves, border
Mountain Laurel		Stangl	1947-1957	

PATTERN	SHAPE	MAKER	DATE	DESCRIPTION
Mountain Nosegay	Candlewick	Blue Ridge		Blue tulip and multicolored flowers
Mountain Sweetbriar	Skyline	Blue Ridge	1950s	Pink flowers
*Mt. Vernon	E-Line	Hall	1941	Wreath with center decal of pink and green flowers; Granitetone; for Sears, Roebuck and Co.
Multi Flori California	Montecito	Vernon Kilns	1935-1937	Petal outlined in blue, brown, green, rose, yellow; ivory ground
Mums		Hall	1930s	Pink mums
*Mums		Taylor, Smith, and Taylor		Pink flowers; black and blue leaves
Muriel	Square; Colonial	Blue Ridge		Yellow and pink floral
Murphy	Teapot	Hall	Early 1940s	Victorian style; see also Benjamin, Birch, Bowknot, Connie, Plume
Nadine	Colonial	Blue Ridge		Floral
Nassau		Homer Laughlin		Border of large roses
Nassau	Concord	Red Wing	1947	
Nasturtium	Shell-Crest; Shenandoah	Paden City	1940s	Bright orange flower
Native American	Montecito	Vernon Kilns	1935-1937	Scenes of the Southwest; soft pastel colors
*Native California	Melinda	Vernon Kilns	1942-1947	Pastels: aqua, blue, green, pink, yellow
Nautical	Candlewick	Blue Ridge		
Nautilus	Teapot	Hall	1939	Seashell design
Navajo		Crown		Navajo design; red banded rim
Navarra	Williamsburg	E. M. Knowles	1955	
Neville		W. S. George		Small rosebuds interspersed on colored border; sold by Sears, Roebuck
New Art	New Art	Homer Laughlin	1930s	Solid colors
New Princess		Sebring-Limoges		
*New York	Teapot	Hall	1920	Gold-decorated line; many sizes
Newport	Teapot	Hall	Early 1930s	Solid colors, gold decoration, or black decal
Newport		Stangl	1940-1942	Blue shading from dark to pale; matte finish; sailboat
Night Flower	Skyline	Blue Ridge	1952	White flowers on dark background
Night Song	Cavalier	Royal		Ironstone; bold patterned border
No. 488	Kitchenware	Hall	1930s	Flower decal
Nocturne	Colonial	Blue Ridge		Rose-red flower; red brushed edge

PATTERN	SHAPE	MAKER	DATE	DESCRIPTION
Nora, see Norris				
Nordic		Homer Laughlin	1977-1978	
Nordic Flower	Americana	E. M. Knowles	1959	
Norma	Colonial	Blue Ridge		Pink and blue flower border, green rim
Norma		Stangl		Della-Ware mark; pear branch in center; rings of color on rim
Normandy	Skyline	Blue Ridge	1950s	Two designs—one man, one woman—on sponged willow background; brown rim
Normandy	Provincial	Red Wing	1941	Blue and maroon bands, later apple blossoms added
Normandy Plaid		Purinton	1936-1959	Red plaid
Norris	Refrigerator ware	Hall	1950s	Water server in blue, canary, green lustre; also called Nora
North Star Cherry	Colonial	Blue Ridge		Cherries on border; red rim
North Wind	Montecito	Vernon Kilns	1948	Dark green and lime
Northern Lights	Futura	Red Wing	1960	Geometric blue
Norway Rose		Homer Laughlin		Floral decal
Nut Tree	Nut Tree	Franciscan		
Nutcracker	Ultra	Vernon Kilns	1940	Brown print border
Oakleaf	Criterion	E. M. Knowles	1955	
Oasis		Franciscan	1955	Mondrian-type design in soft blue and gray
Obion	Candlewick	Blue Ridge		Red and yellow flower; red border
Octagon	Octagon	Catalina	1930s	Solids
October	October	Franciscan	1977	
Ohio, see Miss Terry				
Oklahoma, see Plainsman				
*Old Curiosity Shop	Cavalier	Royal China	1940s	Scenic center design; elaborate border
Old Dutch		Sebring-Limoges		
Old English		Homer Laughlin		Decal scene with castle
Old Mexico	Alara	Limoges		
Old Orchard		Stangl	1941-1942	
Old Provincial		Red Wing	1943	Aqua, brown bottom
Olena-Aztec	Montecito	Vernon Kilns	1937	Floral and geometric Aztec design; blue, green, rose, yellow; ivory ground
Olivia		Stangl		Della-Ware mark
Orange Blossom	Regina	Paden City		
Orange Poppy, see Poppy (Hall)				

PATTERN	SHAPE	MAKER	DATE	DESCRIPTION
Orange Tree	Orange Tree	Homer Laughlin		Raised design on outside of nested bowls
Orbit		Homer Laughlin	1960s	Streamlined design; avocado, brown, and other colors
Orchard	Ultra	Vernon Kilns	1937; 1939	Hand-painted fruit design
Orchard Glory	Colonial	Blue Ridge		Yellow pear and red apple; broken green rim
*Orchard Song		Stangl	1962-1974	Green and orange stylized fruit
*Organdie	Montecito	Vernon Kilns	1940-1958	Overall brown pattern; yellow and brown plaid border; see also Calico; Coronation Organdy; Gingham; Homespun; Tam O'Shanter; Tweed
*Organdy		Homer Laughlin		Pastel border on eggshell; green handles
Oriental Poppy	Colonial	Blue Ridge		Three red poppies; red border
Orion	Colonial	Blue Ridge		Blue flowers; blue and black leaves
Orleans	Provincial	Red Wing	1941	Red rose
Oslo	Mayfair	E. M. Knowles	1954	
Our America		Vernon Kilns	1939	Dark blue, maroon, and walnut brown on cream ground
Our Barnyard Friends	Kiddieware	Stangl		
Overtrue	Cavalier	Royal		Ironstone; bold center design
Paden Rose		Paden City		Large pale rose and bud
*Painted Daisy	Colonial	Blue Ridge		Red, blue, yellow, and green flowers; broken green rim
Painted Desert	Ballerina	Universal	1950	Abstract
Paisley		Stangl	1963-1967	
Palm Tree	New Art	E. M. Knowles		
Palm Tree		Purinton	1936-1959	Two palm trees
Palo Alto	Encanto	Franciscan		
Pan American Lei	Lotus	Vernon Kilns	1950	Lei design on pink ground
Pandora	Colonial	Blue Ridge		Floral design
Pansy		Harker		Pastel flowers
Pantry Shelf	Yorktown	E. M. Knowles		
Paper Roses	Colonial	Blue Ridge		
*Parade	Teapot	Hall	1942	Canary common color; also called Drape
Paradise	Coupe	Homer Laughlin		
Park Lane	Heritage	E. M. Knowles	1955	
Parsley	Salem	Salem		

PATTERN	SHAPE	MAKER	DATE	DESCRIPTION
Partridge Berry	Skyline	Blue Ridge	1950s	Yellow pear-like flower, red berry border
Passy	Ballerina	Universal	1950	Abstract
Pastel Garden	Sabina	Sabin		
Pastel Morning Glory	D-Style	Hall	1930s	Pink flowers
Pastel Poppy	Astor	Blue Ridge		Pink flowers and border
*Pastel Tulip		Harker		Floral decals
Patchwork Posy	Colonial	Blue Ridge		Red plaid; blue plaid flowers
*Pate Sur Pate		Harker		Scalloped border; solid colors
Pate-Sur-Pate	Shalimar	Steubenville		
Patio	Shell-Crest	Paden City	1907-1950s	Mexican decal decoration
Patricia	Skyline	Blue Ridge	1950s	Brown and gray flowers; also called Phoenix
Patrician	Refrigerator ware	Hall	1938	Westinghouse; Delphinium, Lettuce
Pauda (Freesia)	Pauda	Franciscan		Hand painted
Pauline	Astor	Blue Ridge		Yellow flowers; wide yellow and thin brown border
Peach		Pottery Guild		Peaches and lavender flowers
Peach Blossom	Bolero	W. S. George		Sprigs of small pink flowers (Cynthia has same decal on Lido shape)
Peach Blossom	Hallcraft	Hall		Designed by Eva Zeisel
Peach Blossom	Accent	E. M. Knowles	1955	
Pear		Pottery Guild		Fruit grouping
Pear Turnpike		Vernon Kilns		Brown
Peasant Ware, see Hercules				
Pebble Beach	Pebble Beach	Franciscan		
Pedro & Conchita	Montecito	Vernon Kilns	1937	Indian man and woman
Pembrooke	Colonial	Blue Ridge		Yellow flowers; pink dot border
Pennsylvania Dutch		Purinton	1936-1959	Red and blue plaid tulips around border
Penny Serenade	Colonial	Blue Ridge		Red and blue flowers, green leaves, border
Penthouse	Yorktown	E. M. Knowles		Flowerpots
Peony	Colonial	Blue Ridge		Centered large pink flower; pink and green line border
Peony Bouquet	Candlewick	Blue Ridge		One pink and three blue flowers
*Pepe	New Shape	Red Wing	1963	Geometric; Bittersweet, dark bluish-purple, and green

PATTERN	SHAPE	MAKER	DATE	DESCRIPTION
Periwinkle	Astor	Blue Ridge		Two-tone blue flower and leaves
*Petalware		W. S. George	Late 1930s	Solid colors: black, blue, coral, ivory, pink, red, turquoise
Peter Rabbit	Kiddieware	Stangl		
Petit Point		Crown	1941	Flower bouquet, stitch effect
Petit Point		Leigh/Crescent		Floral border, stitch effect
Petit Point		Sold by Montgomery Ward	1936	Decals, stitch effect
Petit Point		Taylor, Smith, and Taylor		
Petit Point Basket		Salem		Flower basket; stitch effect
Petit Point Bouquet	Delphian	Taylor, Smith, and Taylor	Late 1920s	Stitched flowers
*Petit Point House		Crooksville		Decal of stitched houses, trees; also called House
Petit Point Leaf		Crooksville		Decals, stitched
*Petit Point Rose		Harker		Rose border, stitched
Petit Point Rose	Fleurette	W. S. George		Stitched floral
Petite Flowers		Stangl	1970-1974	
Petitpoint		Homer Laughlin	1960s	Floral decal like stitched petit point
Petunia	Colonial	Blue Ridge		Red and blue flowers, border
Petunia		Hall	1932-1969	Pink floral decal
Phacelia	Montecito	Vernon Kilns		Pink flowers
Pheasant	LaGrande	Crooksville		Flying birds; scenic
*Philadelphia	Teapot	Hall	1923	Variety of colors, decals, or gold trim; many sizes
Philodendron	Melinda	Vernon Kilns	1942; 1950-1954	Green and yellow leaf border
Phoenix, see Patrician				
Picardy	Clinchfield	Blue Ridge		Centered man, woman, and ducks; pink border
Picardy	Village Green	Red Wing	1960	Yellow rose
Picket Fence	Yorktown	E. M. Knowles		Brightly colored floral and fence
Picnic	Picnic	Franciscan		
Pie Crust		Stangl	1969	
Piedmont Plaid	Square	Blue Ridge		Brown plaid on yellow swirled background
Pilgrims	Skyline	Blue Ridge	1950s	Figures in center; flowered border

PATTERN	SHAPE	MAKER	DATE	DESCRIPTION
Pine Cone		Harker		Wispy, brown design
Pinecone	Skyline	Blue Ridge	1950s	Pinecones with gray swirled background
Pinecone Spray	Fiesta	Homer Laughlin		Decal
Pink Border	LaGrande	Crooksville		Tiny pink floral border
Pink Carousel	Kiddieware	Stangl	Mid-1940s-1974	
Pink Cosmos		Stangl	1966	Marked Prestige
Pink Dogwood	Moderne	Blue Ridge	1950s	Stylized
Pink Dogwood	Classique	E. M. Knowles	1960	
Pink Dogwood		Stangl		
Pink Fairy	Kiddieware	Stangl	Mid-1940s-1974	
Pink Lady	Vernon Ware	Metlox	1965	
Pink Lily		Stangl	1953-1957	
Pink Morning Glory		Hall		Early decal
Pink Moss Rose		Homer Laughlin	1920	Decal
Pink Mums		Hall	1930s	Floral decals
Pink Pastel		E. M. Knowles		Pale pink and white with pink flowers
Pink Petticoat	Colonial	Blue Ridge		Pink flowers; rim
Pink Print		Sold by Montgomery Ward	1936	Decals
Pink Rose		Homer Laughlin	1920	Decals
Pink Rose & Daisy	Plain Edge	Homer Laughlin	1920	Decals
Pink Spice	Anniversary	Red Wing	1953	Butterfly design
Pinkie	Skyline	Blue Ridge	1950s	Pink flowers; sponged center; green rim
Pintoria		Metlox	c.1939	
Pippin	Skyline	Blue Ridge	1950s	Three red apples; green rim

Plaid, see Calico; Gay Plaid; Gingham; Homespun; Organdie; Tam O'Shanter; Tweed

Plain (Hall), see Queen

Plain	Gypsy Trail	Red Wing	1935	Blue, ivory, orange, turquoise, yellow
Plain-Jane	Lido	W. S. George	1949-present	black, brown, gold, green, red, yellow
Plainsman		Frankoma		Also called Oklahoma
*Plantation Ivy	Skyline	Blue Ridge	1950s	Yellow and green ivy
Playful Pups	Kiddieware	Stangl	Mid-1940s-1974	
Plaza	Regrigerator ware	Hall	1930s-1960s	Water server
Plum	Candlewick	Blue Ridge		Purple fruit
Plum		Stangl	1940	Blue, green, tan

PATTERN	SHAPE	MAKER	DATE	DESCRIPTION
*Plum Blossom	Dynasty	Red Wing	1949	Pink or yellow flower, oriental motif; six-sided
Plum Duff	Candlewick	Blue Ridge		Two plums; gray and gold swirled background
Plum Pudding	Kitchenware	Hall		White bowls with holly decals
Plume	Astor	Blue Ridge		Three rose plums; rose border; light blue rim
Plume	Teapot	Hall	Early 1940s	Victorian style; see also Benjamin, Birch, Bowknot, Connie, Murphy
Pocahontas	Commonwealth	James River Pottery		
Poinsettia	Colonial	Blue Ridge	1950	Hand-painted red flowers, gray leaves
Polka Dot	Colonial	Blue Ridge		Flowers, center, random dots
Polka Dot		Hall	1942	
Polo	Tricone	Salem		Decals
Polychrome A	Montecito	Vernon Kilns	1935-1937	Rims decorated with brightly colored blocks
Pom Pom	Candlewick	Blue Ridge		Red and blue flower; red border
Pomegranate	Montecito	Vernon Kilns	1935-1937	Pink with ivory
Pompadour	Sabina	Sabin	c.1946	
Pompeii	New Shape	Red Wing	1962	Geometric
Pony Tail	Kiddieware	Stangl	Mid-1940s-1974	
Poppy		Crown		Floral center; pastel vinelike border
Poppy	Rainbow	W. S. George		Center design of three flowers
*Poppy	C-Line	Hall	1933-1950s	Floral decals; orange poppies
Poppy	Deanna	E. M. Knowles	1948	Orange floral spray
Poppy	Shenandoah	Paden City		Floral border
*Poppy & Wheat	Radiance; Kitchenware	Hall	1933-c.1939	Orange flowers, green leaves
*Poppy Trail		Metlox	1934-1942	15 solid colors, including Delphinium Blue, Canary Yellow, ivory, Old Rose, peach, Poppy Orange, rust, turquoise
Posey Shop	Triumph	Sebring-Limoges	1944-1945	
Posies	LaGrande	Crooksville		Pastel flowers
Posies	Coupe	Paden City		Abstract flowers
Posies		Stangl	1973	
Potpourri	Colonial	Blue Ridge		Off-centered floral; black line border
*Prelude		Stangl	1949-1957	Stylized flower design

PATTERN	SHAPE	MAKER	DATE	DESCRIPTION
Pretty Pinks	Accent	E. M. Knowles	1957	
Primitive Bird, see Bird				
Primrose Path	Astor	Blue Ridge		Red, yellow, and blue flower border
*Prince	Refrigerator ware	Hall	c.1952	Westinghouse; Turk Blue and Daffodil; also called Adonis
Priscilla	Clinchfield	Blue Ridge		Red and blue flowers, center and border
*Priscilla	Kitchen Kraft	Homer Laughlin	1940s-1950s	Pale pink roses and sprigs of flowers
Pristine	Colonial	Blue Ridge		Blue flowers and leaves, border
Provincial	Kitchenware	Hall	1938	Clay-colored with American Indian
Provincial		Stangl	1957-1967	Floral center; border
Provincial Blue	Poppytrail line	Metlox	1951	
Provincial Bouquet	Tempo	Knowles	1961-1963	
*Provincial Fruit	Poppytrail	Metlox	c.1965-1980	Solid border with cluster of fruit in center
Provincial Tulip		Harker	1959	Cameoware
Provincial Wreath		Harker		Stoneware; Pennsylvania Dutch design
Puppy-Flower	Floral edge	E. M. Knowles	1933-1934	Decals
Puritan	Royal Gadroon	Harker		Plain white
Pussy Willow		W. S. George		
Quaker Maid		Harker	1960s	Dark brown, drips of lighter color
Quartette	Concord	Red Wing	1947	Four solid colors
Queen	Refrigerator ware	Hall		Westinghouse ovenware; Delphinium
Queen Anne's Lace	Skyline	Blue Ridge	1950s	Dark flowers; brown, gray, and green leaves
Queen Anne's Lace	Esquire	E. M. Knowles	1955-1962	Russel Wright; abstract decal
Queen Rose	Coupe	Crooksville		Pastel rose stem; also called Dinner Rose
Quilted Fruit		Blue Ridge	1950s	Fruit design, printed calicos
Quilted Ivy	Woodcrest	Blue Ridge	1950s	Red plaid, black, and yellow ivy
R.F.D.	San Fernando	Vernon Kilns	1953-1954	Brown rooster; green plaid border
Radiance, see Sunshine				
Radiant Ware	Kitchenware	Hall	1940s	Bowls; blue, green, red, yellow

PATTERN	SHAPE	MAKER	DATE	DESCRIPTION
Raffia	San Marino	Vernon Kilns	1953-1954	Green and brown; like tree bark
Rainbow		Hall		Hall's Radiant ware
Rainbow	Rainbow	W. S. George	Late 1930s	Solid colors
Rainelle	Colonial	Blue Ridge		Bold pastel flowers
Raisin	Ring	Vernon Kilns		Drip glaze; solids
Rambler Rose	Aristocrat	E. M. Knowles	1930s	Decals
Rambler Rose		Universal		Rose medallions
*Rancho	Zephyr	French Saxon		Solid dark colors
*Random Harvest		Red Wing	1961	Hand-painted brown, copper, coral, green, and turquoise on flecked dish
Ranger		Stangl		Cowboys and cactus
Ranger Boy	Kiddieware	Stangl	Mid-1940s-1974	
Rawhide		Harker	1960s	Stoneware; dark brown
Raymond	Yellowstone	Homer Laughlin	1926	Floral decal
Raymor		Roseville (Ben Siebel)	1952-1953	Black, brown, dark green, gray, ivory, mottled green, rust; modern
Raymore	Contempora	Steubenville (Ben Siebel)		Three-dimensional rippling; charcoal, Fawn, Mist gray, Sand white
Razzle Dazzle	Skyline	Blue Ridge	1950s	Black, gray, and red leaves; sponged background
Red & Gold		Sold by Montgomery Ward	1936	Decals
Red Apple		Blue Ridge		Center apple; green rim
Red Apple 1		Harker		Small, continuous apple decal
Red Apple 2		Harker		Large, individual apple decal
Red Bank		Blue Ridge		Red and blue flowers; green leaves border
Red Barn	Skyline	Blue Ridge	1950s	Red barn and fence; yellow sponged background; brown rim
Red Berry	Victory	Salem		Decals
Red Cone Flower	Clinchfield	Blue Ridge		Large red flower and bud; green, blue, and yellow leaves
Red Dot	Kitchenware	Hall		Red dot on Eggshell white
Red Ivy		Stangl	1957	
*Red Poppy	D-Line	Hall	1930-1950	Made for Grand Union Tea Company; red flowers, black leaves
*Red Riding Hood	Figural	Hull	1943-1957	Three-dimensional little girl; also called Little Red Riding Hood

PATTERN	SHAPE	MAKER	DATE	DESCRIPTION
Red Rooster	Skyline	Blue Ridge		Red and blue rooster center, red rim
*Red Rooster Provincial	Poppytrail line	Metlox	1955-1980	Red, yellow and green rooster; some solid red
Red Rose		Paden City		Red rose decal, rosebud decal
Red Starflower, see Starflower				
Red Tulip	Candlewick	Blue Ridge		Red tulip border
Red Tulip	Kitchen Kraft	Homer Laughlin		Decals
Red Willow	Colonial	Blue Ridge		Red oriental scene; rim
Red Wing Rose	Futura	Red Wing	1960	Rose
Reed	Gypsytrail	Red Wing	1935	Blue, ivory, orange, turquoise, yellow
Reflection	Four Seasons	E. M. Knowles	1960-1963	
Refrigerator ware, see Aristocrat; Bingo; Emperor; General Electric; Hotpoint; King; Montgomery Ward; Norris; Patrician; Plaza; Prince; Queen; Sears, Roebuck and Co.				
Regal	Teapot	Hall		By J. Palin Thorley
Regal Rings	Queen Anne	Sabin	c.1946	
Remembrance	Citation	Steubenville		
Rhapsody	Colonial	Blue Ridge		Blue, pink, and yellow flowers; yellow border
Rhea	Trend	Steubenville		
Rhonda	Americana	E. M. Knowles	1958	
Rhythm	Teapot	Hall	1939	Cadet, Canary, Chinese Red common colors
*Rhythm		Homer Laughlin	1951-1958	Harlequin colors; simple, modern shapes
Rhythm		Paden City	1936	
*Rhythm Rose	Century	Homer Laughlin	Mid-1940s-1950s	Large center rose
Rialto		Stangl		Della-Ware mark; yellow flowers on blue background
Ribbed, see Flute				
Ribbon	Criterion	E. M. Knowles	1954	
Ribbon Plaid	Skyline	Blue Ridge	1950s	Green and yellow
Richmond	E-Style	Hall	1941	Granitetone; yellow daisies and other flowers
Rick-Rack		Blair		Yellow and brown
Ridge, see King				
Ridge Rose	Colonial	Blue Ridge		Pink flower; broken pink border
Ring-A-Round	Four Seasons	E. M. Knowles	1959-1963	
Ring-O-Roses	Piecrust	Blue Ridge	1948	Red rosebud border

PATTERN	SHAPE	MAKER	DATE	DESCRIPTION
*Ring		J.A. Bauer	1932-1962	Solids: black, burnt orange, dark blue, green, ivory, maroon, yellow; pastels: chartreuse, gray, green, light yellow, olive, pale blue, pink, turquoise, white; also called Beehive
Ringles		Stangl	1973-1974	
Rio		Salem	1943	
Rio Chico	Ultra	Vernon Kilns	1938	Pink border; center floral design
Rio Verda	Ultra	Vernon Kilns	1938	Green border; center floral design
Rio Vista	Ultra	Vernon Kilns	1938	Blue border; center floral design
Rite of Spring		Paden City		
*Riviera	Century	Homer Laughlin	1938-1950	Made for Murphy Co.; solids: blue, dark blue, ivory, light green, mauve, red, yellow
Roan Mountain Rose	Colonial	Blue Ridge		Pink flowers; bold green leaves; pink line border
Roanoke	Astor	Blue Ridge		Red, blue, and yellow flowers
Rock Garden	Skyline	Blue Ridge	1950s	Small blue and gray flowers; gray rim
Rock-Mount		Coors	Late 1930s	Colored tableware and ovenware; blue, green, ivory, orange, rose, yellow
Rock Castle	Skyline	Blue Ridge	1950s	Gray and brown leaves
Rock Rose	Colonial	Blue Ridge		Hand painted; pink flowers and green leaves
Rockport Rooster	Candlewick	Blue Ridge		Stylized rooster center
Rococo	Princess	Paden City	1933	
Rodelay	Tempo	E. M. Knowles	1961-1963	
Romance	Cavalier	Homer Laughlin		
Romance	Regent	E. M. Knowles	1955	
*Ronald Reagan	Teapot	Hall	1970s	Three-dimensional caricature resembling Ronald Reagan
*Rooster (or Game Cock)		Blue Ridge	1950s	Red rooster
Rooster		Harker		Blue, pink; cameoware
Rooster		Stangl	1970-1974	Gold background; rooster center
Rooster Motto	Candlewick	Blue Ridge		Rooster center; "My love will stop when this rooster crows" on border
Rope Edge	Rope Edge	Catalina	1936	Solids

PATTERN	SHAPE	MAKER	DATE	DESCRIPTION
Rosalinde	Colonial	Blue Ridge		Pink, purple, and yellow flowers
Rose	Deanna	E. M. Knowles		Pale rose and buds
Rose & Lattice	Plain edge	Homer Laughlin	1920	Decals
Rose-A-Day	Anytime	Vernon Kilns	1956-1958	Pink rose, pastel leaves, ivory ground
Rose Bouquet	Floral edge	E. M. Knowles	1933-1934	
Rose Bud	Horizon	Steubenville		
Rose Garden	Gray Lure	Crooksville		Rose spray
Rose Garland		Crooksville	1920s	Border of tiny roses
Rose Garland Border		Homer Laughlin	1920	Decals
Rose Hill	Colonial	Blue Ridge		Pink, purple, and rose flowers
Rose Leaf		Syracuse		
Rose-Marie		Salem		Large cluster of rosebuds; platinum edge
Rose Marie		Sebring-Limoges		
Rose O'Day		Vernon Kilns		
*Rose Parade	Kitchenware	Hall	1941-1950s	Cadet Blue body, Hi-white knobs and handles; rose decals
Rose Point	Stafford Rose	Pope-Gosser		Embossed roses
Rose Red	Candlewick	Blue Ridge		Red flowers; green leaves border
Rose Spray		Harker		Allover pattern; tiny pink and yellow flowers
Rose Tree	Criterion	E. M. Knowles	1955	
*Rose White	Kitchenware	Hall	1941	Hi-white body; trimmed in silver with a pink floral decal
*Rosebud		Coors, Golden CO.	1920-1939	Blue, green, ivory, maroon, turquoise, yellow; raised rosebud and leaf design
Rosebud	Horizon	Steubenville		
Rosemont	Victoria	E. M. Knowles	1948	
Roses	Birds; Bolero	Crooksville		Multicolored flowers
Rosetta		Homer Laughlin		Bird hovering over flowers
Rosette	Colonial	Blue Ridge		Blue and yellow flowers; broken pink rim
Rosettes		Harker		Thin sprays of flowers on border and in center
Rosey	Moderne	Blue Ridge	1950s	
Rosita	Ranchero	W. S. George		Rose blossoms
Roundelay (No. 4499)	Trailway	Blue Ridge		
Round-up	Casual	Red Wing	1958	
Roxanna		Universal		Decals

PATTERN	SHAPE	MAKER	DATE	DESCRIPTION
Roxanne		Stangl	1972-1974	Blue flowers and rim
Royal	Teapot	Hall		White; some with gold
Royal Brocade	Forcast	E. M. Knowles	1957	
Royal Harvest	Coupe	Homer Laughlin		
Royal Marina	Sebring	Sebring-Limoges	1944-1945	
*Royal Rose	Kitchenware	Hall	late 1940s-early 1950s	Cadet Blue exterior; Hi-white handles and knobs; silver trim; floral decals
Royal Rose		Harker		Bright single rose decal
Royal Windsor		Salem	1950s	
Ruby	Clinchfield	Blue Ridge		Blue; large red flowers with blue centers border
Ruffled Tulip		Harker		Bright flowers
Rugosa	Colonial	Blue Ridge		Large yellow flowers with brown centers and green leaves

Russel Wright, see also American Modern; Botanica; Grass; Highlight; Iroquois; Queen Anne's Lace; Seeds; Solar; White Clover

PATTERN	SHAPE	MAKER	DATE	DESCRIPTION
Russel Wright		Bauer	1945	Art pottery
Russel Wright	Vitreous restaurant ware	Sterling	1948	Cedar brown, ivy green, straw yellow, suede gray
Rust Bouquet	LaGrande	Crooksville		Fall shades
Rust Floral	Lido	W. S. George		Predominantly orange flowers
Rust Tulip	Shell-Crest	Paden City		Assorted flowers
Rust Tulip	Victory	Salem		Assorted pastel flowers
Rustic		Stangl	1965-1974	
Rustic Garden		Stangl	1972-1974	Orange flowers; green border
*Rustic Plaid	Skyline	Blue Ridge	1950s	Black plaid and rim; sponged background
*Rutherford	Teapot	Hall		Smooth version of fluted kitchenware pot; white with trim, dots, or decals
Rutledge	Colonial	Blue Ridge		Blue bow, red tulips
Saf-Handle	Refrigerator ware	Hall	1938-1960s	Chinese Red most common color; also called Sundial
*Saf-Handle	Teapot	Hall	1938	Canary most common color; also called Sundial
Sailing	Georgette	W. S. George		Variety of boats on border
Sailing	Tricorne	Salem		Decals, coral and black sailboats
*Salamina	Ultra	Vernon Kilns	1939	Scenes of Greenland with girl
Sampler	Piecrust	Blue Ridge	1948	Red flower; green border
Sampler	Victory	Salem		Decals
Sandra		Salem	1950s	

PATTERN	SHAPE	MAKER	DATE	DESCRIPTION
Sani-Grid	Kitchenware	Hall	1941	Decal; Chinese Red, Cadet; Hi-white handle and knobs
Sani-Grid	Teapot	Hall	1941	Contrasting Hi-white handle and knob
Santa Anita	Melinda	Vernon Kilns	1942	Pink blossoms on border
Santa Barbara	Melinda	Vernon Kilns	1939	Brown print; blue and yellow flowers
Santa Maria	Melinda	Vernon Kilns	1939	Purple print; blue and yellow flowers
Santa Paula	Melinda	Vernon Kilns	1939	Pink print; blue and yellow flowers
Saratoga	Skyline	Blue Ridge	1952	
Sarepta	Colonial	Blue Ridge		Multicolored flowers; yellow border
Scandia	Accent	E. M. Knowles	1954	
Scotch Plaid	Coupe	Crooksville		Plaid center design
Scroll	Accent	E. M. Knowles	1955	
Sculptured Daisy	Poppytrail	Metlox	1965	
Sculptured Fruit		Stangl	1966-1974	Marked Prestige; fruit border
Sculptured Grape	Poppytrail line	Metlox	1963-1975	Sculpted grapevine; blue, brown, green
Sculptured Zinnia	Poppytrail	Metlox	1965-1980	Sculpted zinnias; brown, green, orange, yellow-gold on cream background
Sea Fare	Forcast	E. M. Knowles	1957	
Sea Shell		Paden City		
Sears, Roebuck and Co.	Refrigerator ware	Hall		Cadet, hi-white
Seeds	Esquire	E. M. Knowles	1956-1962	Russel Wright; abstract decal
September Song	Forcast	E. M. Knowles	1959	
Sequoia		E. M. Knowles	Late 1930s	Bright floral bouquet
*Serenade	D-Shape	Hall		Sprigs of orange flowers
*Serenade		Homer Laughlin	1940s	Solid pastels: blue, green, pink
Serenade	Classique	E. M. Knowles	1960	
Sesame		Stangl	1972-1974	Brown stylized flower and rim
Seven Seas	San Marino	Vernon Kilns	1954	Brown and blue sailboats
Sevilla				Solids, similar to Harlequin
Shadow Fruit	Skyline; Moderne	Blue Ridge	1950s	Stylized line drawing of fruit; green rim
Shadow Leaf	San Marino	Vernon Kilns	1954-1955	Red and green flowers on green swirled background

PATTERN	SHAPE	MAKER	DATE	DESCRIPTION
Shaggy Tulip	Kitchenware	Hall	Mid-1930s-mid-1940s	
Shalimar	Shalimar	Steubenville		
Shantung	San Marino	Vernon Kilns	1953	Cloth-like texture; brown and green
Sheffield		Salem	1943	
Shellridge		Harker		Gold decal design
Shellware, see Cameo Shellware				
Sherry	Colonial	Blue Ridge		Red and blue flower, border
*Sherwood	Anytime	Vernon Kilns	1955-1958	Brown, bronze, and gold leaves on beige background
Shoo Fly	Colonial	Blue Ridge		Yellow and pink flowers
Shortcake	Lido	W. S. George		Strawberry decal
Showgirl	Candlewick	Blue Ridge		Red and yellow flowers; broken green rim
Sierra		Stangl	1967/1968-1970	Marked Prestige
Sierra Madre	Ultra	Vernon Kilns	1938	Pink, green, blue border
Signal Flags	Piecrust	Blue Ridge	1948	Red and black squares
*Silhouette		Crooksville	1930s	Silhouette decal; dog included
Silhouette	Skyline	Blue Ridge	1950s	Clothlike appearance; various colors
Silhouette		Hall	1930s	Black decal
Silhouette		Harker		
Silhouette		Taylor, Smith, and Taylor		
Silver Rose		Homer Laughlin	1960s	Floral decals
Silver Spray	Accent	E. M. Knowles	1954	
Simplicity	Accent	E. M. Knowles	1955	
Skiffs	Yorktown	E. M. Knowles		
Skyblue		Homer Laughlin	1977-1978	
Skylark	Americana	E. M. Knowles	1959	
Skyline Songbirds	Skyline	Blue Ridge	1950s	Eight different birds
*Skytone		Homer Laughlin		Light blue
Sleeping Mexican	Deanna	E. M. Knowles		Mexican style; man sleeping under palm tree
Slender Leaf		Harker		Gray border; graceful leaf design
Smart Set	Casual	Red Wing	1955	
Smoky Mountain Laurel	Candlewick	Blue Ridge		Solid light blue with dark blue border
Smooth		J.A. Bauer	1936-1937	Solids
Snappy	Colonial	Blue Ridge		Red and blue flower
Snowflake		Homer Laughlin	1920	Decals

PATTERN	SHAPE	MAKER	DATE	DESCRIPTION
Snowflake		Sold by Montgomery Ward	1936	Decals
Snowflower		E. M. Knowles	1956	Russel Wright
Soddy-Daisy	Skyline	Blue Ridge	1950s	Small brown and cream flowers; red and green leaves; allover pattern
Solar	Esquire	E. M. Knowles	1957-1966	Russel Wright; abstract decal
Sombrero		Pottery Guild		Brightly colored fruit in straw basket
Sonata	Skyline	Blue Ridge	1950s	Blue flowers; pink buds
Sonesta		Homer Laughlin	1977-1978	
Songbirds	Astor	Blue Ridge		Eight different bird designs
Sorrento		Homer Laughlin	1977-1978	
Southern Belle	Coupe; Iva-Lure	Crooksville		Large single rosebud
Southern Camelia	Piecrust	Blue Ridge	1948	Pink flower, blue leaves, broken blue rim
Southern Dogwood	Skyline	Blue Ridge	1950s	Hand-painted cream dogwood
Southern Rose	Melinda	Vernon Kilns	1942	Floral bouquet
Southwind	Forcast	E. M. Knowles	1959	
Sowing Seed	Square	Blue Ridge		Farmer; broken blue border
Speck Ware		J.A. Bauer	1946	Gray, pink, tan, white
Spice Islands	Montecito	Vernon Kilns	1950	Map of East and West Indies; sailing ships; marked "da Bron"
Spider, see Spring Blossom				
Spiderweb	Skyline	Blue Ridge	1950s	Various solid colors, flecked finish
Spindrift	Candlewick	Blue Ridge		Center circle of small blue, red, and yellow flowers; thin red border
Spray	Piecrust	Blue Ridge	1950s	Small black and yellow flowers; green leaves
Spray	Coupe	Crooksville		Pink ground; gray and black decal
Sprig Crocus		Hall		Several sprigs on border
Spring	Trend	Steubenville		
Spring Blossom	LaGrande	Crooksville	1940s	Delicate floral sprays; also called Spider
Spring Bouquet		Sold for Montgomery Ward	1936	Decals
Spring Glory	Candlewick	Blue Ridge		Hand-painted blue flower and band
Spring Hill Tulip	Colonial	Blue Ridge		Centered plaid tulips

PATTERN	SHAPE	MAKER	DATE	DESCRIPTION
Spring Song	Cavalier	Homer Laughlin		
Spring Song	Concord	Red Wing	1947	Birds
Springblossom	Regina	Paden City		Large multicolored pastel flowers
Springtime		W. S. George	1940s	Open window with flower trellis
*Springtime		Hall		Pink flowers on Hi-white body
Springtime		Harker		Large single budding flower
Spun Gold		Stangl	1965-1967	
Square Dance	Colonial	Blue Ridge		Party set of square dancers
Squares	Skyline	Blue Ridge	1950s	Three squares and ribbon
Standard		Salem		Narrow floral sprays; blue edge
*Stanhome Ivy	Skyline	Blue Ridge	1950s	Stylized green ivy sprig
Star	Teapot	Hall	1940	Turquoise or cobalt with gold stars
Star Bright	Accent	E. M. Knowles	1957	
*Star Flower		Stangl	1952-1957	Large center flower
*Starburst		Franciscan	1954	Stylized geometric stars
Stardancer	Colonial	Blue Ridge		Two-handled vase with pink flowers
Stardust		Stangl	1967	
Stardust	Skytone	Homer Laughlin	1940s-1950s	Light blue background; stylized flowers
Starflower		Watt	1953-1965	Red flower with yellow center and green leaves
Starlight	Teapot	Hall		Band of stars; some with rhinestones
Step-Down	Coffeepot	Hall		Sugar and creamer; large and small sizes; different handles
Step-Round	Coffeepot	Hall		Large and small sizes; same handles
Sterling, see Russel Wright				
Still Life	Colonial	Blue Ridge		Bowl of fruit
Strathmoor	Colonial	Blue Ridge		Big dark and yellow flowers; broken rim
Stratosphere	Forcast	E. M. Knowles	1955	
Strawberry	Shenandoah	Paden City		Strawberry plant border
Strawberry Patch	Colonial	Blue Ridge		Strawberries; green and blue leaves
Strawberry Sundae	Skyline	Blue Ridge	1950s	Red strawberries; broken green rim
Streamers	Skyline	Blue Ridge	1950s	Ribbons
*Streamline	Teapot	Hall	1937	Canary and Delphinium most common colors; often silver trim
Style	Ultra	Vernon Kilns	1939	Fruit and floral border

PATTERN	SHAPE	MAKER	DATE	DESCRIPTION
Suburbia	Forcast	E. M. Knowles	1956	
Summer Day		Salem		Blue and white flowerpot with floral sprays
Sun Drops	Astor	Blue Ridge		Yellow and orange flowers, centered; miniature flowers border
Sun Garden	San Marino	Vernon Kilns	1953	Butterflies and flowers on green ground
Sun-Glo	Olympic	Harker	c.1955	Harmony House mark
Sun Glow	Forcast	E. M. Knowles	1958	
Sun Porch	Fiesta	Homer Laughlin		Decal; striped umbrella, table scene
Sunbright	Colonial	Blue Ridge		Yellow flowers, border; green line rim
Sunburst	Tempo	E. M. Knowles	1959	
Sundance	Candlewick	Blue Ridge		Large yellow flowers; border design
Sundial, see Saf-Handle				
Sunfire	Colonial	Blue Ridge		Yellow flowers, gray leaves
Sunflower		Blue Ridge	c.1947	Large flowers
Sundowner	Candlewick	Blue Ridge		Two blue and two yellow flowers around plate
Sungold	Candlewick	Blue Ridge		
*Sunny	Colonial	Blue Ridge		Yellow flowers
Sunny Day	Cavalier	Royal		Ironstone; large flower branch
Sunnybrook Farm	Accent	E. M. Knowles	1957	
Sunrise	Woodcrest	Blue Ridge	1950s	Sun rising behind a log cabin
Sunshine	Candlewick	Blue Ridge		Yellow flowers center; thin red border
Sunshine	Kitchenware	Hall	1933	Kitchenware; decals, lettering, solids; blue, Canary, Cadet, Chinese Red, Delphinium, Dresden Emerald, Indian Red, ivory, Lettuce, Marine, maroon, pink, rose, turquoise, Yellow
Sunshine		Stangl		
Surfside	Teapot	Hall	1939	Seashell-type pot
Susan	Skyline	Blue Ridge	1950s	Rust flowers
Susan		Stangl	1972-1974	Gold daisies and rim
Susan	Trend	Steubenville		
Susannah	Colonial	Blue Ridge		Pink and red flowers; thin red border; pink rim
Swedish		Crown		Modern flowers
Sweet Clover	Candlewick	Blue Ridge		

PATTERN	SHAPE	MAKER	DATE	DESCRIPTION
Sweet Pea	Colonial	Blue Ridge		Pastel blue and pink flowers on border; pink rim
Sweet Pea	Empire	Taylor, Smith, and Taylor		Pink decal
Sweet Rocket	Woodcrest	Blue Ridge	1950s	Brown and pink thistles; green rim
Swirl	Coupe	Crooksville		Flower sprigs on border pointing to center
Symmetry	Tempo	E. M. Knowles	1959	
Symphony	Colonial	Blue Ridge		Red flowers; blue leaves
*T-Ball	Teapot	Hall	1948	Square or round; silver; marked Made for Bacharach, Inc. of New York
Tahiti	Triumph	Sebring-Limoges	1938	
Tahitian Gold	New Shape	Red Wing	1962	Gold
*Tam O'Shanter	Montecito	Vernon Kilns	1939	Green, lime, and reddish-brown plaid; green border; see also Calico; Coronation Organdy; Gingham; Homespun; Organdie; Tweed
*Tampico	Futura	Red Wing	1955	Modernistic design
Tanglewood	Colonial	Blue Ridge		Pink flowers, green leaves, allover pattern
Tango		Homer Laughlin	1930s	Blue, green, yellow, and red solids
Taste	Ultra	Vernon Kilns	1939	Maroon fruit and floral border
*Taverne		Hall	1930s	Silhouette decal; serving pieces
*Taverne	Laurel	Taylor, Smith, and Taylor		Silhouette decal; no dog; dinnerware
Tazewell Tulips	Colonial	Blue Ridge		Striped tulips
Tea for Two/Tea for Four	Teapot	Hall		Angled top; no decoration
Tea Rose	Accent	E. M. Knowles	c.1954	
Tea Rose		Purinton	1936-1959	Two red rosebuds and broken dark rim
Teal Rose	Aladdin	Harker	1952	Wide border, large rose
Teataster	Teapot	Hall	late 1940s	For Teamaster; oval; two compartments
Tempo	Piecrust	Blue Ridge	1948	Red and yellow flowers; green rim
Terra Rose		Stangl	1941-1942	Giftware line; dinnerware patterns called fruits or tulip
Terrace Ceramics	Corn Shape	Terrace Ceramics		

PATTERN	SHAPE	MAKER	DATE	DESCRIPTION
Texas Rose	Candlewick	Blue Ridge		Yellow flower
Thanksgiving Turkey	Skyline	Blue Ridge	1950s	Turkey in center
Thermo-Porcelain		Coors		Canary-tone glaze with decal, white glaze with chrysanthemums
Think Pink	Candlewick	Blue Ridge		Two pink flowers, centered; dark pink border
Thistle	Trailway	Blue Ridge	1954	Thistle in center; wide gray border
Thistle		Hall		Muted floral
Thistle		French Saxon		
*Thistle		Stangl	1951-1967	Hand painted; purple and green decoration
Thistle		Universal		Decals
Thorley	Kitchenware	Hall		Small starbursts
Thorley	Teapot	Hall		
Tia Juana	Deanna	E. M. Knowles		Ivory, white background; Mexican decal
Tic Tack	Piecrust	Blue Ridge	1948	Apple, pear, cross-hatched center; broken green rim
*Tickled Pink	Colonial	Blue Ridge		Pink leaves and rim; gray dots
Tickled Pink	Anytime	Vernon Kilns	1955-1958	Pink and gray geometric designs
Tiffany	Accent	E. M. Knowles	1955	
Tiger Flower	Tiger Flower	Franciscan		Pink
Tiger Lily	Colonial	Blue Ridge		Red, yellow flowers
Tiger Lily		Stangl	1957-1962	Decal
Tiny Rose	Casual	Red Wing	1958	
Toledo Delight	Trojan	Sebring	1941-1942	
*Tom & Jerry		Hall	1930s	Tom & Jerry printed on punch bowl, mug
Tom Thumb & the Butterfly		Homer Laughlin		Child's set; decal
Touch of Black	Regina	Paden City		Pastel flower sprays with occasional black leaves
Touch of Brown		Taylor, Smith, and Taylor		Brown and white flowered decal
Tower		Leigh		
Town & Country		Red Wing	1946	Blue, chartreuse, Forest Green, Metallic Brown, rust, Sandy Peach
*Town & Country		Stangl	1970s	Black, blue, green, honey, yellow; graniteware look
Trade Winds	San Marino	Vernon Kilns	1954-1956	Rust and chartreuse flowers on swirled ground
Tradition	Regent	E. M. Knowles	1948	

PATTERN	SHAPE	MAKER	DATE	DESCRIPTION
Trailing Rose	Montecito	Vernon Kilns	1939	Blue and red flowers and leaves on ivory ground
Traveler		Syracuse	1937-1969	Railroad china; white, shaded pink, flying geese
Trellis	Duckbill	Crooksville	1929	Bright flowers on black trellis
Tricorne		Salem	1934	Red-orange; stripes; modern
Trinidad		Stangl	1972-1974	White background; aqua and brown flower burst; wide borders
Triple Treat	Cavalier	Royal		Ironstone; three modernistic flowers
Tritone	Teapot	Hall	1950s	Diagonal triangular sections of colors
Trojan	Trojan	Catalina Gladding, McBean and Co.	1930-1940s	Solids
Tropical	Skyline	Blue Ridge	1920-1957	Brown bamboo with green leaves
Trotter	Coupe	Crooksville		Racing horse
True Blue	Vernonware	Metlox	1965	
Tudor Rose	Sabina	Sabin		
*Tulip	D-Line	Hall	1930s-1950s	Decals; yellow and purple tulips
Tulip		Universal		Decals
*Tulip		Stangl	1942-1973	Blue or yellow tulip; Terra Rose mark
Tulip		Salem		Tulip and bud
Tulip		E. M. Knowles		Bright orange tulip
Tulip		Paden City		Floral bouquet
Tulip		Leigh/Crescent		Vivid tulips
Tulip Tree		Homer Laughlin	1977-1978	
Tulip Trio	Candlewick	Blue Ridge		Three red tulips
Tulip Wreath	Coupe	Homer Laughlin		
Tulips	Kitchen Kraft	Homer Laughlin	1930s	Decals on ovenware
Tulips		Pottery Guild		
Tulips		Taylor, Smith, and Taylor		
Tuliptime	Tempo	E. M. Knowles	1961-1963	Ruffled tulips
Tuliptime	Candlewick	Blue Ridge		Red, yellow, and purple tulips; green border
Tuna Salad	Skyline	Blue Ridge	1950s	Blue and brown fish
Turkey with Acorns	Skyline	Blue Ridge	1950s	
Turtle Dove	New Shape	Red Wing	1962	Two Doves

PATTERN	SHAPE	MAKER	DATE	DESCRIPTION
Tweed	Montecito	Vernon Kilns	1950-1955	Gray, blue plaid; see also Calico; Coronation Organdy; Gingham; Homespun; Organdie; Tam O'Shanter
Tweed Tex	Anniversary	Red Wing	1953	White
Twilight		Flintridge China Co.		
Twin Oaks	Accent	E. M. Knowles	c.1954	
*Twinspout	Teapot	Hall	Late 1940s	For Teamaster; round; two compartments
Twin-Tee	Teapot	Hall		Flat top; decorated in gold or decal
Two-Some	Montecito	Vernon Kilns	1938	Brown bands on cream ground
*Two Step	Village Green	Red Wing	1960	Geometric design
Two-Tone	Ultra	Vernon Kilns	c.1938	Wide border in blue, green, pink
Tyrol	Olivia	Steubenville		Aster, buttercup, carnation, gardenia
Ultra California	Ultra	Vernon Kilns	1937-1942	Blue, ivory, light green, maroon, pink, yellow
Unicoi	Clinchfield	Blue Ridge		Red and blue flowered border
Valley Violet	Astor	Blue Ridge		Small flowers
Vegetable Patch	Skyline	Blue Ridge	1950s	Corn and tomato on black sponged background
Veggie	Skyline	Blue Ridge	1950s	Vegetables
Veggies		Crooksville		
Vera	Ultra	Vernon Kilns	1938	Floral
Vermillion Rose	Triumph	Sebring-Limoges		
Vernon 1860	San Fernando	Vernon Kilns	1944; 1955	Scene of 1860s America in brown; floral border
Vernon Rose	San Fernando	Vernon Kilns	1944; 1950-1954	Yellow rose, blossoms; cream ground
Verona	Colonial	Blue Ridge		Large blue flowers, border
Veronica	Clinchfield	Blue Ridge		Yellow and red flowers and borders in center; wide green outer border
Vestal Rose		E. M. Knowles	1930s	Decals
Victoria	Colonial	Blue Ridge		Pink and yellow flowers; red rim
Victoria	Teapot	Hall	Early 1940s	Celadon only; Victorian style
Victoria	Americana	E. M. Knowles	1959	
Victoria	Montecito	Vernon Kilns	1939	Green flowers and leaves
Victory		Salem		Fluted border
Vienna	Victory	Salem	1940s	

PATTERN	SHAPE	MAKER	DATE	DESCRIPTION
Village Brown	Village Green	Red Wing	1955	Brown
Village Green	Village Green	Red Wing	1953	Green
Vine		Harker		Cameoware
Vine Yard	Vernonware	Metlox	1965	
Vine Wreath	Laurel	Taylor, Smith, and Taylor	1933-1934	Decals
Vintage	Colonial	Blue Ridge		Bold grapes, vine, and leaves
Vintage	Royal Gadroon	Harker	1947-1949	Red and green ivy
Vintage	Accent	E. M. Knowles	1953-1954	
Vintage	Lotus	Vernon Kilns	1950	Purple grapes, brown leaves
Vintage	True China	Red Wing	1960	Floral
Vintage Pink	Poppytrail	Metlox	1965	
Violet	Trend	Steubenville		
Violet Spray	Skyline	Blue Ridge	1950s	Off-centered large and small violet sprays
Violet Spray		Homer Laughlin	1920	Decals
*Virginia Rose	Virginia Rose	Homer Laughlin	1935-1960	Decal; spray of roses, leaves
*Vistosa		Taylor, Smith, and Taylor	1938	Solids: cobalt blue, deep yellow, light green, mango red
Vistosa		E. M. Knowles	1936	Solids: cadet blue, burgundy, red, russet, yellow
Vogue		Syracuse		
Wagon Wheels		Frankoma	1942	Solids: Clay Blue, Desert Gold, Onyx Black, Prairie Green, Red Bud
Waldorf		Sebring-Limoges	1939	
Waltz Time	Colonial	Blue Ridge		Pastel flowers, broken blue border
Wampum	Ranchero	W. S. George		Floral
Ward's Garland		Sold by Montgomery Ward	1936	Decals
Water Lily	Yorktown	E. M. Knowles		
Water Lily		Stangl	1949-1957	
Waterlily	Astor	Blue Ridge		Multicolored pastel flower; blue rim
Waverly		Homer Laughlin	1977-1978	
Weather Bloom	Squared-Off Edges	E. M. Knowles	1933-1934	Decals
Weathervane (No. 4277)	Skyline	Blue Ridge	1950s	House and tree; sponged yellow background; green rim
Weathervane	Forcast	E. M. Knowles	1957	

PATTERN	SHAPE	MAKER	DATE	DESCRIPTION
Wells Art Glaze		Homer Laughlin	c.1930-1935	Burnt orange matte, green, peach, rust, yellow, some ivory with decals
Westinghouse, see Aristocrat; Emperor; King; Patrician; Prince; Queen				
Westwind		Frankoma	1962	Solids
Wheat	Skyline	Blue Ridge	1950s	Three golden wheat stalks
Wheat		Harker	1961	Cameoware
Wheat	Deanna; Accent	E. M. Knowles	1954	Wheat stalks
Wheat	Melinda	Vernon Kilns	1942	Sheaths of wheat and blossom sprays; Harmony House mark and "Exclusively for Sears, Roebuck and Co."
Wheat		W. S. George		Brightly colored wheat stalks
Wheat (Hall), see Poppy & Wheat				
Wheat Sheaf	Criterion	E. M. Knowles	1955	
Wheatfield		Sebring-Limoges		
Whirligig	Piecrust; Colonial	Blue Ridge	1950s	Red and light blue flowers; green leaves and rim
White and Embossed		Sold by Montgomery Ward	1920	Decals
White & Gold		Homer Laughlin	1920	Decals
White & Gold Carnation		Homer Laughlin	1920	Decals
White & Green Persian		Homer Laughlin	1920	Decals
*White Clover		Harker		Russel Wright; engraved design; Charcoal, Coral Sand, Golden Spice, Meadow Green
White Dogwood		Stangl	1965-1974	Marked Prestige; white flowered border
White Gold Ware		Sebring	1940s	
White Grape		Stangl	1967	
*White Rose		Harker Potteries	1940s	Cameoware; blue or pink; outlined flowers in center
Wild Bouquet		Homer Laughlin	1977-1978	Corn-Kraft; made for Montgomery Ward
Wild Cherry #1	Skyline	Blue Ridge	1950s	Rust leaves; yellow cherries; broken green rim
Wild Cherry #2	Skyline	Blue Ridge	1950s	Pink and gray leaves; black rim
Wild Cherry #3	Piecrust	Blue Ridge	1950s	Cherries; yellow and brown leaves; broken green rim

PATTERN	SHAPE	MAKER	DATE	DESCRIPTION
Wild Irish Rose	Colonial	Blue Ridge		Red flowers border
Wild Oats		E. M. Knowles	1955	
Wild Poppy, see Poppy & Wheat				
Wild Rose		Crown	1941	Wild flowers and wheat sheaths
Wild Rose	Regent	E. M. Knowles	1948	
Wild Rose	Princess	Paden City		
Wild Rose	Colonial	Blue Ridge		Pink flowers
Wild Rose	Floral Edge	E. M. Knowles	1933-1934	Decals
Wild Rose		Homer Laughlin		Floral decals
Wild Rose		Stangl	1955-1973	
Wild Rose & Flower	Empress	Homer Laughlin	1920	Decals
Wild Strawberry	Colonial	Blue Ridge		Two strawberries; green rim
*Wildfire	D-Line	Hall	1950s	Hi-white body; floral garland decals
*Wildflower	Floral Edge	E. M. Knowles	1933-1934	Decals
Wildwood	Colonial	Blue Ridge		Red, pink, and yellow flowers, center, border
Wildwood		Stangl		
Williamsburg	Tempo	E. M. Knowles	1961-1963	
Willow	Coupe	Crooksville		Pussy willow stalks
Willow	Willow	Franciscan		
Willow Wind	Concord	Red Wing	1947	Abstract
Winchester '73	Montecito	Vernon Kilns	1950	Western scene on cream ground
Windcrest	Teapot	Hall	1940s	Canary and sponged gold; fluted; high lip
Windfall		Stangl	1955-1957	Canary
*Windflower	Colonial	Blue Ridge		Fanciful red flower with green leaves
Windjammer	Clinchfield	Blue Ridge		Center sailboat; wide blue border; black rim
Windmill		Crown		
Windmill		Universal		
Windmill	Victory	Salem		Decals
*Windshield	Teapot	Hall	1941	Maroon and Camellia most common colors
Winesap	Skyline	Blue Ridge	1950s	Three red apples
Winged Streamliner		Homer Laughlin		Railroad china
Winnie	Skyline	Blue Ridge	1950s	Off-centered red flowers
Wishing Well	Skyline	Blue Ridge	1950s	Well, tree, and fence
Wizard of Oz	Kiddieware	Stangl	Mid-1940s-1974	
Woman in the Shoe	Kiddieware	Stangl	Mid-1940s-1974	
Wood Echo	Forcast	E. M. Knowles	1957	

PATTERN	SHAPE	MAKER	DATE	DESCRIPTION
Wood Rose		Stangl	1973-1974	
Wood Song		Harker		
Wood Violets	Accent	E. M. Knowles	c.1954	
*Woodfield		Steubenville		Leaf shapes; American Modern shades: Dove Gray, Golden Fawn, Salmon Pink, Tropic Rust
Woodhue	Flair	Salem		
Woodland	Round Coupe	Salem		
Woodland Gold		Metlox		Marked Poppytrail
*Woodvine		Universal		Small red flowers, large leaves
World's Fair	Teapot	Hall		Cobalt and gold; trylon and perisphere embossed on side
Wren	Square	Blue Ridge		Bird; broken black rim
Wrightwood	Rainbow	E. M. Knowles	1930s	Decals
Wrinkled Rose	Colonial	Blue Ridge		Pink flower; yellow rim
Year 'Round	Year 'Round	Vernon Kilns	1957-1958	Gray, mocha, and yellow circles
Yellow Carnation	Fiesta	Homer Laughlin	1962-1968	Yellow and brown flowers on white background; yellow rim; Casual pattern; see also Daisy
Yellow Flower		Stangl	1970	
Yellow Matte Gold		Homer Laughlin	1920	Decals
Yellow Matte Gold Band	Plain Edge	Homer Laughlin	1920	Decals
Yellow Plaid		Blair		
Yellow Poppy	Candlewick	Blue Ridge		Off-centered pattern
Yellow Rose	D-Style	Hall		Bouquet of wild roses
Yellow Rose	Minion	Paden City	1952	
Yellow Trim Poppy	Deanna	E. M. Knowles		
Yellow Tulip, see Tulip by Stangl				
Yellowridge		Salem		Multicolored flowers
Yorkshire	Swirled Edge	Metlox	c.1939	Solids, pastels: Delphinium Blue, Canary Yellow, Old Rose, Opal Green, Peach, Poppy Orange, Satin Ivory, Satin Turquoise, turquoise blue, yellow
Yorktown	Colonial	Blue Ridge		Centered bird, apple, and leaves; dark line border
*Yorktown	Yorktown	E. M. Knowles	1936	Concentric Deco shape; solid colors: light yellow, maroon, periwinkle blue, terra cotta

PATTERN	SHAPE	MAKER	DATE	DESCRIPTION
Young in Heart	Year 'Round	Vernon Kilns	1956-1958	Flowers in aqua, charcoal, mocha, and yellow
*Zeisel	Hallcraft/ Century and Hallcraft/ Tomorrow's Classic	Hall	1950-1960s	Solid white or decals; two modern dinnerware shapes designed by Eva Zeisel
Zephyr, see Bingo				
Zinnia	Colonial	Blue Ridge		Red, blue, and orange flowers
Zinnia		Homer Laughlin	1977-1978	
Zinnia	Concord	Red Wing	1947	

We welcome any additions or corrections to this chart. Please write to us c/o Crown Publishers, 201 E. 50th Street, New York, NY 10022.